THE
SUNNYSIDE
WAR

THE
SUNNYSIDE
WAR

by Fred Civish

BONNEVILLE BOOKS™

ISBN: 1-55517-645-3
e.2

Published by Bonneville Books
Imprint of Cedar Fort Inc.
www.cedarfort.com

Distributed by:

Typeset by Kristin Nelson
Cover design by Nicole Cunningham
Cover design © 2003 by Lyle Mortimer

Printed in the United States of America
10 9 8 7 6 5 4 3 2 1

Printed on acid-free paper

Library of Congress Cataloging-in-Publication Data

Civish, Fred, 1931-
  The Sunnyside War / by Fred Civish.
     p. cm.
  ISBN 1-55517-645-3 (pbk. : alk. paper)
1. Coal mines and mining--Fiction. 2. Sunnyside (Utah)--Fiction. 3.
Labor movement--Fiction. 4. Coal miners--Fiction. I. Title.

PS3603.I95S86 2003
813'.6--dc21
                              2003000985

Dedicated to the 1,383 real-life heroes in the Appendix. Twenty men died mining coal in Carbon County in just the one year of this story, and there were fewer fatalities that year because of the strike. In all, over 150 men were killed during this century helping mine coal at the mines of Sunnyside.

ACKNOWLEDGMENTS

The author wishes to acknowledge Orson Scott Card and Wayne Ude for their serious attempts to improve his writing style. Roberta M. Mahin made this novel possible with her constant support and expert proof-reading skills. Jack Presset is a family friend and mentor. Then, there was that old, old, Paiute sheepherder who made the summer of 1947 so memorable.

Finally, there are all those "old ones" who lived so heroically what I had the great privilege of writing about. Without them, there wouldn't be a novel.

Prologue

THE COMPLEAT COLLIERIES
(From the earliest recorded writing about coal mines.
Author unknown.)

Collieries, or the Coal Trade, being of so great Advantage to the crown and the Kingdom, I have thought fit to publish this Short Treatise there of (having not met with Books of that Nature hither to) in order to encourage Gentlemen (or such) who have Estates or lands where in coal mines are wrought or may be won, to carry on so useful and beneficial an Imployment as this is which I need not mention the particulars of both in respect to Fires for private and publick use as also in respect of Revenue it brings in Yearly or in respect of the great Advantage it is, being a Nursery for Saylers, &c, or lastly in respect to its imploying so many Thousands of the poor in those Northern parts of England which are maintained by it who must otherwise, of course, be Beggers.

PREFACE

This is a historical novel, that is, fiction. While most of the names in the novel were real people contemporary to the times, all statements to the main fictional characters, and all interactions with them, are, of course, fiction as well. Even though such statements or actions represent the mood, milieu, and ideas of the time as combed from historical records, newspapers, court records, etc. In short, unless specifically reported as a quote from a newspaper, that person, or company (real or fictional), did not say or do those things, therefore no inference can or should be made about the character or actions of any specific person or company in the book. However, where real names of people or companies are covered, the things which ultimately happened to them are real events. Here also, however, many of the circumstances leading up to the real event itself were created by the author to reflect as accurately as possible how and why the events happened.

Further, whenever events from newspapers are quoted, they are actual quotes from the papers of the time, with the only literary license exercised being some minor rearranging of the specific time during which these were written. Many items from newspapers and other sources were woven into the story as dialogue of characters.

Special mention should be made of Dr. Dowd. Not only was he a real person, but for the most part, the events in the novel about him are part of the lore of this man by those still alive who remember him with fondness and awe. Also, while Utah Fuel was a real company, and did many of the things enumerated in the novel, that company was in no way responsible for the killings herein, which were the responsibility of other real but unnamed companies. With the exception of the fictional depot at Mounds, all other places and structures mentioned actually existed.

The fictional characters are: the Cook family, the Benton family, Tom Carr, Mitch Saxton, Harry Carpenter, Frank Bonatti, Toshio Osaka, Cyclone Henry, Ann Bagley, and Abe Strang. However, even each of these are based on real people or are a conglomerate of the types of things endured by real people during the period covered by the novel.

Finally, some of the main incidents in this work did not actually occur in Sunnyside but elsewhere in the county during the period of the novel, and were moved to Sunnyside for literary purposes. However, the main events themselves are for the most part real events. Therefore, in the judgement of the author, this book accurately reflects the events and period about which it was written, if not the specific characters or companies named in the book, and the specific places where events occurred.

Book I

Hole In The World

CHAPTER 1
HOLE IN THE WORLD

March 1, 1922, was Dan Cook's eighteenth birthday. He awoke with a start, then smiled. Five o'clock whistle sounds good, Dan thought. He threw back the warm, down comforter and rolled out of bed. Today there's a hole in the world waiting for me.

He jumped up, went into the kitchen, got a box of matches, opened the lid on the kitchen range, and lit the newspaper under the kindling and coal. He stood shivering until he made sure the fire was going. Running back to the bedroom, he jumped on the bed and pulled the comforter over himself.

Dan shivered. "Should've put on my shoes," he mumbled. "Floor's an ice skating pond."

"Shut up," Steve said. "Stop talking to yourself."

Suddenly the call of nature outweighed his fear of the cold. He got up, and dressed rapidly. Passing through the kitchen again, he noticed his mother Mary.

"Happy birthday, Son," she said.

"Thanks, Mom," he said, as he rushed to the bathroom. Returning, he felt more relaxed. He didn't remember his mother's pink terrycloth robe being so worn and faded.

"Guess it's been awhile since I helped you cook breakfast," he said.

She smiled, "Don't remember the last time. Nice for me to feel a little heat for a change."

Her smile faded. "Anxious to start the fourth generation in the pits?" she asked.

"It's not a pit mine, Mom, it's a tunnel mine."

"If men are digging coal out of it, it's a pit. Get me some sausage from the porch."

On the screened-in porch Dan took some sausage out of the box with burlap covering on all sides. The burlap insulated it in the winter so stuff didn't freeze. In the summer keeping the burlap wet cooled stuff. He headed back to the kitchen with the sausage.

"Wake your brother up. He'll tend the horses now, since you're going in the mine."

"Sure thing, Mom."

Standing by the bed, he gently shook Steve's shoulder. "Get up, Steve. Come on, Bud. Mom says you have to feed Turk and Clyde."

"Turk and Clyde ain't your business now," Steve spat contemptuously.

"Unless you want Mom on your butt, you better get up."

Back in the kitchen, Dan put the tea kettle on the stove. Besides tea, his dad had a drink on occasion. "A nip now and then eases the ache in my foot," he'd say. His right heel didn't quite reach the ground when he walked. Who could blame a man crippled in a mine accident at age eight for wanting to ease his pain.

Mary asked Dan to tend the sausage. As he stirred the sausage, his dad's accident came rushing into Dan's mind. Caught on the edge of a cave in, a large piece of rock fell on the lower part of Carl Cook's leg. It would take nearly eight months before he could return to work. Carl would forever after walk with a limp.

Dan continued musing. I wonder how dad felt his first day? He was ten years younger than me when he first went in. I wonder how well he remembers getting his leg buggered up? That was a question Dan would never get answered. Miners, in general, thought talking about accidents could jinx someone present. "I'll bet that really hurt. Got to get my mind off accidents," he thought. "Don't want to call one down on us."

Mary looked at Dan brooding over the sausage. "Things haven't changed one bloody bit since England," she said. "First the father goes in the pit, then the son."

"Mom, please," Dan pleaded. "Everybody has to help his family get along."

"God blessed you with the intelligence to be an honor student — but you quit high school three months early to go into the mine. Did it ever cross your mind you could help better with a college education?"

Carl Cook came out of the bedroom. "Happy birthday, Son," he said.

But without waiting, he turned to his wife. "Mary, give the boy a break. You know why Dan needs to work. Wish he could have finished school, but there's a recession on. And remember what the church says about the sweat of our brow."

"I know, Carl. I'm just on edge this morning. Don't know what hurts worse, Dan's not finishing or his starting another generation in the pits. But," she said, with her eyes starting to tear up, "I guess it's as much my fault as anybody's."

Carl looked vexed. "I'll not be having you making it hard on yourself either. We're coal miners, Mary, and that's all there is to it. Want to or not, we have to live with that."

"As Shakespeare said, there's the rub. Living with it's one thing, dying with it's quite another." Mary said, tears welling once more. "One explosion, and none of you'll be living anywhere. I can't live with that."

"Damn it, Mary, I'll not be having you call a catastrophe down by talking about explosions. It could happen, but why talk about it?"

Dan busied himself putting dishes on the table. Back in the bedroom after breakfast he picked up the box containing his new pit clothes. It also held his wide leather belt, leather miners' cap, powder punch, lock for his locker, soap, razor, washcloth, towel, and carbide lamp. He took it to the front door and sat it down. Back in the bedroom, he got his two new picks and a scoop shovel, and sat them by the front door as well. In the kitchen he saw his shiny, new aluminum lunch pail standing alongside his father's beat up one.

The second whistle blew. "Time to go," Carl said.

Picking up his pail Dan paused to look at his mother. "Thanks, Mom. Bye. Love you."

"Bye, son. I love you too. Be real careful till you know what you're doing."

"I will," Dan said and followed his dad. At the front door, Carl reached down and hoisted Dan's picks and shovel to his shoulder. Dan picked up his box and followed his dad off the front porch. As they got closer to the bath house, more and more men joined them.

"Tekonis," John Tennis said in the customary Greek greeting as he came near them. "You new mine baby, huh?" he asked Dan.

"Sure am," Dan replied.

John took out his pocket knife and began cutting a chew off his plug of chewing tobacco. He extended the plug to Dan. "You want?" he asked.

Embarrassed, Dan just shook his head.

"We're Mormons, John," Carl said. "We're not supposed to chew."

"Mormon or no," Dan thought, "first chance I get I will. Most of my friends do."

"Let's hurry," Carl added. "I want to get to the bath house before the crowd." Even with his limp, Carl could move quickly. Dan hurried to keep up. On his way to the bath house, Dan endured good natured ribbing about this being his first day from each person they met.

"Eat your rabbit food for breakfast?" Harry Carpenter asked. "Run fast if it starts caving."

"Up yours, Harry," Dan responded with good humor. Harry was an old friend who quit high school a year ago. Only seventeen at the time, Harry needed written permission to work from the principal. But the principal wouldn't give permits except in hardship cases.

They arrived at the bath house and fell into line behind the other entering miners. Dan felt the warm, moist atmosphere inside the bath house the moment he entered. The steam heat kept it warm so men undressing wouldn't catch a chill.

The miners' pit clothes swung from hooks near the ceiling resembling a hundred hanged men. They filled the air with the sulfur odor of coal and the stale smell of dried sweat. By tonight, Dan's smell would be contributing to the aroma.

Carl pointed to a hanger next to his. "Mitch Saxton gave it up. This was his old one."

"Great," Dan responded, happy to be next to his dad. "That was nice of Mitch."

"Forget it. He's Bob Benton's man from the top of his shiny bald head to the bottom of his flat feet. Do something wrong, and Mitch'll report it to Benton 'fore the shift is over."

Dan looked up and saw his wire mesh basket, with the four hooks under it, suspended from the pulley at the crossbar. His basket looked naked compared to the other miners' baskets. Dan unlocked the thin chain and let it slip slowly through his fingers until it dropped to chest level. He undressed hurriedly, putting his street clothes on the hooks, and his shoes and socks in the basket. He put on his pit clothes, buckled on his belt, fixed his carbide light on his cap and put it on his head. He pulled the chain and raised the basket back up to the ceiling.

"Howdy, young feller," a husky voice behind him boomed. "Happy birthday."

Dan recognized the voice as long time family friend, Tom Carr. He turned around and looked at the barrel-chested, bull-necked man. "Howdy, Tom. Thanks."

"'Lo, Tom," Carl added. "Ready to make a miner out of my cub?"

Dan thought he'd be working with his father. "Tom's going to be my partner?" he asked.

"Yeah. Benton won't let two members of the same family work in the same drift," Tom answered. Then, speaking softly, he added, "Ain't as good a miner as your old man, but there's a thing or two I can teach you."

"Listen, and listen good," Carl said. "No matter what happens the next few days, keep your mouth shut and your eyes and ears open. Tom will do his best to keep you alive until you learn not to make dumb mistakes. Don't do anything until he tells you to."

Dan felt uneasy. "Okay, Dad," he said. He felt subdued when they went to the lamp shack and Evan Jones handed him several dollar-sized brass chips with the number 458 on them. He fastened the chips to the clip on his belt. He tried to keep his mind off the fact that the chips would identify his body in case an explosion burned it or a cave-in squashed it. Of course, chips were also put on coal cars as proof the owner loaded them.

He didn't feel any better as they passed the tipple. It was here the brakeman Glen Post slipped off a railroad car and got his legs cut off. Dan looked up and saw the mine cars standing just outside the tipple waiting to be dumped. He thought of Jack Scott who failed to hear the mine cars coming and got his guts scattered along the mine tracks. Got to stop thinking about accidents, he told himself yet again. They approached the man-trip of cars that would take them into the mine.

Dan looked at the mine portal yawning darkly before him. He felt a chill that was colder than the March air. Bravado replaced the uneasiness. There it is. Like a girl calling with her legs spread. That's what the mine is, a girl been raped ten thousand times. But calling me all the same to do it right.

Dan huddled in one corner of a mine car. He could see little as the hoist lowered the man trip into the mine. There was a rumbling of the wheels on the track close below. He heard the clacking sound the wheels made each time they hit another rail-joint. Softer, but higher pitched, was the rhythmic squeak, squeak, squeak, of the rollers under the steel hoist rope. The noise echoed from the tunnel walls as an ominous low rumble.

Each time they passed a bare electric bulb, a little dawn was followed again by thick and imminent darkness. As the light alternately flared and waned, Dan looked at the faces of the other miners in the car with him. The faces showed no fear. In fact, they didn't show anything. They resembled mannequins dressed in dirty overalls waiting for some magic at the end of the trip to bring them alive. Their only motion was the swaying from side to side as the mine car jostled back and forth.

Dan felt the iron cold of the car seep slowly through his clothes and into his back where he leaned against it. Though traveling no faster than a man could run, the coal seemed to rush past his head on both sides. He felt he was being pushed uncontrollably toward something. He didn't know what.

The cars slowed, then stopped. Dan started to get up. Tom jerked his hand up, grabbed Dan's belt, and jerked Dan back down to his seat. The steel hoist rope had stretched like a rubber band. Suddenly the man-trip was being jerked back up the slope. It moved slowly down again and settled to a stop as the rope found it's neutral tension.

"Okay, now," Tom said. "Didn't your dad say don't do a damn thing till I tell you to?"

"Thanks, Tom. I'd a fallen out on my face sure," was Dan's only reply.

"And maybe got run over by the trip when it came back down again," Tom added. "Ever think of that? When we say don't do anything, don't do anything!" he fairly shouted.

As the miners scrambled out both sides of the trip, they reached up and took their carbide lamps off their caps. Unscrewing the bases of the lamps, the shiny, dark carbide in the bottom was exposed. Each man spit into the carbide giving it the moisture to make the acetylene gas to make their light. Flint on steel, as in a cigarette lighter, ignited the gas. A small yellow flame poured out, and the polished brass reflector in front focused the light.

Tom nodded, and Dan unscrewed his lamp. He tried to spit into the carbide, but no spit would come. His mouth felt as dry as a mouth full of soda crackers. Try as he might, no saliva would come. Someone came up behind him and took the bottom part of his lamp out of his hand. It was his dad. Carl spat into the lamp and handed it back.

"Thanks, Dad," Dan said, screwing the bottom shut. It really hit home. This unlikely pair of Guardian angels were watching him as close as a bull watches a bastard calf.

Carl mumbled a "you're welcome," and headed down the slope.

Without a word, Tom took off into a tunnel to the right, and Dan followed. A short distance into the tunnel Tom began to speak as though he were talking to himself.

"That place where the trip stopped is called a parting. The track leading off a parting is called a siding. The tunnels running off to each side are called entries. There will generally be two entries at each parting." He pointed up, "That's the roof or the ceiling." He pointed to the side of the mine. "That's the rib." He pointed to large, round timbers wedged between the floor and roof. "Timbers are cut from pine."

Dan's mind began to wander as he tried to take it all in. "Pay attention!" Tom demanded. "A miner has to know mines, or he's dead."

Farther on Tom pointed to a tunnel that opened off to the left. "That's a cross cut." A little while later he pointed to the right. "Another cross cut," he said. "The coal left in between cross cuts and main entry is called a pillar. A pillar helps hold the roof up.

"It's pretty safe until the company gets hungry for coal, and we have to start mining out the pillars. That's called pulling pillars. As we move coal out from under that mountain, it gets more and more dangerous until it caves and releases the pressure."

Dan trudged along beside him, trying to remember everything he'd been told. "Tom, why are timbers made of pine?" he asked.

"Because pine is soft wood and easy for us to work with, yet pine is strong."

The two circles of light from their lamps sliced the darkness. Inside the circles Dan could see things, outside the circles was a total blackness. Dan's entire visible world shrunk to only what could be seen in those two circles. He felt the mine around him. He felt the thousand feet of rock above him. Suddenly, things started to close in on him. He closed his eyes for a moment as he walked, and a shudder coursed through him.

He opened his eyes and looked around. He saw broken, grey, slate rock piled between the midget-sized track and the rib. At times the moist warm smell of sulphurous coal smelled as though someone had farted. Here and there between the rails the droppings of horses slowly dried and became just one more source of dust when it was disturbed.

Suddenly a couple of horses whinnied greeting. They seemed so out of place here in the blackness. The horses were at an entry nearly triple the normal width. A pole corral held several of them. Men already there had started hitching some up.

"Good morning partners," Tom said to the horses. "Ready to help us bust our butts?" Then, turning to Dan, he said, "When I started working in the Winter Quarters mine after it blew up, the coal was so low we pulled it out with dogs. Dog haulage we called it."

"God, Tom, how do you mine coal that low?" Dan asked

"On your belly, Son, on your belly. If you're lucky, maybe your hands and knees."

"Yeah, yeah," Frank Bonatti laughed from the other side of the corral. Then mimicking Tom's voice as best as he could, he said, "And some of those low seam mines in England run out under the ocean. You can hear it roaring on a stormy day. You never know when the next pick you stick in the roof will pull a face full of ocean in on you and you'd drown like rats. Dan, don't let him lay that on you. We've heard it till we've got it memorized."

"It's true," Tom asserted. "What do you Dago bastards know about real mining anyway?"

"Easy," Frank chuckled. "Down, boy. You Limey's take your mining way too serious."

Tom turned to Dan, "Cut out the big grey. His name's Ned, and watch out for him. He's hard to handle 'till he gets his first chew of tobacco each morning."

Dan took a halter from a peg, and started toward the horse. Ned's nostrils flared.

"You skittish son-of-a-bitch," Tom said as he came toward Ned with a chew of tobacco. "You're lucky I'm not the kind to flay the hide off your big grey tail with a rope."

Dan saw Harry Carpenter working on the other side of the horse Frank Bonatti was also working with. "Hi, again Harry," Dan called. "Glad to see you workin' in this area. First chance we get, let's talk. Been wondering how you got a release from the principal."

"Didn't get one, but the company hired me anyway," Harry said.

"I don't need one either, I'm eighteen today," Dan replied.

Harry smiled a broad grin. "Happy Birthday, Dan. This is a hell of a way to celebrate."

Now it was Dan's turn to grin. "Can't think of a better way I'd rather spend it, Harry." Then Dan noticed something odd. "When I move, this horse's eyes don't follow it."

"He's one of the blind ones. These horses are kept here in the dark. A lot of 'em go blind. Ones that work closer to the portal are rounded up and taken outside at night," Tom said.

"That's sad. How can a blind horse work?"

"Lad, these horses know the mine better'n any man in it. If your light goes out and you need to get back here, just give Ned his head, grab onto his tail and he'll lead you right back here, or outside. Many a miner has come out after an explosion following a blind horse. The dust and smoke is so thick your light won't penetrate two inches, but a blind horse can find his way."

"That's amazing."

"Tom's mouth to God's ear," Frank called.

"What did he mean by that?" Dan whispered to Tom.

"He means it's God's truth. Now put this bag of oats on Ned. He's less likely to get grouchy about it if he's eating while you fit him with his tac."

Dan held the oats out so Ned could sniff them. He moved a little closer and let Ned sniff again. Ned showed no resistance at all, so Dan put the bag on his nose. In no time at all Ned's harness was on and he'd finished his oats. Tom gave him another chew.

"Whether you chew or not is your business," he said to Dan. "But buy a plug tonight, and carry it with you for the horse." Tom cut off a plug and gave it to Ned. "It quiets him."

"Already got a plug," Dan said proudly patting his pocket. "For the horse," he added just a bit too loudly. Tom just picked up Ned's halter rope and began trudging down the entry.

"One thing we need to get clear," Tom said as they walked. "Outside I'm your friend. Inside I'm going to drive you till you get to be a real miner. Being a miner is a hard way of life. There's a hundred thousand men outside who ain't got the guts for each one of us inside who has. When you going to try chewing?" Tom asked bluntly.

"Hadn't thought about it much," Dan lied.

Tom laughed, "Well when you do, I got a couple of suggestions. At first take a real small plug and spit it out before you start feeling sick. Wait too long, you're already poisoned."

"Do you think it's wrong to chew, Tom?"

"Mormons and others say so, yes. But it's a pleasure, too. Miners have damn few of those. That ain't the main reason though. When we get loading coal, and the dust gets thick, nothin's as good as chew to keep your mouth from getting so dry you choke."

"How about gum?"

"Don't spit with gum. Soon gum's caught so much dust and grit, chewing it'll grind down your teeth. Don't have to chew tobacco. Just put it in and spit."

The end of the tunnel caught Dan by surprise. Ahead were four small mine cars, a large pile of coal blasted from the face, and here and there assorted mining tools. All had been left from the previous day's work. Thankful to be here at last, he removed his tools from his shoulder and looked at Tom. Tom nodded, and Dan added his tools to the pile.

CHAPTER 2

JUST RUN

"Okay," Tom said. "Back to mining. When you come to the face of the entry you're working in it's called a room. Frank and Harry are mining in a room along side of us, driving a parallel tunnel. Tie Ned up by that hay. Looks as if last night's shot brought down a lot of coal. Ought to get eighteen to twenty tons out of it." Tom reached down, picked up a pick. "Oh yeah," he said, noticing Dan's perplexed look. "Coal blasted down's called a shot. State law says only a shotfire's supposed to do it. Law also says they blast only at night when men are out of the mine. What a joke that is. Leaving too many for him, we'd be looking for a new job. So, if you hear someone call 'Fire in the hole!' stand in the center of the room. Wait for his blast to make sure it doesn't knock anything down in your room, especially you." Tom pointed to some equipment near the rib. "We undercut the coal with our picks, drill our holes, and set the powder and the fuses. Drilling's more work than I want to think of."

"How deep do we drill the holes?"

"There's usually eight to twelve of 'em, and we drill 'em six feet deep," Tom answered.

Tom pointed to some paper sacks about as big around as a stick of pepperoni and about a foot long lying alongside the rib. "Those are dummies; the sacks are filled with clay. When you tamp them in the holes behind the dynamite, make sure you tamp them in good and tight with that long tamping stick over there."

Dan looked over and saw a stick about three times as long as a broom handle and twice as big around. On the end was a sort of head that was a smaller than the size of the drill.

"If you don't tamp the dummies good, the dynamite will just shoot the dummy back out the hole similar to a rifle shot. We need to have the dummy stay in so the blast will spread through the coal and knock a lot down."

Tom lifted the pick he was leaning on. He walked over to where the pile of coal was lying. He beckoned to Dan. "Climb up on that pile of coal and tap the roof nice and easy with the head of this pick," Tom said as he handed the pick to Dan.

Dan climbed up on the pile of coal, but the closer he got to the roof, the more he felt the mine was closing in on him. He tapped the roof very gently.

"A little harder," Tom said. "If it's loose, don't want to bring it down on us."

Dan felt the crowding feeling even more intensely than before. It was all he could do to keep from climbing back down off the coal. But he tapped the roof a little harder.

"Sounds solid. Now thump it a good lick," Tom commanded.

Tom's words eased Dan's fear some. He gave the roof a good solid whack.

"Good, now get down here. That's called sounding the roof. Do it several times a day."

Dan's stomach began turning over. "How do you tell when it ain't safe?"

"Can't really explain it 'til you got enough experience." Tom paused, he was trying to find words to explain a sound. He wrinkled his nose and pursed his lips. "Pay attention to the sound, and feel the pick in your hand. If it don't sound good, you better run like hell."

Dan's uneasiness increased. This was too complicated, he'd never learn it. "What if I don't know when the sound's telling me to run like hell?"

"Remember how it sounded today, and how the pick felt in your hand. It's similar to picking a watermelon. With a watermelon, when you tap it, you listen for a mushy feeling. A low sound means the melon's good. The roof is just the opposite. A nice solid sound and feel means the roof's safe. If there's a sort of a whump, a vibrating sound, and the pick doesn't feel it's hitting something solid, that means the roof's bad."

"Seems an awfully dangerous way to find out if it's safe," Dan complained.

"Find a safer way, miners will bless your name forever," Tom said and chuckled.

Tom picked up a scoop shovel and cleaned a small area on the floor. "We're going to set a timber here," he said. "Go get that one over there." Once the timber was in place, Tom stood back.

"Biggest mistake new bunnies can make is thinking timbers hold the roof up. When the mountain above decides to come down, only thing'll stop it is the floor of the mine."

Dan's shoulders drooped, he looked puzzled. He had been pinning his hopes on the timbers keeping the roof up. He heaved a big sigh. "Shit," he said. "If we don't set them to hold the roof up, why bother?"

"Timbers taking weight from the roof make different noises, sometimes cracking and popping, and sometimes what we call singing. That gives us a kind of warning. You gotta learn to sort the sounds timber makes for yourself. If you run every time a timber pops, you won't load any coal. If you think a low moaning sound ain't dangerous, your family might get to bury you."

"Great!" Dan said, and sounded even more dejected, if that were possible.

"Don't worry, Lad. Sometimes these timbers take so much weight they snap in two as a tooth pick would if you pressed it between your fingers, but that don't necessarily mean the roof's coming in. When timbers snap but the roof's good, we just set more timbers." Dan looked in disbelief. "Yes, it's true. I've worked in rooms three or four sets of timbers have snapped."

"You know all this is really crazy? The way to see if the roof is dangerous is to thump on it, but that might bring it down. We don't set timbers to hold the roof up, but to give us warning sounds. If the timbers crack and pop, that could be dangerous but it might not be dangerous if they snap in two."

"It's a puzzle, ain't it?" Tom said. "You can't count on one darn thing in this mine. Yet you gotta rely on everything cause that's all you got! Mining is crazy, no easy trick to stay alive. Especially when you're new. Dan, I'm not saying this to try to scare you, but..."

"Scared? Scared?" Dan cut him off. "Who is scared? I went miles past scared the second I got up on that coal pile with a pick in my hand.

And it's getting worse by the minute." Dan continued, but there was an ironic tone in his voice. There was the beginning of a shift in him. He was no less terrified, but he was becoming more indifferent to it. "If I'm going to wind up dead, anyway, no sense making myself miserable with worry about it."

"That's the ticket," Tom said. "This mine can kill you if you let your awareness wander for just a minute. It can kill you just to show you that you're getting cocky. And it can kill you to show that you've started taking it for granted. But if you learn the mine and its ways you can outsmart it."

"Tom, you're making it sound like some sort of evil thing that's alive and out to get us."

"Ain't saying it is, ain't saying it ain't. But if it is alive, evil ain't the right word. Sort of uncaring about us one way or another. I just got one more thing to say. Once you can just let it all be, you can load coal without going as crazy as the mine is. Now let's cut out the talk and load some coal. I'll load the front car, you load the back." With that, Tom picked up a scoop shovel and loaded coal rhythmically into the front car.

Dan began shoveling. He worked steadily for a while. Later he felt kinks beginning to form in his muscles. But he kept working. They'll never call me lazy, he vowed.

"Slow down some, or you'll never make it through the..." Tom started to say, when suddenly a lemon-sized piece of coal popped loudly out of a rib.

Dan shot out of there. Finally, he realized he was running down the tunnel. Behind him, he could hear Tom roaring with laughter. There was no sound whatever of the cave-in he expected. "Crap," he muttered to himself. Slowly, he walked back.

Tom was wiping tears of laughter from his eyes, his shoulders shaking and his chest heaving. "Glad I didn't get in your way, you'd a probably busted me open. Don't worry about it. Everybody new does it."

Dan picked up his shovel, scooped up some coal, and threw the coal over the car and onto the rib on the other side. Tom laughed so hard he bent over and held his stomach.

"Whoa, ain't we strong though, when we just had the crap scared outta us?" Tom asked. Then Tom's tone turned serious. "Hear this good,

Lad. You ran and you felt the fool. But you wasn't no fool. Whenever you feel like running, run! If there ain't a reason, but you feel like it, just run! Even if nobody else moves, just run! Then maybe someday you'll run when somebody else don't, and you'll get to laugh your own self as you carry his body into the church for his funeral." With that, he turned silent and began loading coal again.

By the time Dan's car was barely half full, Tom had put chips with his number on it on two full cars. But Dan didn't see him. A timber squeaked loudly. Dan was off again.

This time Dan got only a few steps before he checked himself, turned around and started back. Tom had started loading again as though nothing had happened. Dan took advantage of the strength of his fear, and loaded a little faster. Soon Dan was past sweating. His clothes were dripping water. But he'd finished loading the four tons it took to fill his car. He took a chip with his number, 458, off his belt, and put it on his car. As Dan stood back proudly, Tom finished loading his third car.

"Give me one of your chips," Tom said. Puzzled, he did as Tom requested. Tom took Dan's chip and placed it on the car he'd just finished loading.

"Thank you, Tom. But there's no need. I'll be loading my share in a few days."

"With the bun in your mother's oven your family needs all the help it can get," Tom said.

For a moment, Dan didn't understand. Then he tried to speak. "I didn't . . ." he started. "Nobody told . . ." he tried again. "Mom doesn't look . . ." he mumbled for a third time. Suddenly he understood his mom saying it was partly her fault he was going in the mine.

"Forget I told you, Lad. And don't mention it to your Pap. Let's eat lunch."

Still in a daze, Dan sort of walked, stumbled over to where their lunch pails were. He sat down and reached for his pail, removed the top compartment holding his sandwiches. He gulped thirstily from the water in the bottom part of the pail.

"Sure tasted good," he said, breathing heavily as Tom walked over. Dan could only eat two of the three ham and cheese sandwiches his mother packed for him.

Tom inspected Dan's lunch pail. "You goin' to just leave that there other sandwich?"

Dan didn't think so. "Want a peanut butter sandwich from Sue Fuller's boarding house."

"Nah. Just take it, I'm full," Dan said. Tom reached over and took Dan's final sandwich.

"Damn," Dan complained, "My muscles are killing me."

"Don't worry about it," Tom said. "That ain't fatal."

"Glad to find something down here ain't fatal," Dan groused sarcastically.

Tom sat up straight. "Not much sense making light about fatal things. Not that I'm superstitious myself. But somebody smarter'n me said it's best to keep quiet when you're talkin' 'bout things you can't explain. The meaning of anything I say now is outside of words, so you'll have to make your own meaning of it. A little while ago I said you had to stay alive when you don't know how to stay alive. But that ain't all of it. Lots of times in a mine you got to do what you can't do." Tom paused to try to organize his next thought.

"That don't make any sense at all," Dan said in exasperation.

"I know. But human beings is so much more than we got the slightest idea about. We say, I can't do this, I can't do that, and sure as hell, we can't." Tom's emphasis on the last part made it clear to Dan, Tom meant if we think we can't do something, we can't.

"But in the mine, you gotta learn to do what you think you can't." Tom stopped talking for a moment. "I'm just not good at explaining things."

"No, Tom. Please go on," Dan said, wanting to hear more about this.

Hesitantly, Tom continued. "Using an accident as an example is the only way I really know how to explain it." Tom looked decidedly uneasy. It was as if he was watching for a sign from the mine he'd better stop talking. "Say there's an explosion," Tom said as he finished the sandwich and wiped his hands on the side of his pants. "And for some reason me and Ned gets killed. If you sit and wait for somebody to come save your ass, the black damp gas will get here first, and you're dead. So you gotta make decisions quick. You gotta pick something you can't know how it will turn out. Can I make it to the nearest exit without breathing? Had I better take cover because the first blast was just a gas explosion and a ten times worse dust explosion is coming? Should I put up a brattice barricade to keep out the gas and wait for them to come to me?" Tom stopped to take a deep breath, then continued. "Or is there so much stuff blown down and caved in that I will run out of air long before people trying to save me ever get here? Is the mine on fire and my only chance to make it is trying to get out whether I make it or not?" Tom paused yet again, this time he was sweating.

Dan realized this was not just a hypothetical story. Dan just knew Tom had lived through an explosion. He wasn't just talking, he was reliving it as he talked. Dan leaned toward Tom, and started paying even closer attention.

"You can't possibly know which answer is right, but if you're going to stay alive you better pick the right one, and damned fast. And you better get over the idea that thinking about it will solve it. You sit there thinking, and you're dead."

Dan's thoughts were swirling. He hoped there was something coming more solid than what he was hearing. "Tom," he said softly, "how do you pick the right one?"

The question seemed to anger Tom. "You don't! That's the whole point. You got to trust whatever you decide. Trust is greater than you can possibly know. You just decide and then do it, before you even know why you decided it. Decide wrong, you're dead."

"Tom, that sounds awful." Tom now looked more sad than anything else, Dan thought.

"That's life and death in the mines, Lad. Nobody will think the worse of you if you decide you don't want to be part of it."

Dan got the drift of what Tom just said. Now he knew more about mining, he was being given the chance to choose again. Now that he knew, he was unsure how he'd choose.

"Tom, how many ways can the mine kill me?"

"Besides the obvious ones, an explosion, a cave, a bounce, a ..."

"Bounce? I thought that was just little earthquakes we felt in town," Dan interjected.

"Maybe it's felt little in town, but the more the rock in the mountain starts shifting, the worse things get thrown around down here. Even one you don't feel in town can throw you against the face hard enough to kill you, not to mention causing caves. Then you're a trapped rat in a cage. You either run out of air, or die of thirst before they get to you."

"How long does it take to run out of air?"

"Can't say. Depends on how close the cave is, how good your air was to start with, and how many of us there is in the area. And turn off your light, they burn oxygen. Then sit or lie down. Don't move a muscle you don't have to. When you move, you breathe harder." Tom was embarrassed to tell what was coming next, but he went on knowing it had to be said. "Plus movement makes you sweat. Lying down helps cool you off." Tom paused, heaved a sigh, then continued. "When you got to take a leak, piss into your lunch pail or something else to save it. When your dying of thirst, you'll drink your own piss. If it's weak or mixed with the water in your pail, that's okay. But if you don't save it from the very first, it gets so salty it'll kill you or drive you crazy."

Dan's stomach turned at what Tom had just told him, but he knew if he was going to choose to be a miner, he should hear it all. "How many more ways can a mine kill you?"

Tom sat there quietly for a moment, looking sad. "Dan, how many times you heard so and so was killed in a freak accident? Everything down here is dangerous."

"That it?"

"Not really. We got to talk about somebody in an accident." Again Tom sighed. He crossed his arms in front of him and looked down before he continued. "Maybe he's cut in half. Maybe there's blood and body parts all over the place. Maybe he's under a slab of rock that squashed part of him flat. Maybe the roof's still coming down here and there. Maybe the timbers are singing like the whole Tabernacle Choir." Tom paused and looked up, his arms were still across his chest as he sat there. "Maybe you know your partner's dead for sure. Maybe you know the smart thing is to back off until the roof settles down. Maybe there's a thousand tons of rock over where your partner must be."

The hands behind Dan's head were pulling his head a little forward. His voice was intense. "But none of that matters, right?"

"Right," Tom said. "Then you'll decide what has to be done first and you'll start doing it.

19

"Maybe later you will notice that you puked, or messed your pants. But none of that will mean anything, either. You've either saved your partner or recovered his body so the poor family waiting outside can bury him."

Dan crossed his legs in front of him to relieve the tension on his back. "And what else?"

"Not much. Once you can do this kind of stuff, you're changed somehow and you can never go back to what you were before. But until you can do these things, you're not only not a miner, you're dangerous and better off outside. So, what's it going to be? You staying, or would you rather make a living outside. Most people do," he added.

The tone of the last statement gave Dan no hint that Tom was suggesting one way or another. Dan realized he had made his original decision to come in on his own, despite what anybody else thought. Now he realized he still felt the same, but it seemed much more difficult. Obviously, this was one of those cases a person could know in advance.

Dan got up. Then he said, "For better or worse, I'm a miner. Let's get to work."

Tom reached up, turned off his lamp and laid back. "Nah," he said. "Us miners is a little tired. Let's rest a bit more."

Dan sat, reached up, turned his lamp off, but he did not lay back. He noticed the most profound darkness he'd ever experienced. Somehow, it, and everything else, haunted him.

CHAPTER 3

A SNITCH IN MINE

After lunch they hitched Ned to the loaded cars and started out. Tom stopped Ned at the first cross-cut they came to. Dan wondered what was up. Tom handed Dan the reins. "I'll be right back," he said and walked to the next entry. "You in there, Frank?" He called. After a moment, Dan heard Frank's voice. "About time. Thought you'd be here by noon."

"Couldn't help it," Tom replied. "Dan's all jack rabbit. Be back when I find out when Mitch The Snitch will be making his rounds." Tom climbed back up, and took the reins. "Your dad tell you Mitch was Benton's man?" Dan said he did and asked so what?

Tom shot a squirt of tobacco juice toward the rib. "Around Mitch or one of Benton's other snitches, you'd best keep anything you don't want Benton to know to yourself. Giddy up," he said to get Ned going a little faster. "You've got to treat a snitch nice to his face but keep your own counsel." With that, Tom fell silent again till Ned began trotting. "Hey, Ned! Slow down or you'll derail us," Tom commanded and Ned obediently slowed.

"Dad says if the company don't make money we'll all lose our jobs," Dan said to make conversation.

Tom shook his head. He began to almost shout. "Going broke is one thing. No matter how they cry poverty, they ain't going broke. Some owners back east have mansions, and yachts, and the finest cars money can buy. And all of it off the backs of miners."

Dan blinked. "Of course I knew that," he said to the clip clop of Ned's hooves.

"All that luxury is different from just making money. How many men had to work their guts out, or die mining, to keep those scum living as if they was kings?"

Tom thought a moment. "You seen Stanton's new Packard, ain't you?" Dan asked who hadn't.

"Think any Super gets to drive a fine car as a reward for how good he treat's his men? Benton and all blood-sucking company men is the enemy of all honest workers."

They rode quietly for a while. Only the slow clippity-clop of Ned's hooves and the squeaking of the metal wheels on the tracks broke the profound silence of the mine.

"Okay, okay," Tom mumbled to himself. Then, more loudly. "I guess I owe you and Carl this much. I'd give my life for your pap, he's that good a man. But two things we can never talk about or we'd end up enemies. One's the church and the other's the union."

Dan chuckled. "That's right. Never did hear you and Dad talking about those things."

"Anyway, your dad is a scab. There just ain't no other word for it. But he'd give his life for any man in the mine, so we overlook that. But you can bet your butt he ain't no snitch."

Dan held tight to the coal car behind him while he thought about what Tom had said. The only snitch Dan knew personally was Mitch, and Dan was starting to hate him.

"But worst thing about 'em, they all want you to like 'em," Tom said and his mouth screwed up into a sneer. "If you don't pretend you like 'em, they turn vicious. If one gets it in for you, just turn in your time and clear out. If you don't, your work in the mine will be pure hell. You'll get assigned to places with lots of rock, low coal hard to mine, or pullin' pillars. They're so dangerous sometimes a rat's got better sense than to go there."

"Thanks for the warning," Dan responded.

Tom took a deep breath and fell silent again. As Dan stood on the platform of the car they were riding, he thought over everything Tom said. Again and again it came to his mind his father was a scab. Sure his father had worked during the 1913 strike, but Dan was only nine years old at the time. It never dawned on him before his dad was a scab.

Dan had known Tom all his life. And once or twice a week Tom would come to his house for dinner or just a visit. Tom seemed more like an uncle than one of his dad's friends. But Dan never knew Tom hated Mormons. He wondered how many other non-Mormons in town felt that way. A moving light ahead caught his attention. It was Mitch Saxton standing at the parting.

"Hey there, Mitch, you bow-legged old crow. When you goin' to drag your sorry butt down our way and sell us some powder?" Tom called.

Saxton laughed. "Didn't use the last batch to blow yourself to hell. So why waste more?"

"Got me there, Mitch, got me there. Maybe the cub here'll get careless and take care of it. Kidding aside. We loaded most of yesterday's shot, and need more powder."

"Sure thing, Tom. Don't I always take care of you? After I load my pack and take it down to the Three Left district, I'll get to Frank and you right after that."

Dan just kept quiet and tried to keep his face from showing what he was feeling as the two men continued to banter back and forth.

Dan kept his mouth shut on the return trip with four empty cars, thinking over what he'd just seen and heard. He'd grown up respecting Tom. Tom could be depended on to help when anything needed doing around the house. Tom'd always gone horseback riding and fishing with them. He's the one taught me how to hunt, Dan thought.

He went over all Tom said before they got to the parting. Then when Tom saw Mitch, he was all laughs and jokes as though they were lifelong buddies. But Dan knew Tom too well. He couldn't believe Tom was just acting. It seemed he really liked Saxton.

"Whoa," Tom said to Ned as they came to the entry where Frank and Harry were working. "Stay here," he commanded Dan, and got off the empty car. "Okay, Frank," he called into the tunnel. "It's safe." Then Tom walked back toward the parting and sat down against the rib fifty feet down the track. He reached up and turned out his lamp.

Frank emerged from the cross-cut. "Come on," he said. "let's walk a ways."

Dan's heart was pounding. He hadn't the slightest idea what was going on, but the tension in him grew. When Frank stopped, Dan looked at him. "What's going on, Frank?"

"It's time for you to lay your cards on the table. Tom's hiding back there so no one can surprise us. Harry's staying in the room making mining noises to cover us in case somebody is hiding out and trying to listen to us. So it's safe to talk."

Dan licked his lips nervously. "Time to lay what cards on the table?" he asked hesitantly.

"I'm a United Mine Worker's organizer," Frank said with about as much emphasis as he would mention that he was going to buy some potatoes after work. "I talked to your dad. He said it's okay with him if I talk to you about the union. He said a man has to make his own decisions. A strike's coming that'll blow the lid off every mine in the country. You gotta choose which side you're on. Nobody can ride the fence. Either you're for us, or you're against us. Which one is it going to be?"

Dan just looked at Frank. It was against the law for a union man to try to recruit others on the job. If Dan even discussed joining the union here in the mine, he, too, would be a law-breaker. "Frank, what are you doing? That kind of talk makes us criminals!"

Without a word Frank turned and headed back toward his room. Dan ran up to him and put his arm on Frank's shoulder. Frank whirled around, and Dan saw a knife in Frank's hand, held down low with the point toward Dan's belly. Dan jumped back.

"Hey, Frank. I wasn't saying no. You just caught me by surprise. I need some time to think about this. Maybe talk it over with Dad."

Frank's voice dripped venom. "Then we don't want you in our union. Last time it was weak-kneed sisters who talked union but couldn't stand the heat. And they cost us our strike. This time it ain't going to be that way. If you ain't with us, no matter what happens, get the hell away from me." Frank shined his light directly in Dan's eyes.

Dan knew he was being bullied. Not once since he entered the mine had anyone's light so blinded him. He held his hand up to shade his eyes. Dan looked hard at Frank. Knife or no knife, he was not going to be bullied by this man, and Frank might as well know it.

Apparently, Frank got the message. He took his light away from Dan's eyes. "But you still ain't no real miner, and no son of Carl Cook if you can't make up your mind."

Dan's choices came into sharp focus. He could either agree now, or he could forever after be known as a scab. "Count me in," he said. "What do I have to do?"

"Nothing yet, we'll take care of that at our secret meeting." Frank put the knife away. He looked back toward the parting, reached his hand up and passed it slowly in front of his carbide lamp three times. Dan saw Tom's light come on, and Tom walked back to them.

"Figured you would," Tom said to Dan. "Those three lights was the signal you'd joined."

"Fill him in on what's going on," Frank told Tom. He turned and headed for his room.

The whole thing took less than five minutes. But the biggest question on his mind was whether or not his Dad would be really mad he'd joined. How can I help Dad with the new baby when the strike comes? Is the strike for sure? What'll the union want from me? How long will the strike last?

He knew better than to push Tom for answers, though. Tom spoke about things only when it suited him. Dan would just have to wait. Oh brother, Dan thought, I haven't half learned how to be a miner yet, and now I got to learn how to be a union man, too.

"Well, here we go again," Tom said as they arrived at the face. "Ain't we the lucky ones."

Dan barely heard him. It disturbed Dan that Tom hadn't said one thing to Dan yet about joining the union. As far as Dan could tell from the way Tom was acting, it was almost as though the whole thing had never happened. Dan unhitched Ned, led him to the rib where the hay was thrown, and started shoveling coal into the back car while Tom shoveled into the front one. Dan had to work slowly, but he kept at it. During the trip to the parting his muscles had turned to knots. It was all he could do now to fill a shovel full of coal and throw it into the car. Dan's body refused to do any more. Ashamed, he sank slowly to the floor of the mine.

"You did good," Tom grunted. "I'm surprised you did this much your first day."

Dan sat quietly, knowing he would load no more coal on this day. He'd had enough. He had nothing more to give. His sweat had dried up. Coal dust was caked in his mouth, in his nose, in his ears, and in the lines of his face. He took off his gloves and looked at his blistered hands, he was bleeding a little. He was too tired to care.

He began to doubt he would ever get out of here. He began to feel as though this place would be his tomb. Then, for some reason, he spoke. "Somebody's coming."

"Feel him or hear him?" Tom asked, matter-of-factly.

The hair on the back of Dan's neck begin to crawl. He hadn't heard anything, and still could not. Yet somehow he knew someone was coming. "Man, it's spooky in here."

"All mines are, Lad, all mines are," Tom chuckled. "Must be Saxton." Tom reached down, picked up Dan's shovel, and placed it against the rib with his own. "That you, Mitch?" Tom called out.

Saxton was smiling broadly. "Is this me? Is a pig made out of pork? Shame on you Tom, you wore that poor young stud totally out." Saxton was loaded down with large pouches slung over each shoulder, and a smaller one hanging down his back. He resembled a miniature pack mule. He looked at Dan. "Idle hands are the Devil's workshop, Stud. Stand up so I can load you up with sticks of powder."

Dan couldn't stand up. There was nothing left in him. But he reached down inside himself, somewhere, and found the strength. He stood up, took the powder, and wondered where to put it. Tom nodded toward the rib. Dan put the powder down there.

"By the way, Stud," Mitch said. "I want to give you a word of warning. I know there are some agitators around here who will be on your case to join their stinking union. I know you're as sensible as me and your dad. Union guys? Not our kind. Can't trust any of 'em.

"Why, I heard over in Colorado an organizer blew a guy up with dynamite. Organizer was trying to recruit the other guy. But this other guy snitched and told the Super. Blew him to pieces, he did. Never did find all of him."

Tom whirled around, picked up a pick, and began picking at the face. It looked as if he was picking down loose coal, but there wasn't any. Dan noticed Tom's chest and shoulders shaking. He's so mad at Saxton he's trying to control his anger, Dan reasoned. Strangely, however, Tom seemed to be laughing with his face turned away from them that way. "Why were you picking at the face?" Dan asked suspiciously after Saxton left.

Tom smiled a big smile, and chuckled. "I was dressing the face off smooth to prepare it for undercutting it," he said, lamely.

Dan couldn't see why Tom was smiling. He decided to let his suspicions about Tom's laughter drop. "Dress the face?" he inquired instead. "Undercut it?" he added.

"Sure. Before we undercut the coal we pick at the face until it is as smooth and square as we can get it. This helps keep our room running in a straight line, and it helps make sure we get a good clean shot. We can't have one part of the face sticking out farther than another. If it is, the dynamite just blows out the smaller part. But remember what I tell you now. Your life depends on it. Dressing the face real good helps make sure the weight is evenly distributed. Then when we undercut it with our picks, we don't have to worry so much about a slab falling on us while we're under there."

Dan's face grew ashen. "Undercut it with our picks?"

"Yeah," Tom replied. He chuckled again. "It would ruin my whole day if a slab fell down and pinned me under there. That's why only one of us at a time gets under to pick. In case the face sloughs off, the other guy will get his partner out. If he can't, he'll run for help."

Without another word, Tom used his pick to pick out an eighteen-inch-high slice between the coal and the floor of the mine. He kept picking until he was reaching in as far as his arm would stretch. Then, bit by bit, he slithered under the coal to cut deeper and deeper. Finally, little more than his legs were sticking out.

Dan watched, horrified, not believing what he was seeing. After another eternity, Tom began to inch his way back out. Dan hoped Tom was finished. He even started to pray for the first time in weeks. It did no good. God wouldn't hear him this deep under the ground.

Tom's voice turned emotionless. He extended the pick towards Dan. "Your turn."

Dan grew numb. He was certain this was something he could never do. He grew cold. His mind shut off and stopped thinking. Gone were hopes and dreams. Gone were thoughts about life and death. Gone was any emotion he had ever felt. He reached for the pick. Maybe it's me who's going to get raped, he thought.

CHAPTER 4

KEEP THAT WOLF AWAY
FROM YOUR DOOR

Most people rode the train the twenty-seven miles between Sunnyside and Price, but not Bob Benton. He drove his new 1922 Packard, Twin-Six, Touring Car swiftly over the gravel and washboard bumps of the road. He swore at the dust piling up on the shiny deep maroon paint. The dust filtered into the car and soiled his touring coat. The filthy stuff will be getting on my Tuxedo next, he thought.

Benton had the best car America could build. "Ask a man who owns one," the Packard company bragged. Benton's only problem with owning it was an uneasy feeling that to buy such a fine automobile at this particular time might be a little premature.

He came to Nickerson's hill, and the Packard climbed the hill in high gear without skipping a beat. He coasted down the other side and onto the asphalt road surface which started at Eighth East. Price was planning to pave Main Street to Tenth East next summer.

He headed to the Masonic Temple, three more blocks along Main Street on First East.

The alley leading to the back of the temple fit snugly between the fire house and the temple. He turned left into the narrow alley, and slowed the big Packard to a crawl, driving carefully. He made sure he didn't scrape the fenders on either side. At the parking lot behind the two-story brick building, he pulled to the front of the lot so everyone going into the temple would see the Packard.

Since he was early, he took a moment to sit in the car and enjoy it. Benton looked at the back of the temple. He wouldn't call it ugly, but it certainly didn't look anything special. Inside was a different matter. Being inside made him feel important each time he was there. The crystal chandeliers, gold inlaid chairs, plush-velvet couches, and authentic Oriental rugs gave the place an air of real class. There were Masonic symbols, and just enough stained glass at the windows so as not to be gaudy.

Benton liked a lot of things about being a Mason. One that always tickled him was a little sign someone put on the bulletin board by the staircase leading downstairs. The sign read simply, "I love to love a Mason 'cause a Mason never tells." Benton could tell a lot.

With a sigh, he got out of the Packard. He closed the door. He liked the solid sound of it.

A big Studebaker pulled up next to him and parked. Fellow Superintendents for Utah Fuel Company mines, Mark Haywood and Hank Thompson started getting out of the Studebaker. Benton had to admit that while it was no Packard, Haywood's Studebaker was a fine car as well.

Haywood and Thompson both waved a greeting, and Benton waved back. As Haywood crawled from behind the steering wheel, his tuxedo jacket gaped open. Benton caught a quick peek at the pistol Haywood was packing. Benton sneered at the snub-nosed thirty-eight with its black handle sticking out of Haywood's shoulder holster. Benton's forty-four gave him a greater sense of security. He knew if he should ever really be forced to use it, the forty-four would get the job done. With the miners guessing about the big wage reduction coming, trouble would probably break out soon.

Nobody had been shot in Carbon County since the 1911 strike in Kenilworth, when Deputy Thomas Jackson and four Greeks were killed. Earlier, the 1903 strike at Sunnyside had been called the Sunnyside War. If it came to that again, he would be ready.

Even the fact that any labor agitator who got violent paid the full penalty of the law didn't stop the danger. And in Utah they would pay the full penalty, thank heaven for that. A good example was the labor nut, Joe Hill. Hill did everything to keep from being executed after he was tried for murder. He figured the famous songs he wrote, Casey Jones for example, made him special. He said he didn't want to be found dead in Utah.

Hill hoped the letter written by the head of the AFL, Sam Gompers- a plea for Hill's life-would help. And he figured he had the State on the run when President Woodrow Wilson wrote asking for clemency. Utah still shot the anarchist creep. Mormons aren't easily influenced by the wishes of outsiders, I'll give them that, Benton mused.

Benton sincerely hoped Joe Hill's death might serve as a warning to union officials such as Cahill and Morgan. If they kept trying to import their union from Wyoming, they, too, might find themselves dead in Utah. Benton had experience with Jimmy Morgan during Colorado labor troubles, and he didn't like him one bit. In Benton's judgment, the man was deadly. Benton would as soon negotiate with a cobra as with Morgan.

"Nice car," Thompson said when he was out of his Studebaker.

Benton smiled. "It's not a Silver Ghost, but it'll do."

"Did well enough for President Harding," Haywood added. "Rode one to his inaugural."

"I know," Benton replied. "But I'll bet he didn't have to put up with all this dust. Let's get inside. I'm dying for a drink of something stronger than water."

"Last one in is a Mormon teetotaler," Haywood challenged.

Benton wanted a martini and he was looking forward to the evening. Anybody in business, mining, railroading, government, the legal system, or law enforcement in Carbon county would be there. In the relaxed atmosphere where fellow Masons could trust each other, a lot of important things could well be decided.

The only other event more important Benton could think of was the meeting Utah Fuel had scheduled for him with the top brass in Salt Lake City. There he'd find out if he was going to be made General Superintendent of all of Utah's mines. Figured he had it made.

As they reached the back door of the temple, Benton noticed with more than a little satisfaction that Thompson grabbed the door and held it open so he and Haywood could pass through. Benton took it as a subtle sign that at least Thompson had wind of Benton's appointment as Utah Fuel's new General Super. Otherwise, Benton figured, Thompson would not be currying favor by holding the door open. I guess I can eliminate him as a possible rival, he thought. Thompson was used to controlling three hundred men. Holding doors just didn't seem to be the sort of thing a man of Thompson's clout would do.

Thompson's holding the door open also reminded Benton to stay on his toes. He had to keep his eyes and ears open for the subtle meanings of what was going on. He had to interpret it all correctly, or he would make mistakes. He was too new to the area to know all the ins and outs of what people here were, and which of them he could trust. He loved playing this game, and it was a real satisfaction that the Masonic events tonight gave him the opportunity to play on a more important scale than usual.

"Why, thank you, Hank," he acknowledged Thompson graciously as he passed through the door. "I've been told you are a gentleman as well as a scholar." No harm in letting him think I know more about him than I do, Benton mused. Let him think I've got somebody telling me about him.

Once inside, Benton saw Henry Rugerri, the Attorney for Carbon County, talking with Judge Hammond. If Benton did, in fact, become the General Super, it would be vital for him to have a working relationship with both of these men. He stopped, and when there was a lull in their conversation, he spoke to the judge. "Judge, we may have a big problem coming up. I hear that Jimmy Morgan and his boss Matt Cahill have hired Sam King from right here in Price to represent the United Mine Worker's Union. Can we give them their just deserts if they use violence here as they did in Colorado and Wyoming?"

"This isn't Wyoming," the judge snorted. "We lock agitators up around here."

A grimace crossed Rugerri's face. "King can't make an honest living practicing real law. Now he's gone over to the union? Didn't know he was representing them, Mr. Benton."

Benton couldn't help but smile. He hoped to God it wasn't a condescending smile, that would be a mistake.

"I despise King myself," Judge Hammond said. "Him being with the union is news to me as well. He's just the kind who would turn against his own to make a dollar."

Benton felt he'd struck gold by bringing up King's name. Since they hadn't heard about King they might think Benton had friends in high places feeding him info about union activity. The truth was much simpler: he'd heard it from one of his snitches.

Might as well play it up and see where it goes, he thought. "My friends just got the news about King to me," he said. "We figured it was important to the both of you, and that you should know about it right away. Glad I could give something of use to you."

Benton excused himself, but Hammond delayed him for a moment. Hammond advised Benton that County Commissioner William Emerson needed to talk with him.

Good night, Benton thought as he walked away. What a couple of patsies these two are. If they represent the quality of the people running this county I could end up owning the whole place. He was, however, a little worried about what William Emerson wanted. The judge had made it sound important. For some reason Benton was uneasy about it. But all Emerson wanted was to know if Utah Fuel would pay half the salaries for deputies assigned to them when the strike came. Benton refused till he checked with Salt Lake.

No sooner had he finished talking with Emerson than Benton heard dinner being announced. And, instead of going to the bar, he headed straight to the dining room. While the tables were set elegantly, someone not familiar with the real thing would never guess that the glasses were not real crystal, and what seemed to be silverware was only silver plate. The dining room was filling fast. Who to sit with? Then his problem was solved for him. Tom Parmley was motioning for him to come over and sit. Parmley was Super for the Utah Fuel mine at Winter Quarters. Benton had been told Parmley took over Winter Quarters some time after the disastrous explosion back on May First of Nineteen Hundred. The explosion killed two hundred miners.

Benton smiled, took the proffered chair and sat down. "Thanks Tom, I was beginning to have mental reservations that I would find a place to sit." The fact Parmley saved a place for him did not escape Benton. He's currying favor, Benton decided. Good.

Benton placed the fine linen napkin in his lap just as a salad with vinaigrette dressing was served at the same time a German Auslese was being poured as an aperitif. When it came to wine, Benton was neither a label drinker nor a purist of any sort. He simply enjoyed a wine for its own qualities. But to serve wine with a vinaigrette dressing?

Benton raised the glass, tilted it, and returned it to its upright position. He could tell the wine had good legs. He cupped his hand around the back of the glass, inhaled through his nose, and found it had a semi-sweet aroma and a good grape smell. He took a small sip and held it in his mouth, a little on the sweet side but good for the aperitif. He opened his lips a bit, cupped his tongue and let the liquid drain down below his tongue. He sucked some air in over it, closed his lips, swallowed, and exhaled through his nose. To his delight the wine also had an excellent finish.

The main course of the meal was prime rib, cooked perfectly. It was so tender he could cut it with his fork. The Cabernet Souvignon served with the meat dish complemented the marvelous flavor of the meat exactly.

Throughout the meal, Benton made the usual small talk. But once they were fed, it was time to go to work. He turned once more to Parmley. "Been wanting a chance to talk seriously with you, Tom," he said. "I guess now's as good a time as any."

"Want to brag about the new Packard?" Parmley asked in a joking way. But Benton was not about to let a man using humor as a defense put him off so easily.

"Not especially. I was wondering if you'd heard anything about the union demanding we deduct the union dues from the men's wages and collect it for them?"

"Another dues check-off demand this time? Now that you mention it, no, I haven't."

"Me either," Benton agreed. "It's peculiar, too. They've always pressed for it in other strikes. I wonder why they're so silent about it now?"

Parmley was acting a little tipsy. He smiled a sort of drunken smile. "Should I care?"

Benton chuckled, but stayed on the question. He was testing Parmley to see just how deep his knowledge of union matters extended. That was why he asked about such an obscure thing in the first place. "Really, Tom. What's your view on the check-off?"

Parmley paused for a moment, his look taking on a serious gaze. He squinted one eye, and tilted his head slightly to the left. It was almost as if he were sizing up the man who had just asked the question.

Parmley's lips thinned into almost a snarl. "Just because we deduct things such as hospital and medical care, rent, electric bills, and anything our miners charge at the store, the union cheats think we should be their business agents and handle their money for them.

"It's hard enough for me to keep a couple hundred men working without blowing up the stupid mine again. Union interference don't help one bit."

Benton was satisfied. When Parmley did expose what he was really feeling he made no bones about it. He said what was on his mind straight out. No beating around the bush.

Parmley looked hard at Benton. "Why are you asking me this, Bob? You checking on me already? Or have you heard something about me you're checking out?"

The alarms went off in Benton's head. He had greatly under estimated this man. If he didn't do something quick, this could be one big mistake. This time Benton smiled at the man's straightforward manner. "Don't beat around the bush, Tom. Just come right out and tell me what's on your mind." He was gratified to hear Parmley chuckle.

Still smiling, Benton added. "I'll answer the second part first, I've heard nothing but good about you from the people I've talked with." No forced smile this time. With this man, it wouldn't work. Instead, he looked straight into Parmley's eyes.

"As to why I asked the question, the answer is, put yourself in my place. I really don't know the men I have to work with very well. And I don't have much time to learn before trouble gets here. You know yourself how few times we've been able to get together to talk." Benton noticed Parmley seemed to be evaluating every word. "So I asked a question to get to your feelings about the union without coming out first and letting you know I feel pretty much as you do."

Parmley nodded a short, curt nod. "I'll buy that, for now, Mr. Benton. We all do what we have to nowadays to get along. It isn't as it was in the old days when a Super was pretty much god in his workers' universe. The union is seeing to that."

Benton was starting to respect this man. A big grin came onto his face. "A man after my own heart. I think you and I are going to get along just fine. Unless, of course, you keep calling me Mr. Benton. Anything you want to know about me, just ask." The words were barely out of

Benton's mouth before he realized he'd made another mistake. Giving Parmley an opening such as this would make him vulnerable.

"I just want to know, if you'll tell me— is the General Super job a sure thing?"

Benton paused, pursed his lips and thought fast. *If I were in Frank Cameron's shoes, and I wanted to know how straight somebody was, I'd put a man like Parmley to the task. Better not lie to him, though. He's too sharp for that.*

"When push comes to shove, Tom, you sure don't beat around the bush. Up until Frank Cameron was hired and named both Vice President and General Manager for Utah Fuel, I would have said it was a sure thing. Now? Still, I've heard nothing to the contrary."

"Any other answer you gave me would be baloney," Parmley said. Tension seemed to leave Parmley's face, replaced by a genuine smile.

"Why would it have been baloney, Tom?" It was a straight question to Parmley, without any hidden purpose behind it. Benton just wanted to know the answer.

"I know Cameron well. We're both Winter Quarters men who go a long way back. When he plays cards, he holds his cards so close to his chest he needs a mirror on his sleve to read them. Also, he gets a kick out of keeping people on edge about what's coming," Parmley said. He paused for a moment. "My advice to you, as a friend, is that if you do get the General Super job, watch your back. Another game of his is to make sure he approaches from the blind side when he's about to stab somebody."

Benton continued to be amazed at how straightforward this man really was. Since the original drunken grin, there didn't seem to be a devious bone in his body. "Well, Tom, do you realize that if I do get the job, you just gave me enough to hang you if I wanted to?"

"But you won't. You need help to keep that wolf away from your door. He hates my guts already. But have you noticed, I'm still here, even after he became VP?"

Benton broke into a broad grin. "And if I'm made General Super, you'll be here a lot longer yet. That's a promise."

CHAPTER 5

DUES PAID

Benton sat listening to the clicking of the wheels as they passed over joints in the rails, and the occasional whistle of the steam engine. He couldn't shake the uneasy feeling about getting summoned to Utah Fuel headquarters. While Benton was a king fish in Carbon county, at the main offices in Salt Lake he was barely a keeper. Even Frank Cameron was only a little over pan-sized when compared to the sharks in New York who owned both the Denver and Rio Grande and Utah Fuel.

At the previous meeting in Salt Lake, the brass hadn't come right out with what was really on their minds. They held back the most important item on the agenda until sometime during the meeting. Just when Benton started to relax, they slipped it in, almost as an afterthought. It was a useful trick he sometimes used himself.

Then there was Cameron. The minute it was announced that Cameron was not only the new General Manager, but the VP as well, Benton made it his business to find out all he could about him. Since Cameron had a long history in Carbon County, Benton found it easy to find many people who would talk about him.

Hardest to pin down, however, was what Cameron was up to when he went back to the Central District coal mines. There were rumors he set up a riot back there in which twenty-three men were killed.

Before he could ever relax around Cameron, Benton would have to know Cameron's mind inside and out. He would have to know what Cameron was going to think before he ever thought it. That was going to take time and experience. Benton just hoped he would be around long enough to do it.

When the train pulled into the Denver and Rio Grande depot in Salt Lake twenty minutes early, Benton got off and looked around. He was surprised to see Charley Hotchkiss there acting as a chauffeur to pick him up. Benton was sure Hotchkiss would have hard feelings about not being made General Manager. Before coming to Utah, Hotchkiss was the Assistant to the President at the Denver and Rio Grande. When the railroad allowed Hotchkiss to be "borrowed" by Utah Fuel, the natural assumption was that Hotchkiss was either being groomed to take over as the permanent General Manager, or if someone else was named he would return to the Denver & Rio Grande. Now here he was, running errands. Benton wondered how Hotchkiss could let them do this to him.

"Hi, Charley," he called. "Sorry I got you running taxi duty this morning."

"It's good to get out of the office," Hotchkiss replied. "But having to pick you up was a surprise. I thought you would be showing off that new Packard of yours."

"Had a little work to do on the way here," Benton said, patting his briefcase. "You know how it is. Can't drive and work at the same time."

"Nobody at the office knows the train's early, and the meeting isn't set for another forty-five minutes. Want me to show you around the depot a bit?"

"I'm all yours," Benton said. "Lead the way." The main thing on Benton's mind, however, was feeling Hotchkiss out about Cameron's appointment. "I've got to admit, Charlie, I was surprised when they brought Cameron in and made him a vice president. We all thought you would continue on as General Manager or go back to the railroad."

"The way it was explained to me, I am a railroad man. It looks as though the miners' union is better organized and has more influence than ever before. Mines in Eastern Districts have been organized to the point that some operators had to sign union contracts. The money people back east absolutely don't want the union to get that strong in Carbon county."

"So we got Cameron," Benton finished.

"So, we get Cameron." Hotchkiss agreed as they walked. Hotchkiss paused, held out his left hand, and indicated they should go into the door on the opposite side of the hall from the women's lounge. Benton entered and saw a large smoking lounge for men. A door at the back led to the men's restroom. "Shall we?" he asked, pointing to a shoe shine stand.

"Sure," Benton agreed.

They climbed up and sat down, the black shoe shine boy began soaping up their shoes.

Hotchkiss smiled, "Kind of wish you'd brought the Packard."

Benton watched Hotchkiss closely as he spoke. Hotchkiss seemed jovial. "Been thinking of getting one myself," Hotchkiss continued. "I'd enjoy seeing one, maybe drive it."

"Next time I'm up, you got it," Benton said. But his mind was racing. Ah ha, if they're paying Hotchkiss enough to buy a Packard, I wonder what in blue blazes Cameron must be pulling down? "What kind of a car does Cameron drive?"

"He's toying with getting a new Dusenberg," Hotchkiss replied as matter-of-factly as if he'd said Cameron is having a new pair of shoes made.

A quiet thrill went through Benton. He didn't care that Cameron could afford a Dusenberg and Hotchkiss a Packard. What thrilled him was that suddenly the move from Bluestone, Colorado, to Sunnyside seemed a smarter thing than he could have realized. He began to appreciate that with Utah Fuel being owned by the Denver and Rio Grande, it was a more important company than it seemed at first glance. No wonder they would bring in a Cameron to sit on the union.

He began to feel a little more relaxed about the meeting. No matter how today went, having a reputation for being with Utah Fuel during this strike would let him write his own ticket later. By now, their shines finished, they got down from the stand, and tipped the shoe shine boy.

Hotchkiss suggested a cup of coffee and Benton agreed. They passed the barber shop to their left as they headed for the restaurant. Instead of sitting at one of the long, mahogany counters, they sat at one of the track-side tables to watch the train and people outside.

"Bob, how well do you know Cameron?" Hotchkiss asked, after they'd ordered.

"I only met him one time when he came down to Carbon County after his appointment. But I did a little checking with people who know him well."

"What kind of a man is replacing me?" Hotchkiss asked. Then he added, "If you don't mind telling me."

Benton looked at Hotchkiss. Some day Hotchkiss might repay any kindness he was shown now. If he could work him right, Hotchkiss would become one more ally in addition to Parmley. One right in the middle of everything that would be going on.

"Do you want the long or the short of it?" Benton asked.

Hotchkiss leaned across the table toward Benton. He spoke in a quiet tone. "I need to know I wasn't replaced as a political thing, or something I did wrong. Give me the long."

"I really shouldn't tell you this. Charley, if this gets out, you know I'm fired."

"I appreciate it, Bob. You can trust me."

They both sat back as the waitress brought their coffee, then leaned forward again when she left. "Okay, Charley. I understand Cameron's hard as nails. He started as a miner in Castle Gate. The mines still belonged to the Pleasant Valley Coal Company at that time. After Utah Fuel bought out Pleasant Valley, Cameron worked his way up with them. Then he quit about the time of the Mother Jones troubles, hard to pin down the reason."

Benton paused and took time to put sugar and cream in the coffee, stir it and take a sip. "Maybe he had something to do with Mother Jones being thrown in jail down there. That angered the Eastern papers. Our people back there didn't care for it either. Also, maybe Cameron was the scapegoat, for somebody else."

Both men leaned back, picked up their coffee cups and drank some more. Benton was satisfied to notice they were both in sync. That meant Hotchkiss was paying close attention. "After that, Cameron went back East and held some responsible positions in West Virginia. Then he was General Manager for Phelps Dodge at Dawson, North Dakota, when the Phelps Dodge interests invaded that area."

He had to wait for a moment as the waitress came past, tried to refill their cups, got waived off, and left the check. Hotchkiss reached over, and slid it next to his cup.

"Thanks," Benton said, and continued. "Cameron returned to Utah to open up the Cameron mine, which he owned. Later, W. G. Sharp bought out the Mohrland, Blackhawk, and Hiawatha mines to start U. S. Fuel Company. He induced Cameron to be General Manager for U.S. Fuel. Shall I go on, or do you want me to cut to the bottom line?"

"The more I know, the better prepared we can be. Thanks for giving me the details."

"Maybe Cameron was willing to leave his mine because business wasn't too good. Maybe he's better at stopping union influence than he is in influencing men who work for him. Maybe he just wants to play in a bigger pond. Who knows?"

They both leaned back to finish off their coffee, then leaned forward again. "Cameron stayed with U.S. Fuel until he decided to try being his own boss again. Cameron became the principal owner of Liberty Fuel, and opened the Liberty mine. Liberty Fuel started doing pretty good. When Utah Fuel hired Cameron from Liberty, he made his brother-in-law, L.R. Weber, the new president of Liberty."

"So Cameron can still control Liberty, even though he's gone?" Hotchkiss asked.

"Sure looks that way. Plus, he's probably getting more than his share of the money. And in every place Cameron has worked, there were labor troubles." Benton paused so Hotchkiss could get the full effect of what he was going to say next. "And, Charley, not once did the union ever win."

"Is that so?" Hotchkiss said, "No wonder they had to make him a Vice President to get him. Looks as if they didn't simply decide to get a man experienced in labor troubles, they panicked into hiring a tiger."

"A friend of mine calls him a wolf," Benton corrected.

"Yeah, that fits," Hotchkiss agreed. "Our friends back East give away nothing unless they have to. If Cameron didn't have that kind of reputation, why else would they make him a Vice President? They must really be afraid of how strong the union is becoming."

That ended the conversation for the moment. They left the restaurant, tipped a porter to put the luggage in Hotchkiss' car. "You got to remember, Charley," Benton added as Hotchkiss started the car, "the big shots are from back East. The unions there have had some success. In Utah, unions have never had a chance. In addition to what we've got going for us in other places, in Utah we've even got the dominant church on our side. Maybe they've hired a wolf to hunt lambs."

Hotchkiss just laughed. He drove up Third South. As they went by some land being cleared for construction, Hotchkiss pointed to it. "Next year the Greeks are going to build a special cathedral there called Holy Trinity."

Hotchkiss pulled up to the Judge Building and found a parking place. It was a large modern building made of a red/yellowish firebrick; it rose six stories, big for this part of the country.

Once upstairs, they went through the company's offices. Hotchkiss stopped to say something to his secretary. This gave Benton a chance for a quick look around. He'd been there once before, but the quality of the place still impressed him. It bespoke money and power. But if you're going to invite state senators, church leaders, and a governor to your digs, you'd better be able to impress them. Hotchkiss rejoined him. "Seems everyone's already in the main conference room," he said.

It almost floored Benton to see J. H. Young, President of the Denver and Rio Grande at this meeting. Fish didn't get much bigger than this. Something really important was up. During the introductions, Benton was busy trying to size up Cameron and noticed Cameron was sizing him up as well—standard procedure. Benton was careful not to seem too informal with any of them, and addressed Frank as Mr. Cameron.

"Let's cut the polite stuff, Bob. Mr. Cameron was my father. I'm Frank." Then he turned to Hotchkiss. "Charley, how about a little coffee, and a few refreshments for our guests?" Hotchkiss turned immediately and walked out.

Benton could hear Hotchkiss giving instructions to his secretary. The speed with which the coffee, doughnuts, sweet rolls, and bran muffins arrived left no doubt in Benton's mind that Hotchkiss had done a little preparing for this meeting as well as Benton had.

"I was looking forward to seeing your new Packard," President Young said as Benton and Hotchkiss settled around the table. "I think you made a good choice in cars, but a bad choice in timing."

"How's that, President Young?" Benton asked, trying to figure Young's objection.

Young pursed his lips, then spoke. "The recession really hasn't hurt us in the West yet. A strike seems certain to be called around April first. That's when Carbon county operators will announce that increased production costs force us to cut miners' wages. Better not to buy a Packard on one hand, and talk about increased production costs on the other."

"Mia culpa," Benton responded. Now he was ready with his answer. "One reason I bought it was to demonstrate to L.F. Rains how strong Utah Fuel is. I know Rains took an option on coal property next to ours at Sunnyside. He's planning to open a mine in the next canyon over. That would certainly create a competitor for our coal as well as a possible competitor for our coke.

"I figured a Packard would demonstrate to him that if even our superintendents could afford Packards, maybe it would cost him more money than it was worth to go into competition with us. Then maybe he would give up his option."

Young looked at Benton long and hard. "Good response," he said at last. "I can see you've thought your answer through. But let me give you a little word of advice.

"Before you take it upon yourself to solve our problems on your own, you might find it useful to speak with Frank, here, first." Young emphasized the word first.

Benton simply nodded. He got the message loud and clear. He had been warned. Don't do one thing without getting Cameron's approval.

Young pursed his lips, again. This time he paused longer, as if he were weighing the pros and cons of something. He turned to Cameron. "Order that new Dusenberg, Frank. Or maybe a Silver Ghost. Charley, get going on the Packard."

Benton got the other message. Cameron had waited for approval from Young to buy a new car. It was also crystal clear to Benton that powerful as Cameron seemed to be, he wasn't running this company. Maybe Young isn't running this company, either. I wonder who Young has to clear things with first?

Young interrupted Benton's chain of thought. "As for Mr. Rains, you can forget him. We have already dealt with Mr. Rains. As time goes on, Rains will learn he must let his option on the property next to Sunnyside lapse. He will have no choice. The Denver and Rio Grande will refuse to build the twelve miles of tracks he needs to develop that coal he has the option on. Coke he needs will have to come from us. It is a dead issue."

"That's really good to hear," Benton said, and there was relief in his voice. "That's going to make my job a lot easier," he continued. "On what grounds is the railroad going to deny him, President Young?"

Young smiled a devious smile. "You're going to have to watch this one, Frank. He could end up in your job someday. He's already figured out our reasons would have to stand up in court. Otherwise, our railroad would be slapped with a restraint of trade lawsuit.

"First," Young continued, "we will prove to the industrial commission that we don't have enough coal cars to support a new mine. Second, since we let out bids for a thousand cars just last September to handle the business we already have, we cannot afford more cars at this time. Also, as you know, we have to put at least one, and sometimes as many as three extra helper engines on a train to boost it up the grade from Helper to Soldier Summit. We are currently hauling over two hundred and fifty cars of coal a day over the Summit. The many hundreds of cars of freight we also handle taxes our capacity to the limit."

Young pursed his lips again and looked even more smug as he continued. "We can prove that our financial situation at this time will not allow us to purchase the extra engines it would take to move his coal over the summit. As I said before," Young continued, "game, set, and match. Case closed."

"Whew," Benton exclaimed in true amazement.

"President Young has him cold," Cameron said, admiringly. "L. F. Rains and his supposed big money from back East hasn't got a chance. See why it's a dead issue?"

Benton knew he had better respond, and quick. "I see it as clear as a rabbit staring into a coyote's eyes," he responded.

That made Young chuckle. "You Westerners sure have a lot of quaint expressions. A rabbit looking into a coyote's eyes? Never heard that one before. Have to remember it."

How could he have heard it before? Benton thought. I just made it up. "Why, thank you, President Young. Glad to be of service in any way I can," Benton said.

Up until now Cameron had pretty much been sitting back and letting Young do the talking. Now, he leaned across the table just enough to let Benton know he was going to be spoken to, and looked Benton straight in the eye.

"We understand that at your Masonic doings you told County Commissioner William Emerson that you would not commit Utah Fuel to paying half the salaries of any deputies needed for a strike until you talked with us. Is that correct?"

"Yes, Sir. It is," Benton replied, and thought fast. He had prepared to discuss this request by the county commissioners when he got the chance to talk. He had not anticipated Cameron would know about it in advance.

But even more important, Benton now knew who at least one of Cameron's snitches in the county was. In addition to being a commissioner, Emerson was also a Utah Fuel employee. Nor did it escape Benton that Cameron had let him know who this snitch was. Emerson was the only one who approached Benton with this request.

"Why didn't you agree to pay the costs," Cameron challenged.

"The commissioners just assumed that we'd pay half the costs as we did last time. With the recession on, I was not convinced we should pay those extra costs. Plus, I would never commit to such expenses without checking with you first."

"Real smart," Cameron replied.

Benton had wondered why Emerson had pressed him so hard the night of the banquet. Now, he could see it plainly. Cameron used Emerson to set Benton up. If he'd taken the bait and agreed to pay, his hopes of being General Super would be history now.

Cameron still seemed intense. "About that request to pay for the extra deputies," he continued. "When they hit you up about it again, try to stall. Ask them what do they think we pay taxes for?" Benton nodded, and Cameron curtly changed the subject.

"What I want you to do about security is to build a rock shed for a search light up on the hillside overlooking town. We've got an extra large carbon-arc light ordered. Should be down there any day now. The shed needs to be built strong in case some trouble maker with a rifle tries to shoot the light out. When the strike comes, I want that light up and running all night, every night. That should help discourage any of those union rogues who think they can stop production with sabotage."

Benton was logging it all into his memory faster than Cameron was talking about it. "The shed's as good as built," he said.

"Good. At the first sign of trouble, the other operators and I will get Governor Maybe to send in the National Guard." He paused, leaned back, and took a sip of coffee, then he took a bite of roll. "Keep me advised on security matters as they come up."

"Mind if I interrupt with another item?" Young asked. He was still seated and showed no signs of leaving. Then he continued without waiting for a response. "Charley, will you run me down to the station?"

"Sure thing, President Young," Hotchkiss responded.

Without even acknowledging that Hotchkiss had spoken, Young began again. "I want you to know that when I met with the officers of Utah Fuel in New York before coming here, we agreed that along with all Frank's responsibilities as Vice President and General Manager, he is now also the President of the Wasatch Store Company. And is, therefore, over all company stores as well, not just the one in Sunnyside."

Both Benton and Hotchkiss offered their congratulations to Cameron. Cameron smiled smugly, then looked at Young. "Thank you for mentioning that President Young. With your permission, I'll talk with Bob about the matter we discussed now." Young nodded. Strangely Young didn't leave and Benton got a sinking feeling in the pit of his stomach.

"Bob, there is one real problem for our Sunnyside store that needs discussing," Cameron began. "What have you done about the Sunnyside Mercantile Company operating that store at the mouth of the canyon below our property? Don't you think they are really cutting into the business our miners entitle us to? Miners whose wages we pay?"

Oh no, here it is, Benton thought, what he needs to can me. He has me nailed. I was so focused on mining and unions, I totally forgot about merchandising.

"Frank, I'll be honest. I haven't given it a lot of thought. Jack Pessetto has operated that store since long before I came to town. So I just assumed he had worked out some sort of accommodation with the company." Benton felt his heart had stopped.

"Perhaps that accommodation was with old Alexander Cowie, our ex-General Manager. Probably on some personal basis," Cameron said. "Now, however, any accommodation which might have been in existence no longer has any force as far as I'm concerned."

Benton thought fast. "I understand what you're saying, Frank. Jack Pessetto is a Mason. I will talk with him at our next meeting."

"I didn't know he was a fellow Mason of yours. Working with him

45

might put you in a ticklish position. I'll get someone else to handle negotiations with him. Okay with you?"

Benton's heart started beating again. "Whatever you want, Frank," he said with more relief than he could remember having in years. "Let's just say I owe you a favor."

"Don't worry. With your new status, there will be plenty of opportunity for payback."

"New status?" Benton asked, totally unaware of what Cameron was talking about.

"Let me tell him, Frank," President Young interjected, "I'd forgotten about this earlier. But then I remembered it, and that's why I stayed.

"Bob, we're not unaware of the yeoman service you did at Bluestone Colorado before coming to Utah. Labor trouble is labor trouble, I guess, no matter what state it's in. Therefore, we decided that someone new to Utah might help us make our case with the public better than old dogs such as Cameron and me."

Benton held his breath.

"On Charley's recommendation, you are our new General Superintendent."

"Congratulations, Bob," Hotchkiss said. "I guess you've paid the dues to earn it."

During the rest of the meeting, Benton was barely aware of what was going on. So great was the mixture of satisfaction and relief, it interfered with his normally close attention to detail. He tried concentrating, but was barely aware of what else was said.

"Bob, I'm counting on you," Cameron said as the meeting closed. "You're the one down in the trenches. You'll be one of our major tools in squashing the union this time."

Bob's uneasiness on the return train bordered almost on panic. His worry now covered new ground. Getting named General Superintendent was one thing. Keeping the job was quite another. Benton realized he'd just begun to pay dues.

CHAPTER 6

AIN'T SHE SWEET

Once again Benton drove the Packard at fifty over the wash board road. He had to get to the depot at Mounds Junction by 7:00. He really didn't care if Elizabeth had to wait for him.

Mounds acted as the Sunnyside depot, even though it was twelve miles away and in the middle of nowhere. Compared to the depot in Salt Lake, it was a shanty. Still, cattle and sheep men loading stock, freight for the mine, and food for the stores in Sunnyside all combined to keep it a busy place. This morning Benton got a call from the mainline telegrapher saying his daughter had boarded in Denver and would be stopping here.

He arrived only to discover the train would be twenty minutes late. Just when it seemed things in Carbon county were all going his way, his daughter had to be coming home. She would add problems, he knew. He and his daughter had a history of violent arguments. She felt that both she and her mother, Katherine, were better than he was. When she had to leave college she argued about coming to Utah. She threatened to run away if he didn't let her stay in Colorado.

At last the big engine pulled in slowly and stopped, steam spewing from the chamber release valve. For a moment, the cloud of white shrouded the tracks. Out into that mist Elizabeth stepped from her car. Benton had to admit, she looked stunning.

She held out her white-gloved hand for the conductor, who barely touched the tips of her long, slim fingers to help her down. Because of the shroud of steam, she seemed almost to float to the ground. She looked around with disdain. She paused to adjust the little saucer hat above her long flowing hair, then she saw her dad.

To Benton's surprise, she smiled sweetly. He hurried toward her. "Howdy, Princess," he said as pleasantly as he could.

47

As quickly as her smile came, it faded and was replaced with a look of hurt. "Dad, you know I don't want to be here in Utah. It's awful. Can't you send me to another college?"

"Maybe next fall." Benton turned to the porter and gave him a nickel. "Put the bags in the back of the Packard." He didn't specify which Packard. With 37,000 license plates issued in Utah in 1922, this was one of only three Packards in the state.

"Dad, fall is six months away. I can't stand this isolation that long. After we left Green River, I didn't even see a house for over an hour."

"What did you expect to see?" he asked. But what he really wanted to say was that if she paid less attention to boys and parties and more to studying, she wouldn't have to be looking for houses. "It won't be all that bad. You'll enjoy our house in Sunnyside."

"Is it as big as our house in Glenwood Springs?"

"Well, no. But your mother enjoys it. It's a nice town, not the ends of the earth."

Sarcasm replaced the hurt look. "Oh?" she asked. "Then where is?"

Benton did his best to stifle the anger rising within him. But, for his wife's sake, he tried to be civil. "I have a surprise for you. I brought your horse Bonnie here. . . ."

Elizabeth interrupted him in mid sentence. "Bonnie? Really? Oh, thank you!" To his surprise, she hugged him and gave him a kiss on the cheek. Benton was pleased and flustered at the same time. Elizabeth hadn't given him a hug or kiss without prompting for over five years.

"My blacksmith is grooming her and riding her every day, so she will be in good shape."

Learning Bonnie was waiting for her gave her the kind of joy she felt the first time she saw the horse and knew it was hers. "Remember how Bonnie got her name, Dad?"

"Afraid not," he replied, wondering where this was leading.

"Our stable hand in Glenwood Springs was Scottish. When he first showed her to me, he said, 'She's bonnie.' I thought Bonnie was her name. But it'll be no fun riding her here."

Benton held the door to the Packard open for her. "This country grows on you, somehow. Your mother says it's the first time we have really been able to be alone together in a nice place."

"Good for Mom," Elizabeth said. Benton did not respond. He just slammed the car door shut with enough force to raise the head of the porter who was just leaving.

Elizabeth ran her white gloves over the leather upholstery and examined the dials and gauges. "I hate this place, but love the Packard. I'm really glad Mom could help you get it."

Benton didn't know whether to accept the compliment, or to snap back at her for the insinuation he could have never afforded the car on his own. Her rapidly changing emotions, her disdain and insinuations at one moment, and her childlike joy the next left him feeling totally bewildered. He got out of the Packard, walked to the other side. "Slide over," he said as he opened the door.

Elizabeth squealed as a child on Christmas morning. "Can I drive it? Really?"

He gave her the instructions about the Packard he felt she needed. With Elizabeth driving, they headed east toward Sunnyside.

"How far is Sunnyside?" After awhile Benton said about seven more miles. "Are there any good roads around here?" she asked as dust began coming into the car.

Then her problems came rushing back. "Thanks for letting me drive, Dad. Really. But I feel a stranger here. I don't even have anyone my own age with whom I can talk."

"I know," he said, and Elizabeth's heart sank. She knew very well he did not know. "But you have your mother and me. You'll make new friends, and ride your horse. We have parties in town, and a Masonic Temple in Price. You'll go when parties are for families."

None of this was what Elizabeth wanted to hear. "Dad, let me go back to Colorado with my friends. I can be trusted. I didn't do anything terrible in college," she said in a voice she hoped sounded full of contrition. "I was never alone with those boys we sneaked into our bedroom. My roommate was always there. Dad, this's the Twenties, we were just having a little party," she tried to explain. "It's what kids in college do."

Again Benton tried not to let the anger show on his face. "That's what I understand. Yes, that's what the school told me. But, Elizabeth, there are rules and proprieties, Twenties or no Twenties," he added, the anger in him finally starting to win the battle. He knew he was losing control. "Look at the position you've put me in. How do I explain that my daughter is leaving school three months before she finishes her first year?"

His anger mounted. "No matter what I tell people they're going to believe you're knocked up. You'll stay here for the summer to prove you're not."

"Dad!" Elizabeth screamed. She jammed on the brakes, stopped the car in the middle of the road, put her face in her hands, and began to cry.

"Slide over," Benton said. He got out, went around and got behind the steering wheel. He put the car in gear and sped out, leaving a cloud of dust spewing fifty yards behind them. They approached the canyon leading into the town. Elizabeth fought to get her tears under control. She would never forgive him for that remark—never, never, never. She took off one of her gloves, and dabbed at her eyes. She no longer cared what he felt or thought.

She began looking around. Nothing here looked similar to any other town she had ever seen. She decided the only thing left was to run away. She had to learn the place and the people quickly. She wouldn't have a chance if everyone in town was a stooge of his who would report her every movement to him.

Benton realized he'd gone too far. He'd hurt her, and that was a mistake. He only wanted her to understand what she did affected the family and his image. With the kind of people he must work with if he was going to make it as the General Super, image was vital.

He calmed down, and wanted to try to make amends as she sat silently looking out the window. But he really didn't know how. He tried a stab at getting her interested in the town she seemed to be staring at so intently. "Those women we are passing-the ones with the shawls over their heads-are Greeks. We're in Greek town now. They've even got a couple of coffee houses just outside of town on private property. There are also a couple of coffee houses on company property that they lease from us."

Elizabeth looked at the short, dark women in their drab dresses and felt sorry for them. They looked as trapped here as she was. She realized that when she ran, somehow she would have to throw her father off guard. If he knew how really dissatisfied she was, he'd watch her like a hawk. So, she began asking questions. Not because she cared about the answers, but to create the facade that they had an acceptable father-daughter relationship. "What do you mean, coffee houses? Doesn't the company own everything?" she asked, as her dad slowed the Packard for a couple of dirty little urchins who ran into the road.

"They're all private businesses. The large store off to the left just before we entered town is Pessetto's place. It and the others take away business the company should be getting at my store. In my coal camp, the company should own all businesses."

With disgust for him growing, she noticed that almost everything he spoke about had the possessive adjective "my" in front of it. He acts as if he really owns these things.

She noticed Sunnyside not only looked dirty, but smoky. Rows of fires were burning in something off to the right. They looked dangerous. She would have to stay away from there when she ran. "What are those things, with the smoke coming from them?"

"Beehive-type coke ovens. Production from my mine goes into the production of coke."

For a moment, she remained silent and just looked around. She noticed the town laid along the bottom of a narrow canyon with steep cliffs on each side. "What's that big thing over there on those spindly-legged beams to hold it up?"

"That's my tipple. That tunnel with the small tracks running out of it is the portal to my mine. All the main buildings are grouped around the mine. That one," he said, pointing, "is the fan house. It has a huge fan which blows fresh air from the outside into the mine. The long building is our shops where we repair our mine equipment. Those little stone buildings over there are the powder houses where we keep the explosives we use."

"This is really interesting," she said to cover her real motives for wanting to know so much. She continued looking and saw corrugated iron sheds she recognized as stables. Also, there were many corrals. They must use an awful lot of horses. Maybe I can steal one of those to get away. Then she saw more danger--- huge greyish-black piles of what seemed to be smoking rock and dirt. "What are those huge piles of smoking dirt?"

"We call them bony piles. They contain a mixture of rock and coal from the mine. We throw it away. After a while, spontaneous combustion sets the coal in them on fire. Eventually they burn themselves out, but it takes years."

Benton was totally taken in by all her questions. He thought she'd finally found some interest in his world. His own mood shifted. He laughed. "The canyon is so narrow and the cliffs on each side are so high that the old timers say first it's sunny on one side, then it's sunny on the other side, then the sun goes down. That's why it's called Sunnyside."

In spite of herself, Elizabeth smiled. That description fit this place so perfectly. Benton noticed the smile, and decided maybe his tactic was working. He decided to share more with her. The road crossed a bridge. He pulled the Packard to a stop on the bridge. "This bridge is the dividing line between English town and Wop town."

"The mine workings, the post office, the bridge, and the store are a sort of a no-man's land. Everybody in town seems to mix well as long as they are in one of these areas. But when some of the Wop kids and English kids have a fight with each other, it's usually here on the bridge. They have some real brawls. We tolerate it because when you have this many different kinds of people living so close together, there is going to be friction."

Elizabeth thought this was barbaric. Her own feelings showed on her face. Noticing, Benton changed his tone. "But myself, I'm against violence of any kind."

"The houses look terrible. And look at all those outhouses, don't they have plumbing?"

"We're building new houses and replacing the old ones as fast as company profits will allow us to," he said proudly. "All the modern houses in upper town where we live have plumbing and bath tubs." More respect for him slipped away. Squalor and people living in houses I wouldn't keep my horse in, are tolerated if they interfere with profits. Ugh.

"Many of the men we have to hire are lower class scum from all over Southern Europe. They adjust after they've been here a while. The biggest problem is not how they live, but how they think. It was the Greeks who caused the labor trouble over in Colorado in 1913. So we hired labor agents back East to recruit gangs of Wops for us. We brought them in to help break strikes. Now it's the Wops, Greeks, Bohunks, that's causing trouble. Always said it was a mistake to bring in foreigners. We'd hire more Englishmen if we could get 'em. But even many of them are from the bottom rung of English society."

Benton turned off the main road onto a section that shut them off from the sight of the lower canyon. Elizabeth could see a group of modern, brightly painted houses. Each had a nice lawn. She saw him pointing down what seemed a private, tree-lined lane. She looked and saw a large, white, two-story house surrounded on three sides by an expansive lawn. The ginger bread moldings around the windows were a bright green that matched the color of the lawn perfectly. Everything looked newly painted. Flower gardens were here and there. Elizabeth was most taken with one garden that had large yellow roses. As her dad had said, the house was smaller than their home in Glenwood Springs. But compared to anything else she had seen in Sunnyside, it seemed to be a palace.

Behind and off to the left there was another structure, equally as well cared for. Her dad drove the Packard toward this little house. "It used to be a carriage house, but now it's the garage," he explained. "There's your mother waiting for you," he added.

"Stop, Dad, let me out." She got out and started running toward her mother. Katherine Benton opened the screen door and started toward Elizabeth as well. Both of them were smiling and holding their arms out for an embrace. Both had tears in their eyes. Paying no attention, Benton put his Packard in the carriage house.

CHAPTER 7

MORE TIRED
THAN BEASTS OF BURDEN

Once the three of them were inside, her mother hugged Elizabeth again and gave her a kiss on the cheek. They started to talk excitedly. After a few exchanges, however, Katherine proudly began showing Elizabeth the house and garden. Benton asserted he'd wasted enough time already, and would have to get back to work. He left as the other two began their tour.

There were three bedrooms and two baths. Elizabeth was relieved that, at least, she would have her own bathroom. The worry she'd have to share one with her parents was small compared to a fear she had been trying to shut out of her mind. Silly as it would sound to anybody, she'd worried Sunnyside might be so primitive she'd have to use an outhouse.

She had never had to use one in her entire life. But at college, some of her friends had. Their description of the smell, the flies, and the sight below the seat sickened Elizabeth.

As they toured, Elizabeth made appropriate comments about this or that being really nice. Finally, Elizabeth followed her mom back to the main floor.

Adjoining the kitchen, there was a walk-in pantry. "The pantry keeps the heat of the kitchen out of the dining room in the summer," Katherine said. "But most of our cooking is done in the spare kitchen downstairs. Some ladies from the town come in to do most of it. The only thing I have to cook is breakfast. And not even that on holidays."

They went through a rather small hallway that led to the dining room. There her mother seemed especially pleased about two large china hutches filled with truly exquisite china. Also, Katherine brought some of her art collection that she was particularly proud of from Colorado.

On the rear wall was the new water color by John Marin titled Sunset, Maine Coast. On the adjoining wall across from the large picture window were La Peche by Thomas Wilmer Dewing and The Winter Garden by Childe Hassam.

"Mom, do you think anyone in this town will recognize the value of these pieces?"

"It's not important, Honey. I do."

Although their home in Colorado had many more and nicer things, her mother really seemed happy here.

On the basement floor was another kitchen, laundry area, and a storage area for canned and bottled foods. There was also a study for her dad with a billiard table, rifle cases, and a few trophy heads mounted on the wall.

Katherine pointed to a couple of the trophy heads. "Dad and I made a trade-off," she said. "I let him have the heads downstairs if he let me choose the paintings upstairs."

Katherine led them outside. Behind the house was a rise that sloped upward toward the mountain. Up the sloping side of the rise, a cobble-stone walkway meandered back and forth between gorgeous stone wall terraces. They contained grape arbors and large trees. Elizabeth noticed shaded stone benches. At the top, Elizabeth saw an Oriental man bent over planting onions and other early vegetables. "Toshio! Come meet my daughter," Katherine called kindly. "Toshio is a master gardener. He's also my chauffeur when I need to go somewhere and your dad can't drive me. We have a lot of foreign help."

Toshio came hurrying toward them. He stood there quietly.

Katherine changed the subject for a moment, and Elizabeth wondered why. "The people in town seem to admire your father. Your father's office manager tells me that at Christmas many of the Greeks and Italians bring special Christmas confections and wines. Other men bring things such as roasts, sausages, and geese."

Elizabeth doubted townspeople were doing this out of the goodness of their hearts. More likely they were afraid they'd get fired if they didn't. But doing it only because they couldn't help but adore her family? What rubbish. Still, if everyone in town was at his beck and call, she'd never get out of here.

She turned to Toshio. "Toshio, is that what you're called?"

Toshio bowed, and raised his head slightly, "If it please you, I answer to that name."

"Is that right? Do the men and women of town really want to help out and bring gifts?"

Toshio raised almost upright, but his hands were still stiffly at his sides. "Oh, yes, Miss. Everyone in town feels it is a great honor to be able to assist your most esteemed family."

Lying little Chinaman, Elizabeth thought.

"Toshio," Katherine interjected, "this is my daughter, Elizabeth. When she's ready, I want you to take her to the company stables and introduce her to Cyclone Henry."

"Hai," Toshio said. The word came out quick and sharp. He bowed slightly once more. "If I may say so, Mrs. Benton, you have a very beautiful daughter."

"Thank you, Toshio," Elizabeth said. "You speak English surprisingly well."

Again Toshio bowed, but this time it was a slight dropping of the head and shoulders.

"You are too kind. Mainly my children taught me. I am the only Japanese man in Sunnyside who brought his wife and children over with him." My mistake, Elizabeth thought. He isn't a coolie, he's a Jap. Oh, well, no difference.

"Toshio assures me that by the time summer comes and he has planted everything in the garden, we will have all the fresh produce we can eat," Katherine bragged.

"Mine are humble efforts," Toshio said modestly. "Some of the Italian and Greek miners have gardens with outstanding vegetables as well."

"Toshio takes the prizes at the vegetable contest Sunnyside has each fall," Katherine said.

Elizabeth began to rethink her opinion of Toshio, not particularly as a person, but as a potential help mate for escape. Since he was the chauffeur, maybe she could get him to take her somewhere where she could ditch him.

They turned around and started back down the path. "Ganz Durrant is Dad's office manager. He tells us Toshio steals vegetables from the garden. He takes some home to his family, and he sells the rest," Katherine told Elizabeth. "Ganz said I didn't need to worry about it because Toshio would always make sure we had everything we need. I appreciate a man who can make a little extra money as much as anyone else."

As they reached the back door, Katherine turned to Eliazabeth. "Are you sorry to be here, Baby?"

Elizabeth was stumped. If she let her mother know what happened it might cause her mother pain, and she might be on guard as well. If she pretended to enjoy it here, it would really devastate her mother if she had to run away. But she didn't want to lie to her, either. "I'll probably be able to manage until this fall when I go to another college. Mom, don't you have some friends in Colorado, or some other place, I can go to until then?"

Katherine hesitated. "I don't think so. For some reason, your father really is insisting you stay here for a while. Maybe we can talk about it later. But, Honey, you're being here means so much to me."

"Me, too, Mom," she said and reached out and hugged her mother to show her how much she loved her. But she needed time alone to think about what her best move would be. "Mom, I don't want to bother Toshio. Would you tell me how to get to the stables? I can't wait to say hello to Bonnie."

"It's easy. The stables are past the large recreation hall on the left."

"Got to go get my bags from the Packard," she responded. She went out to the carriage house and opened the trunk for her first load of luggage. "Please, Miss," a voice behind her said, and she recognized Toshio. "Don't get me in trouble with your father by carrying those heavy things into the house by yourself."

Apparently she was not the only one watching what was going on around the place.

"As you wish," she said as kindly as she could. But she jotted away in her memory that Toshio was quiet, but very much aware, nonetheless. He might well prove useful later—maybe more help than just a ride somewhere. Toshio brought in her suitcases and took them up to her bedroom; Katherine came upstairs to help Elizabeth put her things away.

"I see you've done your best to prepare my room," she said, looking around. She saw that here and there on the bed were stuffed pillows with crocheted covers. On top of the dresser were small framed photographs of Elizabeth as a child. And propped up against the pillows at the head of the bed was Elizabeth's teddy bear.

"The room looks cute, Mom," Elizabeth said in acknowledgment. "Thanks for hanging up the clothes you brought from Colorado. I'll unpack my suitcases. I'll be all set."

Her mother was trying unsuccessfully to hide her joy. "You're welcome, Dear. Where shall we start?" was the only response she gave. Her mother seemed so anxious to see Elizabeth settled in and happy there was little doubt in Elizabeth's mind how much her mother really loved her. Elizabeth was a little disturbed by how happy her mother seemed to be with Elizabeth's company. That would make running away harder.

"Mom, we'll have plenty of time to visit. But right now I just want to get up to see Bonnie." Disappointment crossed her mother's face, but she left to go downstairs.

Before Elizabeth left, she took her riding clothes from their hangers and put them on. She put on her hat and adjusted it.

She decided that her English riding habit would probably look out of place here in this nowhere backwater. But it couldn't be helped. She chided herself for not having anticipated this. She should have purchased a few Western outfits. On the other hand, she thought, I won't be here that long. She went downstairs. "Mom, I'm going to see Bonnie now. Maybe a ride will relax me."

"Be careful, Honey," Katherine cautioned.

"There's nothing to worry about," Elizabeth shot back over her shoulder as she walked out the door. Once outside, Elizabeth walked down the road toward the mine and through some of the upper part of town. Here and there a woman or two passed with a polite, "Hello," and a quizzical stare. As she passed them, Elizabeth looked at their plain, generally worn dresses, feeling out of place in her fine riding habit. She was a little embarrassed. She wouldn't satisfy the curiosity in their looks by stopping to tell them she was the Super's daughter. They'll learn soon enough who I am, she thought.

Mostly, however, she hated walking through this town. Tucked up against the mountain-side were chicken coops and pig pens. The smell of the town was really ugly.

She was surprised at the large number of children playing noisily throughout the town. They laughed, shouted, and ran around. Elizabeth's spirits buoyed just watching them. Except for her mother, they were the first demonstration of joy she had seen from anyone since the trouble started at college. Ahead lay the little canyon her mother mentioned. There were several corrals with horses in them. Behind was a large open blacksmith shop. A colored man was busily banging on some glowing iron thing between his hammer and his anvil. A small boy stood working the bellows which kept the glowing forge billowing hot flame.

And there, in the first corral, among some large work horses, stood her beautiful black Bonnie. Elizabeth broke into a run. The other horses in the corral shied away from her approach, but Bonnie raised her head, whinnied, and trotted toward the fence.

Elizabeth's heart swelled with love for this horse. She had not suspected that Bonnie would even remember her after six months, let alone register joy to see her. A look of sadness again crossed her face. Running away meant she had to leave Bonnie, again. Bonnie was more than just a friend. As far as Elizabeth was concerned, she was a member of Elizabeth's family. Next to her mother, there was Bonnie. That was all she had. Leaving them again would be hard. But she felt so very out of place here.

Elizabeth crawled through the timber rails of the corral, hugged Bonnie around the neck, and rubbed and petted her all over. While Elizabeth was stroking and caressing her, Bonnie did her best to nuzzle Elizabeth at every move she made.

Elizabeth started for the gate and Bonnie followed her. As she went out the gate Bonnie tried to follow. When Elizabeth shut the gate Bonnie whinnied at her, began to prance, and then ran nervously back and forth along the fence. "Just a minute, Bonnie. I'm not leaving you again. We'll go for a ride in a minute," Elizabeth said in a soothing tone.

Elizabeth headed for the blacksmith shop. "Hi, there," she said to the man with the heavy hammer in his hand. "Do you know where I can find Mr. Henry?"

"I be Cyclone, Ma'am. Y'all must be Mr. Benton's girl."

"Yes, pleased to meet you. You the one been taking such good care of my horse?"

"I be doin' my best, Ma'am."

"Thank you. I'm impressed. I've never seen her looking better."

"Thank you, Ma'am."

"Do you have my saddle and other tac?"

"I be gettin' it for you immediately. But excuse me while I be washin' my hands." Cyclone answered so graciously that she was a little confused by this man. Although he was dirty and his speech illiterate, he seemed to exude friendliness and good humor. There was something genuine about him. He seemed unaware of his sad position in life.

Cyclone interrupted her thoughts by turning to the boy at the bellows, "Hank, you be easin' up on them bellows. This be takin' a while." Elizabeth waited while he washed his hands and muscled arms in the barrel of dirty water alongside the anvil. She couldn't help but wrinkle her nose. Why does he bother? That filthy water won't make him any cleaner.

"Is my saddle, bridal, and everything already here?" She asked.

"Yes, Ma'am," Cyclone said, drying his hands on the dirty towel alongside the barrel. "Follow me, Ma'am."

"Cyclone, stop calling me, Ma'am. My name is Elizabeth," she said as she followed him.

"Yes, Miss Elizabeth."

"And stop being so blasted polite. You can call me Elizabeth without putting the Miss in front of it. Anybody who's taken care of Bonnie this way deserves my gratitude."

"Thank you, Miss Elizabeth. But it wouldn't do if I be too sociable. I hopes y'all understands." Elizabeth thought for a moment, realized what he was saying. She told him she would find a proper way to show him how much she appreciated what he'd done for Bonnie.

"No need, Miss Elizabeth," Cyclone said and broke into a broad smile. "Ain't that what friends be for? Besides, that Bonnie, she sure be one fine little filly. It be a pleasure carin' for her." He stopped in front of a large cupboard, smiled again, and opened it. A bridle hung on a wooden peg. On a large wide shelf below that was a beautiful black saddle. It was inlaid and decorated with pure silver. "Mr. Benton be wantin' to surprise you with it. He be havin' it sent out special from Denver."

Elizabeth took one look at it and knew immediately why her father had bought it, him and his precious image. He wanted everybody to see how classy he and his whole family was. Well, I'm not going to play his Lady Godiva in a silver saddle. It's a little payback time, she thought. "Cyclone, it's just too beautiful. I couldn't ride on that every day. That's a show saddle," she said.

"You be havin' good sense, Miss Elizabeth. Let me be gettin' a regular saddle. But y'all have to be a promisin' to tell Mr. Benton it be you a sayin' y'all wanted a old one."

"I promise," she said. She smiled, and there was a gleam in her eye. "It'll be a pleasure." Cyclone just grinned. Shortly, he had Bonnie bridled, saddled, and ready to go. Elizabeth mounted, and Cyclone opened the gate for her.

"See you," she said as Bonnie trotted out of the corral. Bonnie's head was held high, and she began prancing. Again Elizabeth felt a pang. Running away would mean she'd have to leave Bonnie after she put on such a show of happiness to see her.

Elizabeth rode down through town, and out into the flats below town. She began exploring possible escape routes, but now her heart just wasn't in it as much. Finally, she relaxed and started enjoying herself more than she had since the night of the party in college.

Below the canyon, and past the homes and stores, she turned right and headed toward the base of the cliffs. It appeared there was a canyon that went up toward the top of the mountain. Before she got very far up the canyon, a large herd of sheep filled the trail. An old Indian on a horse and a couple of dogs seemed to be in charge of the sheep. She waved to the Indian, and he waved back. She decided to try the trail another day when things were less congested and with no sheep smell.

She let Bonnie have her head and went wherever Bonnie's fancy took her. Bonnie took her past the mine portal, and began to prance. Apparently, she knew what was coming next. Forty to fifty horses came spilling out of the mine tunnel and headed for the barn and their evening oats. Some whinnied at Bonnie as they rushed past. "So, you little vixen. You've made friends here already, haven't you?" Ahead of the horses,

Elizabeth saw miners getting out of the cars.

She could hardly stand how black with coal dust and dirty looking they were, how worn their clothing was. She watched, torn between pity and disgust as they trudged slowly along, hardly even talking to each other. They didn't resemble anyone she knew, especially the boys at college. Few of the men even looked her way as she trotted past them. They looked more tired than the beasts of burden that came out of the mine before them. Elizabeth put Bonnie away, and turned to leave. The plaintive sound of Bonnie's whinny and her overall dejected look touched Elizabeth's heart. "Don't worry, Baby. Tomorrow morning, I promise, I'll come and ride you to your heart's content."

CHAPTER 8

A TIME TO LAUGH

Elizabeth was back at the stable at eight in the morning. After asking Cyclone's advice, she rode up Number Two canyon. Soon she passed the Number Two Mine which gave the canyon its name. After enjoying the rugged beauty of the canyon more than she dreamed she would, she meandered back to town. She waved to Cyclone and Hank as she rode past, and Cyclone began washing his hands in the barrel. "I'll take care of it," she called. "I need the exercise."

Cyclone grunted. "Promise y'all be tellin' Mr. Benton you be makin' me do it?"

"Of course," she replied. She gave Bonnie a drink from the trough, then put her in the corral. She noticed Cyclone watching out of the corner of his eye. She had no doubt he would be there quickly if she showed the first sign of struggling. Saddle off, she began to curry Bonnie.

Only the loud bangs, the loud clanking, and the whirring of machinery at the tipple distracted from her enjoyment. In most of the town the invasive noise of the tipple was mostly a dull rumble. You got so used to it, you didn't even notice it after a while. But here, with the corral and stables so close, it was almost a roar.

Suddenly, the noise stopped. The cars stopped dumping. The crushers were turned off. The conveyor stopped. And the silence gnawed at Elizabeth's ears. She didn't know why, but she slowed the pace of currying. Then she stopped currying and stood totally focused and waiting—for what, she couldn't guess. She looked over at Cyclone. He was still slowly beating at something on the anvil, but his whole demeanor was that of a man doing one thing, while intensely waiting for something else. The flame from the forge dimmed as Hank pumped the bellows more slowly. Even he was anticipating something.

Just as suddenly as the noise had stopped, the silence was now shattered by the wailing of the town siren. It was the sound everyone was waiting for, but praying they would not hear. Elizabeth dropped the curry comb and slipped the halter from Bonnie. She hurried out the gate and closed it quickly behind her. "What is it, Cyclone?" she asked.

"Be an accident at the mine, Miss. We best be goin' to the mine office." Cyclone took off at a rapid pace, and Elizabeth followed him as best she could. But she soon fell behind. Every door in town opened and every man, woman, and child in town began the trip along the road toward the mine office. It was a silent parade with worry on every face, except for the youngest children. Elizabeth noticed everything said was a quiet expression of hope that no one was hurt badly. It was almost as though speaking about it might jinx their own loved ones still inside. Strangely, although she didn't even know anyone inside, she, too, began to feel the sense of dread manifested in every face.

School let out and the older children began their march. She noticed that while there was haste, no one was running. Things almost seemed to be happening in slow motion.

When she got there, Elizabeth noticed the stoic look of worry on each face, and she could not help but feel it more and more herself as more and more people arrived. They stood as close as they could to the office, then turned so that soon every eye was on the portal of the mine. Elizabeth turned her attention there also. She didn't know why she was looking. A tall man on a horse arrived at the portal. He got off his horse and began talking with some other men standing nearby. For a moment she considered that her status as the daughter of the Superintendent would allow her to go into the office to ask what was going on. But this might add negatively to the already intense feelings of people standing there so solemnly.

"Pardon me," Elizabeth said to a handsome young boy standing silently beside her. "Who is that man who just came up on a horse?"

"Doc Dowd," he said. Then, without pausing, he added, "My dad and brother'r in there."

"Sorry," Elizabeth consoled him. She saw the look of worry on his face.

"What's your name?" Elizabeth asked, not wanting to intrude on him further, but feeling a need to break the tension she was feeling. He told her it was Steve Cook, then fell silent again.

64

Elizabeth continued watching. She heard moans and groans escape from the throats of people in the crowd as the doctor remounted his horse and trotted away. She looked at them; many of them were trembling and off to the side she could see a woman vomiting on the ground. Her eyes jerked once more to the portal. A horse-drawn hearse was pulling near to the mouth of the mine. Suddenly she felt about to cry. But there were no tears in any one else's eyes. Some had their fists clenched and were holding them over their hearts. Many foreign women were fingering their rosary beads and silently praying. Unable to stand the tension, again she intruded on the Cook boy to ask why the office didn't tell them what was going on.

"The office don't want to say only so and so is dead, when it turns out there is more than that," he said in faltering speech, stopping every now and then to look at the portal. And all the while he spoke, his voice caught as though speaking were great effort. She knew she wouldn't be intruding on him again. An hour passed, then another.

In spite of everything else, she had the sense that just being here somehow helped these people. After what seemed an eternity, the hoist began rumbling. Soon a trip of cars issued from the mine portal. A number of men riding the trip jumped out of their cars as it slowed, then stopped. They lifted an inert form on a stretcher from the rear car. It was covered with a grayish blanket.

Ganz Durrant came out the front door of the office, and stood on the porch. Every eye was instantly on him, every ear straining to hear. Every heart stopped beating. "Mrs. Carpenter, would you please come in for a minute? I need to talk to you about your boy."

A gasp went through the crowd. Harry Carpenter's mother fainted.

But to Elizabeth's bewilderment, others showed more than just signs of relief. Strangely, Elizabeth noticed most of them became a chattering, enlivened mob. A woman the age of Elizabeth's mother went running up on the porch and said something to Durrant, then came rushing toward them. Elizabeth looked at Steve Cook. Obviously, he knew the woman. Before she even got to where Steve and Elizabeth were standing, she shouted, "It's okay, Steve. Ganz said Tom, Dan and Frank Bonatti ain't hurt." Tears of joy were streaming down her face. She grabbed Steve, and they hugged each other.

Steve began laughing, "Then it's only Harry. Old Harry Carpenter's dead as a mackerel."

"How can you make such a joke?" Elizabeth blurted out. The other two just turned and glared at her. She opened her mouth to tell Steve how unfeeling his comment was. A voice behind her kept her from saying more. She turned and saw Cyclone.

"Miss Benton," he said again, in a soft voice that still captured her full attention. "Bonnie not be havin' her oats yet. You be ridin' her pretty hard, and she be needin' oats."

"Sure," she said, knowing he'd commanded her to leave, and followed him to the stables.

"Miss Benton," Cyclone said as they walked. "Don't be feelin' too hateful to young Steve Cook. I not be havin' words to explain what happen' here, but I be tryin', if y'all want."

"Please," Elizabeth agreed. Obviously, Cyclone's words and actions told her that her anger at Steve Cook had been out of place. She was most anxious to find out why.

"Well, it be like this. He be relieved his dad or brother not be dead. He be so relieved, he be feelin' happiness more than anything else. Later, he be truly mournin' poor Harry with the rest of the town. He be young, not used to hiding his real feelings. Us older ones be careful not to show too much joy, but joy be what we feelin' in our hearts. But the tears of joy and relief runnin' down people's faces be no different than Steve a laughin'."

"How can that be?" she asked, her mind in a blur. Joy, at such a time? It was absurd.

"Y'all be understandin' only if y'alls own loved one be in there. "

"I'm trying to understand, Cyclone, but . . ." her words trailed off. She was thinking so hard she wasn't paying attention to walking. She tripped on a rock in the road.

Cyclone instinctively put his arm around her to steady her. A moment later, he jerked his arm back as if he'd touched a hot poker.

"I be knowin' Miss Elizabeth," he said to try to cover what just happened. "It be one of them things y'all got to experience your own self, 'thout that it be past understandin'."

He stopped walking to make his point, and they stood there in the middle of the road. "Everybody what be there today, besides the Carpenters, be happy Mr. Durrant called her. For some, it be a time to laugh. That just the way it be in a coal camp. I be hopin' y'all never be forced to be understandin' all this your own self."

"Thanks, Cyclone," Elizabeth said. They reached the stables. She noticed a look of pain on Cyclone's face. She couldn't tell if he were grieving over the Carpenter boy, or if there was something else.

Nothing in Elizabeth's life had prepared her for the emotions all of this had forced upon her. Suddenly, her own petty worries didn't seem important.

That evening at the Cook home, Mary busied herself making supper. She tried to keep her mind off things by staying busy. But it was no use. Harry's death ate away at her soul. Nothing she could do would remove the fear that someday it might be Dan or Carl, or, heaven forbid, both. "If that happens, I'll go crazy, I know it," she thought. She did her best to calm herself. From many past times, such as this, she'd learned a trick to momentarily ease her mind. She'd think of totally insignificant things.

She wondered why the company store was called the Utah Wash Rag Store. Nobody seemed to know, except that Utah Fuel Company had another wash rag store in Summerset, Colorado. But that brought up another question for her. If this was the Utah Fuel Company, how come they had a mine in Colorado? Oh, well, she mused to herself. What can you expect from a state where the state tree is the Colorado blue spruce, and where the state bird is the California gull?

Her hands were shaking as she dredged the steak in flour and began frying it in the heavy cast iron skillet. When the steak was cooked, she removed it to a platter. She made the gravy. She began to cry softly. Some of her tears fell in and became part of the gravy.

"Making gravy, Hon?" Carl asked as he came into the kitchen. Mary was glad to have someone to talk to, at last. That always helped.

"Yes, and poor gravy it's going to be," she answered without turning around. "What with the happenings this afternoon, I didn't have time to prepare a proper meal. Steak, potatoes, the gravy, and a little canned corn is about the best I can manage," she continued, as she surreptitiously lifted her apron and wiped the tears from her cheeks.

"That'll do just fine. How's my best girl? You doing all right, Darlin'?"

Then, in spite of the dozen vows that afternoon not to make things worse for Carl and Dan, she said, "Doin' alright? Now that I've got two men in the mine to worry about?"

Tears began flowing again. Her voice started shaking. "Harry was such a sweet boy. His mother told me he helped her in the kitchen and could cook almost as good as her." Carl did not respond. He sat at the table and opened the *Deseret News*. Mary's misery cut him to the bone. But, what could he do?

"I smell something good cooking," Steve interrupted as he came into the kitchen.

"Did you wash your hands?" Mary asked.

"Of course I washed my hands. I just picked my nose. Would I pick my nose with dirty hands?" Steve asked, a smirk on his face. Mary reached for the hot pad by the stove and threw it at him. Then, in spite of herself, she smiled.

"Well, go wash them again. When you finish, get back in here and mash the potatoes for me. I've already put in the butter and the milk. Carl, Benton's daughter...." she started.

But Steve interrupted her. "Yes, Master," Steve said, grinning as he left. But the grin was not as much in humor as it was in satisfaction. He was happy he'd made his mother smile.

"Need any more help, Mom?" Dan asked as he came in.

"No. Dinner will be ready in just a minute," she said as she poured the gravy into a bowl. "As soon as your brother's through with the potatoes." Steve came back and worked rapidly on the potatoes. He finished shortly, and stood aside so Mary could spoon them into a bowl. Dan took his accustomed place at the back of the table.

Steve looked at his father. "Dad, did Mom tell you about old man Benton's daughter?"

"I tried to tell him, but he had his nose stuck too deep in that newspaper."

Carl looked up. "Tried to tell me when?"

"Two minutes ago, that's when."

Carl thought back, confused again for a moment. Then he remembered she'd started to speak before Steve interrupted her. "Okay, Hon. Let's start over. What happened?"

"You tell him, Steve," she said. "I'm too upset right now to make much sense."

Steve pursed his lips. "Well, when we found out you and Dan were okay," he paused. "Mom and me, we . . . well, we hugged and was happy. Then that daughter of Mr. Benton's said we were making fun of Harry being dead. She told us to stop it." Carl was beginning to get upset about it for his own reasons. "I really wasn't paying too much attention until she started speaking ugly to us," Steve continued.

Carl thought for a moment. "I'll apologize if Benton mentions anything about it to me."

"You want to apologize for something his daughter did?" She paused a moment, and wiped some sweat from her forehead. "Afraid you'll lose your job?" she asked.

"What did she say, exactly?" Dan asked. Then helped himself to some corn and potatoes.

"I don't really remember, it happened so fast." Steve replied. "She said something about how could we be so happy you and Dad were alive. Then she looked at us real hard, and was about to say something else when Cyclone took her away."

"Don't pay no attention to her, Mom," Dan said. "The fellas say she got kicked out of some high and mighty college back East. I doubt she's terribly easy to get along with if they kicked her out of college. And she's strange. I saw her yesterday after I got out of the man trip. She was wearing English riding clothes and riding a Western saddle. Pass the bread and some butter, please. As to her telling Mr. Benton, the fellas say her dad isn't too happy with her right now anyway. He must be having trouble with her, too."

His mother seemed to settle down. Then, in a disjointed logic Dan did not follow, she said, "Just shows how different they are from us. How's the bread, Son? I just baked it. "

"Best part of the meal," Dan replied.

"How? Different, I mean, Mom," Steve asked.

"If you're born with a silver spoon in your mouth is what I mean. All those fancy clothes. We would buy some plain clothes or furniture with that much money. Or we'd buy some decent food to keep Dan's and your dad's strength up on a hard day at the pit."

She handed Dan the platter of meat, but he just passed it on to his father without taking any of the steak. Carl pretended not to notice, as did his mother and Steve. They were all aware that seeing a gory accident might cause one to pass the meat for a while. Many was the time Carl had passed the platter, sometimes for as long as a couple of weeks. But this was different. This was Dan's first time and Mary was suddenly no longer able to pretend that a young boy not being able to eat meat was a normal thing.

"Was it pretty bad, Son?" she asked.

"Yeah," Dan said without taking his eyes from his plate.

"What happened?" Steve asked, unable to curb his youthful curiosity.

Carl shot Steve a disapproving look. "I'll tell you what happened," he interjected, not wanting Dan to be forced to recount the details so fresh on his mind. "Tom told me; a bounce came. The bounce knocked Tom and Dan down, but their room didn't cave.

"At Frank's room it was a different story. The bounce knocked out the timbers. Part of their roof came down. Frank was pinned between the rib and the car. He was protected from the cave by a slab of rock that rested on one side of a car. Frank was under the slanting rock and it kept him from getting killed."

"Wow," Steve interjected. He put down his fork and leaned closer to his father.

"Harry got knocked backwards, and about twenty tons of rock and coal fell on him. Tom said that right after the bounce when he and Dan started to get up, Frank's horse came running into their room dragging the timber he was tied to before the bounce."

Dan just kept eating. Mary started crying silently again, but Steve was all ears.

"That's when Tom knew Frank and Harry was in trouble." Carl turned to Dan. "You can be proud, Son. Frank told me you did real good your first time."

Dan put down his fork. "Thanks, Dad," he said. "All my life I wondered if I would have the guts to go in under a cave and get somebody out. What I learned today is that I did." He paused, looked down at his plate, picked up his fork, shrugged his shoulders, and spoke softly, "This time. Next time, who knows?"

"I know what you mean," Carl replied and picked up his fork and started eating again.

Dan looked at his mother. He knew his mother loved horses as much as he did. "Mom, I swear that horse came to get us. It was the saddest thing. His eyes were rolling back, his nostrils were flaring, and his ears were flat back against his head. But, Mom, that horse was not panicked so bad it didn't know what it was doing." Tears began streaming down Dan's cheeks as well. "That horse knew we was closest to Frank and Harry and it came to get us. One of the things I'll never be able to forget about is the desperate look on that horse's face as it tried to tell us to come help. And when we got there, it just stood there until we could get Frank out." Dan paused to try to get his tears under control. His voice got even huskier. "Mom, that horse was crying with happiness when Frank got up."

It wouldn't do to let his family see him cry. He got up and rushed into his bedroom.

CHAPTER 9

LITTLE BROTHER AND SIX NEPHEWS

Dan was glad to see Saturday night. He was tired. He had been working two weeks now, and while most of the soreness was gone from his muscles, he was still exhausted by the end of each shift. He could not do the one thing he most wanted to do right now, rest. Instead, he had to go to the union meeting and join up.

But he'd given his word to keep where and when it was a secret. It was upsetting to lie to his family about where he was going. Yet he could see no other alternative but to lie.

Rubbing the sleep from his eyes, he went into the kitchen. His mom was doing dishes and his dad was sitting at the table reading the newspaper. His father seemed tired, too. He turned the pages slowly, and didn't seem really interested in anything he was reading. "Dad, I can't seem to relax," he said. "Think I'll take a long walk down in the flats to clear my head." Mary stopped doing dishes, looked at him, and smiled.

His father didn't even look up from the newspaper. "Sure, son. Want some company?"

"Nah, maybe when I get there I'll just sit and relax a while." Dan couldn't think of any other way to cover how long he'd be out. His mother smiled again.

"Be careful, Son," Carl said. Dan felt he wasn't fooling anybody. Why did his mom keep smiling, and why did his dad tell him to be careful? He walked down the road.

Walking past the last few houses, Dan kept his eyes open for John Tennis. He saw John sitting on the stairs of his front porch. John was a fairly small man. He smiled and Dan could see he had a couple of teeth missing. "Tekanis," John called. "You for walk?"

"Tekanis," Dan responded. "Sure am, John."

"Want John go?" John asked, as he got up, not waiting for an answer.

"Sure thing," Dan agreed, "glad for the company." But the whole conversation was a charade. Dan hadn't known the way to the meeting. Frank Bonatti said it would be best if neither he nor Tom took Dan. People might wonder why Dan was getting so chummy with them all of a sudden. Tom suggested John Tennis could be the one to show Dan. Frank agreed the Greek was a good choice. Since John lived at the end of town, they probably wouldn't meet anybody on the way out of the canyon. John seemed in no particular hurry to go anywhere as they sauntered past the remaining houses in town.

The two men passed a couple of pool halls, and the Greek coffee houses. Every time they passed a coffee house John looked at it with what Dan surmised was longing, or perhaps anticipation. Finally, the canyon spilled into the flats like water coming out the wrong end of a funnel. Once past the mouth of the canyon, it opened up wide and fast. From there on, it was nothing but sage brush and cedar trees. Except for a few little hills.

Finally, John turned a little to the right and headed for the store and other buildings of Joe Pessetto's Sunnyside Trading Company. Dan just sort of tagged along. Small John might be, but there was a sense of compact power in every step, every movement. A life of loading coal leaves its mark. At Pessetto's, John led Dan past the store, too. Shortly, John pointed to a horse trail which paralleled the road. "Maybe, I think, walk there."

"Must careful," he said as they headed up the trail. "All different way come. Some road come. Some tracks come. Some trail come. All different time come." Dan understood the need for secrecy. It was legal for union men to meet except on company property. Huge difference, however, between legality and being moved to a dangerous part of the mine.

Apparently John noticed Dan's silence. "When join union, fight Mormon dad?"

"No. Dad says a man makes up his own mind. Mom thinks the union is our only chance."

"Carl scab, but good man. Everybody know."

"Thanks, John," Dan replied and began to puff a little as they climbed a small hill.

John pointed to a large flat rock. "We sit," he said. "We wait. Later can go." He reached into his pocket, got out a plug, cut some off, and offered it to Dan. Dan accepted, and tucked the plug between his teeth and his cheek. John cut his own plug and put it in his mouth. "You smart boy, union join young." John spat a stream of tobacco juice from the newly installed plug. It was caught by a stand of bunch grass. "Yes," John said, nodding his head in agreement with himself. "Smart like scab dad, Carl. I not know," John said.

Dan didn't have too much trouble following Greek, or Italian, or any of the other dialects he had grown up hearing in Sunnyside. But occasionally their way of speaking made it a little difficult to know what they were trying to say. "Know what, John?"

"I not know you mother she union. She pretty good man, too."

"You mean because she thinks the union is our only chance?"

"No think. Union is only chance. John know. Before here John, Colorado, Ludlow." All his life Dan had heard how the national Guard had massacred a tent town in Ludlow. But this was the first time he ever had the chance to talk with someone who was actually there. He was eager to find out about it.

"I guess Ludlow was pretty bad."

"Terrible," John said. A sad look came onto his face. "John friend Louie Tikas shot. Then Louie face rifle butt smash. Frank Snyder shoot Louie, face smash."

"I'm sorry, John. I knew how I felt when Harry got killed."

"More," John continued. "Machine gun she almost get John. Damn good train man blow train whistle. Train she start. Train she move slow. John hide behind train. Train she move. John move too. Everybody come." John paused to spit. "Get outta there."

Dan could picture the strikers running for the train and crouching on the opposite side from the machine gun. Again the sad look. "Not all get out. Man name Frank Snyder, he kill James Fyler, Frank Rubino, John Bartolotti, Carlo Costa."

"Oh my gosh," Dan said in amazement, "It truly was a massacre."

"More. When tent town everybody go, below tent dig, boards put across, make a cellar. When shoot start, everybody go under boards in tent. National Guard mans. He name Karl Linderfelt. In court say he burn tents. Court say when tents burn, air go. In cellar Cedelina Costa, no can breathe. She afraid come out. Machine gun shoot, tat, tat, tat, tat," John said, imitating as best he could, the sound of the machine gun. "Of course Cedelina Costa die. She kid Lucy, die. She kid Onafrio, die." John was now looking down, and shaking his head slowly back and forth with each name as he continued. "Same Lucy Petrucci, die." John was not crying, Dan noticed. But there were tears in his voice. "Same Patria Valdez, die. She kid Mary, die. She kid Eulala, die. Same Cloriva Pedragon, die. She kid Rogerlo, die."

Finally, John just stopped talking. He sat there with his head bowed, his hands in his lap. Dan was quiet himself. He knew some women and children had died at Ludlow. But the look on John's face, his tone of voice, his tolling off the names one by one, all brought the horror of it into Dan's soul. "I hope they hanged them."

"No." John said softly. "Court say, not guilty."

"You must hate them, John."

"No," John said, spat again, wrinkled his forehead in an attempt to find the right English words. "John hate lies. But must work, must feed family. Only coal mining this country."

"I don't think I really understand what you are saying," Dan admitted.

"John young, have friend old country. Name him Gust. Must do right thing Gust say. John say, how know right? Gust say eef John's kids she hungry, no can feed, John must steal bread. Gust say John must do. Gust say maybe John steal bread from Gust. Gust say eef Gust kids not hungry, Gust try catch John. Gust fight John."

Dan just sat trying to absorb it. He held up his hand to stop John, and repeated back what he thought John had said. "If your kids are hungry and there is no other way to feed them, you may even have to steal your friend's bread. If his kids are not hungry, if he catches you, he will fight with you because it's right for him to protect what is his."

"You smart boy. More. Eef John kids she hungry, Gust kids she hungry, John steal bread, Gust say catch John, eef Gust can, put John in hospeet. But eef John kids not hungry Gust kids she hungry, John steal bread, Gust catch, Gust keel John eef he can." When Dan said he understood, John replied only with, "Smart boy."

Dan sat quietly thinking all that over for a while. He understood it, all right. He knew that with the Greeks, the word kill, when used in the context of a real wrong done, was not merely a figure of speech. Somehow this helped Dan feel better about having to lie to his family. Obviously, certain things were wrong under all circumstances. But sometimes in life one must do a little wrong to achieve a greater right.

Dan suddenly realized John's story almost made him forget what John had said about hating lies. "Guess I'm not too smart," he said. "What about hating lies?"

John chuckled. "Smart Boy. Smart say don't know every ting. But, of course. Company say, no have bread, sorry, must steal you kids bread. Company lie. Company have much bread, kids no have enough bread. John hate company lie." Dan was almost stunned. In his halting English John had made clear what had taken Tom a long time to get across. The company was stealing bread from the mouths of hungry kids.

John had said that to steal bread from hungry kids when the person stealing was not hungry could result in a killing. "How do we kill the company, John."

"No can kill company. No such ting, company. Company many mans together work. Company just name. Name for lies top boss say. If believe lies top boss say, must stupid!"

"But isn't the company the men who own it?"

"No. Benton company. John company. Scab dad company. You company. No can kill."

Dan lifted his shoulders, he held his palms up, "Then what do?" he asked, not noticing he had taken on part of John's way of speaking.

John's face lit up. "We strike!!"

It was getting late, the sun had finished setting. Dan could hardly wait for the meeting to begin. He was ready to fight, to strike. He was ready to band together with others to fight the lie. Fight, with others, in every way possible. "I wish the meeting would start."

John looked at him without answering. Dan could tell something he said didn't please John. "What's wrong, John?"

"John one more ting say. Different old country. Greek gun like for family protect. Old country if no gun, everybody bread steal. John this country come. John tink eet same old country. John go Ludlow. John buy gun. Nobody she going steal John bread, John tink. John happy. Ludlow friend buy gun, too. Friend happy, too. Friend say gun she little brother, bullets she six little nephews. Friend name Louis Tikas, name same before tell you. John bury Louis, Ludlow." John spat yet again, and sat silent.

Finally, John spoke once more. "But America no old country. Now time we meeting go. Fight, yes. But no keel. We keel peoples, National Guard keel peoples, keel strike too."

In the early dusk they headed up a wide dry wash with high banks on each side. The wash headed into a narrow canyon. Walking rapidly now, they came to Bill Lyons and Joe Padriva. The pair were standing up on the banks holding rifles. Dan stopped, a little surge of fear coursed through him. Caught, he thought. But John just waved to them, and kept on walking. "They watch," John said. "Nobody meeting surprise." Dan started walking again. He also waved a greeting to the lookouts, and each of them waved back.

The wash curved, and past the bend it opened up and flattened out. There was a large bonfire, and several smaller fires for warmth and light. The walls of the wash behind them with its several curves made it obvious that the fires would be hidden from anyone in town, or on the flats below. Some men were seated on rocks. Others were standing, or seated on rough benches made from cut pinion pines with rocks under them as supports. Dan was surprised to see about three hundred men jammed into the area.

Dan recognized most men at the meeting. He and John sat on a log near the back. Some of the men in attendance were a surprise to him. Especially many fellow Mormons, some of whom waved to him and smiled a knowing sort of smile. Earlier, if he'd had to guess, he wouldn't have guessed more than a tenth of them.

"What are we waiting for, John?"

"Big shots," John said. But before he could explain further, Frank Bonatti came up to them.

"Got your five dollars?" Frank asked.

Dan reached in his pocket. He fished out his five-dollar gold piece and handed it to Frank. Dan was excited, but Frank acted as if he was selling a pair of shoes or something. "Sign this," Frank said, extending

Dan a half sheet form with Dan's name already written on it. Dan took the pencil Frank was also proffering, and signed. A smile finally broke out on Franks' features. "Welcome to the United Mine Workers of America."

Dan handed the paper and pencil back. "That's it?" He asked. "Isn't there some sort of ceremony or something?" He expected to at least have to swear to something.

"That's it," Frank responded. "We're not held together by some oath or other. It's what's in your heart that makes you a member. How good a member you are, only time will tell."

When Frank left, Dan turned to John. "What were Bill Lyons and Joe Padriva doing as lookouts?" Dan asked to pass the time as they waited. "Bill is a cattle man when he's not acting as a mine Guard one place or another. Joe works for Sod Nelson at the store."

"Smart, huh?" John asked. "If spy come, see two miners in wash, spy know meeting must be. If spy see Bill, see Joe, say what doing? Bill say, see miners. Tink maybe meeting. We looking. If meeting find, Big Boss tell."

Dan shifted his rear end on the log. "That is smart. Nobody would ever take Joe and Bill for union lookouts. I'll bet after he sent them off he'd come up here and warn us."

"Smart boy," was again John's only comment.

Just then there was a slight commotion behind them. Dan turned around quickly, and the log under him scraped his back side. He saw Tom Carr and five men coming up the wash. To Dan's surprise, they were dressed in suits and ties. Dan had never seen Tom in a suit.

"Who are they?" he asked John.

"Not analtos. Good men. Men lead union, truth tell."

"Analtos? What's that."

"Saltless. But wait you. John see friend English talk good." John walked over to a young Greek Dan did not know. The two of them talked a moment, and they both came back.

Dan was sorry he'd asked about analtos because as the well dressed men got near the front, there was a commotion. Dan heard loud laughing, and saw back slapping and hand shaking going on. He was more interested in finding out what was happening there. But John was not to be denied. "Andy Vullis friend John. Andy English talk better."

Andy stuck out his hand, and Dan noticed Andy was much younger than John, but dressed in the same old country style. Andy's handle bar mustache first drooped, then turned up at the ends. "Pleased to meet you, Andy." Dan said as they shook hands.

"Likewise. John asked me to explain analtos to you. What John means by analtos is literally translated as saltless. But the term, when applied to men, is a metaphor for those pink-cheeked Americans who hide their tempers and are usually dressed in suits. They act courteous, and speak softly to your face. But turn your back and they'll skin you."

"Yes, yes," John agreed. "In old country say, how feel, must show on face. America much analtos. Never trust analtos. No face show what thinking, dangerous." Dan was silent. Analtos had been digging at him all his life, he just didn't have a name for them.

Tom raised his arms and those standing sat down. Those talking began to get quiet. "Okay, you trouble making bums," Tom's voice boomed over the throng. "This is what you've been waiting for." Then, pointing to each visitor in turn, Tom said, "This is President Cahill and Jimmy Morgan from District 22. You all know Ed Dobbins our area organizer, and Jay Ramsey, our district official."

Tom put his arm around the shoulder of the man standing to his left. "For those of you who don't know my friend Sam King here, I suggest you put your hands in your pockets and hold onto your money. Sam's an attorney." Laughs and cat calls broke out.

Dan could see that being dressed in a suit definitely made Tom feel uncomfortable. Tom's tone changed. "But thank heavens for him. He's our union attorney from Price."

"Now without further ado, here's President Cahill."

"Are you the rabble I'm here to rouse?" Cahill asked. Calls of, "Right!" and "You betcha," answered his question. Also, hushed whispers among the crowd interpreted the comment of the speaker into such languages as Spanish, Japanese, Austrian, Greek, and Italian. Every man knew the importance of what was to be said. Every man wanted to understand fully, whether it was spoken in his native tongue or not.

"For those of you who don't have the slightest idea what I'm talking about, let me explain. Before this strike is over, I will be called an outside rabble rouser. I will also be called a trouble maker and I will be called an out-of-state Bolshevik and anarchist." Shouts of denial broke out. Cahill raised his hands above his head, to quiet the crowd.

Cahill broke into a broad smile. "I not only admit it, I am proud of it. Proud if by Bolshevik you mean somebody willing to fight to see working men get their share. Proud if by anarchy you mean being against government by industry and for the rich."

He paused to look seriously at the crowd. "But make sure you understand me. The union is not out to overthrow the government, and it's not communist, and neither am I."

Shouts of, "We're with you," and "Let's make some trouble," rang out.

Cahill pretended to be upset. "You men shock me. Do you mean you're going to believe me, and not believe them? Not believe that I came sneaking over from Wyoming just to get you good, honest, but stupid, Utah men to do our trouble-making business?"

"Never," and "Down with 'em," and other cries such as, "we'll show 'em," rang out from the group. Cahill left the front. He walked among the miners, shook hands with many, hugged others. He was received as a long lost brother returning to the fold.

When Cahill worked his way back to the front, he looked determined. "I don't need to bend your ear about unionism. I've walked amongst you and pressed the flesh with you. I want you to know I am honored to be here." With that, he sat down on a log.

Tom stood. "Now, for those of you who don't already know him, I'll introduce Jimmy." Jimmy Morgan stood up. Dan noticed that Jimmy's suit fit him perfectly. Dan thought it looked expensive. Morgan seemed a strong, well built, working man, in a suit or no.

"My comments will be about as short as President Cahill's," Jimmy said. Dan smiled to himself. Things weren't proceeding anywhere near the way he thought the meeting would go. First there was no initiation ceremony, and now it looked as if there wasn't even going to be the long speeches he'd expected. "I already know most of you men," Jimmy continued, "and the District has no worries about your determination, or your strength. Jimmy paused long enough to take off his suit jacket, fold it and lay it over the log he had been sitting on. He was wearing a short-sleeved shirt. Dan noticed Jimmy's bulging biceps. If there ever is a fight, Dan thought, I want him on my side. "What I want to discuss with you is the different kinds of dignity," Jimmy said. "The kind of dignity I'm talking about has to do with self respect, and pride. But it's more than that, it has to do with respect for others and responsibility as well.

"An industrialist thinks his dignity is in direct proportion to the huge profits he makes." Shouts to the contrary interrupted him, but he also raised his arms to quiet them. "No, my friends, profits aren't wrong. Profits are the American way. No right-thinking person can believe there can be jobs and work without profits." The crowd grew hushed as Jimmy continued. "What you were booing at, however, was the obscene profits many companies make. You were booing that top management not satisfied with just profit. They want power over the lives of you men as well. They think that adds to their dignity." Jimmy paused for a moment.

"Then you see local management, Supers, foremen, and others without real dignity of their own. They kiss up to the big shots, if necessary, to share the big shots' power. They hope in this way to make everyone believe they, too, have dignity." To Dan's surprise, Jimmy returned to his log. He folded his coat into a small bundle, and sat down.

"I'm not finished," Jimmy responded to their questioning looks. "But think about it," he said in a voice so soft not all could hear. His words had to be passed back from the front. "People stand to fight. Or one man will stand to lecture others who are sitting. That is not my way. I have come to reason with friends, and I can only do that sitting amongst you."

He paused, reached into the breast pocket of his shirt, took out a cigar, lit it, and puffed smoke into the air. "The reason for this meeting is that those of us not good at kissing up have learned we must band together. We cannot stand up alone to those who think they are better than us. There are too many of them, and they are too strong."

He paused to take another puff. "We've got Greeks and Dagoes who in their own lands hate each other. We've got Limeys and Huns who just spilled each others' blood in the Great War. We've got Japs and Chinks who have despised each other for longer than this has been a country. We've got Pollocks, Bohunks, Niggers and Spicks. And, and," he repeated for emphasis, "Yes, we have men from Utah and men from

Wyoming working together in enough different languages to put the League of Nations to shame."

Once more he paused, to let all that sink in. He took another puff, or two. The crowd was hushed, intent on every word. At last, he continued. He spoke as softly as before, but the look on his face turned intense. "Now a moment ago I talked about dignity, and I wanted to prove a point to you. I used words such as Dago, Spick, Nigger, and Hun. Words that in other circumstances could get a man killed for using them. But there was not a murmur from you. Why?" he asked. But still the crowd was hushed.

"Because I used those words with dignity, the dignity one miner sees in another, the dignity one friend sees in another, and the dignity one family member knows is in another family member." Once more Jimmy paused. Once more he puffed on his cigar. Once more he waited. That gave Dan time to think it over. He smiled. He understood.

Jimmy began speaking again. "I dare any industrialist, any financier, any government big shot, or any boss to come out here and call you those things. That I can and they can't, proves we, here, all of us, share a dignity of comradeship that all their money, or all their kissing up, or all their luxuries cannot match."

"Bingo," Dan said to himself.

"And they hate us for it," Jimmy concluded.

Dan realized he'd spoken too soon. This last thought took him by surprise. It explained so much about the seeming hate, or at least disdain, those in authority displayed toward those under them. The rest of the group sat quietly. Many of them looked around. Some noticed others they did not like in the crowd. But Jimmy's words had softened that. Individual dislikes and hates were being set aside. A dignity they had not realized they had began to form concretely in their minds.

Sam King stood up. "You all know about the trumped up charges the companies and the courts use to defeat union men and organizers alike. This time, I feel, we are prepared to handle most of them. They will use dozens of petty charges which in your wildest imagination you'd think nobody would believe," he said. Sam put his hands on his hips.

"Let me give you just one example," he said. "When miners go on strike, what happens? They are out of work, right? In the last strike, when the president and the secretary of Winter Quarters were arrested, what were they charged with?"

No one cared to guess. "Isn't it obvious? They were charged with vagrancy," Sam said. "Let me warn you what to look out for. They'll try to charge you with carrying concealed weapons, disturbing the peace, vagrancy, assault, and more. My job will be to defend you against all that. But make no mistake, the cards are already stacked against us. If you actually did any of those things, you're going to pay a fine, go to jail, or both."

"I'll kill anybody tries that," someone from the crowd shouted.

Jay Ramsey jumped to his feet. "Sit down, Sam," he commanded. "I'll handle this." He stood glaring at the crowd. Then he shouted, "Hey wise guy who said that, stand up!"

A tall, lanky man Dan did not know got sheepishly to his feet. Jay strolled leisurely over to him and reached out to put his arm around the man's shoulders. The man shied back away from Jay's outstretched arm.

"For land sake man," Jay said. "Ain't you got the word yet? We're all brothers here."

"My brother used to kick the crap out of me," the man said. The crowd hooted. The man grinned, "Regularly," he added and was again regaled with laughter.

"What's your name?" Jay asked. The tall man said it was Mike Harding. "Mike, my friend, I ain't that kind of brother." Lots of laughter. "Will you step back over to the front with me?" When Mike agreed, Jay led him to the front and again reached out his arm. This time he encircled Mike's shoulder without resistance. "Mike, do you know why I'm so steamed?" Mike said he supposed it was because he talked about killing somebody. "You got the brass ring on that one," Jay said, and began looking fiercely at the crowd. He turned his head first one way, then another. "Hear me good. There won't even be talk of killing in this union, or I promise you, I'll quit on the spot!"

Shouts of, "No!" and "You wouldn't do that to us, Jay," rang out.

"I swear. I have seen too many strikes busted when some hot head shot somebody, and that was all the excuse the governor needed to send in the Guard. Confound it, we won't lose again that way." Jay took his hands from around Mike's shoulder. He pretended he was holding a rifle.

He pointed at one man. "Bang, you're dead." He pointed at another, "Bang, you're dead. Get the picture? Any of us start shooting, they got more guns than we can ever muster. I don't want to see any more of us killed in a strike."

Jay raised up to his tallest, and looked toward the men in the back. Dan thought Jay was looking directly at him. He couldn't understand why. Jay cleared up the mystery. "John Tennis over there can tell you. We were both at Ludlow. I had the blood of more than one friend on me that day."

He paused. He looked around, then more softly. "My friends, this ain't no baby crap. If we start violence of any sort, the main things that are gonna die are some of you, and our strike." With that, Jay took his seat. Tom stood. "Meeting's over," he said.

But nothing was over higher up on the mountain. An old pair of eyes, watched all below. Old the eyes might be but they were as the eyes of an eagle. Everything that existed down there in the land of his youth came under his scrutiny. Anyone looking for the man would have a difficult time. He wasn't invisible, but his total lack of movement created that illusion. He sat within the branches and the shadow of a moonlit pine. When all below returned to normal except for the dying embers of the fires, he returned to the tent by his sheep, lay down, and began to remember.

At first the men sneaking through the canyon disturbed him. Then, as they cut down trees, moved rocks, and laid fires he began to wonder. Finally with their fires lit and men seated around them, Billy Neyah calmed his spirit. He began to feel other spirits around him, and the spirits of the men below. They were good. He thanked Mother Earth for the sign. Fires below made lights in the night which should not be there. That was an omen. But Mother Earth had taught Billy to wait for four such omens to be certain. That way, he could not be deceived if Shadow laid a false sign in front of him once his quest began. Even before he came here from near The Devil's Backbone, he was sure this was the place Mother Earth had chosen to fulfill her plan for him. Now he was more sure than ever. Although Paiute, deep in his heart he felt the words of the Navajo, "All is in beauty."

CHAPTER 10

WEAR THAT DRESS

Elizabeth really didn't want to attend her mother's card party that night. "Honey," her mother said, "you've spent so much time on Bonnie you've neglected the townspeople. We have to be sociable. It's expected of all Supers and their wives."

"Fine for you and dad," she said. "I understand people wanting to kiss up to the Big Boss. But why me? I only know a couple, and have nothing in common with any of them."

"We didn't know them when we first came here, either. But they're nice people. You'll see. All of them have wondered when they'd get to meet you." The more her mother spoke, however, the more sure Elizabeth was that she didn't want any part of it.

"So?" Elizabeth asked. "Is that any reason to drag me out and display me like a show horse?" Elizabeth knew she'd gone too far. The angry look from her mother made it obvious. "Okay, I'll go." Then she added, "And, Mom, for your sake I'll try to enjoy it."

Katherine smiled. "Thank you dear, I appreciate it. Got to go now and see how Mrs. Padriva is coming with the roast lamb." When Katherine came back, Elizabeth asked if there was anything she could do to help. Her mother declined, saying everything was under control. Elizabeth remarked she was going upstairs to take a bath and then dress before the guests got here.

Her mother pursed her lips in thought. "That's good," Katherine agreed. "Tell you what," she said, "put on the ruffled, pink dress I brought from Colorado for you."

Elizabeth scowled. "I'm old enough to choose my own clothes, Mom. I left that dress in Colorado in the first place because it makes me look as if I were a teenager."

"You are a teenager, Dear," her mother said.

"I'm almost twenty," she shot back over her shoulder as she went upstairs. When she finished her bath, she decided whether her mother liked or not she'd put on her slinky black dress she'd bought at college. Low cut, and in strategic places, as was the style in college, she wore no corset, although some'd think that not proper. "Also," she thought, "wish my breasts weren't so big."

She decided to go downstairs, and see what her mother's reaction to the dress would be. Her mother took one look at Elizabeth and started crying.

"What's wrong, Mom?" Elizabeth asked, truly concerned. "Do I look that bad?"

"Nothing, Baby. Really. You look stunning." Her mother sniffed a few times, picked up a napkin from a card table, and wiped her eyes. She looked at the napkin. "Oh, no," she said. She showed the napkin to Elizabeth. "Look at this, I've ruined my mascara."

Elizabeth dabbed her mother's face here and there with another napkin. Her mother's tears had touched her heart. "Why were you crying, Mom?"

"I knew your growing up would come soon enough. I just didn't think it would be tonight." Elizabeth felt a surge of joy at her mother's tribute. Her mother turned and picked up a stack of place cards from a table, and said the place cards were in the order how people should sit. She handed the cards to Elizabeth and asked her to call off the names so she could put them at the appropriate places. Katherine would proudly make some comment about those she knew.

The first name Elizbeth read was E. Jones. "His first name is Evan," her mother said. "He is Commander of the Sunnyside American Legion." When they came to Mrs. Galbraith, her mother interjected, "Her name is Emma." When they came to Mrs. J. Meese, Elizabeth was advised her name was Patsy. When they came to J. Meese, her mother had another comment. "His name is Jimmy. Jimmy is in charge of the St. Patrick's Day dance. The American Legion sponsors it. It will be on the twentieth of this month, I think."

Elizabeth was most interested in who would be sitting with her. She scanned ahead in the cards again, and discovered that one of the men seated next to her would be Dr. Dowd. She was pleased that here, at least, was someone she had seen. But the memory of him at the mine portal reminded her of things she'd rather forget.

Benton came into the room; he looked at Elizabeth; anger crowded his face, "Get back upstairs and put on something that doesn't make you look like a hussy!" he demanded.

The remark cut deep. Elizabeth began to cry. That's twice he's practically called me a whore. Doesn't he have any respect for his own flesh and blood? Loud, angry, utterances between her mother and father forced her thoughts away from herself. Her parents were arguing.

"She's not decent," Benton said.

Earlier her mother had sounded assertive; now Elizabeth heard her mother sound strident. "She is too decent! That's the style now." Her dad's insult faded as Elizabeth watched and listened.

"Style be damned! I'll not have a daughter of mine looking that way."

Katherine folded her arms across her chest. "She'll choose her own clothes!"

His next comment almost wavered. "Not in my house."

"It's our house, too. I swear, Robert Benton, if you cause her any more grief, you'll be sorry. I'll go upstairs, and if she has another one that pretty, I'll put it on myself."

Elizabeth was surprised. Her mother dared speak to her father in that tone of voice? And on Elizabeth's behalf? Benton's muscles at each side of his forehead began to twitch. "Suit yourselves," he spat, and stormed out. Elizabeth was elated. At least her dad knew he couldn't make those kind of remarks in the presence of her mother. Impulsively, Elizabeth reached out, grabbed her mother and pulled Katherine to her in a heart-felt hug.

The door bell chimed, interrupting any further discussion they might have had. One of the ladies Elizabeth had seen downstairs opened the door. First to arrive was the tall man Elizabeth saw at the mine. "Honey, this is..." Katherine started to say.

"Doctor Dowd," Elizabeth finished. "It's a pleasure to meet you." It did not escape Elizabeth that he was also looking boldly at her cleavage.

"Damn glad to meet you at last," he said, continuing his stare.

"Now Doctor, we're going to watch our language in front of

Elizabeth and the other guests, aren't we?" Katherine asked in a pleasant enough tone.

Dowd smiled. "As you wish, Madam," he said no less pleasantly. "But Mother Jones says, 'Profanity is prayer to the working man.' Mark Twain thinks it's even better. He commented that profanity sometimes provides a relief denied even to prayer."

"Well, you're certainly no working man, Doctor," Katherine tried one more time.

"The hell I'm not," Dowd replied and winked at Elizabeth. Katherine gave up. She guessed she couldn't change him in one evening. More guests arrived, and Katherine left to greet them.

Dowd glanced at Elizabeth again, this time more boldly. Elizabeth felt even more grown up in her dress. Feeling impish, "What do you think of my dress?" she asked and smiled slyly.

"Damn fine dress, that" Dowd said. Katherine returned in time to hear the remark and suggested he watch that cradle. And smiling, she added, "By the way, where is your good wife?"

A little of the wind seemed to be taken out of Dowd's sails. "Sorry, the wife couldn't make it. She wanted me to give you some lame excuse but the truth is, she has diarrhea."

"Sorry she couldn't come," Katherine said. "I had her paired up with Jimmy Meese; now I'll have to make some adjustments. Maybe I'll pair him up with Mrs. Harvey."

Apparently over his pique, her dad re-entered the room. He headed straight for the doctor. "Doc, you heard about a union meeting tonight?" Dowd replied negatively. "Heard rumors there was a secret meeting, trying to confirm it. Want something to drink?" Benton asked.

When Doc said that Scotch and water sounded good, Benton left to talk with Mrs. Naylor. She had kindly consented to bring drinks for the guests. Elizabeth saw her mother return. "If you don't mind teaching a novice to play Five Hundred," Elizabeth said as her mother came up to them, "Mom has assigned me to your table."

"Well, what with Mrs. Dowd not coming, perhaps . . ." Katherine began to object.

"The matter is settled," the doctor interrupted.

Reluctantly, Katherine had to leave yet again. More guests arrived.

Dowd turned to Elizabeth. "I enjoy teaching novices," he said, and the double entendre was not lost on her. The stirring grew. But, to her chagrin, once more she began to blush. For the life of her, she couldn't think of a good way to put Dowd in his proper place.

Dowd lifted his arm slightly, indicating the direction of the stairs. "Shall we?' he asked. Without objection, Elizabeth took his arm and accompanied him downstairs. Then, Elizabeth led Doc to their table. As yet, no one else was at the table. Doc gallantly pulled out Elizabeth's chair. As he leaned a little forward to push it in after she was seated, Elizabeth burned. She felt his eyes searching her. This time more fully, more wantonly.

Doc sat, reached across the table, and picked up the place card from the plate opposite him. "Damn," he said for the eighth time. She asked what the problem was. "Your mother has assigned T. C. Harvey as my partner. He's a lousy card player,." He paused to think a moment. "Oh, well, your mom doesn't know all the town folk yet. No harm done," Dowd said graciously. "All the more reason to concentrate on teaching you," he added.

Again the double entendre. He's lascivious, wonder if some of the ladies in town enjoy having their breasts examined by him. As she blushed at the thought, she really started searching for a good way to shut him down. "Dr. Dowd, in small towns do all doctors take such an interest in the daughters of their peers?"

Doc reached up and held the front of his chest with both hands as though clutching a wound. "Touche," he said. "You got me," he added, then smiled.

Apparently, her ploy worked. Tom Harvey and Mrs. Varner joined them, forestalling any comments Elizabeth might have had.

Elizabeth was grateful that just then plates of food were brought to their table.She had to admit the lamb, pilaf, and cheesecake were delicious. After dinner, Elizabeth even learned to enjoy the card game. She was soon bidding and playing her hand without help. It was not all that much different from bridge. The party turned out an enjoyable affair.

As the party was breaking up, she also enjoyed a conversation with Patsy Meese. Her husband, Jimmy, came over to join the conversation. Elizabeth was able to utilize the information her mother had given her earlier. "I understand you are in charge of the St. Patrick's Day dance." "He sure is," Patsy said proudly. "And you must come. Jimmy is putting together a Mysterious Moon. We're going to have a grand time."

"Yes, do come," Jimmy agreed. "And wear that dress."

However, on the night of the St. Patrick's Day dance, Elizabeth did not wear the slinky dress. Perhaps to please her mother, or perhaps because she felt all her other dresses were just too chic for a coal camp dance, she wore the ruffled, pink one.

After she put on the dress, she went downstairs, and was pleased by the smile on her mother's face. Her mother explained everybody in town would be there. The beeping of the Packard's horn signaled it was time to leave.

The recreation hall was a large, two-story, stone building. As the Packard drove up, Elizabeth saw a long covered porch at the front of the second floor of the recreation hall. It ran the full width of the building. A number of people were standing around and talking.

Inside, it was, at best, interesting, at worst, tacky. There were crepe paper streamers everywhere, and green paper shamrock cut-outs of every size decorating everything. The front two thirds of the hall was set up with long tables. The "Mysterious Moon" was simply decorated card board boxes placed over the lights. Quarter moon cutouts on each side of the boxes served to dim the room and give everything a soft, shadowy effect. Under the basketball net at the rear of the hall, a raised bandstand held some musicians.

Apparently the Bentons had arrived late. The band was playing, and a number of people were dancing. Elizabeth noticed some of them were about her age. As the dancers noticed her family, couple by couple they stopped dancing. Soon, even the band stopped playing. Evan Jones mounted the front of the bandstand, turned around and raised his hands.

"Ladies and Gentlemen," Evan said. "As Commander of the Sunnyside American Legion, I want you all to welcome Mr. Robert Benton, his beautiful wife, Katherine, and their lovely daughter, Elizabeth. Thank you for coming," he said to them. At which Benton bowed his head slightly in acknowledgment. Elizabeth noticed the smiling faces, and the eagerness of the applause. Hypocrites, she thought.

After coming off the bandstand and conferring with some people, Jones again mounted the bandstand and raised his hands. "Now, take your seats at the tables. Dinner will be served. Our red-headed sea cook, Gilligan, has prepared an Irish feast. He's made nettle soup, Irish stew, soda bread, Irish potatoes, corned beef and cabbage, and for desert that all time favorite, Irish tipsy cake."

Bob and Patsy Meese came toward them. "With your permission, Sir," he said with great formality. "As I am presiding over this dance, I request you sit with us at the head table."

Benton turned to ask his wife if that would be okay. "I'd be pleased," her mother answered. Her dad grunted something about that it would be fine with him, too. Two small tables wcre being combined near the bandstand. Soon they were all seated. Elizabeth tasted the nettle soup. It was strange, but delicious. She noticed those seated at head tables were being served individually, the rest were being served family style.

After the meal, as the last dish was taken from their table, Jimmy Meese stood up. "Presiding, though I may be," he said, "Duty calls. I'm on K.P."

Elizabeth asked what K.P. was, and Patsy answered. "He means he's going to help wash dishes. It's called Kitchen Police in the army."

On total impulse, Elizabeth asked, "Mind if I help?" Immediately, she noticed her father's look of displeasure. Her mother quickly placed her hand on top of Benton's.

"What a nice gesture," her mother said. "The only problem is your father and I will have to be leaving soon. Do you wish to stay, or would you rather go with us?"

"I'll see that she gets home safely, Mr. Benton," Jimmy assured him.

"Well, okay," Benton agreed. "But take good care of my little girl, Jimmy," he added. The tone of Benton's voice made it clear, it was not a request.

"I'll see that he does, Mr. Benton," Patsy Meese said, and the scowl left her father's face.

Elizabeth followed Jimmy into the kitchen area. By the time she got there, she noticed that Jimmy's offering to do dishes was more a matter of form than of reality. There was already a line well-manned by women and youth of the town. A few were scraping dishes into garbage pails and putting them in a sink. A young man was busily rinsing them with a hose attached to a faucet over a sink. Others were taking the rinsed dishes and putting them in a sink full of hot soapy water.

A lady came toward them. "I'm Mrs. Galbraith. Remember? From your mother's party?" Elizabeth smiled and although she couldn't remember her, she did remember something about her. "Oh, yes," she said. "Your first name's Emma."

Emma smiled, happy at being remembered. "If you don't mind putting on an apron, you could go over and help Dan Cook. As he rinses each dish, you can stack them and then it will be easier for the girls to get them in the wash sink. Would that be okay?" she asked.

"Of course," Elizabeth agreed. As Mrs. Galbraith helped Elizabeth put on the apron, Elizabeth heard the band beginning to play again, and wished she had kept quiet about the dishes. It would have been more pleasant to be out there listening and watching.

Mrs. Galbraith led her to the sink where the dishes were being rinsed. "Dan, this is Elizabeth Benton. You lucky little rascal. She'll stack them for you."

"Pleased to meet you," Dan said, and Elizabeth detected a surly tone. Elizabeth began to stack the rinsed dishes, and noticed a scowl on Dan's face. Strange, she thought, he doesn't even know me. Wonder what's upsetting him. Then, she remembered. "Are you Steve Cook's big brother?" she asked, hoping against hope for a negative answer.

"Yes," Dan answered.

Elizabeth began to blush and feel guilty. Remembering what she'd said to Steve. She kept stacking dishes for a few moments while she formulated her next words. "Are your mother and Steve here tonight?" Dan said they were, and Elizabeth continued. "I'm so glad. Before I leave tonight I intend to offer her and Steve my deepest apologies."

"Why would you do that?" The question indicated doubt she would lower herself to do such a thing. "You being the Big Boss's daughter and all," Dan added.

Once again she kept on stacking the dishes. Finally, she spoke, "Please try to understand. I was sick and upset at what I saw the other day. Without thinking, I lashed out at the first person that crossed my path. That was your brother. I'm sorry."

"Don't owe us an apology," Dan replied, at least part of his scowl was beginning to fade.

"I do." she replied. "I realized it when Cyclone told me of the mistake I'd made."

Dan reached for a dish. "Cyclone is a good man," Dan said, and the scowl eased more. Then he added "Do you really mean it?" Elizabeth asked what he meant.

"Do you really mean you were personally upset a miner was killed in the mine?"

Why would he question that the death of anyone would upset me? What does he think I am? "Of course I mean it. That is exactly what I mean. Of course it upset me. And another thing, I hated the way everyone had to stand for hours waiting to find out it was the Carpenter boy." Elizabeth's words came out in a rush. Finally, she was able to really talk with someone about it. "And something else. The cold way Ganz Durrant called to Mrs. Carpenter made me sick."

Dan was aghast at Elizabeth's words. What if somebody heard? What if they told Benton? What if they think I caused her to be so upset? Elizabeth caught the look on his face. She guessed correctly what it was. It floored her to realize the townspeople could be so afraid of her father. She looked around to see if anyone was listening.

"Thank you for listening to me," she said somewhat too loudly, just in case. She lowered her voice, "I want to apologize to you, personally, as well."

"Really," Dan began, he paused to hand a dish to Elizabeth. "Why Miss Benton."

"Please call me Elizabeth, Dan. I appreciated you're telling me what's on your mind," she added, flipping her hands over the sink to shake off some of the water on them.

Dan thought for a moment. Inwardly, he chuckled to himself. How can I tell her what's really on my mind? A broad smile came onto Dan's face. You don't just come flat out and tell the Super's daughter she's got a great-looking figure.

"What's so funny?" Elizabeth asked.

"Nothing really," Dan replied, stalling for time to think. "I'm just glad you feel the way we do." He heaved a big sigh of relief to have been able to answer so quickly.

Elizabeth picked up the sigh, however. *There's more going on here than meets the eye. I wonder if he wants to flirt with me. Maybe he's afraid to try because I'm Dad's daughter.* The next thought made her chuckle. *Maybe I ought to send him to Doc Dowd for lessons.*

"When I first came here tonight I was afraid I would be bored to tears. But now with the music and everything, I'm really tickled. When we're finished, would you please introduce me to your mother and Steve so I can make amends."

They continued spraying dishes and stacking them a while longer without saying anything. Once Elizabeth had to jump back because the spray bounced off one of the dishes and almost got her. Then, the music from the other room enticed her. It seemed to be calling to her, reminding her of better days at college.

Something caught her eye. There was flirting going on between the boy and girl picking up the sprayed dishes. Each time they passed each other something new would happen. One time the girl returning empty-handed, thrust out her hip, and bumped the boy loaded with dishes as he passed. Another time both turned toward the other and they slid by sideways. Elizabeth did not miss the deep look into each other's eyes as they slipped by—a little too closely. Elizabeth realized this was not simple flirting. These two were in love.

"Last pile," the girl bringing the dirty dishes to the sink said. Then the girl started to take off her apron in preparation for heading toward the dance. *For a small coal town in the middle of nowhere, there sure are a lot of buxom girls,* Elizabeth mused as the young girl raised her arms to get the apron off. Elizabeth stole a glance at Dan, his eyes were glued between the upraised arms as well. The appreciation in his gaze had an entirely different quality than Elizabeth's complimentary thoughts about the girl.

Dan looked back at Elizabeth. From the look on her face, he knew he'd been caught. He began to blush. *What a surprise,* Elizabeth thought when she noticed it. He worked so silently at finishing the dishes, his sudden speaking startled Elizabeth.

"That does it," he said. Then he added, "Want me to find my mother now?" He wiped his hands and began taking off his apron while he waited for the answer.

"No better time," Elizabeth said as she started doing the same. She was aghast at herself. Consciously, with no show of modesty, she raised her arms just as the other girl had done. Let him look, she thought. What can it hurt?

Dan took a quick glance and averted his eyes. He pretended folding his apron was important. He put his hand on her back to guide her to the dance floor. Oh my gosh, she's not wearing a corset. His feeling of guilt turned into a twitch of pain in his groin.

Elizabeth spotted Mrs. Cook immediately, and without further guidance, headed toward her. Dan trailed behind, trying to get his emotions under control. If this kept up, he was definitely going to get himself into a lot of trouble. Elizabeth's apology was respectfully given, and graciously accepted. But Elizabeth still insisted on apologizing to Steve as well. Mary Cook thought for a moment. "You two stay here, I'll go get Steve. Why don't you dance while you wait?"

Elizabeth had been itching to get onto the dance floor all night, but now that the actual moment had come, she felt a little shy. Dan was flat-out worried he would seem a country bumpkin to her if she didn't know his style of dancing. They stood facing each other. Elizabeth felt like a third grader. The orchestra started playing "Over The Waves." Not knowing what else to do, Dan reached out his arms. "Shall we?" he asked, hesitantly.

"Love to," she replied with a slight tremor in her voice. She was pleased to find Dan waltzed beautifully. She closed her eyes to better enjoy the music and the rhythm of the dance as Dan whirled her about the floor. But something else began to creep slowly into her consciousness. She was enjoying his hand holding hers, as well as his hand at her waist. She remembered his look at the girl with the apron.

On impulse, Dan pulled her a little closer to him. As their bodies touched, Elizabeth quivered. Dan held his breath as he felt her against him, moving against him. Wow, he thought, I don't care if Benton strings me up by the balls. She's worth it. The music stopped, and they held each other a moment longer than they should have.

Elizabeth forced her mind out into the rest of the room, away from the touch of his hands. She could still feel his solid young body against her. His muscles are iron, she thought. Then she saw Mary Cook coming toward them, with Steve in tow.

A sense of relief flooded her. That dance had been just too much. She wondered what was wrong with her. How could she have let this happen? How could she have been so one with this boy she just barely met? It wasn't decent.

Again the apology was accepted, and again the band started playing. To Elizabeth's great relief, Jimmy Meese showed up asking for the honor of a dance. Then it was T. C., whatever-his-name-was, and following that it was Evan Jones.

As she danced with each of them, and made polite conversation, two things were on her mind. Then she made a silent vow. She was not ever, ever, ever going to make the same mistake her mother had. She would not allow herself to fall in love with someone beneath her. Look at how much it had cost her mother.

Doc Dowd was her next partner, and the desire for a drink was so over powering she decided to ask him at the first opportunity.

She didn't have to worry about him looking at her cleavage this time. A new worry took it's place. At every opportunity Doc seemed to "accidentally" bump one of her breasts with the side of his arm, or put his hand a little two far forward on her side as he twirled her on the dance floor. But he was so slick about it Elizabeth couldn't say for sure it wasn't an accident. And his unconcerned chatter as he did it gave her no evidence he was doing it on purpose. Soon she began waiting for the next slight touch. She was beginning to feel absolutely wanton.

Love the way you dan. . ." Doc started to say.

"Oh, there you are," Patsy Meese interrupted. "We've been looking for you, time to go."

"I think so, too," Elizabeth responded gaily with a glance at Doc. She turned so Doc's hand covered her breast entirely, and left him standing as she walked toward Patsy. Let him think that one over for a while.

CHAPTER 11

LAW AND ORDER

Benton decided against a group meeting on Friday. Some things shouldn't be discussed with everybody. He had Durrant schedule each person individually, with the men who worked in the mine scheduled early, so they could get back to work. He sat sleepy-eyed, but the coffee was helping. A soft knock on the door. "Come in," he said.

Mitch Saxton entered and stood stiffly just inside the door. "Good morning, Mr. Benton." Benton mumbled a greeting and pointed to the chair in front of his desk where he wanted Mitch to sit. Mitch sat in the chair as stiffly as he'd stood. He definitely looks ill at ease, Benton thought. That's good. Benton flipped through some pages on his nearly full legal pad. Then he raised his eyes and looked at Mitch.

"I was wondering what you're hearing about union activity?"

"Don't have as much information for you as I should, Sir. Either activity has slowed down some, or the men have stopped talking union around me. Since my last report very little's been going on, with the exception of one incident."

Shifting in his chair, Benton leaned back and looked Saxton straight in the eyes. "Mitch, if I'm going to have a man able to move around his district in the way you are, I need that man to be bringing me information. Understood?" Mitch sat up even straighter in the chair. His back was no longer touching the chair at any point, and he nodded rapidly. Benton let him think that over for a bit. He reached for his legal pad, leafing through it as though he were looking for something. "You might want to become a little more aggressive. Accuse people of being union, then bring back to me what they say. Bad-mouth the union around someone you suspect, then report their response."

"Yes, sir. I see that maybe I haven't pushed hard enough."

Once more Benton flipped through the pad, Then looked at Mitch.

"Things are heating up. I need to know everything that's going on, and I need it quick. Tell Durrant I said to schedule you here twice a week, unless something really important comes up. If that happens, I want you to come out of the mine immediately. Understood?" Benton paused, looked down at his fingernails, and then once more back at Saxton. "And, Mitch, I strongly suggest you bring me a lot more at your next meeting than you brought today."

Mitch relaxed a little but not much. "You can count on me, Sir."

"I know I can, Mitch. Or I would already have someone else in that powder monkey job, and you'd be pulling pillars." Once more Benton paused to let the full impact of his words sink in. "Before you go, what was the incident you mentioned?

"Nothing I can accuse anybody of, just yet. As I told you before, old Sam Preston, and Old Man Stevenson worked during the last strikes. I'm pretty sure we can count on them again. But they were talking about something when I came up. It made me suspicious how fast they stopped talking when they saw me. I definitely caught the word union, and the word sun or son, in their conversation."

"What's your interpretation?"

"Mr. Benton, it is only fair that we have some proof before you take any act . . ."

Benton cut him off in mid-word. "I'll be the one to judge what's fair and when to take action! Get on with your story!"

Saxton paused, then surreptitiously, "I"m not completely sure. But if I had my bet, I'd bet they were talking about Old Man Preston's sons John and Leigh. Or on the other hand, it could be the Stevenson boys, or even both."

Benton paused and pursed his lips, then licked them. "That's good, Mitch," he said finally. "We don't always get all the information we need all at once. Get back to me when you're more sure, even if it has to be an educated guess." Bob paused to finish off the last of the coffee in his cup. "Both the Prestons and Stevensons are Mormon. I'll make sure my friend in the church has a talk with the boys."

Benton was gratified that Mitch was following every word, to make sure he didn't miss anything. Saxton is well motivated all right, Benton thought. Benton continued. "Since the boys don't work in your district,

I'll have someone else keeping an eye on 'em."

Benton smiled. "You're a good man, Mitch. Love to spend a bit more time shooting the breeze with you, but I have a pretty full schedule."

"Yes, Sir," Mitch said. He stood up briskly, and headed for the door. "And thank you, Sir," Mitch said as he opened the door to leave.

As each of his snitches came in and gave his report, Benton made notes on his pad. As with Saxton, none had much to report. Eagerly, he searched for the confirmation he felt was in his notes. Then, as he suspected, there it was. Benton was elated. Nobody was bringing in anywhere near what they usually did. Mitch Saxton hit the nail on the head, the union men had stopped talking union in the mine. The only logical explanation was the union was definitely preparing for a strike, and the men were being quiet about it. He'd seen it before. Once the organizing phase was over, things seemed to quiet down. Once lit, a fuse makes very little noise as it burns. Today he'd confirmed the fuse was lit.

The big boys back East might still be debating whether there was really going to be a strike, or if the union was just bluffing. But Benton knew.

He got up, went out to the wall phone, gave the handle a twist, and gave the operator Cameron's number in Salt Lake. He was shaking with excitement as he waited for Cameron's office to answer. He gave his report quickly and succinctly. Then he got off the phone. From the response he got, he knew Cameron would want to contact the people back East immediately.

As Benton was returning to his office, Sod Nelson arrived. "Let's go on in, Sod," Benton said. "Have a seat." Glancing at the note pad, Benton took a little time to let his excitement wear off and concentrate again on the business at hand.

"Need to know how you are doing profit-wise at the store the last month or so," he said.

Nelson looked as uncomfortable as Mitch had. "I can't give you an item by item report on that. Sorry, I put them on the train yesterday, as Mr. Cameron asked me to do."

Benton's face turned dark. "Sod, don't you think I should have been advised about that?"

Nelson's voice was quivering. "Sorry, Mr. Benton. I just naturally thought since Mr. Cameron was made the new President of Wasatch Stores, he'd keep you advised."

Benton got up from his desk, walked to the door, and in a voice that sounded deadly, he spoke out to Durrant. "Ganz, Sod will be leaving now. He'll be back in half an hour with a report on how the store is doing profit-wise. Look it over, and if you think it's okay, send him on in to me. If he doesn't have good information, just fire him." He walked back to his desk, sat down, and picked up the pad. Out of the corner of his eye, he saw Sod slinking out of the office. He sat thinking how Cameron had blind-sided him about the store once, and that was definitely not going to happen again. Benton called Durrant into the office. Durrant came and mentioned Benton had sure lit a fire under Nelson.

"Sod's been a little complacent lately. He's good at his job, but we can't have anybody getting too laid back just now. I don't have time to nurse anybody along. Who's next?" Durrant had no sooner said Abe Strang was next when someone knocked on the office door. "Come in, Abe," Benton called as Durrant got up to leave.

"Good morning, Boss," Strang said as he came in and sat in the chair Durrant just vacated. A cheeky fellow, Benton thought. He'd been told when he first came to Sunnyside that Strang was not your typical miner. Strang was gruff, kowtowed to no one, and was the best master mechanic in the state. Benton's informant said the two possible courses were either keep him, or fire him first thing. Benton had decided to keep him. Good men were hard to find.

"Good morning, Abe. Want a cup of coffee?"

"Sounds good," Strang responded.

"How do you want it?"

"Sugar in the morning turns my stomach, and if I wanted milk, I'd buy a cow. I want my coffee straight from the coffee pot." Benton called for more coffee, and an extra cup. Benton made small talk while they drank their coffee.

"You know, Abe," Benton said as he finished the last of his coffee, "When I first came here I was told that you were worth your weight in gold, I can really depend on you."

"Some say that about me, yes. But mainly, I finish what I start, or I don't start it."

Braggart, Benton thought. But, compliment paid, he turned to the business at hand. "How's the shed for the searchlight coming?"

"Good. I've got Horace Naylor supervising the Italian stone masons. Men from the maintenance shop are running a power line up there. When the light comes, we'll be ready."

"Good, Abe. I expect the light to arrive in the next day or so. Keep on top of it. Did you come up with a cover story as I asked?"

Strang smiled. "I put out the story that we'd be putting pumps there for a water tank we'll build further up the hillside. It's supposed to give the boiler a steadier supply of water because of better gravity feed."

Benton thought it over for a minute. Keeping Strang had been the right decision. "Good thinking, Abe. Just one more thing. When the strike starts, the maintenance shops have to keep running. Let me know right away if any men you absolutely need go out on strike."

When Abe left, Benton looked over some mine inspector reports until he heard Nelson talking with Durrant. Benton contemplated letting Nelson stew a little longer, but there was too much to do. He put a stern look on his face, got up, walked to the door.

"He ain't got the details, Bob. But over all it looks good to me," Durrant said.

"Guess he's still got his job --- for awhile," Benton turned and beckoned Nelson in. "Well," he said, without offering Nelson a chair.

"Profits are still right up there, sir, although, we have slipped about three percentage points in the last two or three months, because of the flyers Pessetto's been handing out."

"Why wasn't I advised of this?" he almost hissed. He noticed Nelson was trembling.

"Sir, it started before you came here. Right after old Alexander Cowie quit as General Manager, Pessetto started putting out these flyers."

"Give me some examples of what's on those flyers."

Nelson reached in his pocket. He pulled out a flyer. "Here it is, sir. If you want, you can see for yourself." Benton declined, so Nelson began reading. "He's selling lamb stew meat for twelve and a half cents, chops for twenty and eggs are a quarter a dozen. Those are very popular with the Greeks. Pork roast is twenty cents, but pot roast is only fifteen."

"Okay," Benton said, "I get the picture."

Benton began to see why Cameron was upset. Now, how he wished he'd made the store a top priority. Leaning back in his swivel chair he put his hands behind his head. "As in the past, on the day of the strike, all strikers will be paid off in full and released from their jobs. Your job is to make sure you know which miners owe you money. Then, get a list of who owes what to paymaster Rudy, so he can deduct it from their wages when they're paid off. Make sure you get it to him early so he has plenty of time to figure what the strikers owe us."

"Even for non-strikers? That will make it real hard on some of our loyal men." The words were no sooner out of Nelson's mouth than he realized he'd just contradicted a man who would tolerate no contradiction.

Benton's anger started to rise, but he was in too good a mood to let something this trivial ruin it. "I appreciate the loyalty of our good men, too, Sod. My experience in Colorado taught me a valuable lesson, however. We can't take the chance that some who do not strike at first, will stay just long enough to charge a bunch of food. Once they have hurt us that way, they join the strike. It's becoming a union trick."

"Hadn't thought about that," Nelson said.

Another thought occurred to Benton. "Will Pessetto give strikers credit?"

Sod said that Pessetto would. That made things even worse for Benton. "Any questions, Sod?" Nelson just shook his head, turned and left. There goes a man I can now depend on Benton thought.

A knock on the door pulled his mind back to the present. "Come in," he said, and watched to see who it was. He saw the star on Ovie Rasmussen's chest before he saw the man, and knew it was the town marshal.

"Sit, Ovie. We've got a lot of things to talk over." Without waiting for Rasmussen to be seated, Benton continued. "We're starting to make our final plans for a strike now. Can we count on what's-his-name, the Justice of the Peace, if we gotta make some arrests?"

Rasmussen nodded. "We've always been able to count on Judge Mathis."

"I figured as much. A town with the history of Sunnyside has to have some pretty solid people. Any new men we have to hire?"

"I'm lining some up," Rasmussen said. He paused, looked down, then raised his head. He was leery about mentioning the next subject. "Could we get a machine gun?"

Benton frowned, and was about to refuse forcefully, but decided he'd hear Ovie out first. "What in heaven's name for?" was all he asked.

"A machine gun would be mighty handy to have in case of trouble. And, after Ludlow, having a machine gun mounted will scare the beejeses out of the strikers. Maybe even keep them from trying something they might otherwise try."

Now it was Benton's turn to think. He sat back in his swivel chair. In spite of his first impulse to reject the idea completely, Rasmussen made some good points. "I'll consider it. But, Ovie, you can bet your bottom dollar I will not tolerate another Ludlow in my town." There was no way he was going to tell Rasmussen that he couldn't agree to it without first clearing it through Cameron. "When you mentioned other things strikers might try, were you referring to sabotage?"

"Yeah, and strikers attacking scabs in mass."

Benton looked straight into the other man's eyes. "Ovie, we have no scabs. We have loyal employees, and we have trouble-making foreigners. Don't forget that."

Benton shifted in his chair. "Ovie, what I'm going to tell you now had better stay with you. We're not building a shed on the hillside for pumps. A searchlight is coming. That's what's going up there." Benton was pleased at the surprised look on Rasmussen's face. Apparently Strang's story had circulated, and was being believed. "How many men do you want at the light at any one time?"

Rasmussen thought for a moment. "At least two. One to point the light, and one with a rifle to protect the light and other company property."

"Good. Now run down for me what your current thinking is on how many new men we will need. You can get the exact number to me later."

"Yes, sir. Well, off the top of my head, besides the three deputies we have now, can't see how I'd man the light without at least six men, if I work 'em overtime. Plus, I'll need at least six more if there's going to be a tent town. We'll set up a Guard post between the tents and town. That will take at least six more men. In addition to the Guard post, and the men on the light, I think we need six additional men for mobile patrols in town. I would need no fewer than eighteen, all told."

Benton was not pleased. "That's a lot of men, Ovie."

"Yes, but that should about cover us. I could probably get by on a little less if there's no trouble. But my feeling is we can prevent trouble with a good show of strength."

Benton was agitated. That's bad. How can I ask Cameron for that many men when production will be down during the strike? "Ovie, I want you to work out the schedules of the patrols in random and over-lapping patterns. That way no one can figure out in advance when or where our men will show up. Also, I want it set up so that one time the men may patrol on horses, another time on foot. We'll keep 'em all guessing."

"When can we start hiring?" Rasmussen asked.

Benton leaned back and clasped his hands behind his head. He began going over his schedule, and repeated it aloud. "Tuesday I go to Price to meet with the county commissioners, Wednesday I have to tour Utah Fuel's other operations in the county. Thursday I'll drive to Salt Lake, and come home Friday. I'll probably get back too late to do much that day. Unless things really heat up and we have to do something sooner, probably a week from today will be the soonest we can start hiring.

Rasmussen looked worried. "I won't have time to get things ready."

Benton smiled. "Don't panic, Ovie. There won't be any trouble early in the strike. It will take a few days for the men to get settled in a tent town. Besides, you've got a week to start talking with people now. You can promise them, without an unforeseen problem, they'll start on the first day of a strike. Got anybody in mind?"

"A couple. Bill Lyons worked for us in the past. He's a little iffie right now. He's a close friend of Jack Dempsey, and Dempsey just sent him a prize bull for Bill's herd. I don't know if he will be willing to come, but I'll try. Maybe we can get William Cook, and Howard Mathis. They're good men."

Driving the Packard to Salt Lake Thursday morning was such a joy. The weather was dry, the snow melted from Soldier Summit, and much of the roads had recently been graded.

It took him only five hours to cover the entire one hundred and fifty miles between Sunnyside and Salt Lake. No easy trick given the condition of some of the roads, and all of the little towns in Utah Valley. Finally, he parked in front of the Judge Building.

At the company offices, Benton was surprised to discover he would be the only one meeting with Frank Cameron. As he went into Frank's office, Frank motioned Benton to a chair. "We've got too much to cover for a group meeting," Cameron explained. "And some of it is just nobody else's business."

"Know what you mean, Frank. Just went through that myself," Benton replied.

Cameron surprised Benton. "When we're through here, I've got you booked into a room at the Newhouse Hotel. And you can drive me down there in that fancy car of yours. I'll even pop for dinner. Your information yesterday is worth a Porterhouse."

Bingo, Benton thought. "Thanks, Frank. I'm glad it was useful to you." Benton began to relax. "And a Porterhouse sounds good to me," Benton agreed.

"Good," Cameron grunted. "Where do you want to start your report, Bob?"

"County Commission. I had a meeting with them Tuesday regarding their paying for deputies. They are really stone-walling it."

"Yes, I know," Cameron said. "The operators agreed we'd all take a stand against our paying this time. Also, the report I got is that you did very well making the case for Utah Fuel."

Benton thought Frank's network must be everywhere. "Frank, I've been doing my very best to get an information network set up ever since I came to Sunnyside. I feel pretty good about what I've accomplished so far. But compared to you I'm a piker. You've been here only a short while, yet you have your finger on everything. How do you do it?"

Cameron chuckled, pleased at a compliment he knew was real. "Got one real advantage over you, Bob. I'm an old Carbon County man, and many of my people have been with me for years. But, I'll give you one piece of advice. Never trust the man you're most certain you've got under your thumb. He'll turn out to be an enemy every time." Cameron took a sip of coffee, before he continued. "That's the key," he said. "I don't know why it works, the enemy will be the one who you're most convinced is at your beck and call."

Benton sat thinking deeply. One by one he began going over those he worked with. Who in my organization am I most sure of? And how do I shut him out of important stuff?

"What's your assessment on paying half the cost of deputies?" Cameron asked.

"If we don't, the union will stir up the people about all the extra taxes they have to pay."

Cameron looked thoughtful. "When you get back to Carbon County, tell them Utah Fuel will pay for every other deputy hired, provided we get to pick all the deputies." He emphasized the word, "all," and Benton did not miss this addition to his plan. "What's next?" Cameron asked, apparently satisfied this subject was handled.

Benton decided to bring up Watson's request. "Rasmussen wants a machine gun."

"And you agree with that?" A frown crossed Cameron's features. The machine gun seemed to catch him by surprise.

Seems his spies aren't everywhere, Benton thought. "Yes, Sir, I do. Putting out the word that we have a machine gun might just be enough of a show of force to keep any trouble from happening. Also, having one on hand in our armory might just give us the edge we need in the months to come if things get real ugly, real quick."

Cameron leaned back in his chair. "I'm against it. I've run mines in Carbon County for twenty years, and I never needed a machine gun. Further, there is no way I am going to let Utah Fuel be involved in anything similar to what happened in Ludlow."

Benton was prepared for this, too. "I hear that, Frank. I visited Ludlow right after it happened. It was enough to make anybody sick. The machine gun is totally your decision, that's why I brought it to you. But there is one aspect of Ludlow I wonder if you've considered?"

"What's that?"

"Because of Ludlow, miners out here have a hate for the companies that is not exceeded anywhere in the country. When I visited Ludlow I heard conversation after conversation that they would get even, that there would be a day of reckoning."

Benton paused to give Cameron a moment to think it over. "There are an awful lot of ex-Ludlow miners working in Carbon County."

He pressed the point; he wanted to get it all out before Cameron could object again. "What if the strike goes on longer than we expect? What if things start to turn ugly and some of those men decide on revenge? Or maybe even worse, what if a whole bunch of them are so afraid Ludlow might happen to them, they decide the only way to protect themselves is to attack us first?"

Cameron leaned forward, picked up his cigar, then put it back down. He put his elbows on the desk, laced his fingers together, and rested his chin on them. "Buy Watson his new machine gun, and order three more besides. One for each of the other supers. But, Benton, I don't need to warn you, it's your reputation on the line if something unfavorable to Utah Fuel happens with those guns."

Got him. "I am very clear about that, Frank. But I feel strong enough to think it's worth the risk." At this time he wasn't about to tell Cameron his plans for making certain Ludlow would not happen in Carbon county.

Cameron was nodding his head up and down. "Maybe we made the right choice in a General Super. In addition to the information you gave me yesterday, you even bring me something you know will be a hard sell. You're not just a yes man, Benton, and I need such men."

Cameron's eyes narrowed to slits. His voice became almost deadly. "But, don't rest on your laurels. I expect a top man in your position. And I demand no less."

Benton got the message. "I'm not the resting kind, Frank," he said. "Never will be," he added.

Just when Benton was feeling good about Cameron's compliment, Cameron leaned forward and looked him in the eye. "Is Pessetto taking company scrip at his store?"

Benton paled. "Don't know, Frank," he said, and thought fast. "Our scrip says plainly that it is good only in our stores. Also, since it would be against federal law for him to use our scrip as money in his store, I think there is very little chance of it."

"But you don't know for certain? Benton, what am I paying you for? And you don't think it's likely Pessetto is taking our scrip and someone in your organization is buying it back at a discount, then skinning the company for the difference?" Benton knew he'd been had.

Cameron didn't wait for an answer. "One more incident of this nature and we might have to rethink your appointment as General Super."

"No, Sir. You don't," Benton paused. "You don't have to warn me, that is," he added. He's got me rattled now. I can't keep ahead of him. How in the world can anyone think of every twist, turn, and devious possibility he can? I've probably had it. I can never keep ahead of such a man.

"Well," Cameron said, scowling. "It's out of your hands now anyway. You can forget about Pessetto. He's my problem."

Chapter 12

Saturday Night

"Wake up, Dan, wake up!" Steve said as he shook his brother's shoulder. "Can't you hear the whistle?"

"Leave me alone. I'm not going to work today."

"No, Dan. It's the whistle, get up."

"Forget the whistle for crying out loud. I'm on strike."

"No, Dan, it's three o'clock in the morning. Something's wrong, get up," Steve pleaded.

Sleep gone, consciousness returned. Dan woke wide-eyed. He grabbed his clothes. Steve did likewise. Dan heard commotion in his parents' bedroom as well. In a moment more, every light in the house was on. Dan looked out the window and saw other lights coming on all over town. The family converged at the front door.

"What could it be?" his mother asked. "The mine isn't working."

"Could have blown just the same," Carl said as they reached the street.

People from all over town ran down the street. Dan looked in the direction they were running. The mouth of the canyon showed the rosy glow of a night fire.

"No!" Carl cried out. "Jack Pessetto's place must be on fire. It's too far out to be anyone else." As one, the family joined the groups hurrying toward the fire. As they passed the first shed where hand-pulled hose carts were housed, the shed was empty. So were the three successive fire sheds after that.

"I hope they get there in time," Mary puffed.

"No chance," Carl said. "It's already too big! Look!" he said pointing to the right, where the mouth of the canyon opened up before them.

Every one of Pessetto's buildings was on fire. As they got closer they saw the fire carts all standing in a row, resembling four cannons lined up for battle. But no fire hoses were pulled out, and hardly anyone was around the carts.

"What's wrong, Carl?" Mary asked, pointing to the carts.

"What's wrong?" Carl asked as they slowed at the first cart.

"They're useless," someone said. "No water or fire hydrants down here," he added.

They stopped at the ring of the crowd. Dan watched in amazement. His gaze swept from the fire at the store, to the larger warehouse, to the garage, to the stables, and to Jack's house. All were burning furiously. Every now and then, something inside the store would explode, and a big ball of flame would shoot a hundred feet into the air.

"It's a burn-out," Carl said. "No doubt about it. I hope to high heaven they catch the crooks that did it."

"I hope Jack and his family are safe," Mary said.

"He's okay," a voice beside them said. "They're in Salt Lake to a Shriner's convention."

Dan turned, and for the first time noticed Frank Bonatti standing next to them.

"Hi, Frank," Dan said.

Hypnotizing as the sight of the burning buildings were, Dan looked around. Several cars from town were parked here and there along the road leading to Pessetto's. Dan spied what he was looking for. The big Packard was shining in the firelight.

"Be back in a minute," he told his family. "I'm going on around that way."

He could not take his eyes off the fire as he walked. He stumbled frequently. He stopped and gasped with the rest of the crowd as one wall of the warehouse caved in, sending a galaxy of sparks shooting into the night air.

Shortly, he was near the Packard and saw Bob Benton, his wife, and Elizabeth standing there a short distance in front of him, looking at the fire. Elizabeth still had on her thin nightgown. Dan stood behind. He was riveted by the sight of her silhouette, her long, shapely legs slightly spread beneath the silky material of her gown.

"Heaven help us," Benton said to Katherine. "I sure hope no one tries to blame this on me." Dan could see that now definitely was not the time to speak with them. He turned, saw a couple of people he knew and headed toward them.

"Guess old man Benton got him good," Joe Padriva was saying.

Dan stepped next to him. "I just came past the Bentons. Said he sure hoped no one would try to blame this on him."

Padriva shook his head in disbelief. "What would you expect him to say? Hey, look everybody, see the fire I started?"

Dan had believed the upset he heard in Benton's voice. "No, really. He really seemed upset. Really, I don't think he was faking it."

"Come with me," Joe said. "I got to talk to you."

"Why?" Dan asked.

Joe just put his index finger to his lips indicating silence, turned and led Dan away. They climbed the hillside until they were huffing and puffing. Dan was getting more anxious by the minute to find out what Joe wanted. Dan stopped and pointed to some rocks they could sit on.

"Good idea," Padriva said. "We can see the fire and the crowd both."

"Why did you bring me up here?" Dan asked anxiously.

Joe looked at him blankly, then laughed. "Biggest fire I ever seen. Forgot we gotta talk."

"Well, talk," Dan demanded a little impatiently.

"Don't get uppity with me, you Limey kid. Or you'll never find out."

"Sorry. But you seemed so anxious down there you got me nervous."

"You should be, that's why I gotta talk to you."

Dan was losing patience. The rock under him was cold. "Well get to it. Talk."

"You know my wife cooks for the Bentons?" Dan nodded that he did. "She told me that the day after the dance, there was an awful argument about you. Benton kept shouting he wouldn't have his daughter frater, fraternest..."

"Fraternizing?" Dan suggested.

"Yeah, that's the word. Benton told his daughter to keep away from all coal miners in general, and you in particular."

"Why?"

"How should I know? You should know. What'd you do? Feel her up or something?"

Does everybody think I'm some kind of pervert, he asked himself. "I didn't do anything, I swear. I just danced with her one time, that's all."

"My wife says you must of did something. Benton's daughter acted mad at you, too." Dan protested he couldn't think of a single thing he'd done to upset her. But his heart sank. Probably cause I pulled her too close to dance. Stupid, stupid, he said to himself.

"Look!" Joe exclaimed. "Look at that." Something else had exploded, or fallen. Thousands of sparks were shooting up into the night air. Exciting as the sight was, Dan was far more concerned with what Joe was telling him.

"Did your wife say anything else?" Dan asked.

"What? Oh, you mean about her being mad at you. No. She just told me the girl said she'd rather fall into an outhouse than be caught with anybody that far below her station, whatever that means." Joe grinned. "And that tore it. My wife says Benton jumped up and ran out as if some- body shoved a jalapeno up his butt. Then Mrs. Benton started crying and demanding to know where her little girl ever learned to use that kind of language." Apparently Joe had said all he was going to on the subject. Once again Joe shifted his attention to the fire. Dan tried to watch it as well. It was the biggest fire he'd ever seen, too.

There was an ache in his chest when he saw the Bentons pile into their Packard and leave.

Joe jerked his arm toward the fire. "Look out!" he blurted. "Look at that." Dan looked and saw the four walls of the store all caving in at once. The collapsing walls somehow blew a hot ball of fire toward the spectators. They scattered in every direction, some bumping into others, knocking them down.

Dan jumped to his feet. His family was down that way. But the fire never quite reached where people were standing. Slowly the downed people got up, and the rest began returning. Dan sat down on the rock again.

He figured he owed Joe something. "Thanks Joe for letting me in on that."

"Da nada. It's them against us, right?"

"Right!" Dan said. Then he vowed never again to give Elizabeth the chance to turn against him this way. I'd rather fall through the floor of an outhouse.

Higher up on the hillside, the old pair of eyes was again watching a scene far below him. He was busy chanting his thanks to Mother Earth and Great Spirit for the second omen. Lights in the night for the second time could mean only one thing. He still didn't know when, but this would be the place. He was sure of it. Two more omens and it would start.

He looked up. "Suhdee'u tuhchunee," he said in Paiute. He was telling the meteor overhead that it scared him. It was the third sign, and such a powerful one. Could anything else match this? He thanked Mother Earth for making each sign greater than the last. Now, more than ever, he was certain when Mother Earth's plan came, it would be big medicine. This third sign was so magnificent, and so close to the second sign.

Both Dan and Joe had looked up. Just as the fire had been the biggest they'd ever seen, this was the brightest shooting star they had ever seen. It spread light from the mountains on their left, across the entire valley, and all the way to the mountains on their right. Dan had almost ducked, it seemed so close. "That's spooky," he whispered.

BOOK II
STRIKE

CHAPTER 13

STRIKE!

On Monday, after Pessetto's fire, nearly nine hundred men in Sunnyside went on strike. In the rest of the nation over half a million men stopped working. Benton walked into the office meeting room. Already seated were Ovie Rasmussen, Abe Strang, and Sod Nelson. "Okay, boys, I've established the dead line from the creek to the cliffs, and from the back of the store to Lower Bridge. It contains all the shops, and we'll see anybody sneaking in."

Ovie Rasmussen smiled. "Rest assured, Boss, any striker we find there will be visiting Judge Mathis quicker than he can stop bleeding." Benton cautioned him against unnecessary roughness, with emphasis on the word "unnecessary." Rasmussen agreed

Benton picked up a pencil and drew a line through the first item on the pad. "Abe, is the searchlight operational?" When Strang, in his usual gruff manner, said it was ready and tested, Benton drew a line through that item. He asked Rasmussen if his men had been trained on it.

Strang answered the question. "Bet your life. Ready and trained. One thing, though. Ovie asked if I'd supply the man on each shift to work the light and he would supply the guard. He figures mechanics who don't go on strike won't be all that busy, and I agreed."

Benton was pleased. "Good plan. I want the light to sweep around the deadline area often. Thanks, Abe." Drawing another line, he turned to Nelson. "Sod, turned in your list to Rudy?"

"Yes, Sir. I stopped credit after our last meeting. The excuse I used was that all our ledgers were sent to Salt Lake. I have a list of some of the men still working who have been stocking up."

Benton nodded in approval. "Good, give me the list." Nelson opened a folder, took out the list, and handed it to Benton. Benton looked over the list, nodded his head at a few names, and shook his head back and forth at others. "I was checking to see how accurate our information was. Most of the names have been identified, but some were new to me." He handed the list to Rasmussen. "Ovie, I want you and your men to keep an eye on every name on that list. It's possible they were buying canned goods for some other reason than going on strike later. Maybe they're planning to stay at work to cause trouble, and need the groceries in case they get caught."

Benton picked up a pencil and drew a line through several more items. "Okay. Abe, Sod, I won't keep you from your duties. I want to talk with Ovie."

As they left, he turned to Ovie, and his eyes narrowed. "Where's the machine gun?"

"It's in a cabinet in the Armory."

"Is it a sturdy cabinet, and is there a lock on the cabinet door?" Rasmussen nodded affirmatively. "What else is in the cabinet besides the machine gun?"

"Ammunition for that, our other ammunition, and five shotguns."

Benton paused, pursed his lips, and thought for a moment. "Find somewhere else to store the other ammunition and the shotguns. But make sure they're under lock and key as well. When you get all that other stuff out of the cabinet, bring me the keys. I want every key to that lock. If you're not one hundred percent positive I have all the keys, buy a new lock." Benton let that sink in for a moment, but kept his gaze on Rasmussen. "You can forget about the machine gun. I will be the only one who can give an order to unlock that cabinet. Do you understand?" Rasmussen nodded his head. "Don't take this personal, Ovie. I gave the same instructions to my other superintendents. They are sending me their keys as well. In a dire emergency, they'll call me and I'll give permission to cut locks."

Benton drew a line through a couple more items. Without looking up, he spoke again. "Another thing I want you to do. Get the word out that we have the machine gun. Don't make that part a threat, just sort of informational. Hint that we have it set up and we will use it if there is any sort of organized violence against us." Again Rasmussen nodded.

Benton drew a line through another item. "If there weren't so many veterans among the strikers, I'd not have bought that gun in the first place. During the war they learned how to attack. Find out who of your men was a fighting veteran, and have him train the others how to stop them." Benton drew another line. "Now let's talk about your staff. How's the hiring coming?"

"Couldn't get Bill Lyons. It's the wrong time of year because he has a lot to do with his herd right now. Says if the strike drags on, or we really need him, he'll come. I got Art Webb, Lorenzo Young, and Bill Cook. Know them well, all are experienced. Top hands in this sort of situation."

Benton paused. He really didn't want to bring up this next subject. But desperate times call for desperate measures. "Any of the men got any, uh, special talents?"

"Webb is a tough customer. Also, I hired Lorenzo Young from over in Emery County. He has a reputation as a man we can count on to be firm with the strikers. Know what I mean?"

Benton pursed his lips. "He's a trouble-maker, might stir up some, uh, excitement if we need him to?" Rasmussen nodded in agreement. "How about the others? Any special talents there?"

"Haven't had them long enough to know. When I know them better, I'll give you a report."

Benton asked Rasmussen their names, and Rasmussen rattled them off. "Scott Faucett, Jack Gentry, Jesse Halverson, David Adamson, Warren Peacock, and Ralph Young."

"Have them all deputized by Sheriff Kelter as soon as possible." When Rasmussen said that was already handled, Benton sat, mentally counting. "That's only nine."

Rasmussen shifted in his chair. "You told me to go easy at first. I figured Strang supplying men to operate the light would save at least three. With our night watchmen, should do us for now."

Benton agreed, as he relaxed a little. He hadn't realized Rasmussen was so smart. *Ovie really is a top man, the best I've got. I can trust him to handle security without too much oversight.* Something clicked in Benton's memory. *Cameron! That sneaky double-talking crook Cameron. He only pretended to be surprised about the machine gun to throw me off. Ovie already cleared it with Cameron before he asked me. What do I do now? Now that I know Rasmussen's a snitch?*

"When will we need more men?" Rasmussen observed probably not till tent town was set up. By now, Benton had formulated his plan for shutting Rasmussen out of the loop.

"You're a good man, Ovie. I couldn't have set things up better myself. These last couple of weeks must have really been a strain on you," Benton said, throwing out bait to see what would grab at it. Rasmussen supplied the needed information.

"Well, the wife has been complaining that I'm not spending enough time with her and the kids."

Benton set the hook. "Who is the best man among the new group you've hired?"

"Without a doubt, Art Webb. I was lucky to get him," Rasmussen bragged.

Benton suppressed a smile and kept looking sincere. "Can he think on his feet in a tight situation, and keep his mouth closed when he has to?"

"I've known Art for years, and he has never let any of his employers down."

"I think you're right, Ovie. I think you were lucky to get him." Rasmussen hadn't put up much of a fight. Benton knew now was the time to reel him in. "Tell you what, my friend. Make Webb your Chief Deputy, second in command, and offer to pay him a little something extra. Work out the details about the pay with Ganz. Then start giving him some of the extra load you've been carrying. Your wife and kids deserve to have a good man around more."

When Rasmussen really seemed to go for the idea, Benton reasoned he could keep Webb in reserve. When he really needed Webb, he would call him in, double the pay Rasmussen gave him, and tell Webb he was really in charge. Let Cameron try to figure that one out.

Benton drew a line through several items on his pad. "Just one more thing. I don't want my daughter riding alone. I'll try to ride with her some. But can I call on you to have a deputy go with her fairly regularly?" Rasmussen saw no problem with that. Benton concluded the meeting.

On his walk home, Benton found himself whistling. He was in a good mood. Too bad it didn't last. He went through the front door and saw Elizabeth sitting on the couch. He told her about his plan to protect her with an accompanying guard on her rides. "Oh, no! That's no fair!" Elizabeth shouted. "Riding Bonnie is the only chance I have to be alone."

"Even so, that is the way it is, young lady. Remember, I was the one who had Bonnie shipped out from Colorado, and I can have her shipped back."

"Daddy, you wouldn't do that to me, would you? Bonnie is the only real friend I have."

"Well, probably not. But Elizabeth, you really try my patience sometimes."

"Sorry, Daddy. Daddy, I have so little fun out here. Wouldn't be fun to ride with a guard."

Benton had not forgotten her remark last week about not wanting to marry below her station. He knew she wanted to add, as you did Mom. Lower class that he was, he had her worried.

"Fun has nothing to do with it, Elizabeth. Keeping you safe is my responsibility. You have no idea how nasty things can get during a strike. The matter is settled. Where's your mom?"

Elizabeth looked surly. "In the kitchen."

As Benton held his meeting, the Union Committee was meeting as well. They knew they'd be put out of their homes, and most would have to go to a tent town. Not all nine hundred would be living there. Some had friends or relatives they would stay with. But the committee figured well over 2,500 of the men and their families would live in tents.

They set the site for tent town just below where Pessetto's place was burned out, and busied themselves making all the plans they could to assure the move would go as smoothly as possible. By the time the initial planning was done, it became obvious that a lot of work would have to begin right away if tent town was to be ready in time for the move.

Dan got the word the committee wanted everybody down to the site, and headed out. Frank Bonatti caught up to him as he walked. Past Pessetto's they came to the flat area where assignments were handed out.

"Why do we need assignments?" he asked Frank.

"Do you think a tent town builds itself, or do you think it just grows up overnight, like mushrooms? Somebody's got to dig holes for outhouses, and stuff such as that. You're going to be on my crew planting gardens," Frank said as he turned and headed off.

Dan went looking for Tom. Dan wondered about Tom's assignment. He asked Tom what he was in charge of. Dan guessed that whatever this bull-necked, deep-voiced, tough-as-nails man had been put in charge of, it would be dangerous.

Tom shuffled his feet in the dirt. "Games," Tom replied. "Once we move into tent town, one of our biggest problems is going to be keeping everybody busy. You probably think laying around a tent town sounds sort of great. But that gets old really fast. Then the trouble starts."

"What kind of trouble?" Dan asked.

"Can't talk now. Got to start the meeting." Tom turned to walk off, Dan fell in along side of him.

Dan wondered why it was Tom who's starting the meeting. "You some sort of union official?"

"Didn't you know?" Tom asked. "Thought you knew I'm president of our local." Surprised, Dan said he wished somebody had told him.

As they walked, Tom elaborated a little bit. "Your first strike can be pretty confusing. One minute you're bored to death, and the next minute somebody from tent town starts a fight. These men are used to working hard every day. Having nothing to do wears on them."

Dan thought it over a bit. "Tom, I never saw you play a game in my whole life."

"Well, I used to. I was pretty good at soccer when I was a lad. But that ain't the point. Keeping people busy, that's the point."

As they walked, every time they passed someone, Tom waved to them. Tom continued. "Some of these guys ain't going to want to play games. They picked me because I'm the most unlikely guy they could think of. When those guys see me playing, it won't be so bad for them to play, too. Anybody still won't play after that, I'll have a little talk with them." They walked to a flat place, and Tom whistled at some men further away.

Dan was a little upset now. He reached out and put his hand on Tom's shoulder. "Tom, do you realize what you're telling me?" Tom just looked at him questioningly. "You're telling me playing games ain't about having fun."

Tom nodded his head up and down forcefully. His lips tightened. "You got that straight." Tom stood up on a rock. "Okay, you mugs, listen to me!" he shouted. "John Tennis, security, meet over by that burned out shed there," Tom said and pointed to where he wanted them to go. Then in rapid fire order, he barked out the rest of the details, and indicated their meeting place.

Dan was amazed at the completeness of the organization. Things he had taken for granted all his life: helping his mother wash clothes and hang them on the line to dry, was now under someone's direction. In his mind, he had always pictured a tent town as a group of tents scattered around. He could see now that the emphasis was more on the word town, than on the word tent. Tom continued giving directions. "Andy Vullis, picketing, meet on the other side of the shed."

By the time Dan met with his crew, marked off the various garden plots, and got his instructions, it was dark. John Tennis came by and told everyone not to go back to town in a bunch. They were to space themselves out. There were some questions Dan wanted to ask about picketing. He found Andy and they started back toward town together. Suddenly they were illuminated in the glare of the searchlight. Andy stopped walking.

"Man," Dan said jerking his hand up to shade his eyes. "That thing will blind you." The spot stayed on them for a moment, and then began it's random searching.

"Why'd you stop?" Dan asked.

"Get used to it," Andy said, unperturbed. "Benton has a couple of his goons hid around here. Every man coming back to town will have the light turned on him to identify him, and have his name written down in a book. When the light hits you, stop. That way, the men at the light know you're aware they've seen you. If you just keep walking, the light will continue to follow. Try to hide, a couple a goons will be out looking for you. Cross the dead line, they'll shoot you."

"That's good to know, thanks."

High up on the mountainside the voice cutting the night air was that of an Indian chanting. Billy had been chanting since dark when a sign unlike any other he'd ever seen pierced the night sky. It was a night-time eye of Great Spirit. Everything in its path turned from night to day.

This is the place, this is the time, Mother Earth's plan will be fulfilled. All is in Beauty. All he wished was that he could live a few more years so that in the winter story telling time, he could tell his people about this time, this place, and that light. He knew it was going to be a good story. Must watch, he said to himself. Don't want to miss the first part of my quest when it starts.

Next morning, Dan helped his mom with breakfast dishes. Dan felt useless. He couldn't even help Frank with the gardens. They wouldn't plant until John Varner could bring a team from his farm and plow the fields. He was beginning to feel lazy.

He went into his bedroom and came out with his Thirty-Thirty. "Think I'll do a little hunting," he said to his Mom. He didn't tell his mother he was going after a deer, but he didn't need to. With the Thirty-Thirty, he was hardly after rabbits. He saddled Turk, threw his canteen over the pommel, and put the rifle in the saddle boot, and headed out.

Dan didn't expect he'd have much success either, because most of the deer had gone high up by now. But maybe he could catch a straggler still hanging around. Two thirds of the way up, he passed a herd of sheep which were being watched by an old sheepherder sitting under the shade of a tree. He noticed the shepherd staring as he rode by. The intense gaze of the man bothered Dan a little, so he waved to see what the man's response would be. The man smiled and waved back. He's an Indian, Dan thought, and rode on.

For the next little while, Dan used every trick he'd been taught to spot and shoot a deer. He cut fresh sign on a trail, and circled above it. A young buck came prancing along. Slowly, he raised his rifle and shot. The downed deer thrashed a little, then lay still. Dan sat quietly, for a few moments to give the deer a chance to die, then walked slowly toward it, set his rifle on a rock, and pulled out his hunting knife to cut its throat and bleed it.

"Did you offer thanks to deer spirit yet?" a voice behind him asked. Instantly, Dan checked his rifle and saw it was too far away to be of any use. He whirled around with the hunting knife in his hand. The old Indian stood on the trail a few feet behind him. "Easy, Little Friend," the Indian said. "The Indian wars ended years ago." He raised his hands to show he was not armed.

"What'd you say?" Dan asked, not having heard because of being startled.

"I asked, did you offer thanks to deer spirit yet?"

"No, I didn't," Dan said, not at all sure what the strange old man was talking about. The Indian told him to get back to his work, and he would take care of it.

Dan moved to the other side of the deer so he could keep his eye on the Indian. The old man was dancing and singing a chant. Dan began dressing the deer. There was a strange and compelling beauty in the man's dance and chant. Dan was almost sorry when the Indian stopped.

Coming over to Dan, the Indian extended his hand. "Hello," the Indian said. "My name is Billy. Want some help?" Dan stuck out his right hand, and noticed it was covered with blood. He pulled it back and began looking for something to wipe it on. The Indian laughed. "Shaking hands is the white man's custom anyway." He paused, looked at his feet, then continued. "The white man doesn't believe this, but Indians do. Nothing happens by accident, everything has a purpose. Please, shake my hand."

Unsure, Dan extended his bloody hand, and Billy looked down at their hands as they shook. "Good. Now the deer's blood and spirit have joined us in friendship," Billy said. Then, before Dan could even ask what was going on, Billy said, "Do you want help or not?"

"Sure." Dan said. "My name is Dan Cook," he told the Indian as they began to work. Billy did not reply, nor did he say another word as they labored. Dan offered Billy the fresh liver. He took it and the other organ meat as well. Then left a little piece of each meat on a rock.

After loading the meat sacks on Turk, and heading back toward Billy's camp, Billy spoke for the first time since he'd asked Dan if he wanted help. "Good to meet you, Dan Cook," Billy said. "It's a good sign we meet with you doing as we did in the old days, hunting for food. I've waited to meet you for a long time."

Dan was a little worried. He's been waiting to meet me for a long time? Is this Indian crazy? What Dan was thinking must have shown on his face, because Billy laughed. His laughter was soft, and melodious. It seemed to come from all over him at once rather than just from his voice. Dan voiced his earlier question. "What'd you mean you've been waiting a long time?"

"Tell you later. Now, back to my camp," Billy said.

124

"Why'd you leave a little piece of liver and that other meat?" Dan asked.

Billy laughed once more. "Ah, that's for little brother coyote, unless a crow gets to it first. The Paiute call the crows the cleaning people," Billy told Dan as they approached Billy's camp.

"How interesting," Dan said appreciatively. "I've always wanted to learn more about the Paiute."

Soft laughter. "Oh, you will."

Dan pulled Turk to a stop. He asked what Billy's last name was. Billy reached up and scratched Turk between the ears. "I'm called Billy Neyah. Neyah means, that person. White men can't pronounce the Indian name of my youth." Again Billy laughed.

Dan was charmed by the unusual things this man was continually saying. It was obvious Billy wasn't crazy. "You sure laugh a lot," Dan said. "And you still haven't told me what you meant about waiting for me. And what'd you mean I'll learn about Paiute?"

"Ah," Billy said. "There is my camp. Want to stop awhile for a drink and a little to eat?" Billy asked, as he looked toward his camp. "It will give us some time to talk." Dan agreed, and after they arrived, he unsaddled Turk. It had not slipped by Dan that Billy never seemed to answer a question directly. He either said, "Later," or he changed the subject. Mostly, he didn't talk. Dan looked over the camp. There were some of the expected camp items such as a tent, fire, and Dutch ovens. But compared to the camp outs Dan had been on, it was almost stark.

Billy showed Dan a small spring and offered Dan some water. "You already know many Indian ways," Billy said as they walked the few steps back to camp. "One is to be patient and let things happen by themselves. But now I will tell you what you wish to know." Billy looked around, his eyes moving slowly. He never seemed to look at any one thing for very long, yet he seemed to see everything. As he looked, he began to speak again. "Mother Earth sent me to find the answer to a question, and she sent you to give me the answer."

Puzzled, Dan figured he might as well play along. "Sure, what's the question?"

Billy was again smiling broadly, "The question is, why is the white man who has everything so miserable, while the Indian who has nothing is happy?"

Dan's first impulse was to argue that he wasn't particularly miserable, and he knew many white people who were happy. But this would lead nowhere. He thought for a minute. He spoke as kindly as he could so as not to hurt the old man's feelings. "Sorry. I haven't the slightest idea."

Billy smiled and looked down at the ground. "I know. But you will give me the answer. Mother Earth has said so. Let's forget it for now. Just think you've met a crazy old Indian. That is true, and the rest will just happen."

Billy pointed to a large rock by the fire. "Want to sit?" he asked. Dan sat, and Billy started rummaging through some boxes and a Dutch oven. Soon he handed Dan an enameled tin plate heaped with sour dough bread and lamb stew. Dan looked at it appreciatively. He hadn't realized how hungry he was. "You sure speak English good."

At first Billy did not reply, and just ate. Dan began tasting the food. Either it was delicious, or he was a lot hungrier than he thought. "Where did you learn English so good?" he asked again.

"When I was a boy I had a friend named Mericat who came to live with us after his people were killed in Mountain Meadow massacre. Then, later, a Mormon missionary, came to stay with us for a while. He taught me a lot, too." This piqued Dan's curiosity. It would be just too bizarre if this old Indian were also a Mormon. He asked Billy if he was Mormon. "At the time we thought the missionary was a nice man. He wanted to baptize us, so we let him," Billy answered.

"I don't understand. You didn't believe, yet he baptized you?" Billie smiled, waiting.

"Because it pleased him. When we were around him, we talked of Jesus Christ. When we were among ourselves, we talked of Mother Earth and Father Sky." Billy sat on a log by the fire. Finally, Billy put his plate on the log, and looked at it. "I followed you, you know."

"Yes, I know. Why?"

"Ah," Billy said. "The white man's question, why." He was smiling so broadly that Dan ceased to take offense at anything this strange man said. "I followed you to see what kind of man Mother Earth sent me. You stalked your game with care and skill. Although young, the methods you used are ancient. Mother Earth has sent me a hunter." Billy smiled again.

"From the the sureness of your shot, and the way you held your knife, probably a warrior, too. But that remains to be seen."

Dan was very pleased. "I've had good teachers," he said modestly.

"Yes, but none of them have taught you respect for the spirit of animals." Billy smiled, and took a drink of water. "Not knowing about the spirits isn't your fault. In your culture it is hard to learn such things." Dan just looked at him with a quizzical look on his face as Billy continued. "Being a warrior is not judged only by going into battle. It is judged by having the courage and spirit of a warrior. I don't know your spirit well enough to judge that."

Spirits again, Dan thought. Is this all he thinks about? I'd rather learn more about the Paiutes. Billy sat silently, with head bowed for a couple of minutes. Finally, Billy looked up. He was not smiling. "I had a dream a while ago. It disturbs me. I dreamed of two men in a cave. One had a little light coming out the top of his head. All I could see of the other was his two legs sticking out from under the wall of the cave."

Dan was astounded. Billy had just described how it would look to somebody watching him while he undercut the face in the mine. He started to speak, then stopped. Dan thought a bit of the courage it took for him to crawl under there to start picking. "I think maybe I have a warrior's courage, and a warrior's spirit," he said, humbly. "But I don't know for sure."

Billy was smiling again. "Among the Paiute one never talks of himself or his power. Others will believe he thinks too much of himself." Dan realized there was no way he was going to have a normal conversation with this man. Billy's thoughts and ideas jumped from one thing to another, wove in and out, and came back again. But Dan was beginning to appreciate it.

Billy stood up. "I must tend my sheep now. We will talk more next time we meet." Dan knew that as kind and soft as this man's words were, he'd been dismissed.

"Thank you for the food and the help," he said. "I hope someday I'll be able to get back up to see you." But he doubted it because of the strike, planting gardens, and taking turns on the picket line.

CHAPTER 14

Now You Know

Dan had a lot on his mind as he rode toward town. He did not consider himself miserable. He did not want to disappoint the old Indian, but Billy's Mother Earth had sent him on a wild goose chase. Of that, Dan was certain. Billy was interesting, to say the least. There was a peacefulness and sense of self assurance in the old man. The soft way he spoke, the strange way he had of saying things, the different kinds of smiles and grins that played across his craggy old face made him fascinating to be around. Dan decided maybe Billy was similar to John Tennis, only more so.

A sudden noise jerked him out of his intense thoughts. He looked up and saw Elizabeth on her black horse riding up the trail toward him. Oh brother, Dan thought, some warrior I am. Anybody can sneak up on me. A few steps more and the horses closed the distance between them. The horses stopped with their noses close together, and sniffed at each other. Dan waited for Elizabeth to speak first. What Joe Padriva told him was still very much on his mind. He resented her even being on the trail. Now he would have to deal with her, once and for all.

Elizabeth, however, was excited. First, she was wearing jeans and a blouse. Since she had not put on her riding clothes, no one suspected she was going to sneak out on Bonnie. She thought maybe Cyclone would stop her, but he hadn't said a word. Now she was meeting the very person her father had forbidden her to see ever again. This was her lucky day—her dad would throw a fit.

"Hi, Dan. What are you doing roaming around the hillside?"

The calm, peaceful time with Billy was long gone, and Dan had no desire to be humiliated. Fear of her father made him speak politely, however. "Perhaps we shouldn't talk. I understand Mr. Benton said you were supposed to stay away from me."

A scowl crossed Elizabeth's face. "Who told you that?" Elizabeth demanded. Bonnie whinnied.

Now Dan had another worry. If he told Elizabeth what he knew, she would guess it came from. Mrs. Padriva. She'd be fired, sure. "My dad said he'd heard it," he lied. Then he added, "He said he was told somebody at the office heard your dad talking about it."

"When you get to know me better," Elizabeth said, "you'll learn Mr. Benton's daughter seldom does what Mr. Benton says."

Dan couldn't believe his ears. "Uhh." Dan stammered. "You mean you don't want to stay away from me?" Dan noticed that the horses, at least, seemed to be getting along well together.

"I thought I made it clear. Dad's telling me I shouldn't see you makes me glad I am."

Dan was in utter turmoil. She's driving me nuts, he thought. She snuggles against me when we dance; she leaves me flat to dance with someone else and never comes back; she tells her dad I'm below her; and now she's glad to see me.

Elizabeth could see that her remark hadn't helped his mood any. But her own mood was too good to let him spoil it, so she changed the subject. "Guess I was stupid to ask what you've been doing. Got deer meat in the sacks?" Dan mumbled an excuse about a sheepherder giving him some mutton. She smiled. "Sure he did. Just wouldn't do to let the boss's daughter know you were poaching deer out of season, would it?" Dan scowled. He figured she would probably tell her dad. "Dan," Elizabeth said in a soothing tone, "don't worry. I won't tell Dad."

Reassured, Dan smiled sheepishly. He reached down and patted one of the sacks, "Damn fine mutton it is, too. Probably taste as good as a yearling buck."

He was pleased when she smiled. He agreed when she asked if she could ride back with him. Elizabeth turned her horse around, and side by side they started down the trail.

"My horse's name's Bonnie, what's yours?"

There was pride in his voice when he told her his horse's name was Turk. Dan's obvious affection for his horse impressed Elizabeth, it gave them something in common. "Old Turk here is part Arabian." The two horses stepped closer to each other. Dan's leg momentarily brushed against Elizabeth's leg. She felt the sudden desire to get to know this young man better.

"Dan, you sure you don't mind riding with me? You really didn't seem very happy to see me." Dan explained that he felt today had been a lucky day for him. He spoke briefly of getting meat for people in town and meeting a strange Indian. "Best of all, meeting you," he added.

Elizabeth ignored the compliment. She wanted to find out if they had anything else in common. "Tell me about the Indian." She listened intently as he told her all he could remember. She found it genuinely unusual and interesting as well. She pumped him for the answer the Indian wanted, but Dan assured her he didn't have a clue.

They decided to go their separate ways before they got to town. Elizabeth apologized and said she definitely didn't want him to get into trouble just in case one of the deputies was out looking for her. On his part, Dan had no desire to let a deputy catch him with a poached deer. So splitting up now was definitely a good plan. But Dan felt a sense of deep disappointment as he waited on the trail for her to go on ahead.

When sufficient time had elapsed, he began riding again. At Pessetto's old place he took the sacks off his horse and hid them in one corner of the burned-out stable. Then he covered them with sage brush. Once he got into town, he stopped at Tennis's and told him where he could find the little bundles. John thanked him profusely and promised to share it with others needing meat.

At home, Dan was tired and took a bath. He was barely dressed when there was a loud banging at the door. He heard his mother open it.

"Quick, where's Dan?" Tom Carr's voice boomed. Everyone in the family converged on the front room. "You'd better run quick, Dan. Benton's goons are after you," Tom said.

Mary put her hands on each side of her face in shock. Carl began looking fierce. Steve looked bewildered. Dan's face blanched, and his voice quivered as he asked if Tom knew why, even though Dan knew the answer. "Don't know, and no time to explain," Tom replied.

Just then there was another knock on the front door. "Open up!" a voice on the other side of the door commanded. "It's Ovie, and I've got to talk to Dan." Mary's hand was shaking as she reached to open the door and invited him in. Rasmussen and another man came into the house.

Rasmussen ignored everyone. "Pack only what you need right now, Dan. Come with me."

Mary stepped in front of Rasmussen. "Why, Ovie?" she demanded.

"Dan was seen riding on the hillside with his daughter. Mr. Benton says to move Dan to the boarding house where Sue Fuller can keep an eye on him, since you folks can't seem to." Then, turning to Carl, Rasmussen said, "Sorry, Carl. Benton says next time it happens you're fired."

Thoughtfully, Rasmussen volunteered to wait outside while Dan got ready. Inside the house there were tears, apologies, and deep expressions of regret. It was everyone's expressed hope that when things cooled down, Dan could move back. But nobody believed it.

As the family went out on the front porch, Tom turned to Rasmussen. "I've visited here long enough," Tom said. "It's time I get back, myself. I'll go with you." But try as Tom might to cover the real reason he wanted to accompany them back, everyone guessed. Mary looked relieved and Carl looked at Tom with gratitude in his eyes.

A surly look came over Rasmussen's features. "If we were going to work him over I'd never come in the house and talked so politely."

"Good to know, Ovie," Tom said. "As I said, got to be getting back myself anyway."

When they arrived at the boarding house, Sue Fuller was kind, and seemed sort of sad. She said she already had a room ready for him, and Tom helped him put his things away. Dan began telling Tom he hated being away from home. "Don't worry about it, lad. Won't be here long."

For the first time, a glimmer of hope grew in Dan. "Mr. Benton will let me move home?"

"No. I mean they are already making plans to throw us all out of town."

The next morning Dan missed not eating breakfast with his family. Tom slouched over his plate next to Dan. Dan had one friend here, at least, but it was poor consolation. Dan had to admit, however, Sue Fuller's food did taste great. At home there was generally only one kind of meat. Sue Fuller had patty sausage, link sausage, ham, and bacon. Suddenly, Ganz Durrant came into the room, called Sue aside, and talked in a hushed voice to her. Every eye was on the two of them. Then, Ganz stalked out.

With a distraught look on her face, Sue turned to the tables. "Well, there goes the nice peaceful breakfast me and my girls worked so hard to prepare," she said as her voice shook. "Mr. Durrant just said anyone not showing up to work today will go to the mine office to draw their pay. You are discharged on the grounds that you abandoned your jobs. And you'll all have to move out."

Groans, moans, and looks of anger greeted the announcement. "Oh man," somebody said. "Now we're not strikers, we're fired miners." The few scabs staying at the boarding house just sat

Sue cleared her throat a couple of times. "Since the company owns the boarding house, only men working for Utah Fuel can stay here."

"How long did he give us?" erupted from someone at the far end of a table.

"Five days," Sue said. "But a week's board and room will be deducted from your wages. Ganz said it'll take a couple of days to clean up your rooms when you leave." Murmurs of subdued anger filled the dining room. Dan looked once more at the faces of the men around the breakfast table. Even if he had not known most of them, he would still be able to sort the scabs from the strikers. The righteousness of the scabs, the despair of the others would have made it obvious.

Sue walked over to where Dan and Tom were sitting. She spoke softly. "Dan, could you see me when you're finished eating?" Sue led Dan out of the dining room and into the kitchen. "Dan, I'm sorry. Mr. Durrant wanted me to make it very clear to you that you won't be allowed back into your dad's house. Not today, not ever. Also, Mr. Benton said he would take it as a great favor if you did not stay the full five days."

Dan recognized the "favor" as the demand it was. He felt rebellious as he walked back into the dining room. He wanted to smash something.

Tom looked up unhappily as Dan returned. "Finish your breakfast, lad."

"Can't. Mood I'm in it'd twist my guts. Benton wants me out right away." Suddenly, he hated ever having laid eyes on Elizabeth. She had caused his family problems ever since she came into town. Quite a price to pay for one dance and a mile ride.

Getting his pay was no easy task, either. So many strikers were there before him that Dan had to stand in line for three hours before he got to the pay window.

As Dan pocketed his money, Tom came up to him. "After you left, I got a hold of Frank Bonatti. We'll be setting up about a dozen tents today. You can use one." Tom reached up and put his hand on Dan's shoulder. He gave it a squeeze of friendship. "You'll have a tent to yourself at first. When everybody else moves, we'll assign you some tent mates."

Dan knew he was being taken care of, and wondered how he'd have made out if Tom was not his friend and wasn't the president of the local. Tom removed his arm, and looked questioningly at Dan. "As you know, we've been picketing since the day after the strike, but until we get better organized they're only letting certain people on the line. Frank said he wants you to take a turn."

Dan gave an approving nod. "Lead me to it!"

"Ha, you wish! Lead yourself to it," Tom said with dry humor, and laughed. "I ain't your wet nurse." He turned serious again, "But be careful going past the guard shack. Benton's goons have been aggressive with everyone leaving town today. When you get to the picket line, find Andy Vullis and tell him I sent you."

"I'm on my way. Thanks, Tom." Dan hurried out of town.

"Hold it!" a voice commanded as he passed the guard shack. "Where do you think you're going?" Dan stopped in his tracks as one of the new deputies stepped out of the guard shack with a rifle leveled at Dan's belly. "What's your name?" the man demanded.

"Dan Cook."

A man inside the guard house checked a list on a clipboard "A striker," he informed the man outside. "A trouble-maker, you mean," the man with the rifle said. "Want to start some trouble now? Or are you chicken?" Dan felt the anger rising; he clenched his fists. Remembering what he'd heard at the union meeting, he slowly unclenched them.

"No, Sir, Mr. Deputy. I ain't chicken. And I ain't stupid enough to let you push me into a game with everything in your favor."

"I saw your clenched fists. You got yourself under control this time, but my time is coming."

"If you say so," Dan said, and felt pride in the fact that this time, he had not let them get to him.

"I say so. My name's Art Webb. You better remember it. The day you lose control, I'll nail you."

"If you say so," Dan said, and smiled. "It's been nice meeting you, Mr. Webb." There was a sneer in his voice. Webb raised his rifle butt and stepped toward Dan.

"Hold it, Art!" the man in the shack shouted. "Don't let him push you into anything. Benton'll be peeved if we start it."

Webb stopped in his tracks. He looked back into the guard shack. "Right you are, Lorenzo." Turning to Dan, his face showed a menacing smile. "I can wait. But I'll remember you Cook."

Once more Dan started toward the picket line. He realized he'd come very close to serious trouble. Not to be taken by surprise again, he looked down the road as he left the shack. The guard shack was at the edge of company property. Past that, it was less than half a mile to where tent town would be. There were coffee houses on the left, between the railroad tracks and the road. On the right was the Ambrosio orchard. A little lane bisected the orchard and led to the small rock house the Ambrosios lived in. A quarter of a mile further on, the road ran through the middle of what would become tent town. At the end of that, Dan could see the picket line.

He quickened his pace. Once there, he immediately saw Andy Vullis standing with John Tennis, and walked over to them. "Tom sent me," he said.

Andy tensed. "Did the deputies at the shack cause you any trouble?" Dan was proud to say they tried, but he wouldn't let them push him into anything.

"You smart boy," John Tennis said. "Too, you lucky. Before John this kind man see."

Andy looked toward the shack, the worried look still on his face. "John's right," he agreed reluctantly. "Benton has brought in some real scum."

"I tell you," John said, "same like Ludlow. Must careful. No careful die union mans."

"Come on, my friend," Andy said as he put his arm around John's shoulder. You're just afraid Ludlow is still following you. Forget it, this is Utah. We won't let them box us in as they did there. Andy had a confident look. "I can tell you for certain that Bob Benton doesn't want Sunnyside to become a Ludlow any more than you do, John."

"How do you know that?" Dan asked.

"Union snitch," Andy answered. Then he looked at Dan. "Ever been on a picket line before?" Dan just shrugged his shoulders, and Andy smiled. "Stupid question. This's your first strike. Well, just sort of hang around and watch. We're just picketing the road. We'll set up the railroad picket at Mounds tomorrow."

"Railroad? How do you picket a train?" Dan had visions of the pickets actually going aboard. He listened intently as Andy explained they only picket both sides of the track at the spur off the main line. Andy said trains coming to Sunnyside have to stop there and switch to the Sunnyside tracks. People riding on both sides would see the pickets' signs. "Hell, Andy," Dan interjected. "Mounds is clear down by Twelve Mile Wash. How do we get down there?" Andy explained that those with horses would ride them. Others would start early and walk. Later the union would also be setting up a camp there. The people picketing would stay a couple of days, then rotate out.

Again, Dan was taken with the completeness of the organization. Everyone except him seemed to know what to expect, and what to do. They all sounded a lot more confident than he felt. Andy and John excused themselves and went over to talk with other pickets. Dan was ready for something to happen so he could start getting back at them. What he did mostly, however, was just stand and wait. Then he sat and waited. Then he stood again, restlessly.

He noticed everyone else was doing about the same. Nobody was even holding up picket signs, or anything. Some signs were piled together, handles up. Finally, dust could be seen coming up the flats. Everyone was suddenly moving, grabbing. The pickets closed off the road several deep.

"Okay, boys," Andy shouted. "We don't want anyone hurt. We'll try to stop them long enough to talk with anyone inside the car. But for crying out loud, let's not get anybody hurt. If they don't slow down, get out of the way." Dan stood alongside Andy and said he didn't think the union could close off a state highway the way the pickets were doing. "We can't. We will give way when we have to. It's sort of a glorified game of chicken. But there is no law against trying to stop someone on the highway to talk to them. If they won't stop, they won't stop."

"John! John!" Andy shouted and started pointing at George and Harry Kocolakis. Dan looked and saw both men holding signs up high, their shirts had raised above their belt buckles. Both of them had pistols sticking out above their pants.

John ran across the road. "Give! Give!" he demanded. Then without waiting, he reached over and jerked the pistols from the men's belts. He ran a few feet to the side and threw the pistols into some sage brush. John turned around and started back just as the car got close and started slowing. "That was close. Too close!" Andy said as the car stopped. Dan saw the word, "Sheriff" painted on the side of the car.

With unhurried movements, Sheriff Kelter got out, three deputies carrying rifles scrambled out. With rifles pointing in the air, the three deputies stood at the front of the car. Kelter sauntered over to the picket line. Then an abrupt change came over his entire demeanor. "Clear the road!" he demanded brusquely. "We don't want trouble, but we'll give you plenty if you don't"

The men blocking the road gave way rapidly as Kelter began to walk slowly toward Sunnyside. Kelter looked intently at each man as he passed. Once past the group, however, he turned around to face the assembled men again. "You know it's against the law to block the road. I'll give you the benefit of the doubt, you'd have moved if I'd kept on coming." Kelter stood, hands on hips, glaring at the men. "Listen close," he barked. "Governor's orders! All foreign-born strikers will here and now turn in their guns!"

The strikers just stood looking at him. Some shuffled their feet, others put their hands in their pockets, but no weapons were forthcoming. "Who's in charge here?" Kelter demanded. Andy stepped forward. "You Greek?" Kelter asked. Andy nodded. "Then you tell the rest of your kind that if they are not citizens they will surrender their weapons right now." Clicking sounds thundered in Dan's ears. He jerked his head toward the car, and saw the deputies chambering shells into their rifles. Kelter's voice was a snarl. "Have I got your attention, now?"

Kelter pointed to Andy. "You better do what I said and start talking with those Greeks. Any Wops here speak English?" he asked without waiting for Andy to respond. Sam Farlino raised his hand. Kelter's eyes, full of threat, flashed momentarily into Sam's. "You tell your Dago brothers the same thing I told the Greek," he demanded.

Andy still hadn't moved. "Sheriff," Andy said, and there was authority in his voice. "If you'll step back to your car, and give us a few moments to talk, we'll handle this matter for you."

Kelter started to speak, then stopped. Without another word he walked back to the car. After a flurry of conversation the Zulakis brothers, Andreas and Mike, each held pistols in the air. As the deputies came to collect them, young Sonny Fratto turned in an old, rusted hand gun as well. Satisfied, Kelter and the deputies got in the car and headed toward Sunnyside.

This was what a strike was about? People lining up on roads trying to keep out scabs? Police demanding weapons, and strikers meekly turning over firearms? Then cops leaving with threats of what would happen if any more weapons were found? And all the while Dan knew there were at least two more guns out in the bushes. The puzzled look must have shown on his face.

"It's moves in a chess game," Andy said. "Did you see what that old clunker Fratto turned in? If you could find ammunition to fit it, it would probably blow up in your face." Dan had seen the weapon, and knew Andy was right. There was a rebellious streak to Andy's words. "It was all planned, of course." Andy said the only surprise this morning was that Kelter, himself, had shown up.

"Then what was all that argument between you Greeks?"

Andy laughed. "Hey, Gus!" he called to Gus Delabanis. "Show him your gun."

Gus laughed, reached behind his belt and pulled out a pistol at least eighteen inches long. It was so badly rusted that it made Fratto's pistol seem the latest issue. "What we were arguing about was how many pistols we were going to have to give up to impress Kelter. We decided the Zulakis boys would each turn over a good weapon to satisfy him. But, if only a couple of loud-mouthed deputies showed up and started demanding weapons, they'd only get Gus's."

"I guess I'll learn as I go along . . ." Dan started to say, but shouts interrupted him. More dust came, but this time from the direction of

Sunnyside. Bob Benton's big, maroon, Packard was heading out of town. Filthy shouts erupted in English, and in other languages as well.

"Easy, guys, easy," Andy said. "No violence!" he commanded. "Get back!" he said as a couple of men stepped into the road. "We don't bother cars going out of town." The car did not even slow down at the guard shack, but kept on coming. As it roared past, Dan saw that Bob Benton was not in the car. Elizabeth was driving, and Toshio the gardener was her passenger. Dan's pain of being thrown out of his home welled up in him, and he shot her a fierce look. During the rest of the day they stopped a half dozen cars, and threw insults back and forth.

CHAPTER 15

IT'S MY TURN

Next morning, not yet fully awake, Dan stretched and yawned. Suddenly he felt confused and disoriented. Then, when he cleared his head, he remembered he was sleeping in a tent. He was swept by an intense feeling of loneliness. He missed his family. He rummaged around in the jumbled mess of things that were brought to make life in a tent as nearly civilized as possible. Getting out what he needed, he fixed breakfast and then began organizing equipment and supplies. When he was through, it was still a hole. Thank goodness it was a big tent.

As he worked he began to feel a little less sorry for himself when he realized none of what happened to him the last couple of days was an accident. It had all been his choice. Not, maybe, at the time it was happening, but it all started back that day he told Frank to count him in. It seemed, looking at it from that angle, everything about to happen would be his choice, too. From now on, he vowed, his choices would always be to do whatever it took for the union.

He decided to go back into town and had to smile. Yesterday he wouldn't have even thought about choices, so intimidated had he been by the power of the company and the day's events. He sauntered back past the guard shack. The bullying of the guards barely upset him, knowing what to expect and the kind of men they were. No way he'd be the one to give them the excuse they were so obviously looking for to beat up some poor fellow and run gloating to Benton. And he knew the errand he had set for himself would make them furious if they found out about it. Dan was going to visit his mother, and arrange for his brother to become a union spy.

Yesterday Tom mentioned he wanted Frank and Steve to be couriers for the union. Said he'd already cleared it with their dad. When the town was sealed against strikers, Steve would ride out a couple of times a day.

139

He'd bring messages from union people in town, meet Dan, and pass them on. And visa-versa for messages the strikers wanted to get into town.

"Hi, Mom," he said as she came rushing out onto the porch to meet him.

"I was so worried when you didn't come by yesterday," she greeted, wiping tears from her eyes.

His first impulse was to make an excuse. But going to the picket line had been his choice, too. "All in all, it couldn't be helped," he said. "How are you?" She pretended to be fine.

There was a new easiness in talking with his mother. "How's Dad and Steve?"

Dan's whole manner and tone of voice caught Mary's attention. She paused, didn't answer him right away, and then looked at him. She said they were okay, and said he seemed changed, somehow. Dan just smiled. He looked confident. "Nothing to worry about, Mom. It's a change for the better." Dan felt really mellow for the first time in what seemed ages. "Guess a son can't hide anything from his mom. Come here and give me a hug."

Throughout the rest of the visit, not a single thing interfered with the good feelings they shared in that hug. He told her he already had the tent set up, and that it would be livable. He shared with her how well tent town was organized. She relaxed even more when he explained how dedicated the union was to preventing violence.

Gladly, she gave her permission for him to take Turk. She also agreed to have Steve come to see him right after school. He took his leave after another long hug. Then, to his delight, his mother kissed him on the cheek. "Keep your nose clean," she said. Dan smiled. He felt peaceful. Her phrase was a family code to take care of one's self, stay out of trouble, and keep safe.

As he rode Turk to the guard shack, he stopped, expecting unpleasantness. There wasn't any, really. Two different deputies were on duty. "You Dan Cook?" the one outside asked. He wasn't even carrying a rifle. Dan admitted he was, with a smile on his face. The deputy shuffled his feet, looking embarrassed. "Art Webb said for me to tell you that if you ever try passing this guard shack without stopping, he really is going to shoot you." Then, in a voice that sounded a lot more friendly warning than a threat, the guard said. "If I was you, I'd believe him."

Even this did not upset Dan too much. By now he expected such talk from Webb. Once more Dan smiled. "You can tell Mr. Webb not to worry." The deputy looked relieved. It astonished Dan that the deputy didn't seem any more eager for trouble than Dan had been as he rode up. "See you later," he called as he rode off.

When he got to tent town he put Turk in Pessetto's old corral. He went to his tent, and looked around, trying to figure out how to rearrange things better. The ten-by-twelve-foot tent was furnished with a small camp stove for cooking, three fold-down cots, a kerosene lamp, and a table. Dan rearranged things the best he could. Even though the tent was his alone for the time being, he kept his things in one area to make room for the others who would be moving in.

Frank Bonatti popped his head in. "Did the best I could for you on such short notice," Frank said.

"We want you at the next committee meeting. I'll let you know when we schedule it. Get over to the garden as soon as you can," Frank continued. "Everybody else is already there."

Dan said he was ready now and the two of them started out. Dan was amazed at the size and the completeness of the garden. It was more a small farm. It was arranged in sections. Carrots would go here, lettuce there, and tomatoes in yet another area. Not only did they have seeds, but there were hundreds of little sprouting plants in flat boxes about the size of a folded newspaper. Frank put Dan to work planting cabbage with a couple of other men who were already at work.

"Where did we get all this stuff?" he asked as Frank was leaving.

"We have friends in town and in Price. Since you're goin' on the committee, now's as good a time to tell you as any. You know Toshio, don't you?" Dan nodded. "He's been a union friend for longer than I've been in town. The Super think's Toshio steals vegetables from their garden to sell. Truth is, he checks with us to see who is most needy, and gives them the vegetables. In Benton's car yesterday, he went to Price to get seeds and have the starts sent up."

"Well, I'll be! A man right there to keep an eye on Benton even in his own back yard!"

"He ain't all. Cyclone Henry is another. And that reminds me. You talked with Steve about being a messenger yet?" Frank questioned.

"No, but I left word with Mom to have him come down as soon as school is out." Frank told Dan to look him up as soon as Steve arrived, and headed out. Dan stayed busy the rest of the morning.

When they broke for lunch, he grabbed a couple of sandwiches and went looking for Tom. "What they got you doin' this mornin'?" Dan asked as he sat down beside Tom.

"Been laying out the baseball diamond. The ground is as bumpy as my mother's washboard. Had to scrape it with a team and a blade. Wish we had the water to plant grass. Dust's awful."

After lunch, Dan had barely started planting turnips when Steve came riding up. Steve grinned. "I thought strikers laid around on their backs and took it easy."

"Fat chance," Dan said as Steve got off his horse. Steve wanted to know what was up and why the urgent message to come straight here after school. Dan looked around, saw Frank, and motioned for him to come over. "Just a minute, Steve," he said and waited for Frank to get to them. "Frank, I'm going to talk with Steve now about that thing. I thought it would be good for you to be here, just in case he has any questions."

"Good idea," Frank said, then hesitated and looked around. "But..."

"But what?" Dan asked.

"But, I don't see Tom. He should be here, too. Lets go find him." The three of them left to find Tom. Steve tied his horse up under the first tree they came to. After spotting Tom, Frank motioned them to go off where others wouldn't hear them talking.

Steve was looking more animated by the minute. "You're sure acting mysterious," Steve said. "Whatever you guys got up your sleeves, I like it already."

"Don't be in too much of a hurry, young man," Frank advised him. "What we want you to do will involve some personal risk." Looking chastised, Steve looked first at Dan, then back to Frank.

"Well, okay, what is it?"

Tom looked serious, "We want you to run messages back and forth from Sunnyside to Tent Town." Steve seemed disappointed, and asked if that was all. "It's enough," Tom said. "If the company catches on, the goons will probably work you over, school kid or no school kid."

"Count me in," Steve agreed much too quickly to suit Dan.

"Smarten up," Tom said in exasperation. "This ain't a kid game. If we didn't need you so bad, I'd call the whole thing right now!" Turning to Dan, he said, "Try to keep the kid safe."

Tom and Frank exchanged glances. Frank nodded. Tom spoke in quiet tones. "We want you and Dan to each ride out on your horses at set times. You from town, and Dan from here. The Guards will get suspicious if you ride straight here from town. Usually, you'll have to meet somewhere else, except in emergencies, such as over in the flats below the coke ovens."

Dan was paying close attention. "We can work it out as we go along, and it's probably best if we have a number of meeting places," Dan said. Frank agreed that was a good idea. Then Frank turned once more to Tom, and mentioned he still had some doubts about it.

"It's the best shot we got, Frank," Tom said. Then he added, "I've known both these boys all their lives. They're fine lads, Frank." Frank seemed satisfied.

"Steve, Toshio and Cyclone will be your contacts," Frank said. "Start getting friendly with Cyclone right away, so nobody will be the wiser when you talk with him at the stables." Steve wanted to know how to contact Toshio. "You don't," Frank cautioned. "Toshio and our man inside the mine will pass on any messages they have to Cyclone."

Once more Frank looked at Tom. Then he looked back at the boys. "I have to tell you another name, also." Tom was smiling as the cat who ate the canary when Frank turned to Steve. "Our inside man is Mitch Saxton. And the reason you have to know that is if anything happens to Mitch, we have to be told immediately, just as quick as you can get here. If, heaven forbid, it happens, forget about secret meeting places. Forget about getting found out. Get around the guard shack somehow, and come straight here. Got it?"

"Yes, I do," Steve said, much more soberly. Frank's urgency about what he should do if something happened to Mitch helped Steve realize the seriousness of what they were planning.

But Dan was incredulous. "I'll be jiggered. And in our whole district in the mine, he's the one we've tried to be most careful around. And he really is a snitch! But for the union!"

Noticing Dan's surprise, Tom began laughing. "Frank, I've got to tell you this. Remember that first day in the mine when we were pushing Dan pretty hard to join the union?" Frank thought a minute, then he nodded "Well later, Mitch came along and told Dan a cock and bull story about a man in Colorado who got blown up because he informed on a union man. Frank, I thought I'd pee my pants. I thought for sure Dan would figure out why Mitch was warning him about snitches. When he didn't, I was trying so hard not to laugh I had to grab a pick and start pounding the face with it to get myself under control."

"You clown," Dan said. "You really were laughing. And I told myself you were just mad."

Tom was still chuckling. "Sorry, Dan," Tom apologized, but he didn't sound sorry at all. "But when we get a greenhorn in the mine, who can resist having fun with him?"

"I'll have to remember that," Steve said.

When Frank and Tom returned to their work, Dan and Steve began making plans. They picked up Steve's horse and headed up to the corral to get Turk. They decided that every time they met at a regular meeting, they'd decide when and where to meet the next time. Dan saw an old, bent, five-gallon can lying alongside the corral. He picked up the can and turned it upside down on the corner pole of the corral. "You should be able to see this can from up the canyon a good ways before you get to Tent Town. It will be my signal that we need an emergency meeting. We'll meet at the top of the cut below the coke ovens."

Dan asked Steve to bring down his foot locker. Steve agreed, and said he'd make a couple of trips back and forth bringing any supplies Dan might need. That way, Dan reasoned, the guards would get used to Steve coming down to meet his brother.

After Steve left, Dan didn't want to go back to camp. Most of the crews had gone back to town except the ones putting rough timber planks on the floors inside the tents which had been set up. So there weren't a lot of people to talk with, and Dan didn't want to spend the rest of the day alone in a tent. He sat on his horse, feeling a displaced person with nowhere to go.

He started aimlessly riding, but soon became aware that he was going to see the Indian. Now was as good a time as any to get questions answered. He might not have time later. To his amazement, the Indian had supper ready when he arrived. Dan noticed two plates on the camp table. Dan had the eerie feeling he was expected.

"Not mystery stuff," Billy advised him without looking at Dan. "I could hear you coming up the trail twenty minutes before you got here, and I put on another plate. I don't get a lot of visitors up here. Can't imagine why," he said with a bewildered look on his face, and Dan laughed. But Dan noticed Billy's eyes were on the table as he talked. Dan remembered the last time they met. Billy rarely looked directly at him and he never looked Dan in the eyes.

They talked of general things during the meal. Billy told Dan about life being hard for the old Paiutes. This land was so poor that much of the year the Paiute moved around in small bands of six or eight people, just to find enough food to keep alive. Except when they gathered together in the fall and winter, they had no villages as other Indians. The other Indians lived in better country that would support more of them in one place.

Then he began speaking of what the different clans did when it got cooler. "When the heat broke, and some rains came, we would get together again as a clan. Some clans would meet one place, some another, but always by some body of water."

Billy said different clans gathered at different places such as Panguitch Lake, or along the Virgin River. His clan would gather along the Price River. Billy said his particular clan was called the Squawbush Water People. Or, in Paiute, Suhuh' Vawdutseng. But since the white man couldn't pronounce it, they called them the Sheberitch clan. Billy spread his arms wide. "We were the largest clan of Paiute. We lived all the way from near Price to what you now call Monticello.

"One winter about fifty years ago, my clan was gathered together for a pow-wow. It was a time of dancing and singing." Billy got up, moved over closer to the fire and sat cross legged once more on the ground. He motioned for Dan to join him. "Stories always sound better by the fire," Billy said as Dan came over and sat down. "There are two versions of the story about that pow-wow. The Indian version, and the white man version. Which one do you want to hear first?"

Dan didn't have to think twice about it. He said to give the Indian version. Billy looked at the fire as he talked. "At this pow-wow, the wives of two powerful medicine men got to arguing. They had big power, big medicine."

"What kind of power?"

"A medicine man must never talk about his own power, or it turns shadow. Then he will have to leave the clan. Other people can talk about it, though. Well, after the wives got to arguing, the two medicine men got brought into it. Soon they were arguing, and after that the people in the clan started taking one side or another. These medicine men had the kind of power that let them put curses on the other side, and people started dying."

Dan found this just a little hard to swallow, but he tried to pretend he was believing what he was being told. Billy looked at him, smiled, and interrupted his story long enough to put some more wood on the fire. Billy sat down again. "The people started to say Mother Earth cursed this land because of the argument. So they left. Some went north to be with the Ute, and some went south to be with the Southern Paiute."

Billy paused, and looked into the fire, took a deep breath and heaved a sigh. "To this day other clans tell the story of how medicine power wiped out a clan of Paiute." After a minute or two, Billy spoke again. "Now for the other version. The white men say they all got small-pox."

It seemed, however, Billy was through talking about Indians for a while. Through subtle suggestions, more than direct questions, Billy got Dan talking about himself. Billy was especially interested in what a strike was. After Dan described it as best he could, Billy paused to get up and break some bread, throwing pieces here and there. "For the birds and chipmunks," he explained. "It's getting close to night, and they want to load up before they go to sleep."

Billy put a finger to his lips, signaling for Dan to be quiet. Then slowly he pointed down the trail. Dan turned his head to look, and saw a coyote slinking up the trail toward them. Billy spoke in hushed tones so he wouldn't frighten the coyote. Dan watched the coyote keep coming, and sat transfixed. He had never seen a coyote get this close to people before. Near the top of the trail, the coyote looked up. Dan could swear that, for an instant, their eyes met. But only an instant because the coyote whirled, crouched, and started to slink toward the nearest tree.

"I think he is afraid of you," Billy said. "He's not afraid of me because we're friends. I throw little scraps of meat out for him. My sheep dogs make sure he leaves the sheep alone. Hey, Little Brother Coyote," Billy called. "Don't be impatient. I'll be with you soon enough."

Billy put more wood on the fire. Then he rummaged around in his pockets, fished out a pipe and some tobacco, and started filling the pipe. "Indian smoke 'um pipe, now," Billy said with such mockingly good humor that Dan could not help but catch his mood. Billy put the stem of the pipe into his mouth, reached out, got a small burning branch from the fire, and lit the pipe.

When Billy began to puff contentedly, Dan looked at Billy's face. He guessed it must have at least a thousand wrinkles. After Billy puffed a couple more times, he reached up with his hand over the pipe bowl, and absentmindedly fanned some of the smoke toward himself. Dan just watched, knowing Billy would speak when the fancy struck him. Sure enough, he began again.

"Paiute believe that smoke is cleansing." Again puffs, fanning, and relaxation without talk. Finally, Dan realized Billy was talking to him again. "Thank you for coming, Dan. I'm not saying to leave, you're welcome to stay. But I have things I must do."

Dan smiled. "When I come back, it's my turn to supply food."

CHAPTER 16
DOC DRIVES THE PACKARD

"It's a fine automobile," Doc Dowd said. "No doubt about that. But as for me, if I could find a horse that went forty miles an hour, I'd never own a car."

"You're crazy, Doc. It's one thing to be a character, but quite another to be nuts. Of the hundred people who spoke of this Packard, you're the only one said they'd rather have a horse!"

Doc Dowd laughed as they pulled into the alley between the fire house and the Temple. "Well, you know me. The moment I find myself agreeing with the majority, I change my opinion."

"You're definitely weird, Doc," Bob said as they got out of the Packard, and headed toward the back of the Temple. Suddenly, Jack Pessetto emerged from the back door. His face meant trouble.

Bitterness spilled from him. "You Bastard!"

"Jack, I"m sorry your . . ."

Jack cut him off. "You burned me out! You're not getting away with it."

"Jack! Jack!" Benton fairly shouted. "On my oath as a Mason! I didn't burn you out."

Pessetto thought less than a second. "You're a liar. You did it, or you know who did."

Benton raised his right hand to the square as if taking an oath, "I swear, Jack." Benton's face was pale. "Frank Cameron was only going to send down someone to negotiate with you."

Jack reached into his shoulder holster. Bob went for his own gun, but he was too slow. Jack's gun pointed at his chest before he touched his pistol. "You're a dead man," Jack said.

Doc Dowd stepped decisively between them. The barrel of Jack's pistol was nearly touching Doc's chest. "Calm down Jack. You lost your business, don't throw your life away, too."

"Get out of the way, Doc. I'm gonna kill him." Jack reached out to move Doc aside.

Doc's words came out in a rush. "Your wife and kids, Jack! Think of them!" Pessetto hesitated. "Who'd take care of your kids?" Doc asked. The gun wavered.

"Move out of the way, Doc. I don't want to shoot you, but, honest to God, I will if I have to."

"I'm not moving," Doc said, spreading his legs a little to more firmly stay planted just where he was. By now more people were arriving, and seeing what was going on, they scattered, or made sure they were behind Pessetto. Doc spoke calmly. "Look, Jack. Look at the people around here. First you shoot me, then you shoot Benton, and one of your bullets glances off and kills somebody else. How many Jack? How many?"

Reason began to replace Pessetto's hot passion. "Should've shot first, asked questions later."

Doc reached a hand up and put it on Pessetto's shoulder. "I know. But it's really best you didn't."

Jack thought a moment. "My kids're the only thing between you and the undertaker's table."

Jack turned, walked around them, and took a step toward his car. Relief flooded Benton. He started to say something. But before a word came out, Pessetto whirled and smashed a fist into Benton's face. "Negotiate that!" he said as Benton crumpled in a heap on the ground. "Sorry to interrupt your evening, Doc. Better take care of the pile of garbage. I think I loosened his teeth."

"How the mighty have fallen," someone said, as the crowd closed in, now that the danger had passed. Doc Dowd bent down and helped Bob to his feet. Doc reached into his pocket, got out his handkerchief and held it to Benton's mouth to keep the blood from getting onto Benton's suit.

"Let's go inside where I can have a look at you," he said.

"No, get in the car. We're going home," Benton mumbled through the handkerchief.

"Don't forget who the doctor is here, Bob. I may be on your payroll, but I still give the orders when it comes to doctoring." Doc paused to give Benton a moment to think about that. "We have to go inside where I can look at you." Benton reached into his pocket, got out his own handkerchief and held it to his face. He was still a little unsteady as he followed Doc. Once inside the bathroom Doc had Benton open his mouth so he could look at his teeth. "Seems there's no real damage," Doc said. "Want me to get Doc Goetzman, the dentist?"

"Forget it," Benton said. Bitterness poured from him. "The second I'm finished here, I'm going to get Sheriff Kelter. I want him arrested," Benton said. His face grew ugly. "I'm going to have that creep thrown out of the Masons if it's the last thing I do."

Doc didn't respond immediately. He placed his hand on Benton's chin and turned his head so he could inspect the outside of Benton's jaw. "Just a contusion, nothing to worry about," Doc said. He let go of Benton's chin, and when Benton lowered his head, Doc looked him in the eye. "Remember what I said about being on your payroll, but in charge of doctoring?" Benton nodded. "Consider this a prescription. You are not going to get Jack thrown out of the Masons, arrested, fined or anything else of that nature." Benton's nostrils widened, and he started to object. "Think about it. If you try getting even, you will be admitting he whipped you. Any charges you bring against him will get you no sympathy from anybody."

Doc could see Benton was listening, so he continued. "You're in a tough spot here. Half the county probably thinks you burned him out. Remember, Jack grew up here, you didn't. He's got many friends. They'll figure you're too chicken to take him on one on one. They'll believe you're trying to get the Masons or the courts to do your dirty work for you."

Doc's argument slowly turned the tide away from Benton's need for revenge. He could see the logic in what Doc said. "Besides, it just wouldn't do for everybody to think my boss is a cry baby as well as an arsonist." Benton glared at this statement, but the smile on Doc's face was healing. "What you'll do is put a big smile on your face, go out there and tell everybody you know exactly how Jack feels. He's just suffered a terrible loss, had to strike out at somebody."

"I don't feel like smiling."

150

Doc stopped smiling. "Then go and fake it till you make it."

In spite of himself, Benton smiled at Doc's remark. "You really are crazy, Doc. You know that?"

"Some say so, yes," Doc admitted and returned Benton's smile. "But that makes two of us."

"Think I'm nuts, huh?" Benton asked as he headed for the door to the restroom. He caught the importance of the idea Doc was expressing, and quickly improved on it. "Watch me. I'm going out there and sympathize with the best of 'em about a fellow Mason who's had terrible trouble. I'll even propose a fund be set up by the Masons to help him in his hour of need."

Once out of the restroom, things went pretty much as Doc said they would. First thing Benton did was to head for the bar to get a drink to kill the pain, and calm himself down. Then, before he returned to the bar, he headed out to speak with the people necessary to begin collecting the fund.

Later, by taking the high ground, many even sympathized with Benton. And, out of the goodness of their hearts, they were willing to forgive Jack Pessetto, too, as Benton had. It only took four martini's, and then Benton really wasn't feeling much pain. Commissioner Henry Tidwell came up with County Commissioner Eugene Santsci, and commiserated with Bob about Pessetto. Bob made it clear he wanted no action taken against the poor man, and the subject of their conversation changed. Finally, Santschi mentioned a proclamation that was going to be issued.

Now Santsci had caught Benton's interest. "What proclamation, Gene?"

"Apparently Governor Maybe doesn't trust local men to keep him informed of what's going on down here. He sent down Major Elmer Johnson, the head of the National Guard, to keep an eye on us. Major Johnson brought a communique from the governor. It's supposed to be based on reports of pickets everywhere in the county," Santschi said. He reached into his inside coat pocket and withdrew a sheaf of papers. He flipped past the top few, chose a page and handed it to Benton. As Benton took the paper, Santschi pointed to one section. "This part says it all."

Benton read, "A condition must be brought to prevail in Carbon County where any man can work at any place where he chooses to accept employment, without intimidation or threats being used against him. This condition does not at present exist."

Tidwell seemed upset. "This ain't about the union letting scabs in. It's written instructions to us to restore order. Now what are we going to do?" Tidwell asked, rhetorically. "We sure as hell aren't going to get the pickets to go away by just telling them to." Benton asked if they'd decided on any particular action. "Kelter has even told the strikers it was the governor's direct order that all non-citizens have to turn in their guns," Tidwell said. "But that ain't calmed things down a bit."

Now both Tidwell and Santschi looked dismayed. Without giving them anything to feel better about, Benton said, "I guess you'll have to go back to your drawing boards and figure out something else to create the condition the governor says must be created." Benton rubbed his hand along the side of his face, and grimaced. "You're going to have to excuse me while I go get another drink. Poor Jack was so upset he really nailed me. Hurts."

As Benton was getting his next drink, out of the corner of his eye, Benton saw Harold Cooper, the editor of *The News Advocate* talking with one of The Advocate owners, Joseph Borboflio. He walked over to the two men, and waited until they had finished their conversation.

"Hi, Hal. Hi, Joe. I just wanted to thank you, Hal. We read your article about the Sunnyside Saint Patrick's Day dance. You made my little girl really happy."

"What part of the article referred to her?" Cooper asked.

"That part about one of the most popular young ladies of the town helping do the dishes."

"Good. Evan Jones wrote the article, and told me who did what."

"Seems I'll have to thank Evan, too," Benton observed. His duty to stay on the good side of the newspaper done, Benton figured it was time for another drink. To make a graceful exit, he said. "Thanks again. My daughter has been really bored. Your writing about her cheered her up."

"Wasn't she in college?" Cooper asked.

"Yes, but her heart just wasn't in it," Benton lied. "You know how difficult kids that age can be."

"I've got an idea that may interest you," Cooper said. "If she's all that bored, maybe she ought to come see me. I have a vacant position, and she might just fill the bill."

Benton asked how she might help him. "My proof reader, Miss Bagley, quit to be the secretary for the Chamber of Commerce. I could try her out as the proof reader. It wouldn't be a full time job, or anything. We're a weekly. Only need her a day or so a week."

Benton was starting to warm to the idea. Getting her out of the house more often would give everyone a break. "Sounds interesting. I'll talk with her about it in the morning. Let you know."

That seemed to satisfy Cooper. "Good. Let me know one way or the other."

"Deal. I'll let you know in the morning, one way or another," Benton agreed. He rubbed his jaw. He was in pain. "Think I need another drink." But, he picked up the drink and there was a tap on his shoulder. He turned around. There was Tidwell again, and a stranger.

"Bob, this is Major Johnson." Benton stuck out his hand. "Major Johnson, this is Bob Benton. He's the General Superintendent of all the Utah Fuel mines in this area."

Benton shook hands with the major. "Pleased to meet you, Major. Henry was telling me earlier you'd come down from the governor's office to help us."

"Likewise," Johnson said. "I've heard about you and your new Packard."

Benton hoped he hadn't heard about the fight with Pessetto as well.

"Bob, Major wants to know if picketers are affecting work at Utah Fuel," Tidwell said.

"What can I say?" Benton asked, and shrugged his shoulders. "The picketers are keeping a lot of men away from work who want to work. There is no way even half of the men out on strike at my mine are strong union members, but the union has made them afraid to go to work."

The major paused as the bartender came up. "Scotch and water," he said. Tidwell said he'd have a martini.

Once more, the major turned attention to Benton. "I didn't think many men would be union, if left to themselves," he said. Turning to Tidwell. "Other mines being affected?"

Tidwell was pleased. He'd prepared just such a report, in case someone asked. He put on an official look, and began in a dry voice. "It depends on the day, Major. Spring Canyon is only putting out twenty-five percent or so. At Peerless only forty out of a hundred men are working, and Rains is only putting out five hundred tons a day which is about a quarter of what is normal for them. Storrs is about fifty percent, but the Kinney mine is closed down completely."

"Is that all of the mines on strike?" the major asked. He seemed bored as Tidwell named others.

"You will have to forgive me," the major interrupted. "I'm not a mining man. You folks will have to teach me a lot before I make my first report to him."

"You have our full cooperation, Sir," Tidwell said, solicitously.

Benton felt Tidwell was making a fool of himself. Also, there were a lot more important things which should be talked about than the number of mines. "If I may say so," Benton interjected, "what makes these strikers and picket lines so troublesome is that the strikers are primarily foreign-born, non-English speaking men who hardly represent most of our miners. By itself, that's bad enough, but we've got trouble-makers from Wyoming stirring them up."

The Major nodded his head. "That's what I've heard. Wasn't that true in past strikes as well?"

"It's always been that way," Benton assured him. With that, Benton finished his drink, held up his glass, looked at the major and Tidwell. "Buy you another round?" When they agreed, he motioned to the bartender. "Bring us tee martoonies," he said, paused, pretended it was a joke, and laughed. The two other men joined in the laughter. "And a watch and scotter, for the major," he said, to try further to make the first slip seem to be a joke.

Even after the Major and Tidwell left, however, Benton continued to drink. His words were becoming slurred as he stood at the bar and talked with Judge Hammond. Yet another hand on Benton's shoulder caused him to turn. This time, he turned more than a little unsteadily. Doc was standing there, and without saying anything to Benton, he looked directly at the judge.

"Hate to interrupt you, Judge, but I've got to pull Bob out of here.

Got a Greek lady in Sunnyside that's about to drop any time now. I have to check on her before I can go to bed." Benton suggested the Doc have one for the road before they left. "Sorry. It's important. You wouldn't want me to let Frank Cameron's business slide, would you?"

Just the mention of Cameron sobered Benton up slightly. "Jeez, you can be a real wet blanket."

Doc turned to the Judge, "You know, Judge, if I were charged with that in your court, I'd have to plead guilty as hell." The judge laughed.

Benton hiccupped, "You got that right, " he said.

"Guess you better go with him, Bob," the Judge agreed.

Benton finished his martini in one gulp. "Okay, Doc. I'm all yours," Benton said.

Dowd led Benton out of the building. Outside Benton began fishing around in his pockets for his keys. Doc just stood, patiently, and waited. Finally Benton found the key ring, and held it up to the light while he tried to pick the key to the Packard. Doc reached out and took the keys.

"What you doin' here?" Benton demanded. "You think I'm too drunk to drive?"

"Not at all, but on the way down you promised me I could drive on the way back. Don't you remember?" Benton searched his memory, the best he could, and didn't remember that. Better play it safe and not let Doc see how drunk I am, he thought. Dutifully he got in.

A few miles up the road Doc pulled the car off to the side of the road and stopped. Benton opened his door, hung his head out over the running board, and puked. He got his blood-stained handkerchief from his pocket and wiped his mouth. The incident was repeated a number of times. When he got home he passed out on the sofa.

The next morning Benton told Elizabeth about the conversation he'd had with Harold Cooper and asked if she wanted to try it. Thrilled, she jumped at the chance. Her dad suggested she might accompany Toshio to Price, and see about the job right away.

They were barely out of town when once more she talked Toshio into letting her drive. It was easier this time than the morning of the strike, when he'd gone to Price for seeds. As they drove she briefly considered using the trip as an opportunity to run away. But she remembered how furious she was at her dad for kicking Dan out of his home.

Somehow she'd get even. But she couldn't get even if she ran. Then and there, she decided not to do it. At least not now.

As they pulled into Price she was again reminded of that last trip. What surprised her last time was that Price was not a typical coal town. It wasn't too different from the many county seats she had seen in the Midwest. "Where's the newspaper?" she asked as they reached the pavement. "There are two," Toshio advised her. "You will be going to *The News Advocate*. It's on down Main street a ways. But, with your permission, I need to stop at the other newspaper first. It's called The Sun." Elizabeth asked why. Toshio looked apologetic, "More seeds."

Toshio returned, and they proceeded to *The News Advocate*. Once inside, Elizabeth noticed a strong smell. After meeting Harold Cooper, she asked what the smell was, and he told her it was the ink. "Not only does it get everywhere," he complained. "We have to spend all day smelling it."

He asked Elizabeth a few quick questions, and seemed satisfied. He went to get what he called galleys. He brought back some strips of paper of various length with printing on them. Each strip contained one article. Elizabeth was surprised. She thought she would be going over a newspaper to look for mistakes. Cooper was smiling at her, and there was something about the way he smiled that reminded her of Doc Dowd. "I can't say for sure that I can hire you," Cooper said. "We'll have to test you first. These galleys are just for practice. I have already proof-read another set. Here's a book on proof-reading symbols. Take these home and proof-read them."

Elizabeth couldn't believe it would be that easy, but Cooper was looking at her and smiling again. She still had no idea what she was supposed to do. "How, exactly, do I proof-read them?"

"Check with Ann Bagley at the Chamber of Commerce office in the county court house. She used to be my proof-reader, instead of a book she's got cards with the proof-reading marks." The only advice he gave her was to buy a good dictionary if she didn't already have one. As they prepared to leave, Cooper gave Toshio a couple of boxes of seed. Then he turned to Elizabeth once more. "The sooner you get the galleys back, the sooner you start working." After assuring him she would do her best, she and Toshio left to find Miss Bagley. On the way, Toshio mentioned while she was with Miss Bagley, he would go to the county agricultural office and see the county agent to get some more starts for the garden.

All these seeds, and now more starts? Elizabeth smelled a rat. "Okay, Toshio, what's going on?"

"What do you mean, Miss Benton? You, yourself, heard your father say for me to get seeds to distribute to people in town."

She knew Toshio was rearranging the truth, if not downright lying. "Toshio, I am getting the feeling that there is more going on here than meets the eye." Toshio just looked at her, and as far as Elizabeth could tell, he wasn't having a thought in the world. Now she knew what was meant by Oriental inscrutability. "Toshio, I hope someday you will trust me enough to let me know things you might not want somebody else to know. I'd hoped we were, well, friends."

"You are a very perceptive young woman," Toshio said without changing expressions. "I, too, hope that someday our friendship progresses to the point we can share secrets with each other."

When Elizabeth found the right office at the court house, she walked in and told the beautiful girl at the desk she wanted to speak with Miss Bagley. "It's Ann, to you, Honey. You must be Elizabeth. Cooper called. My, you're sure a lot prettier than I expected you to be."

"I had the same thought about you," Elizabeth said, blushing just a bit at Ann's lavish praise. We're getting off to a great start, Elizabeth thought. Ann didn't spend much time talking about proof reading. Instead she gave Elizabeth some cards showing the various proof reading marks.

"And I mean this," Ann said as Elizabeth left. "If you don't come to see me every time you're in town I shall be very put out. Next time we'll go down to the Queen City for lunch."

On the way back to Sunnyside, Elizabeth tried again. "Okay, Toshio. If you won't share secrets with me, I'll share some with you. Do you know what my dad did to Dan Cook?"

Again the inscrutable look on Toshio. "Everyone in town knows, I think. Sunnyside is too small for that to stay secret." Elizabeth asked if he knew why her dad made him move. Toshio looked at her. His eyelids narrowed to almost slits. "It is said your father saw you riding with Dan Cook and forbids you ever to see him again."

Elizabeth seemed relieved. "That's right. But, Toshio, I generally don't do what my father says."

She broke into tears. "Oh, Toshio, what am I going to do? Dan's a nice boy. How can I tell him I had nothing to do with his getting thrown out?"

Toshio spoke softly, "I'll see what I can do."

Gratitude flooded over her, but she knew she couldn't let him take such chances on her behalf. "Thanks, Toshio. That means so much to me. But I can't let you do it. We both know why."

Toshio pursed his lips. He let out a sort of deep breath and guttural sound. "You asked about the seeds. I'm not a miner, so I can't belong to the union, but many of my countrymen do. Let's just say I'm a sympathizer. That is why I delivered most of the seeds to the strikers, as I will most of those I got today." Almost stunned, Elizabeth asked if he realized the risk he was taking by telling her this. "Not so risky it would stop me from helping my friend with her problem."

That whole evening Elizabeth's mind and emotions were as jumbled as they had been that first day in Sunnyside. She understood why the miners would go out on strike. If they won, they'd have a lot to gain. But why would this gentle man risk so much to help them? If he were discovered, at the very least he'd be fired and kicked out of his home. Then what would he and his family do? He had nothing to gain, and everything to lose.

She tossed and turned in bed that night, and could not sleep. The enormity of Toshio's sacrifice in helping her was more than she could bear. If something bad happened to him because of that, she would never forgive herself. Then another thought crossed her mind. She smiled to herself as a plan began to form. She slept soundly.

CHAPTER 17

IT'S THE RIGHT THING TO DO

The next morning, set up with her pencils, her dictionary, her proof-reading cards, and the galleys all lying on the desk in her bedroom, Elizabeth felt she was a newspaper woman already. She flipped through the galleys to find a short one to correct. The headline proclaimed, "Mines Working; No Disturbances Here." How interesting, she thought as she started reading, my first article is about Utah Fuel. She continued reading. Then sat back bewildered.

"This is wrong," she said aloud. Her mother was just passing in the hall, and asked what was wrong. "Mom, come in here for a minute, please." When her mother came in, Elizabeth showed her the galley. "Mother, this article is all wrong. It says the Utah Fuel and the United States Fuel mines are all working as steadily as the demand for coal will permit. It says only the Panther mine at Heiner is closed, and that's because the men are on vacation from work for the present. Mom, the men are on strike, not vacation."

"You said these were just for practice. Maybe it's an old article."

"No, Mr. Cooper said they were copies of articles he'd already proof-read for Thursday's paper."

"Well, call him and ask him. I'm sure a newspaper would have a telephone."

Elizabeth agreed. She went downstairs, and stationed herself in front of the varnished telephone box on the wall. She lifted the heavy ear piece off its cradle, and gave the handle a good solid twist for a couple of rotations. When the operator answered, she spoke into the long, tube-like mouthpiece mounted on the front of the box. She identified herself to the operator and asked for *The News Advocate* in Price. Shortly, Harold Cooper was on the phone. His voice sounded tinny in the ear piece.

"Mr. Cooper, I really hate to trouble you with problems before I'm even hired, but I don't know how to correct the very first article I tried." He asked what the problem was. "Well," Elizabeth said, and took a deep breath, "the proof-reading cards Miss Bagley gave me only tell how to correct errors, punctuation or spelling. The cards don't tell me what to do if it's wrong."

There was a pause on the other end of the phone. "How do you mean, wrong?" Cooper asked. His question sounded as if it were an accusation to Elizabeth. She regretted having made the call.

"I don't know about the other mines, but it says all Utah Fuel mines are working steadily. At Sunnyside we have very few men working."

"I guess," Cooper said and paused. "I guess I didn't make myself clear. The proof-reader corrects only errors in the typesetting. The editor corrects any errors in fact and how it's presented." Elizabeth asked what he meant by presented. "That's a subject you don't have to worry your pretty little head about right now.

"*The News Advocate* has several owners. All the owners, except for a large coal company which puts up part of the money to keep us in business, are well-respected business men. Our articles must present news in ways that are in harmony with the needs of our owners. Every newspaper knows what its basic philosophy is, and prints its news in harmony with that."

Elizabeth couldn't believe it. "I thought the newspaper's job was to print the truth."

Cooper was no longer even trying to sound friendly. "Our job is to print that part of the truth in harmony with our basic philosophy. Otherwise, readers are confused and they do not know where the paper really stands." Elizabeth realized that Cooper was losing his patience, and she feared she'd blown any chance for the job. Besides, all he was giving her was double talk for lying.

"You're young, and such things are probably pretty confusing to you," Cooper was saying. "Tell you what, I'm pretty busy right now. Talk it over with your dad, he can explain it to you."

Elizabeth's thoughts were in turmoil. Well, I don't care if they are lying, I want this job. What she said was, "Thanks, Mr. Cooper, I'll do that."

"Good," Cooper said, and Elizabeth thought he sounded relieved.

"And if he gets you straightened out, come on back in and we'll do our best to put you to work.

"Oh, by the way," Cooper said. "Give my regards to your dad, and remind him he's guest speaker at our next Chamber of Commerce meeting."

Well, there it is, Elizabeth thought as she went back upstairs. I either go along with their lies, or don't bother coming back in. Nothing to talk over with her father. By the time she was again ready to start proof-reading, she approached the galleys differently, and with much less joy.

She re-read the article to see what other "harmony" was being "presented." She read, "Scofield and Kinney are completely quiet. There has been no disturbances and none is anticipated. Up Spring canyon the first of the week men from several of the mines stayed away from work."

"Ah ha," she said, "canyon" needs to be capitalized. She reached for her card to find out how to mark the correction. Next she noticed there should probably be a comma after week. Soon she was absorbed in finding mistakes and how to correct them. She finished in less than an hour.

After lunch, Elizabeth decided that even if she could not ride Bonnie alone, at least she could go up, curry her, and exercise her around the stables. At the corral, Cyclone came over.

"Sorry, Miss Elizabeth, but your father be tellin' me to be tellin' him right away if you be takin' Bonnie out without somebody with you." She advised him she was just going to curry and exercise Bonnie, and this seemed fine with him.

Young Steve Cook came riding up, got off his horse, and started talking to Cyclone. When he finished, he remounted his horse and started off. Elizabeth waved at him, calling him over.

"Yes, Miss Benton?"

"Steve, I am awfully sorry my dad made Dan move out. I didn't have anything to do with it. I didn't even know about it until the next day. Would you please tell that to him?"

"Yes, Ma'am, but there's no need. He already told me it's your old man . . . uh, your father's fault, not yours." Elizabeth paused. She gave Bonnie a couple of quick brushes with the curry comb. She thanked Steve, and asked him to set up a time and place to meet Dan, and personally apologize. Steve's eyes flashed an angry look. "No, Ma'am, I won't do that."

Elizabeth realized that if Steve was to be of use in helping her, she would have to win him over first. She spoke in soft, friendly tones. "Why not? And stop calling me Ma'am for heaven's sake. To you, I'm Elizabeth. You and I can be friends, can't we?"

Steve definitely seemed less angry, and his tones softened as well. "Elizabeth, I can't tell him you want to meet him cause your dad'll fire my dad if you're caught with Dan again."

Elizabeth couldn't believe it. "Oh, no! He couldn't." Steve said he'd personally heard Marshall Rasmussen say that. She was beginning to believe it. "I hate him!" she spat. "Now, more than ever, I really need to speak with Dan." Steve said he couldn't gamble with his dad's job. He told her she'd be doing their family a favor by staying away from Dan.

Elizabeth hated what she was hearing. "Steve, I won't jeopardize your family," she said. She noticed that some of the tension left Steve's body. His shoulders relaxed, and he looked relieved. "I like you all too much," she added.

With that, Steve smiled. "Thank you. I believe you about Dan getting throwed out. I'll tell him." He whirled his horse and took off at a trot.

Elizabeth continued to curry Bonnie. Then, without putting on a saddle, she hopped on her, and rode her around the stables. All the while her mind was racing. She had to implement her plan, but how? Toshio already said he wasn't a member of the union, but maybe he could help. There had to be a way to do what she'd decided. More than ever she had reason to make her Dad pay.

After exercising Bonnie, she wiped her down and thought of a possible solution. She would sound out Cyclone to find where his sympathies really lay. She would ask him why he thought someone who had nothing to gain themselves was helping the union. She'd have to be very careful not to expose Toshio. Cyclone was smart and would know she was talking about him.

When she finished Bonnie, she walked over to where Cyclone was working at his anvil. "Cyclone, I already think I know the answer, but I want to ask you a question."

"Askin' be good," Cyclone responded, concentrating on the horse-shoe he was making.

"Why would a man risk everything when he has nothing personal to gain by helping the union?" Cyclone look worried, and kept hammering away. He asked her what she meant by that. "For example, let's say this friend of mine didn't belong to the union himself. But he sympathized with them, and did things for them that could get both him and his family into serious trouble."

Strangely, Elizabeth noticed Cyclone was hitting the horseshoe with such force he was bending it out of shape. He didn't answer her, but kept pounding. Finally, he turned to Elizabeth, and there was pleading in his eyes. "You a goin' to be tellin' your dad?"

She did her best to cover the surprise. But there was no question as to what she had stumbled onto by accident. No worry about her words exposing Toshio now.

"You know your secret is safe with me," she said. "But," she said, glancing at the boy at the bellows as if to indicate they'd better be careful in front of him. Cyclone's whole body seemed to radiate relief and good humor. He stopped pounding and walked over to the bellows. He began to ruffle the boy's hair with his hand. "Old Hank, here, he be as steady as they come. His pappy be a union man." Cyclone walked back to the anvil and looked at the mass of unrecognizable metal on it. He began talking to himself out loud. "Now look what you be a doin', you old fool."

Cyclone looked at Elizabeth, smiling broadly but seeming a little embarrassed as well. "I plum be forgettin' you be askin' Cyclone a question." He put the metal from the anvil back into the forge to reheat it. "A man be a doin' that kinda thing cause it be the right thing to do."

"Thank you, Cyclone," Elizabeth said, but she didn't believe it was all that simple. There could be many more reasons. Her vow to make her dad pay for the way he'd treated Dan was one. But Cyclone made sense. Even better than getting back at her father, Cyclone had given her a better reason to do what she planned. It was the right thing to do.

"Cyclone. How helpful would it be to the union to know what is going to be printed in *The News Advocate* a couple of days before it came out?"

"You be joshin' old Cyclone, right?" He seemed almost confused. "You be askin' old Cyclone how important it be to be a knowin' what your enemy be thinkin' two days before he even be a sayin' it?" He just shook his head. "I reckon it be about the most important thing there be."

Cyclone's response thrilled Elizabeth. Suddenly she realized her idea was a lot better than she hoped it would be. Now she would help the union. But not just to get back at her dad, that was petty, but because it was the right thing to do. She found joy in that thought all the rest of the day.

Now he's got to hire me, Elizabeth thought the next morning. He's just got to, so much is riding on it now. She worried that maybe she hadn't done the galleys right. Anxiously, she went over them one more time as she waited for Toshio to bring the Packard around.

Once away from town, Toshio stopped. Without saying a word, he got out, and went around to the passenger's side. Eagerly, Elizabeth slid over behind the wheel. Driving was a thrill for her. As she drove, she told Toshio exactly what she planned to do, and asked him if he could talk to the right people to get it rolling. He assured her it had already been handled.

She sat, feeling almost stunned. Toshio explained. "Yesterday, Cyclone came to me and told me what you said. I told some people I know, who contacted the district officials. I understand they were even happier than Cyclone." Elizabeth was getting more pleased with herself by the minute.

Elizabeth paused to think. She had hoped they might just want to know what the articles were going to say. It had not dawned on her that they might be able to take action to overcome the effects of the article. But the more she thought about it, the more sense it made. Then, another thought struck her. In anguish, she blurted out, "I'll just die if he doesn't hire me, Toshio."

"He will. You're so pretty he'll want you around. Being Benton's daughter is no little thing in and of itself. You will probably overhear many things which would be useful." Toshio turned a little more serious. "Give Cyclone or me details of anything that might in any way hurt the strike or the men involved," Toshio said as they pulled into Price.

At this, Elizabeth felt momentary confusion. I just told Cyclone yesterday afternoon, for heaven's sake. Now Toshio is laying it out for me as though they've been discussing it a week. Elizabeth began to have a far greater respect for the union. "I see a lot of people are in on this," she said.

Toshio smiled. "Organized labor means they are organized, Elizabeth." He pointed to the county courthouse. "Want to pull over there and park?" Elizabeth asked if he needed more seeds. "No. I thought you might want to show Miss Bagley the work you've done on the galleys?"

"Why would I want . . ." Elizabeth started to say, then stopped. "Oh, I see. You really are a sly one, aren't you?" Grinning, he got out and opened the door to the Packard for her.

Inside the office, Ann smiled an impish smile. "I certainly will not look at those to see if you've done them right," she asserted. "Until you buy me a cup of coffee." Soon, seated in a diner three doors down from the courthouse, they'd ordered coffee and hot rolls. Ann spread the galleys in front of her on the table. She looked at them intently. She made only a couple of corrections. "Perfect," she said. Then Ann paused long enough to get a package of cigarettes from her purse. After taking one, she put the pack on the table in front of them.

"I'm so glad! I want this job so much," Elizabeth said and nodded toward the cigarettes. "Could I?" she asked. Ann said it was her coffin, and she could drive another nail any time she wanted.

Then she turned more serious. "May I ask you something?" Elizabeth waited until her own cigarette was lit before nodding her head. "Why on Earth are you so eager to get that job? You don't need the money, and, frankly, Cooper is a bear to work for."

Elizabeth stalled for time to think of a good answer. "It gets me out of the house."

Ann still looked skeptical. There was obviously something on her mind. "Fair enough. What did you think of the articles?" Pleasantly as she could manage, Elizabeth said they were interesting. "They're a pack of lies. You know that or we can't be as good friends as I thought we were."

A little shocked, Elizabeth looked at Ann. "Why wouldn't we be good friends?"

"Don't let the fact I work at the Chamber of Commerce fool you into thinking I'm something I'm not. First, I hate those creeps. Second, if I've judged wrong, my job is already in jeopardy for telling so much to Miss General Super's Daughter."

Elizabeth smiled. She knew she'd liked this girl from the moment she laid eyes on her. She put on what she hoped was an angelic look that said that she, of all people, must always tell the truth. "What makes you think I won't tell?"

Ann grinned back. "I know the "Miss Holier Than Thou" type of look well enough, heaven knows. You just don't have it. And give up trying to fake it." Elizabeth looked smug as the waitress brought the coffee and rolls. Both girls sat quietly, except to say, "Thanks." As the waitress worked, Elizabeth thought about herself, and how much she'd changed.

"You know," she observed, as the waitress left and they could talk again, "Barely over a month ago, I might have had that look." Ann said it was lucky they didn't meet then.

On the way back to the office, Elizabeth waived to Toshio sitting patiently in the car. "Why don't you get your own car," Ann suggested. Elizabeth said she might just do that.

Things went just as well at The Advocate. After Cooper gave her a new set of galleys to correct, he asked her to go over to the wall and read the published list of The Advocate's owners. He said he wanted her to be very clear who she was working for. While she was standing there, Elizabeth volunteered to come in twice a week, if that was okay. With an approving glance at her fanny, Cooper agreed that would be just fine.

On the way home, Elizabeth was in a good mood. She and Toshio really enjoyed each other's company. They had become more than friends. Again she thought of the difference between doing something for a higher purpose, and doing something just to irritate her father. Too bad, this new idea would drive him nuts.

When she got home, the first thing she did was to glance around to make sure her father wasn't home. The second thing she did was tell her mother all about getting the job. As Elizabeth had expected, her mother was really pleased for Elizabeth.

Finally, Elizabeth took a deep breath and looked at her mother.

"Mom, never in my life have I asked you for a really big favor." Elizabeth noticed her mother's brow wrinkle as she spoke. Her mother agreed she had not, but ask, Honey, it's yours. "I need a car."

"Perhaps you're right," Katherine said, then thought for a few moments. "Okay. I helped him buy the Packard. So I guess he can't object too much if I buy my daughter an automobile as well." Elizabeth threw her arms around her mother and hugged her with more love than she had ever felt before. When Benton came home Katherine asked him if he wanted a drink. Once it was fixed she winked at Elizabeth.

"Honey, Elizabeth has to have her corrections back to the paper in the morning, and I have some shopping to do. Would it be all right with you if we took Toshio and the Packard with us? I may need his help." Benton nodded, looked at the drink questioningly, and sampled it gingerly.

"What will you be shopping for?"

"A little something to help Elizabeth do her job, and a surprise for you."

"Hardly wait," he said without much enthusiasm.

Elizabeth was so excited she could hardly contain herself. During dinner, her dad even mentioned her animated mood. Elizabeth declared it was excitement about getting the new job. "Glad I found it for you," her father said, and seemed to be really happy for her. You old coot, she said to herself. It's a strange world. Now he's being nice to me.

She hurried through dinner and excused herself. Outside Toshio was just finishing up. Elizabeth told him they were going to Price again early tomorrow morning.

Next morning the five o'clock whistle woke Elizabeth. It was the first time she'd heard it since she got used to it a couple of days after arriving in Sunnyside. Even her mother seemed excited. She came into Elizabeth's bedroom just as Elizabeth finished her make-up.

"I thought it would be nice if we had breakfast in Price," she said. "The New Grand Hotel, down by the train station, has a very good restaurant. I'm told a lot of the train men eat there.

"Give me just a minute. All I have left to do is brush my hair and we will be on our way," Elizabeth said. Her mother said she'd tell Bob they were leaving. Outside, Toshio backed the Packard out. He was still warming up the engine as the two women left the house. He jumped out of the car and opened the back door for them.

Toshio bowed to Katherine. "I thought you'd appreciate a nice warm car when you came out," he said. Katherine offered her thanks, as the two women got into the back seat. Toshio helped them spread the lap robe over their laps. They were on their way before Benton was even out of bed.

"Mom, when we get to Price would it be all right with you if we dropped by the Chamber of Commerce office? I have a friend I want you to meet. Her name is Ann. She has been showing me how to proofread, and I kind of owe her a meal." Her mother agreed.

None too soon for Elizabeth, they finally pulled in front of the courthouse and parked. Toshio got out and opened the door for Elizabeth. At the office Ann said she had already eaten breakfast, but she'd be happy to join them, and have a cup of coffee, and maybe a roll.

Before they could even order, Elizabeth told Ann they were going to buy a car. After they ordered, Ann asked if they were buying a Model T. "Heavens no!" Elizabeth said. "Some of my friends in Colorado call me Liz. I can just hear them now saying, 'There goes Liz in her Tin Lizzy.'" Elizabeth looked at her mother and suggested something such as a Reo, or perhaps a Studebaker. Katherine felt Elizabeth should have something smaller.

"How would a coupe or something work?" she asked, happy everyone was so excited. Ann asked if she could make a suggestion, and told them the Durrant Motor Company had just put out a new runabout in its Star line, and thought it was much better looking than a Ford.

While they drove Ann back to the courthouse, she gave Toshio the directions to the sales agency. They barely walked in the door before being met by a salesman. Katherine explained what they wanted to look at and the salesman led them to a model he had on hand. "It's got four cylinders and a one-hundred-and-two-inch wheel base," the salesman said.

"Gee, that's nice," Elizabeth agreed. Looking at her mother. "What do you think? I love it."

"How much does it cost?" she asked the salesman. When he said three hundred and forty eight dollars, Katherine asked if that included an electric starter. When the salesman said a starter would cost an additional one hundred dollars, Elizabeth's heart sank. "We will take it with a starter," her mother said.

Elizabeth squealed with delight and started jumping up and down. "I've got me a Star!" she said.

"You got a what?" her dad almost screamed when he was told. Katherine hurried to mention they had considered a Studebaker or a Reo at first, but Elizabeth's friend talked them out of it. Benton stood tapping his foot on the floor. He glared at them, but then the look softened. "Women," he snorted and headed down to his den. "Get two of 'em together and nobody's safe."

CHAPTER 18

UNION BUSINESS COULD WAIT

As Dan rode out of town on Turk, Dan saw Doc Dowd on a porch. He stopped to say hello. Doc sat in a rocking chair on the porch of the ramshackle old house. "Been watching," Doc said. "People parading out of town are a pitiful sight. Women carrying bedding, women pulling little wagons of food, children holding onto their mothers' skirts and crying. Men with poles rigged as stretchers are carrying heavier stuff out..."

Before he could continue, Ovie Rasmussen walked up with two of his men. One was carrying a rifle. With a vicious edge to his voice, Ovie told Doc it was time for the family inside to vacate company property. "Not on your life," erupted from Doc. "I told Benton I got a Greek woman in the late stages of pregnancy. She is not leaving this house until I say so."

Rasmussen's manner seemed as though the situation had already been settled. "We all talked it over, Doc. They've had a week to get ready."

Rasmussen tried a different tack. He spoke glibly, and said then he had no choice left but to arrest her. "And it'll be your fault, Doc. Actually, we were supposed to arrest anybody not out by eight this morning. But Mr. Benton was kind enough to extend that until ten o'clock."

Doc reached down, picked up the double barrel shotgun he'd laid on the porch alongside the rocking chair, and pointed it at Rasmussen's belly. "Okay, come get her. But you get the first barrel, Ovie. The second barrel is for any other idiot that sets foot on a step."

Fear flared in Rasmussen's eyes, his nostrils widened. "Doc, put that thing down."

"Well, that's the only way you're going to get her. As you said,

What's it going to be?" Rasmussen stammered something Doc did not catch, but Doc'd had about enough of this. "Make your move or get on out of here. I may be busy soon."

Rasmussen scowled. He looked at his two deputies, one of them shrugged. Rasmussen looked back at Dowd. "I'm going to have to report you for this, Doc," he said stridently.

As Rasmussen moved his men back up the road, Dan nudged Turk in the flanks to get him moving again, then stopped. "Would you really have shot him, Doc?" Dan asked.

A devious smile made it's way across Dowd's features. "We'll never know, will we?" Again Dan was about to leave. "One more thing," Doc said. "You wouldn't have a couple of shotgun shells on you, would you?" he asked before an immense smile broke out.

Dan just shook his head back and forth. "You're a real card, Doc. See you later." On his way to Tent Town, Dan couldn't help but wonder if Doc was just joking with him, or if he had faced down Rasmussen and those two deputies with only an empty shotgun.

Once at his tent, he put the last of his stuff away, met his other two tent mates, and went out to see where to find Tom. Tom's tent flaps were down, so Dan knocked on the tent pole. Tom's voice boomed, "Who goes there, friend or enemy?" He laughed. "Give a password."

Dan thought quickly, and said, "Dago Red." Tom laughed and said to throw the bottle of wine in first. Inside, Dan saw Tom sitting on the only bed and wondered how come Tom rated a tent by himself. "What happened? That ugly face of yours scare your tent mates away?" Tom said the union didn't have to pay his way, he'd bought this one himself. He said he was too used to being alone. If he could stand other people around all the time, he'd a got married. Dan laughed. Tom pointed to a chair, and told Dan to sit down. He said he had something important to talk about. Dan didn't care for the tone of Tom's voice, but he sat. "You sound worried," Dan observed.

Tom agreed he was. He thought for a moment, "Don't know the best way to tell you this, but you ain't going to like it since it could cost your dad his job." Now Dan really began to worry. Tom took a deep breath. "Okay. Here's the short of it. Did you know that Elizabeth Benton is passing important information on to the union?" Dan looked at Tom in amazement as he continued speaking. "Seems she got so mad at her pap for throwing you out of your house, she started helping us, just to get even." Dan couldn't believe it. "Seems you sure charmed her." Tom turned serious again. "That ain't important. What's important is she is supposed to give info to Toshio or Cyclone. But now that's changed."

"Yeah?" Dan asked, but he was starting to get a sick feeling in his stomach. The seriousness with which Tom spoke made Dan wonder what it was that kept Tom beating around the bush. "I ain't going to get my dad fired," he said.

"Don't get ahead of me, Dan. You need to know why we're asking. The district people thought it over, and decided it was too dangerous for her to talk union around Toshio and Cyclone. Her, and Cyclone, and Toshio are too important to us to get any two of them wiped out as informants if somebody overhears them." Dan spat out that he guessed his dad wasn't important to the union. "Stop it, Dan. Don't make this any harder for me than it is already. You know that ain't the truth. Think I'd be talking about this I hadn't cleared it with your dad? Your dad asked me if it was important enough to risk him getting fired if you're caught, and I told him it was." Dan was incredulous. He couldn't believe his Dad would risk getting fired. "Maybe now you'll understand why nobody in the union holds it against your dad for being a scab. But," Tom hastened to add, "I told your pap if you get caught and he gets fired, when we win the strike we'll get his job back."

Dan knew he'd meet Elizabeth. How could he refuse? But he couldn't bring himself to speak the words that might put his dad's job in jeopardy. After all, there was a baby coming. The best he could do was ask, "How do we keep from getting caught?"

Tom stood up, put his hand on Dan's shoulder in friendship. "That's one of the reasons you was chose. You're a good horseman, and a savvy kid. Elizabeth's got a new automobile. We figured you could ride out of town, and meet her where you won't get caught. Your first meeting with her is scheduled tonight, down on the road to Big Spring Ranch." Tom sat down on his bed again, and looked sadly at Dan. They sat for awhile talking. Tom filled Dan in on some of the other news. The town had been sealed, and no strikers could enter. One man per day could go to the post office to bring back everybody's mail. And he'd have to be accompanied by a guard.

Dan's mood was ugly as he went over to the corral. By now, school was out and Steve should be showing up for their regularly scheduled meeting. Dan threw the saddle on Turk and rode out to meet Steve. When he got to the draw below the coke ovens, Steve was already there. Steve had a worried look on his face. "What's up?" Dan asked.

"The good news is that a lot more men are going to join the strike. Bad news is Benton got word that some of the scabs he brought in are planning to bolt and leave town. Benton has his goons going out and telling everybody wives can go, and so can kids, but not the men."

Turk stood nose-to-nose with his stable mate. They seemed to be catching up with each other as well. "Thanks, Steve. I've got to get your information back to camp right away."

"Sure, Bud. Tomorrow, same time?" Steve suggested they meet early since he didn't have to go to school on Saturday. "Got to go now. Union business can't wait," Dan said.

Strangely, back in Tent Town, neither Frank nor Tom seemed that upset. They told Dan this type of thing frequently happened in a strike. Especially if the strike was really hurting production. Tom told Dan to go lie down and rest. Elizabeth would not be meeting him till after eight.

Dan tried to rest, but it did not come easily. Right after dark the sweeping of the searchlight flooded the outside of the tent. He got up, saddled Turk, and headed out.

It was only a half-hour ride to Big Spring Ranch road. Elizabeth was to meet him about a half a mile down the ranch road. He was pleased that nobody passing by on the main road a half mile away would be able to see them. He rode back and forth, making sure nobody else was in the area.

After what seemed to be hours, Dan saw lights turning off the main road. The vehicle was heading directly toward him. He started Turk trotting toward the lights.

Elizabeth saw the figure on the horse ahead of her. She heaved a sigh of relief when she recognized him. She pulled the car off the road, turned off the lights, and waited for him. She watched as he gracefully dismounted and walked over to her open window.

"Did you see anyone else around?" He said only jack rabbits. Elizabeth asked him if he wanted to get in. "It was nice of you to meet me like this," she said as he entered. "I know what you are risking, and that means a lot to me."

Dan's first impulse was to complain about her dad, but this was union business. He wouldn't let his own fears about his dad's job stand in the way of that. But Elizabeth noticed the look on his face and asked him what was wrong. "Nothing really. I'm just so afraid we'll get caught."

Elizabeth's heart went out to him. She knew how he'd been hurt because of her. She slid across the seat and kissed him. He did not pull away. Her arms encircled his neck as the kiss became more than just friendly. Feeling her emotions for him, she jumped back.

Dan jerked away. "What are we doing? I'm sorry, Elizabeth. I'm really sorry."

"Don't be," she said, feeling the rush of blood to her cheeks. She hoped the moonlight was not bright enough to reveal her blushing. How strong her feelings were for him. She had never felt this way. She wondered what he must be thinking.

The second she kissed him, he knew what he wanted. Lord, how he wanted it. The realization filled him with shame. "Please forgive me. I respect you too much to act this way." She told him there was nothing to forgive. A faint smile came again to her face.

Doing his best to remember why he was here, "We need to talk about union business..." he started to say. "God, you're beautiful."

Again the rush of blood to her face. "I'm glad you think so," she said softly. To ease the pain in his voice, she reached out and ran her hand across his stubbled cheek. He raised both hands and put them on her shoulders. He held her, and looked deep into her large blue and frightened eyes. She did not pull away. He continued staring into her eyes, the moon putting a faint pinprick in each one. He pulled her toward him again, he would not be denied. She was breathing heavily. Passionately, he kissed her. She felt his hand caressing the front of her. Then she felt his hand moving lower. All the while their hot young lips were compressing. Softly he kissed her cheek. Slowly his lips traced the path his hands had just taken.

He pushed her back over on the seat, and she did not resist. Without even thinking, he was on top of her, entering her. All thoughts of anything else ceased to exist. She shuddered as it began. She moaned softly and shuddered again.

Finally, he collapsed onto her. "I can't believe it," he said as his breath calmed.

"How could I stop you?" she asked. Admitting to herself for the first time that she had wanted him from the moment he touched her at the dance.

"This is your first time, isn't it?" he asked.

She hesitated a moment. "Yes," she lied, more to put him at ease than to deceive him. Dan said it was his first time, too. "I never guessed it would be so wonderful," she said. This time she was telling the truth. Last time hurt. "We can't tell anyone what we did."

"I'd rather die first," he whispered.

Dan sat looking at her. Already, he felt the stirring within him again. He reached over to kiss her. Apparently, union business could wait. The moon was setting and the the sun lightening the Eastern sky before he remembered why he was here. When she told him she had nothing to report but just came tonight to apologize to him, Dan withheld the comment that this was some apology. She said that when she could meet him again, she'd send word with Steve. Then Dan began to worry about what Elizabeth would say to her folks. Elizabeth said she'd tell them she was having such a good time with Ann, that they talked so long they fell asleep.

Hesitantly, lovingly, they parted. Dan hurried back into town. He was relieved when no one seemed to pay any attention to his return. What he wanted to do was crawl into bed and dream of Elizabeth, but this was Saturday, and he had his early meeting with Steve.

Dan rested for a while, but was afraid to drift off to sleep, even for a moment. Later, he rode out across the flats with a full heart. He started knowing some things he might have only considered a guess before. He knew Elizabeth either loved him or would love him soon. He could not get his mind off the night before. By the time he got to the meeting place, once more Steve was already there. He'd unsaddled his horse, and was sitting on a rock under a large pinion pine. First thing Steve did was to ask where he'd been. Then Steve observed that he looked tired.

"Didn't sleep much last night with that spotlight making the tent brighter than daylight. Guess maybe I'll get used to it," Dan said, hoping his face wouldn't give away what had really kept him awake. "Anyway, I slept late. Just woke up."

Steve spoke in a rush. "Got a message for Tom and Frank. Jimmy Morgan and J. D. Ramsey tried to get into town yesterday. But Benton's goons intercepted 'em and turned 'em back. The goons set up a road block at Twelve Mile Wash." Dan said this was so important he'd better get back.

Morgan and Ramsey decided to try again the next day. Jimmy and his group would ride the train as far as the water stop at Big Spring Ranch, and a car would take them into town. It worked as planned and when the men in the car got to camp, the strikers were already gathered at the baseball diamond. Tom began the meeting by quieting the crowd, as usual.

Ramsey had some good news for them. He said seven hundred thousand dollars was returned to UMWA by the Supreme Court. In 1914, courts in Arkansas ruled that the union was responsible for two riots in which company property was damaged. They fined the union the seven hundred thousand dollars. The union put the money in escrow and appealed to the Supreme Court. Now the Supreme Court had ruled the union was not responsible and the money was returned.

The audience appreciated this good news. It was the first they had received for quite a while. Ramsey then explained how the money would be used. He said he hoped that when operators saw all this money for strengthening of strikers, they might be more willing to negotiate.

When it was Jimmy's turn to speak, he said the union wanted all its men to keep current on what was happening around the rest of the country by reading the newspapers. Jimmy felt this was important, first of all, so miners in Sunnyside would not begin to feel they were all alone in this thing. He said it was important for Sunnyside men to see that any thing done anywhere that could be blamed on the union was being picked up and printed nationwide. "So don't you fellows do anything stupid that'll get in the papers all over the country." As Jimmy finished his remarks, Tom and Dan went forward to see if Jimmy and JD would be leaving right away, since the goons below wouldn't bother them. "Stay Strong!" Jimmy called as his car left.

CHAPTER 19

UDU'VUTS

Next morning Dan's meeting with Steve came and went; nothing new was going on. He asked if another meeting with Elizabeth was set up. The negative response disappointed him.

He whiled away the morning working in the garden. All day he worried that maybe now Elizabeth was ashamed to meet him, except for union business. Heavy with worry about it, and not wanting to keep the boys in the tent awake another night, he rolled his bedding into a roll. He told them he would not be back that night. He saddled Turk, tied the bed roll behind his saddle, and rode up to the Greek coffee house. Some of the men offered him glasses of wine. Because he didn't speak Greek, Dan just shook his head. He purchased some Greek bread, some sweet pastry that was sticky with honey, and had the man fill a large pickle jar with stew. As an afterthought, he got a bottle of wine for Billy. He put it all in the saddle bags.

Billy had hot coffee ready when Dan arrived. Dan got out the food he'd brought and put it on the camp table. Billy tried the stew tentatively, took another bite, and then began enjoying it lustily along with the big chunks of bread. He opened the wine, poured a cup full, and enjoyed that.

"Good to see you smile," Billy said. "I had a friend who never smiled. It was Coyote's fault."

Coyote's fault? Billy saw the quizzical look. "Coyote is the one who messed up Wolf's world so things were not perfect and beautiful." By now, Dan knew the signs of a story coming on. It followed some outrageous statement. Billy would look everywhere but at Dan.

"It was back in the days when Wolf and Coyote still walked on two legs. Toovuts, that's what we call this god-like creator wolf; he was the pure and virtuous one." Billy took another drink.

177

"Toovuts is not the four legged wolf we know today. Toovuts wanted everybody to live forever, live in harmony, and to love one another all the time. Coyote was the only other being around in those days before anything else was created." Billy paused to break up some bread. He whistled for his dogs, and gave them some of the bread. They enjoyed it immensely. Billy held his hands up, open palms forward to show the dogs his hands were empty. Billy explained that every time Toovuts wanted to create something, Coyote would would screw up what Toovuts wanted.

Billy paused, and looked somewhere near Dan. "Would you enjoy putting some wood on the fire?" As Dan did so, Billy continued. "That's why the world is the way it is. We know how we want it to be, but because of Coyote, it turns out different." Dan asked if Coyote was like a devil. Billy thought this funny. "Devil? Paiutes have no Devil. Just evil spirits.

"Would you call yourself a devil?" Billy asked. But continued before Dan could answer. "Coyote's disposition is a part of all men. You call it human nature. Would you call human nature the devil? Mother Earth and Father Sky, are of Toovuts' way. That is a part of us, too."

He paused to look at the fire, and spoke again. "Coyote was not evil. He was impish and naughty. Coyote just wanted things his own way," Billy said, and paused once more to sip wine. "Toovuts didn't hate Coyote because Toovuts thought to hate was wrong. But he was, well, disgusted, or sad. Nothing was turning out as he wanted, so he went away. Left Soonungwuv with us."

"Where'd he go?" Dan asked.

"Where is your God?" Billy asked in return. "Since Toovuts went away and Soonungwuv was still here, many Paiute pray to him." At yet another inquisitive look from Dan, Billy continued, "Soonungwuv is another of our names for Coyote. We have others, depending on what aspect of him we are talking about." Billy began digging around in his pockets, finally coming up with the pipe and tobacco he was fishing for, and started loading his pipe.

Dan asked why Paiute believed Coyote was still with us. "Ah, the white man's question, why. The only answer I can give you is, udu' vuts."

Dan asked for an interpretation of that last word. Billy reached for a stick from the fire to light the pipe. "Can't," he said, puffing on the pipe to get it going. Once again he was doing the little ritual with his hands, fanning the cleansing smoke toward himself.

"I can't, because there is nothing in English that gives the same idea as udu'vuts."

Dan said he understood because the Greek word analtos couldn't be translated directly into English either. But he asked Billy to give him a general meaning. "Udu'vuts means, that's the way it is. Or maybe, it's that way. Also, how could it possibly be any way other than the way it is? Or, perhaps even, how else could it be in a world created by Coyote?" Dan nodded his head, and said he could see the problem.

But Billy seemed unsatisfied with how Dan had understood what he was saying. "That's only a small part of understanding the word. The meaning isn't as important as the effect of the word. The effect is that there is no sense wondering about it, or fretting about it. That's just the way it is. Its effect creates peace in the heart and harmony with the world. As when I said white man is unhappy. I meant the Indian has a happiness and harmony the white man cannot comprehend. That is the happiness I'm seeking the answer to." Billy puffed, and fanned more smoke toward himself. "You're staying the night, of course," he continued. Dan nodded. "Good. A full moon was a magic time for the Old Ones." Billy had mentioned magic a number of times. Dan asked him if he would talk a little more about it.

"Some of the Old Ones did real magic. Real magic is being able to do something that you don't know how you did it," he said. He got up and took his turn at putting more wood on the fire. When he returned, he sat cross-legged on the ground. "It is also the power to make things for good happen. As the time the Shivwits medicine man, Toab, stood in the middle of the Cedar Indian's fire. When everyone came to see, he told them they must stop raiding each other's camps to steal children for slave trade to Mexicans. That's how taking slaves stopped for the People. At least that's how the story goes," Billy said.

Finally, he spoke, "My time is running short. I can feel it."

Dan was shocked. What did Billy mean? Dan's mind was a jumble. Billy always seemed to have deeper meanings to everything he said.

179

"Billy, you don't talk in a straight line. I can't really pin down the meaning of most of what you say."

Billy was not smiling. "Pinning down is the white man's way. They want to pin things down, to understand them." Dan observed that wanting to understand things was only natural. He asked if Billy never needed to understand. "Not really. I want to know how things are. How hot it gets in the summer, how cold in the winter, how late in the spring a particular pot hole dries up. Our lives depend on these things. Understanding why these things happen changes nothing."

"Okay, I give up. Why such and such is true doesn't change that it is true." Billy just nodded. Then he said it might be a good thing to do for one to make one's bed. Without saying a word, Dan got up and did what Billy thought it would be a good thing to do. When he finished, he lay down on top of the bed and felt that tonight he would sleep well.

Dan woke with a start just after daylight. Apparently Billy had been out checking the sheep and made some noise upon his return. Still in his clothes, Dan sat up. He noticed that Billy must have thrown a blanket over him sometime during the night. But the memory of a dream also hung around the edges of his consciousness. As he concentrated on it, he remembered seeing some sort of fire. It was all rather vague. Maybe the fire was in the sky, he couldn't remember for sure. But while the details were unclear, the dream was strangely haunting.

"Did you dream?" Billy asked. The spooky feeling again coursed its way through the hairs on the back of Dan's neck and his arms. He nodded. Billy got out his pipe, lit it and started fanning smoke. "Tell me what you dreamed, and I will tell you what it means."

"I dreamed about a fire."

Billy puffed and made more smoke. "Have you had many dreams about fire?"

Dan thought it strange Billy would ask this. "Not much," he answered. "At least not since I was young. I used to dream about fire or an explosion coming out of the mouth of a mine. That dream always scared me. But I also dreamed fairly often about the peaceful happy times we would have around a bonfire at Sunnyside Days, up in the canyon."

Billy looked thoughtful. "Mother Earth has given you the power of

180

fire. You also need never worry about dying in an explosion because fire cannot kill you." Dan just sat and looked at Billy, disbelieving. Billy saw the skepticism in Dan's eyes. He nodded. "I could have told you this before because it was fire and a light in the sky that brought you to me. But it was important that you discover your power was fire before I could tell you."

"What is the power of fire, and what do I do with it, Billy?"

Billy finished his pipe before answering. He knocked the ashes out in the usual way. "Udu'vuts. And you will do with it what you do with it. What more is there for you to know? You must never tell anyone you have this power, or fire will become shadow for you. The rest of your life know that fire is your friend, and you have the power of fire."

Dan did his best to reconcile Billy's ideas, but nothing seemed to have changed. If he had a new power, he certainly couldn't feel it. Finally, he rationalized that, as with most superstitions, it was best just to forget it. He had to admit, however, it felt good to be told he had a power. But why couldn't it have been something useful, such as the power to be a leader? Then another thought crossed his mind. He really hoped he had the power of fire. Because if Billy did know what he was talking about, at least Dan would never die in an explosion. That was very comforting.

Billy looked toward the east, then slowly turned his head looking at the rest of the sky. Finally, he looked somewhere near Dan. "If you would care to come with me, there is something I have to do." With that, Billy turned and went inside his tent.

Dan put on his shoes. As Billy came out of the tent he was holding a long stick nearly as tall as Billy. The top of the stick was festooned with long black feathers with white tips. With the stick, he pointed to a similar stick lying on the ground alongside Dan's bed.

"When I was out this morning I found that old stick, there. It was of no use to me. You can have it if you want it. I probably woke you up when I threw it down beside you." Dan stood up and picked the stick up off the ground. It had apparently been a branch on a quaking aspen because it was very light, but it seemed strong as well. It looked as though the rough spots on it had been smoothed and, strangely, it had a good feel in his hands.

"Thanks, Billy. What's it for, and don't tell me udu'vuts."

"Call it a poking stick. You poke around under branches, and bushes, and rocks, and things to see what's there. Or you could call it a walking stick to help you up and down mountains. Then, maybe it's a snake stick." Billy laughed. "When you're carrying it and you see a snake, you can reach out and move your little brother away from you so he does not strike you as you pass by."

Dan could not keep the good humor from rising up in him. "Speaking of snakes, I wish I could get an answer from you that was straighter than a snake's back."

"Udu'vuts," Billy said and chuckled some more. Dan asked if the Paiute had a name for such a stick. "Yes," Billy said looking suddenly serious. "Translating from Paiute, the name for it is, stick," he said and burst into almost uncontrollable laughter. Then pointing to the glow over the mountains, he said, "We must hurry, it is almost time."

He walked a few yards out of camp, went to a clearing which offered a majestic view of the flats below and mountains off to each side as well as behind him. He sat cross-legged and laid his stick alongside of him. "Sit, if that is something you'd care to do," he said. Dan sat and waited. In a few minutes, the first ray of the sun burst over the mountaintop off to their left. Billy picked up his stick and started chanting first in one direction, and then another. He used his stick to pound the earth along-side his feet in rhythm with his chanting. As his feet moved him from place to place the stick kept its cadence as he continued to chant.

Dan noticed that much of the chant was a repetition of a string of syllables said over and over again. Finally he stood up, copied as much of the chant as he could, and used his stick to keep the cadence as well. Billy stopped chanting for a moment. He looked down at Dan's stick, and Dan looked down, not knowing what to expect. Billy reached for Dan's stick and turned it over so the smallest end was up. Then he held the stick out at arms length. "A tree grows this way," he said. .

Dan held the stick out as Billy had done. "A tree grows this way," he repeated, as Billy had done. And when Billy began chanting again, Dan kept the small end of the stick pointing up.

Billy stopped as abruptly as he'd started. He reached over, picked up his rifle, and headed for camp. "It doesn't matter," Billy said. Dan just smiled, he knew one outrageous thing or another was coming. Billy looked at his sheep up on the hillside. "It doesn't matter so much what you say. We were chanting beauty into the world, and the words are not as important as your experiencing the spirit and beauty of things as you chant."

They had deer steak for breakfast. Dan asked Billy to talk about chanting beauty into the world. Without preliminaries, Billy picked up his now empty galvanized plate and banged it suddenly on the table. Dan jumped. "If the noise woke you, maybe you'll see things," Billy said.

Dan got the message. He had been so involved in trying to do what Billy was doing, and remembering everything Billy was doing, he had looked at nothing earlier. Dan began looking around. He looked at the valley below with the sun's still long shadows contrasted against the bright areas where the sun shone. High on the mountain top, the dark green of the trees stood luminescent against the deep blue sky. Four huge black ravens came cawing and soaring overhead. Everything was inde-scribably beautiful.

Billy pointed to the ravens. "Remember? Those are the cleaning people," he said matter of factly. Dan continued looking. Even the rocks were beautiful, some with their huge sharp-edged masses recently caved off from the cliffs, and some small and rounded and glistening in the sun.

Billy said that one thing about chanting worried him. Dan asked what that was. "I do not know if there are still others chanting beauty into the world. I have been told that when there is no one left to chant beauty, the beauty will no longer be. That saddens me greatly." Dan acknowl-edged Billy's remark with pursed lips and a nod of the head. He, too, would be saddened. As he continued looking in awe of the great beauty all around him, he began to feel the beauty of the spirits living there as well. In all, it was the most glorious morning he had ever seen. "Udu'vuts."

CHAPTER 20

THINGS ARE DIFFERENT

Elizabeth and her father rode together in the Packard on this trip to Price. He had to attend the Chamber meeting. He was making small talk, but she was brooding about the new problem that was about to ruin her life. He looked at her, "You're not paying attention to a word I'm saying."

She reached her hand to the dashboard to steady herself as he took a curve too fast. "No, Dad. I'm not ignoring you. I heard what you said about the meeting." Then Benton said she could at least nod her head, or grunt, or something. "Sorry, It's just that while you were talking, I was wondering how I could meet my friend at the courthouse."

"Walk, for heaven's sakes. It's not more than half a mile there from the newspaper." She agreed, the exercise would do her good. Then, trying to change the subject away from herself, she asked why the car was called a Packard Twin Six. "Because it has twelve cylinders, six on each side."

She had too much turmoil going on to really care. "Oh," she said, and returned once more to her problem. "Please, God. Don't let me be pregnant." But she knew she was. When Dan made love to her, her period was somewhere around a week overdue. But that was not unusual. She had been late many times, and usually didn't give it a second thought. This morning she threw up.

She began to mentally count up the time. Her trouble began the night she left college, and she was here about a month before the strike started. The strike had been on over two weeks. That meant she was around a month and a half pregnant. Baby would come in late November.

How she had wished she hadn't given in to Michael's pleading that last night before she left college. What a mess. Maybe if she could get back to Colorado, she could have the baby, give it up for adoption, and no one would ever know. She looked at her father, desperation in her voice. "Dad, I can't stay here. I just can't. You've got to send me back to Colorado."

"That's a closed issue!" Benton said, and the anger in his voice told her it was no use pushing it. But for Elizabeth, it was not a closed issue. She would either have to leave to hide her shame, or kill herself. In Glenwood Springs when a friend had a child out of wedlock, the entire town ostracized her and the girl's mother committed suicide. Now, I'll really have to run away, she thought, returning to her plan the first day she got here. I'll get in my Star, and take off. No one will have any idea where I've gone. She could leave a note telling her family not to look for her. I'll say when I know what I am going to do with my life, I'll tell them where I am.

Then she began to worry that perhaps they would still find her if she were with a friend of hers. But if not to friends, where else could she go? She had heard about societies that helped young girls in trouble. She tried to remember the name of one in Denver she'd heard about, but it had slipped her memory. No matter, she thought, I can find it. She would have to save some money, but that wasn't going to be too hard. It would be a few months yet before she started to show. Some of the panic began to subside. She could take her time, make her plans, and not leave before she had to. That way, she would not be gone so long and maybe nobody would suspect.

When she arrived at the paper, she had another thought. Maybe if I learn enough about newspapers, I could even get a job in Denver to help pay my way. Inside, she got her galleys and asked if there was a desk she might work at for a little while. She quickly glanced at any galleys which might be of use to the union. She read them first.

The first was a United Press wire service item from Indianapolis. Then she came to a galley that shocked her. It was a statement quoting Frank Cameron. He announced that only a small number of the company's employees were affiliated with the UMWA and that no general eviction of strikers was being made. He went on to explain that Utah Fuel only evicts bootleggers, gamblers, agitators of violent methods, and undesirables. Finally, Cameron said in the past week the company had only had to evict probably a half dozen such individuals scattered throughout their various camps. Sure, Elizabeth thought, the liar had already moved everybody else out before that.

Furious as this made her, however, she could not get her mind off her condition. The more she thought about it, the more she began to regret she had ever let Dan make love to her. She regretted even more that at some time she had told him that this was her first experience. It didn't seem much of a lie at the time because it was only her second. Now, however, she knew she could never let him make love to her again. If word somehow got out that she was pregnant, everybody would blame him. She could never ruin his life as hers had been ruined. But what was she to do? If she kept meeting him on union business, everybody would still think the same thing. Her first inclination was to tell the union she had changed her mind, no matter how important she was to them. But then she thought of all those families in the tents. Cameron was proclaiming to the world that they did not exist. She hated him.

Then she began proof-reading other items. After an hour she told Cooper she was going home for the day. She picked up the galleys and said she'd finish them at home. When she arrived at the courthouse, Ann was waiting for her. To keep what was really on her mine from showing on her face, Elizabeth smiled. "Did you know that according to Frank Cameron, the only people Utah Fuel has moved out of company housing are bootleggers, gamblers, and agitators of violent methods?"

Anger flashed across Ann's face. Her words carried an undertone of deep seated anger. "Surprised at discovering the truth according to Frank Cameron, are you?" Ann asked. She spoke Cameron's name with utter contempt. Then, strangely, the sudden emotion faded as fast as it came. Ann grinned, "Come on, lets go get a cup of coffee."

Elizabeth followed her out. "Where are we going?" she asked. Ann said she'd had lunch, but she'd pop for coffee. Elizabeth agreed. Once seated, and coffee ordered, Ann turned to Elizabeth. "I didn't tell you everything about why I quit at The Advocate." Elizabeth's interest was aroused. "I couldn't stay and be part of the lies by the likes of people such as Frank Cameron. But Cooper's nothing but a flunky for the operators. He hunts for anything he can use against unions. He reprints only negative articles from Salt Lake papers or the wire service." Elizabeth sat drinking coffee as she listened. She nodded when Ann offered her a cigarette, and paused to light it. "Every time I think of Frank Cameron, my blood starts to boil," Ann spat.

"With so many things to hate, why Cameron in particular?" Elizabeth asked. A look of sadness came over Ann. She said her dad was killed in the Winter Quarters mine when she was ten. Elizabeth could see Ann's grief. "I'm sorry. What happened?"

Unable to be consoled, Ann pulled her hands gently away from Elizabeth. "Cameron suspected Dad of being a union man. He put Dad to work pulling pillars with another guy they suspected." Again Elizabeth said she was sorry. "One week before Dad was sent there, the State Mine Inspector had declared that section of the mine unsafe for men to work in." Elizabeth was aghast. "Do people go to jail for that?"

Ann's laugh was bitter. She spoke coldly, every detail of the event burned into her memory. "Justice of the Peace W. W. Mackintosh held a coroner's inquest. The three members of the coroner's jury were Horace Parry, J. P. Curtin, and James Adams. Every single one of them were paid employees of a coal company." Ann took a couple of sips of coffee. She puffed her cigarette, pursed her lips, and blew out a thin stream of smoke. "They ruled it was my dad's fault. They ruled he came to his death 'by negligence in not protecting himself, and being in a part of the mine he should not be in at the time.'"

Elizabeth couldn't believe it. Angrily, she stubbed her cigarette out in the ash tray. "But he had no choice, Ann. If he hadn't gone to work where Cameron said he had to, he'd get fired."

Ann paused. She drank some coffee. "Welcome to the wonderful world of Carbon county and Utah Fuel," she said. "After Dad died, Utah Fuel was so very kind as to let my mother run their boarding house. She nearly worked herself to death, but the little money she got kept us alive. Then . . ." Ann paused. She used her old cigarette to light a new one. She puffed the cigarette, sipped from her coffee cup, and looked hard at Elizabeth. "There is no way I should tell you this, but heaven knows I've got to tell somebody." Ann put her coffee cup down, and laid her cigarette in the ash tray. She looked into Elizabeth's eyes. "Then, when I was fifteen, the Super called me in and reminded me how hard my mother had worked all those years. He said how truly sorry he would be to have to let her go, unless . . ."

A sick feeling began to come over Elizabeth. "Unless what?"

"Oh, come on Elizabeth. Do I have to spell it out for you? I shouldn't let it bother me so much after all these years." She shuddered. "But I can't stop thinking about it, even now. That fat old man." Ann lit a cigarette with the half-finished one she still had in her hand. She seemed to be trying to put that memory behind her. Finally, bitterness still in her voice, "After the first time I couldn't stay there and let him do it to me again."

In rapid order, Ann told her how she'd lied to her mother. Told her she couldn't stand Winter Quarters any more, went to stay with a relative in Price, and finished high school.

Elizabeth sat quietly for awhile. She didn't know what to say. Finally, she looked at Ann, and tears formed in Elizabeth's eyes. She mumbled how sorry she was, and reached out once more to take Ann's hands in hers. This time Ann did not pull back. A sickened look came to her features. "I can't tell details, but sometimes I still have to work with scum such as that. I hate 'em all."

Thinking Ann was speaking of the people at the Chamber of Commerce, Elizabeth began to get another idea. Elizabeth leaned over so no one else could hear even though the cafe was practically empty. In a quiet voice, she asked, "How would it be to be able to get back at them for a change?" Ann looked eager. Elizabeth knew she should check with someone else first. But in so doing she could never tell them the intensely personal information Ann had shared about herself. Elizabeth plunged ahead, boldly. "A while ago, you told me something no one else knows. I trust you as much," she paused for effect, "I'm a union spy."

"What?" Ann asked, not comprehending what Elizabeth just told her. "What do you do?"

"I'm just starting, but I let the union know what the paper will print before its published."

Ann was almost jumping up and down with excitement. "What a good idea. I wish I'd thought of it," she said, paused, and looked around. "That's ironic, and I'd be getting back at them in ways you couldn't even imagine. But let's get out of here. I want to hear all about it."

Elizabeth didn't protest as Ann left a tip and paid the tab. They left the cafe, and found one of the benches outside the depot to sit on. As soon as they were seated, Elizabeth's brows furrowed as she developed the idea. "There's no question you get to see and hear stuff the Chamber is doing that the union would want to know." Ann said it happened all the time since they're always trying to get at the union, one way or another. Elizabeth was thrilled. She waved off a cigarette Ann proffered. "Naturally, I'll have to check with the right people, but they'll accept you or they'll lose me. From this moment on, consider yourself a union informer as well."

Ann stood up. "I'm a little late. Let's start walking back. When can I meet your contact?"

"You can't. We've got to be real sneaky about this. You can imagine what would happen to me if we got caught, let alone what would happen to him. I really don't know the best way for you to help, but I'll ask today." Just then, the Packard pulled up, Benton honked his horn.

"Got to go," Elizabeth said. "You'll be hearing from me very soon." Ann said good-bye, and waved as Elizabeth got in the car. She was as preoccupied on the way home as she had been on the way down. What to do? Meet Dan tonight. How? I could have Cyclone get a message to Steve. But how can I get out to meet him on such short notice? She thought fast.

"Dad, what did you think of the new secretary for the Chamber of Commerce?" Her father said she seemed very attractive but he hadn't pay a lot of attention to her. "She's the girl Mom and I went to breakfast with the other day," Elizabeth said, then decided to throw in an extra zinger. "Mom really likes her. Would it be okay with you if I went back down there this evening to have supper with her? She says Bishop some-body or other will be speaking at the Methodist church tonight, and she invited me to come." Her dad didn't even pause to consider it, and said it was nice she was starting to make friends here.

When she got home, she went up to the stables to exercise Bonnie. She told Cyclone what had happened with Ann. Of course she left out a lot of the details, such as what had happened to Ann when she was only fifteen. Cyclone seemed excited about the prospects for this new help for the union. She arranged it with Cyclone to tell Steve that she would be waiting for Dan at the usual place half an hour after dark. Once done, there was nothing to do but wait.

While she waited, she hand-copied the important points from the galleys to give to Dan. There were three different reports on coal production. Elizabeth supposed that by showing what little demand there was for coal, and how much was being mined, they could discourage the union. Taken together it almost seemed as though the companies were saying the strike was having no effect at all. When it was time to leave, she got in her Star and headed out. When she got there, he had already arrived, unsaddled Turk, and was sitting on a rock.

It upset Elizabeth that he looked so happy. The first words out of his mouth as he got in the car were, "When you didn't come to see me the last few days, I thought maybe something was wrong. I thought maybe you weren't coming. Are you angry with me?"

Figuring that there was no better time than right now to do what she had to do, she began. "No, Dan, I'm not angry. But what happened the other night must never happen again."

Dan looked shocked. "Why? You really are mad at me, aren't you?"

"No, Dan, I'm not angry with you. But I have reasons I can't tell you." Dan looked desperate. Stung by her words, he pressed to find out what he'd done wrong. He wanted to find out why. First he asked if she didn't like him, or was it because he was a miner?

Elizabeth felt no joy in what she had to say. She knew it would hurt him, and it wasn't his fault. While she couldn't explain, at least he deserved to know the fault was hers, not his. "Dan, it would surprise you how much I care for you. Given how different we are, I wouldn't have believed it possible. But you don't know me. If I let you love me, it'd ruin your life." Dan insisted nothing could stop him from loving her. Nothing Elizabeth could say could shake his conviction that there was something wrong with him, or that he'd done something wrong.

She gave up. "Fine, no matter what I say you won't believe it's not your fault. But in a couple of months I will be going away. You might as well know it right now. I don't have any choice in the matter." Elizabeth's eyes quickly filled with tears. "Oh, Dan," she said. "It's so hopeless."

Dan reached out, took her in his arms and kissed her. She did not pull back. He finished the kiss, and then held her back at arms length. "Not only do I love you with all my heart, but you love me as well, or soon will. The Indians have a saying, udu'vuts. It means that's the way things are."

"If only things were diff . . ." she started to say. Uncontrollable sobbing stopped her. Dan tried to kiss her. She pushed him away. "No!" she said emphatically. But her voice held no blame.

That night, he fought for sleep. His turmoil about Elizabeth was an indescribable pain in his heart, his soul, his very being, such as he never knew existed. And it got worse as time went on. For the next month the union had him meet her three times a week. Every time they met, he would tell her how much he loved her, and she'd tell him she'd be leaving soon.

On their last meeting Elizabeth began to sob "I hate you, Dan Cook," she screamed. "You said I would fall in love with you and I have. It will break my heart when I have to leave."

"Then don't go. Please!" He'd begged, but to no avail. Then she added what was most hurtful of all. She said she would be leaving in a month. So, once again as he had so often lately, he thought of the mess they were in. And again, he said a silent prayer he had said a hundred times, "Please, God, don't let her go."

Next morning Dan had nothing to do for the day. He wasn't standing security watch. It wasn't his turn to man a picket line, so he decided on doing what he usually did at such times. He would visit Billy. But this time he would take two food baskets up to him. Dan busied himself gathering things he figured Billy would enjoy. In addition to what he could scrounge elsewhere, one Italian lady even gave him a freshly baked loaf of Italian bread. In all, there were cans of fruit, a small sack of beans, a small sack of rice, a can of coffee, a tin of tea, two jars of strawberry jam, the loaf of home-made bread, and two dozen fresh eggs.

What made Dan want to see Billy this particular day was not Billy's good humor. Dan was in no mood for that. Nor was it Billy's teaching him the ways of the Paiute. Sometimes Dan felt Billy's stories only made it harder for him to live in his own society. It was Billy's aura of peace and self certainty that Dan sought. He paid little attention to guiding his horse, but Turk had been this way before. Dan sat on him in deep reverie thinking about Elizabeth and feeling anguish about it all. He didn't pull himself out of this trance-like state until he saw Billy, stick in hand, standing at the head of the trail.

Dan dismounted, put the baskets on the ground and unsaddled Turk. He couldn't contain the anguish in his soul. "Billy, I'm so confused," he started almost immediately. "I'm in trouble, and I want your advice on what to do." But Billy held up his hand to stop him, and fished for his pipe. Sure enough, in a moment Billy was fanning smoke toward himself.

"Are you sure you don't smoke?" Billy asked. Then without waiting for an answer, he said, "Too bad. We really need to smoke together." He stopped, looked pensive, and Dan waited. Finally, Billy started speaking again. "It has been said that when Mother Earth is already working with someone who has a problem, it is not wise for another to offer opinions."

Dan walked over by the fire and sat on his rock. He was getting sick of this. There was no one else in the world he could turn to, and now Billy wouldn't even listen to what his troubles were.

Billy came over, sat on the log, and looked up at his sheep. "A friend once told me, we never need to wonder what Mother Earth is doing now, we need only look. When we look hard enough we see that everything is Mother Earth."

Dan was quiet for a moment. He tried to look as Billy was suggesting. It was hopeless. He didn't even really know what looking meant. He considered for a moment that everything was Mother Earth. He really didn't know what this meant either, but somehow it all made him feel better.

Billy tilted his head to one side. "Sometimes I find it useful to look at what people are doing instead of what they are saying. Especially when they are saying one thing and doing another." Dan moved from the rock to the ground, and crossed his legs. Billy got up for more wood. "Sometimes we think we know how things are going to turn out because of the way they seem now," Billy said as he put the wood on the fire. "I find that no matter how they seem now, everything ends up according to Mother Earth's plan."

Billy looked over to where the saddle was. "What do you have in those baskets?" When Dan told him it was food, and Billy asked what kind, Dan smiled. "What I thought you would enjoy."

As Dan went to get the baskets, Billy put more wood on the fire. Dan carried the baskets over and put them on the camp table. "All of it is yours. It is a gift from the people in Tent Town. It's Mother Earth's plan," he added. Billy looked very pleased. Even his wrinkles seemed to be smiling. Without saying anything else, from one basket Dan got out one of the jars of jam, a can of peaches, and the loaf of bread. From the other he got out the eggs and the can of coffee. He opened the peaches and the jam, and then began using his hunting knife to cut the bread.

"It will be nice to have fresh coffee grounds. I'll make some coffee, and fry the eggs," Billy said and grabbed the empty coffee pot sitting beside the fire. As they ate, Billy made such noises of enjoyment over the fruit, bread, and jam, Dan began to feel better.

As they finished eating, Billy looked at Dan. "I have already told you how my people felt this land was cursed, and left. Mother Earth sent me back to this country to chant the old chants, to sing the old songs, and to dance the old dances. There is much joy in my heart that Mother Earth lets me do this. I tell you this because I know my time is very short. Mother Earth has told me so. I also have great joy in my heart to have lived so long, and seen so much. I have great enthusiasm as I follow the river which leads to the path of the spirits."

Dan's heart started to knot up. Once again the pain was intense, just as it was each time Elizabeth said she was leaving. What in God's good green earth could Mother Earth's plan be in Billy leaving? Then, he realized Billy had already told him he was old. Old things die, udu'vuts. But Elizabeth is young, she's full of life. The thought, full of life, seemed almost to scream at him. That was it!!! Elizabeth was pregnant!

Billy got up for more wood. "I must tend my sheep, now," Billy said, as Dan was about to speak. "It soothes me to remember that the river which leads to the path of the spirits is called life."

Dan knew what path he would follow with Elizabeth, but Billy was a different matter. "Billy, some of the things you say worry me. Will I see you again?"

Billy laughed. "I am old, my memory is poor. I don't remember you telling me the answer to the question Mother Earth sent me to find. Please refresh my memory."

Dan laughed also. "But if my not giving you the answer to your question is what's keeping you here, I'm never going to tell you."

"Yes you will," Billy said, looking into the fire. "You really have no choice."

Billy was still smiling. "Now I must tend my sheep." Sadly, Dan took the empty baskets, saddled his horse, waved to Billy who was rummaging around in his tent. As he started down the trail, the sound of flute music floated from behind him and enveloped all in front of him. As Dan rode away and the beautiful flute music faded, he figured out what to tell Elizabeth the next time they met. He would tell her that people say the first child can come any time, the second takes nine months. Then he would arrange the marriage he hoped Mother Earth had planned for them.

CHAPTER 21

ONE GOOD REASON

Elizabeth sat at a desk at The Advocate and pretended she was correcting the galleys. But her mind was elsewhere. The emotional pain she felt kept her skipping from one terrible thing to another. *What's the use of wishing I don't love Dan? What's the use of wishing I weren't pregnant?* Thoughts of moving to Colorado were awful. Yet she must, and soon. *She'd never love anyone as she loved Dan. But there was no other way. I'm going crazy. I've thought these same things over and over a thousand times, and every time I end up more miserable than before.*

If she told Dan she was pregnant, she was sure he would marry her, but when the baby was born early, he'd know she'd lied to him and the baby was not his, and hate her for it. Or at least, he would wonder about it the rest of his life, and never really trust her again. Either way, what chance would there be for real happiness now? *If only she could abort.*

Finally, it was time for lunch with Ann, but even this held no joy for her. She wanted to be alone, but being alone was driving her crazy. Then another thought crossed her mind. She would tell Ann, and at least hear what Ann had to say. That might help. But she knew she wouldn't. She was too ashamed. There was just nothing to do but to go ahead with her plans for Colorado. *I'm going out of my mind! I've got to stop thinking about this,* she vowed once again.

"Warn your people to watch out," Ann said as they settled around a table at the Queen City Inn. "I'm catching pieces here and there that the supers are going to step up the action."

They waited until the waitress brought their water, and left the menus. "What do you mean, step up the action?" Elizabeth asked when the waitress left. Ann said it was nothing she could put her finger on, but plans to get the Guard definitely weren't working.

"What it's going to take is some violence. They're going to start it and blame it on the union." When the waitress came, they ordered veal cutlets. "Everybody is complaining about the cost of the deputies. They're in a real panic," Ann continued, getting out a cigarette and lighting it.

"They're going to have a hard time manufacturing an incident they can throw blame with," Elizabeth said. "The union has been hounding their men not to get egged into any violence." The waitress returned with the salads and coffee. As they began to eat, Elizabeth felt a little queasy. This salad dressing tastes so greasy. I hope I don't throw up.

Elizabeth couldn't stand it any more. Her eyes flitted back and forth. She turned as red as the tomato in her salad. She looked at Ann. "I'm pregnant," she blurted out in desperation. Then she began to cry softly. "I'm so ashamed. What can I do?"

Ann stopped eating in mid bite. She thought for a moment. "No problem. Marry Dan. There is a saying around here that any girl who reaches twenty and isn't pregnant hasn't been drinking Carbon County water." Elizabeth felt her face flushing. It was too late to turn back now. She told Ann the child wasn't his.

"Oh, no! Whose is it?"

Elizabeth explained how on the last night of college she had let a boy make love to her. When Ann said to marry him, Elizabeth said that was impossible. The waitress came with the cutlets.

Ann leaned forward, and lowered her voice. "No problem. Marry Dan. Tell him it's his."

Elizabeth had gone over these arguments in her mind a hundred times. "He'll know, when it's born eight months after I first let him make love to me."

"So? Maybe you'll be lucky and it will come a little late. Anyway, if you don't tell him, he can never know for sure." Ann took a taste of the cutlet, and dropped her fork on her plate. Elizabeth hadn't even pretended she was going to eat. She said with her luck it would probably come early. And even if Dan didn't know, he would always suspect.

"So?" Ann said, "Life is hard. Besides, what other choice do you have? You can't have the baby without getting married. Your life around here would be unbearable."

Elizabeth told Ann of her plan to run away and put the child up for adoption. Ann decided to try the cutlet again. She chewed a couple of times, swallowed, dropped her fork on the plate once more, and looked at Elizabeth. "We already know more about each other than anyone else in the world. I won't let you run away alone. If you go, I'm going with you."

Relief flooded Elizabeth. This was something she hadn't thought about. She wouldn't have to be all alone. "Oh, Ann! Would you really do that?" Ann said she would, but it made more sense to marry Dan. Worry was back on Elizabeth's face. "He'd know, and think I'm a slut."

Ann said she wasn't hungry and suggested they go where they could talk without interruption. Elizabeth agreed. Ann took Elizabeth's hand. "Even if Dan thought that, and I doubt it, would that be worse than giving up the child in your belly, and feeling guilty the rest of your life?"

Elizabeth sat upright in her chair. Until now, this was another thing she had not considered. But Ann was right. Of late she sometimes stopped thinking of it as a thing, and thought of it as "my baby." Now it was clear. Any decision she made would affect the baby as well. After leaving the Queen City, the girls sat in the Star to talk. Elizabeth finally noticed that all they accomplished was to go the rounds over and over again on the same things she'd been thinking of for weeks. Parting, Ann urged Elizabeth to consider what would be the most sensible thing.

All the way back to the paper, however, one thing uppermost in Elizabeth's mind was Ann's question. Was it better to have Dan think she was a slut, or give her baby up? By the time she got there, she was clear on one thing. She now only had two options. One would be to marry Dan and hide from him it was not his, so that he could love it. And the other was to go to Denver, have her baby and keep it. Somehow, with Ann's help, she would make a life for her child. If Ann went with her, Eizabeth felt she would have a fighting chance.

Back at the paper, she gathered up the galleys she still had to correct. She told Mr. Cooper that she would be leaving, but he asked her to wait a minute. "While you were out to lunch that agitator from Wyoming was in here to get me to print the union's demands for settling the strike. I sent him on his way. The typesetter is just finishing my response. Take it with you."

Outside, Elizabeth sat in her Star, and read the galley. She was anxious to find out who the "outside agitator" had been. The headline read, "No Outside Advice Needed. An imported parasite from Wyoming, whose name we did not catch, and for which we did not give a rap, visited *The News Advocate* to tell us how to run the paper." She was disappointed there was no name in the article. But the reference to Wyoming meant it could only have been Morgan or Ramsey. The rest of the editorial went on to say he was politely told to go to the dickens. Then it said, "An impartial, respectful, and courteous hearing would be given to any committee of bonafide Carbon County miners level headed and disposed to obey the law, but we have no time to waste on hired agitators."

The worst was the last part, however. "These outsiders claim they are running the strike in Carbon County and that the lawless and foreign element will follow them. Therefore, women and children are being shot at on public highways, and men are being intimidated. The suffering public can draw its own conclusions as to who is responsible. As for foreigners who care nothing for the law and for human life, they cannot tell *The News Advocate* anything about the strike or anything else."

She started the car, put it in gear and headed out of town. She was anxious to get this information to Dan. She stopped at their meeting place and Dan came toward the passenger side of the car. Elizabeth reached over and rolled down the window. "Don't get in the car," she said.

"Elizabeth, we have to talk."

"Then come on around to my side where we can talk. I've got a couple of things to tell you. Then I have to be going." She rolled down the window on her side as Dan walked around. Dan was not smiling. He listened intently as she told him about Ann's warning and the editorial. "Got to go now," she said when she finished. She started rolling up her window.

"Elizabeth, I know you're pregnant," he blurted out before she had the window even half way up.

How did he know? "Who told you?" she asked angrily. Ann was the only one she confided in about her pregnancy. Dan put both hands on the window. He said nobody had to tell him. It was just the only thing that made sense. What now? Elizabeth worried. If he knows, who else has figured it out? She had to get out of Sunnyside before everyone knew. "Get in the car," she commanded. "Your knowing doesn't change anything. I'm still leaving."

Hope faded from Dan's face. Once inside the car, Dan turned to her with love in his eyes. "You can't leave. I love you. We'll get married."

She felt no joy in his suggestion, "Impossible," she said. Dan said that was ridiculous and that people got married every day. Flustered, Elizabeth considered it for a moment. But the possibility raised too many questions. "How would you support us? Where would we live?"

Now Dan's manner turned confident. "The strike has to be over soon. We'll move back into town. I'll work hard to make extra money. I'll finish high school, and maybe go to college."

Still hesitant, Elizabeth asked another question that burned within her. "Why do you want to marry me?" Dan just shook his head. He couldn't believe she could ask this question. He asked her to deny how many times he'd said he loved her. "It's just puppy love, you'll get over it," she retorted. Dan fidgeted on the car seat. Then he asked her if she didn't mean it when she said she loved him too. Now it was Elizabeth's turn to fidget. "Dan, it's true, I do love you, but . . ."

Dan interrupted her. "Is that puppy love?"

Again, for the second time today, Elizabeth was taken back. Dan's question made her realize the depths of her love for him. Her love was not puppy love. It was real and lasting. "No, it isn't puppy love. It's something else. It's pain. All loving you has brought me is pain in my heart."

Dan hung his head. He could not argue. His loving her had been the source of pain in his own heart. He looked deep into her eyes. His voice filled with certainty.

"I admit our love brings pain," he agreed. "But, Elizabeth, think how much worse that pain will get if you leave." Dan paused to let that sink in. "When are we going to get married?"

How I wish it were that simple, Elizabeth thought. She reached out and touched his arm. "Dan, I can't answer that right now. There is so much to consider. Could you give me a little time?"

Dan felt an explosion of joy. She hadn't said no. He couldn't help the good humor in his voice as he answered her. "Sure, take all the time you need. Up to eight months or so." Elizabeth was still in such turmoil, she never even noticed the joke. She told him one of the reasons she needed time was to find out what her family would think about it. She reminded him if her dad didn't agree to it, he'd fire Dan's dad. Joy gone, Dan thought fast. "Why'd you bring that up?" he asked, petulantly. "Besides, he'll find out anyway as soon as you start showing."

Elizabeth challenged with "Not if I leave before then." Dan had the sudden urge to cut his tongue out for that last remark. Now I've got her thinking about leaving again. "We'll find a way. We've got to," he said.

As they parted, Elizabeth told him to be patient for just a couple of days, and Dan promised he would. By the time she got home, Elizabeth's mind was almost made up. Ann was probably right. What other chance did she really have? Maybe in the end Dan would turn against her and the baby. But she was becoming so sure of his love that she doubted it. He's a good man.

Once inside her house Elizabeth rushed to her mother. "Mom, we have to talk."

"Yes, dear," her mother said. "Now's as good a time as any. What is it, you look so serious."

With fear in her heart, Elizabeth just blurted it out, "Dan Cook wants to marry me."

"That's nice. I'm so relieved."

"Mom! I tell you I'm going to get married, and all you can say is you're relieved?" Her mother just smiled and asked if Elizabeth really thought she could hide what she did most mornings in the bathroom. She reminded Elizabeth she'd had a child and recognized the symptoms. Elizabeth rushed to her mother and threw her arms around her. "Why didn't you tell me you knew? There are so many things we need to talk about."

Elizabeth's mother looked sad about not having talked with her daughter. "I figured you'd tell me when you could. I didn't want to make things worse for you."

Elizabeth dropped her head. She told her mother it couldn't be much worse. Her mother put her arm about Elizabeth's shoulder. "It worried me when you didn't tell me. Now you've told me. I'll stop worrying about you running away."

Elizabeth was astonished at how much better her mother knew her than Elizabeth ever dreamed. She turned to hug her mom. "You mean . . ." Elizabeth started to say, but broke into tears. She held tight to her mother. She finally got herself under control. "You're not ashamed of me?"

Katherine didn't need to pretend understanding and forgiveness. "Why would I be ashamed of a daughter who's done nothing in her life that didn't happen to me?"

"You?" Elizabeth asked, aghast that her mother would confide this.

"I love your father, and he loves me. I only hope you and Dan love each other as much. Beautiful."

Beautiful or not, Elizabeth knew she wasn't out of the woods yet. "But, Mom, how can I tell Dad? You know how he feels about Dan, and he'd fire Mr. Cook for sure."

A tone of assertiveness crept into Katherine's voice. "I think not. You leave your dad to me, Honey. You and I have too many other things to start planning. You shouldn't have to worry about him." After her dad came home, Elizabeth did all she reasonably could to stay out of his way. She did not want to say or do anything that would make it harder for her mother to talk to him. But the dreadful scene she was expecting never took place.

Maybe she will tell him when they go to bed, Elizabeth reasoned. As time passed, she became more sure of it. When finally she went to bed, she lay straining to hear any sign of the uproar she knew would come. She supposed her mother was waiting till tomorrow.

Katherine turned over in bed and looked at her husband. "Bob, do you remember how violently my parents were against you marrying me?" A slight look of concern showed this unexpected question disturbed Benton's mood as he said he did. Katherine reached over, and put her hand on her husband's arm. "Honey, what would you do if Elizabeth said she wanted to marry Dan?"

Benton shot upright in bed. His eyes glared outrage. He hissed when he spoke. "No! I'll give her a hundred reasons why she can't, and..." But his wife interrupted him. Katherine smiled her most engaging smile. "Honey, I can give you one good reason why she should, and why you will do nothing to stop it."

BOOK III

WHAT TROUBLEMAKER
REALLY MEANS

CHAPTER 22

WHAT TROUBLEMAKER REALLY MEANS

Benton was furious. Last night his family had dropped their little bombshell. This morning he was told half a dozen scabs sneaked out of town, cutting the trickle of coal the mine was producing even more. He sat at his desk, drumming his fingers waiting for everyone to arrive for the emergency meeting. As each came in, he just glared at them, Mitch arriving last.

Benton glared at each man individually. "Okay," he said finally, "what happened?" Nervously, Rasmussen explained the men must have evaded the search-light, weren't seen by the patrol, and got by the guard shack. Benton exploded. "What am I paying you for?"

Rasmussen blinked a couple of times. He began looking at his feet. "Boss, we're staffed to keep men away from the mine workings, not to keep men in." Benton clenched and unclenched his fists on top of the desk. His anger was not eased. "Boss," Rasmussen continued, "it'd take an army to cover every way out. There's a hundred ways if somebody goes along the mountainside."

Benton's knuckles were turning white. "Get wise, Ovie! You're telling me we'll be losing men any time they want to go, and there's not a thing we can do to stop it?" Rasmussen said the only answer was to seal the town with a fence, then patrol to make sure nobody cuts it or goes over it. "Ovie, you know that would cost a fortune." Rasmussen argued it'd been done in other strikes. The excuse was always to protect the workings from stikers, but everybody knew the real reason.

Abe Strang leaned forward in his seat. "Okay, Abe, spit it out." Strang said it wouldn't cost all that much if his men did it, and they ran it straight across the narrowest part of the canyon, with only one open space for the train to get through. That could easily be watched.

Mitch raised his hand. "May I suggest something?" Benton looked at him and nodded. "It would take a little more fence, but if you ran it across the canyon just behind the Guard shack, the men in the shack could watch the train opening as well."

For the first time since he sat down, Benton smiled. What Mitch said was a good idea. He asked if Mitch had any more. No one guessed Mitch wanted the miners who were still working to be fenced in. Discontented men don't load much coal, and it would serve the scabs right. "Just one. If a small fire got started somehow at one of the company sheds, we would have our excuse to put up a fence to keep the saboteurs out." Strength returned to Rasmussen's voice. He added that a fire would be one more excuse for bringing the Guard in.

Benton smiled again. "Good idea, Mitch." Benton's smile became a sly grin. "Now, I wonder which of those scum will be sneaking in here to start a fire?" he asked, and looked directly at Rasmussen. Rasmussen just nodded, almost imperceptibly.

Benton focused on Mitch. Mitch was a good man. He had a good head on his shoulders and Benton trusted him. His eyes flickered for a moment. Trust him? I'll be. . . Bastard Cameron's right again. There was a quick twitch around Benton's eyes.

Webb cleared his throat. Seeing that Rasmussen was in good favor again, Webb decided to put his two-bits in. "Mr. Benton, I suggest starting to put a fence around Tent Town. It might spook them into doing something stupid."

Benton leaned back; he put his hands behind his head and stretched. "Something to think about, Art," he said. "Tell you what, boys. You got four hours to be back in my office with your plans. I'll want to know who'll be doing what, and how long it's going to take you."

He leaned forward on his desk. His voice took on its deadly quality once more as he looked at the men. "But your plans had better not let any more men out of my town. Or I know a bunch of other jobs I'll be filling. Hold on. I'll be right back," he added as they got up to leave.

Benton was gone only a couple of minutes, and when he returned, he sat down, and looked at Rasmussen. "Ovie, Ganz is making you a list of every new man we've hired. Pick it up from him on your way out. Then I want you to go up to the store and tell Sod that I want all purchases charged to those new men. That should take you no more than twenty minutes to a half hour. Then high tail it back here." Rasmussen nodded and he and Webb turned to leave.

Benton's voice could not have been more pleasant. "Mitch, stay a couple of minutes will you?" For an answer, Mitch just sat back down in his chair. Benton began doodling hang man's nooses. Finally he spoke pleasantly to Mitch. "I want you to draw your pay. Be out of town by nightfall."

A sardonic smile crossed Mitch's broad, tough face. "Who told on me?"

"You're good, Mitch. I got to give you that. After your suggestions about the fence and the fire I was sitting there thinking you seemed to have the best head on your shoulders of anybody here. Too bad you're not on our side. I trusted you."

Mitch stood up. "I guess you're not going to tell me who ratted on me. Oh, well, see you later."

Mitch started out. "As I said, you're good," Benton declared, then added, "but we're better."

As Mitch left, his first thought was just to run for it. No way he was going to let Benton sucker him into stopping at the paymaster to draw his pay. But he'd heard Benton tell Rasmussen to be back in twenty minutes. That would give him ten minutes to throw his stuff in a bag. Once he got moving, they'd never catch him. He ran all the way to the boarding house.

Sue Fuller looked at him wide-eyed. "Get out of here, quick," she hissed. Mitch looked up, and saw Young and Webb coming out of the kitchen, their faces contorted with hatred. He turned to run back out the door, but two more goons were coming in that way. He was trapped. His mind racing, he headed for a corner where they couldn't all get to him at once.

In the second it took them to get to him, Mitch knew he'd been set up. When Benton left the office before the meeting broke up, he'd left a note for Rasmussen. Then Benton had talked with Mitch long enough so that Rasmussen could get things arranged. Mitch knew it was hopeless. But, by damned, before they get me, I'll show them what trouble-maker really means.

Young was the first one to Mitch. Young was carrying an eighteen inch piece of lead pipe. When he raised it to strike, Mitch jabbed his fingers into Young's eyes. Young screamed, dropped the pipe, and jerked his hand to his face. Webb jabbed a fist toward's Mitch's face. Mitch ducked under it, snatched the pipe from the floor, and smashed Webb's knee with it on the way up. As he straightened up, he saw Webb fall to the ground, then begin unbuttoning the flap on his holster. Mitch threw the pipe so hard Webb howled in pain as the pipe hit his chest. Mitch's eyes flitted around, looking for another weapon. He grabbed a nearby chair, then holding it in front of him, chair legs forward, he charged the two men rushing toward him from the front door.

Stunned by the quickness of Mitch's movements, the two men jumped aside so as not to be impaled by the chair legs. The force of Mitch's charge carried him between them, and right on out the open front door. He threw the chair away as he hit the porch running. Shocked, he saw a horse saddled and waiting in front of the boarding house.

Mitch scooped up the reins, and bolted into the saddle. He turned the horse, kicked it hard in the flanks, and the horse took off at a dead run. Movement off to his left caught his eye, and he saw Cyclone high tailing it back to the corral. Mitch wasn't sure whether he felt the bee sting in his shoulder first, or heard the gunshot first, but he knew he'd been hit. He began zig zagging the horse to confuse their aim as more shots blasted the air behind him. He looked back and saw them running, but the speed of the horse was losing them fast. The guard shack, Mitch thought. Now the guard shack. What to do? Then, almost as though he'd planned it out before, he headed for the creek. He jumped the horse off the bank into the stream of water below, and went racing along the bed of the creek. He went unnoticed by the guard shack, passing below their line of vision. Hey, Mitch thought, I could move an army past them here, and they'd never know it. He reached for the pommel of the saddle to steady himself as the horse stumbled on a rock. His hand slid off the wet pommel. Mitch looked down. The pommel was covered with blood. So was the front of him. He was getting unsteady in the saddle. He pulled the horse to a walk.

He looked at all the blood. Must've been hit something bad. He was having a hard time seeing. He began to lose feeling. They got me after all. Better'n getting beat to death.

He fell out of the saddle and lay face down in the creek. The water carried away even more of his precious blood, and even that warmth Mitch had been so famous for.

The goons finally got there, picked up his body, and rushed it surreptitiously to the guard shack. It'd be kept there till they got their story straight on what happened. Making a case against Mitch wasn't going to be too hard. Doc bandaged Young's eye, and Webb would limp for a month.

The next morning, Dan had to wait for Steve way too long. Something was wrong.

At noon, Elizabeth's car came up the road with dust boiling up from each side. She would blow her cover for sure. As she came by him she barely slowed; her window open. "They've sealed the town," she called as she went by. Going a little further, she made a U turn and came back. Dan could see she was crying. "Mitch is dead. Meet me by Big Spring."

Dan didn't believe it. Mitch dead? Nah, she couldn't have said that. But Elizabeth's tears and her voice demanded he believe it. He waited till Eizabeth was back on the main road. If anyone was watching, he didn't want it to seem she said something to him.

How could it be? Tom, Frank, and John were waiting. They'd seen Elizabeth's car.

"What's up?" Tom called before Dan even got to them.

"Mitch is dead," he called back. "And Benton sealed the town."

"Mine accident?" Frank asked, hopefully, as Dan stopped alongside them.

"Don't know," Dan said, and wiped a tear from his eyes. "Got to meet Elizabeth at Big Spring road. Find out then."

Tom said he would go with Dan to get the information. Then Dan would go down to give the information to Andy's pickets at Mounds. Tom would bring the word back to camp. They rushed to the stables and saddled their horses. A sudden disturbance on the road through camp caught their attention. Tom mounted, and the two of them rode out to see what the trouble was. A crowd of men were gathered around a car that'd just come back into camp. Frank was waiting.

Frank looked irate. "Six men were turned back by Benton's goons who've blocked the road to Price at Twelve Mile. The goons said nobody'd be let in or out of Tent Town." Just then another uproar at the front of the camp caught their attention. They headed in that direction. The goons were building a fence.

"Ride on up there and see what's up, Dan," Tom said. "They like your dad. Maybe they'll talk with you." Dan rode toward the men. Lorenzo Young, with a white patch over one eye and the other blurry from Mitch's last desperate contribution, strutted out with a rifle pointed at Dan.

"Hold it right there!" Young commanded. "If you want to know about that scum Mitch Saxton, little messenger boy, get back and tell them that he was caught stealing company powder. He'd take more from the powder sheds than he signed for. He was stashing it in the boarding house to blow up the tipple. Sue Fuller found it." Ugly didn't describe the look on Young's face.

Young started speaking again. "Tell that scum of yours, Saxton assaulted the deputies when they tried to arrest him, and they killed him in self defense."

Dan clenched his fist. Young cocked his rifle. Dan looked with hate-filled eyes at Young. "You're lying, and you know it. Mitch Saxton didn't steal any powder. You murdered him."

Instead of the attack he'd expected from Young, the man just smiled slyly. "Everybody knew you'd all say that. But we got company books and witnesses about the powder. As to his resisting arrest, he almost blinded me, crippled Art, and bruised two of Art's ribs with a pipe he had. We can prove it wasn't murder. Now get on back and tell your scum. And tell 'em we're building a fence to pen them in like the pigs they are."

Dan rode back to camp, and people bunched around to hear his news. He gave them Young's message. An uproar followed. Some screamed the company was getting away with murder. Others swore they would not be penned in like pigs. The biggest problem, however, came from the ones who were going for their guns to avenge Mitch.

Suddenly a shot rang out. As Dan's head jerked toward the source of the noise, others hit the ground. Tom sat on his horse, his rifle pointing in the air, a little wisp of smoke coming out of the barrel. Tom put the rifle back in it's saddle scabbard. Cries such as, "What the hell did you do that for?" and "You trying to scare us to death?" rang out from the men as they got to their feet.

"Now I've got your attention, boys, keep quiet for a minute and listen. Frank, John, come up here." As the two men came forward, Tom spoke again. "Don't be letting Bob Benton herd you around. Nobody here loved Mitch Saxton better'n me. If Mitch was here he'd tell you Benton wants nothing more than to stampede you into doing what could get the Guard called."

John Tennis moved over by Tom. "This same Ludlow," he said. "Already best man I ever see killed. No more! Must guns keep, no shooting. Fence? Who give shit? We let build. Front, okay. One side, okay. But build here creek or back side, not okay. They build day, we night go, wire cut little pieces. All sides cut, but front, no cut." Tom agreed that a fence in front would keep the Guards from getting to camp as well as keeping camp people away from town.

Tom's horse moved. "Me and Dan should have been gone a half hour ago."

They rode quietly. Mitch's death made Dan feel numb. And he wanted to meet Elizabeth alone, to see if she'd marry him. Having Tom along messed that up.

"Sorry we're late," Dan said when they met her. "I'll be going down to the railroad pickets. Tom will relay anything new you got back to camp." What Elizabeth had to say, however contributed little to what they already knew. She, in turn, was shocked at Dan's report from Young. All she had known was that Mitch was dead. She couldn't believe her father had ordered Mitch's death.

Elizabeth dropped her eyes. "I know what you all think," she sobbed. "And I know Mitch was murdered as sure as I know my name. But whatever happened, I know my dad didn't order it."

Tom looked sad. Some things about one's family are impossible to believe. "I know, Elizabeth. Things probably just got out of hand. Anything else we should know?" Tom asked.

Elizabeth raised her head. There were still tears in her eyes, but she was no longer sobbing. "Steve got turned back every way he tried to get out of town. The only reason I could get out was because I'm Benton's daughter. You're going to have to find some other way to get information."

Sadly, Dan said good-bye to Elizabeth and headed on down to the lower picket line. He had hoped she would give him some sort of signal as to what she was thinking, but nothing came. At the picket line, Andy Vullis was there with a contingent of Greeks. It took a lot of talking from Dan and Andy to keep them from getting guns to avenge Mitch. It was not easy for these hot blooded men to let a thing such as Mitch's murder go unanswered.

Finally, talking it over they decided the men now on the picket line would stay there. If they didn't, they'd get stuck in Tent Town. Then there'd be nobody to picket at Mounds. Andy told Dan to go back into town and tell them of this decision. "See if they can help us with food and bedding. I'll send men to Price on the train to bring back as much as we can afford."

It was getting dark as Dan started his trip. Once more the moon was rising. It looked almost full and there was plenty of light. He decided to follow the tracks back into camp. He settled into the saddle and the rhythm of the horse. He gave Turk his head, and closed his eyes.

A change in the sound of Turk's hooves woke Dan. A moment ago they'd been a rattle in the gravel on the railroad bed, now they sounded softer. He opened his eyes and saw Turk had turned off onto Big Spring Road. He moved the reins to turn Turk back, but Turk wouldn't turn. Looking down the road he saw Elizabeth's Star. He patted Turk. "Good boy."

Elizabeth saw him coming, got out of the car, and ran toward him. As they met, Dan threw himself to her side. She came into his arms. The moonlight glistened off her hair as they embraced. Breathlessly, they pulled apart and looked into each other's eyes.

"Yes," she said. "Yes, Dan Cook. I will marry you."

They spent the rest of the night talking, making love, and making plans. Both agreed they shouldnt't be married by a Mormon Bishop, or a Methodist Pastor. That'd cause hard feelings. Dan's family'd want one Elizabeth's family the other. The chose a Justice of the Peace in Price.

When Dan asked how soon they'd be married, Elizabeth answered, "In June."

Dan asked why not now? With the baby coming, the sooner the better. Elizabeth understood, but we're going to have to make plans. Two more weeks won't make any difference."

"It'll seem like forever. Let's do it June first."

That decided, they began to speak of where they'd honeymoon. "You're a queen, and I can't give you the castle you deserve. But for our honeymoon we'll take Turk and Bonnie, saddle a pack horse, and I'll take you into Castle Country."

Elizabeth was fascinated by what he mentioned. She asked him to tell her about it. It was the one place on earth Dan loved best. He explained to Elizabeth that Castle Country was in the northern end of the San Rafael Swell. "It's not only the most beautiful, rugged country you've ever seen, it's mysterious. As mysterious as Mother Earth which brought you to me."

.

CHAPTER 23

LET'S GET AWAY

What a way to start off a Sunday! Dan had hardly closed his eyes when the town siren woke everybody up. Smoke was coming from somewhere up Number Two canyon. The fire was in an old shed where a few old tools were stored. It'd been converted into a makeshift barn for the cow that kept the Bentons in fresh milk and cream. Luckily the cow was not inside the shed.

Once the excitement of the morning passed, Dan settled down to the boredom with occasional moments of horror or fright which strikes are made of. Going to see Billy was always one way out. When he arrived, he tried not to speak of it, then, not being able to hold it back, Dan finally told of the trouble in town, and that a friend of his was shot. "The company is getting away with murder."

Billy got up, went to his tent, and came back with a long sheepskin sheath. He pulled a flute from the sheath. This was the flute he had heard Billy play before. Billy handed the flute to Dan. Dan looked at it and saw it was made of a dark, burnished wood. "I have carried that flute for over fifty years. It is a Lakota flute. I play it when I need to think, or to please the spirits that are nearby," he said. Then to Dan's surprise, Billy added, "And now I give it to you."

To accept it would be unthinkable. It obviously meant so much to Billy. "No, Billy, I couldn't."

Billy was not pleased. "You have no choice. I have passed it on to you."

Dan put the flute into the sheath. He knew he'd treasure this gift forever. He got up, and put the flute into his saddle bag. When he returned, Billy was sitting cross-legged by the fire, still fanning smoke. Then Billy mentioned he must tend to his sheep, and asked if Dan wanted to accompany him. Dan knew this was his cue to leave the old man alone with his sheep and his memories. He declined the offer and said it was time for him to go back.

It was around three when Dan put Turk in the corral near the camp. As he started walking down the incline toward the tents, Andy Vullis came jogging toward him. "Do you mind getting on your horse again and going to get John?" Andy asked. Dan asked Andy what was up as they returned to the corral to re-saddle Turk. "After Young came down here this morning, he borrowed a car to go home to Huntington for the day. Some guys from Price said Young's car broke down, and he was in Price raising hell, and trying to provoke strikers into a fight."

Andy continued looking tense. "Young came by here just now. He was making all sorts of threats as he went by. I think John should know about it." Dan finished saddling Turk. Mounting, he looked down at Andy and asked where John was. Andy said John went to the Ambrosia ranch to buy a steer to slaughter for the people in camp.

Dan replied. "That's John for you, always thinking of others." Suddenly, two shots rang out. Dan spurred Turk and started up the canyon on the run. Near Ambrosia's orchard, he could see someone lying in the road. It was John! He jumped off Turk alongside the prostrate form. His feet slipped in the blood. He almost fell. John was mumbling something in Greek. Dan reached down, and lifted John to a sitting position.

"Damned Ludlow," he said. "She get me." A rattle escaped his throat and his form went lax in Dan's arms. Dan laid him back on the ground, reached up, and closed his staring eyes. People rushed in from everywhere, from the ranch, from coffee houses, from tents. Some were crying, and some were screaming in Greek. Dan heard a number of them shout Young's name.

First Mitch, now this? Grief stricken, he looked down at the form lying in the darkening blood. "Father," he said, "now you can rest in peace." Dan stood, jumped on Turk and started up the canyon on the run. Blind anger filled him. I'll catch that murderer Young. Only that was on Dan's mind as Turk approached the guard shack as fast as he could run.

Art Webb stepped out. He pointed a rifle toward Dan and shot once in the air. "Stop or I'll kill you," Webb screamed. Dan kept going. Webb raised the rifle again, and shot again. Dan felt Turk crumble beneath him.

Dan lay on the ground, his leg pinned under Turk's body. Slightly dazed, he felt the hard, cold, steel of Webb's rifle barrel pressed against his temple. "Next time," Webb hissed, "no more Mr. Nice Guy. Right in the head is where you're going to get it."

Webb suddenly took a couple of steps back toward the guard shack. Dan raised his head and saw a group rushing toward him. Webb shot once into the air. The group stopped. "Get this scum out of here, but I swear the first man who tries to pass this guard shack will be lying dead next to him. Then get that piece of horse dung he was riding out of here as well."

"Where are you hit?" a voice asked. Dan raised his head. It was Tom.

"Ain't hit, ain't hit," Dan said. Face contorted with grief, "Tom, he killed Turk."

"I know, Lad. Just take it easy." Tom began trying to lift the saddle enough to free Dan's leg. "Way you're covered in Turk's blood, I thought you was a goner for sure."

"Tom. Never mind me, go help John," Dan said, not remembering he'd closed John's eyes.

"John is past helping, Lad. Andy and some of the other Greeks are taking care of his body." Other men helped Tom lift Turk enough to get Dan's leg out. Dan tried to get up.

"Don't move," a voice commanded. "Until I check you out." Dan looked up. Tears still made it hard to see. It was Dowd. Doc began squeezing Dan's leg in one place or another and asking if it hurt each time he applied pressure. "Nothing broken," Dowd said finally. "You can get up now," Dowd said. "I got to get going; got to go check the Greek."

A team was secured to drag Turk's body to its burying place. The men in town pitched in to help dig a huge grave before Turk's body got there. A couple dozen kerosene lanterns and lamps ringed the grave, giving the working men light. They cast an eerie light over everything. Men put their arms on Dan's shoulder and told him they were sorry; women hugged him and cried.

Dan appreciated this show of care for him and his horse, but it made him feel guilty. All these people should be over with Mrs. Tennis. "Good-bye, little brother," he said as men began filling the grave. "I'll miss you." Again, uncontrollable tears. Dan looked up from Turk's grave. He saw Elizabeth coming toward him. Reaching out his arms, she came into them.

"Oh Dan, I'm so sorry," she said.

"Honey, they shot John and they killed Turk."

"I know, Darling. I got here as quick as I found out."

"Let's get away from here," he said, nodding toward the filling grave. "I can't stand it anymore."

Elizabeth took him out in the flats in her Star. Dan just held on to her and cried. Elizabeth tried a time or two to console him, but it was no use. When he could speak again, he thanked Elizabeth, told her how much he loved her, and asked her to take him to camp. He had to see Mrs. Tennis.

There was a large group of people around her tent, and they made way as Dan came toward them. He poked his head inside the tent to offer his condolences. Mrs. Tennis' grief had deformed her features. Her wailing was so loud it could be heard throughout the camp. He wondered how he could feel so badly about losing Turk, when others had lost so much more.

Next morning in his cot, he wasn't sure he wanted to go on living with this pain. He knew he had a lot to live for. He thought of his future with Elizabeth, but the pain stayed. He felt hopeless.

What was the sense loving Elizabeth or anyone else when it could all be snatched away in a second? He loved his family, and now he could not even be with them. What was the point in calling a dead man father, or a dead horse little brother? His feeling of kinship to them only made the pain worse. "I wish I had never met that crazy old Indian. I wish I'd never had a horse. I wish John was just a Greek that lived at the end of town. I wish Mitch was still a snitch."

But what would life be without them? All of a sudden he knew the privilege and joy of knowing John and Mitch, and the pleasure Turk gave him was so great he would gladly suffer this pain every day for the rest of his life, rather than choose not to have known them.

Now he could get up. The pain was there just as intensely, but the nature of it had changed. Pain was the price one sometimes had to pay for the good things that happened in life. Now the good man John had been, the true hero Mitch was, and the love he felt for his horse could never be taken away from him, pain or no pain. "Udu'vuts," he said.

Dan got out of bed, dressed, and climbed the hillside to where the sun hadn't risen. He sat on a rock and began a conversation with his departed friends. With tears streaming, he told them how much he loved them, and how much joy they brought him. "I don't know if your spirits are together, or if there is such a thing as a man needing a horse in the afterlife. But John, Turk is the best horse you ever see. Turk, John is a good man. He will take good care of you. I give you to each other's care. Mitch, if you are with them, you can all share."

The rising sun crept over him, and he thought of the Indian up on the hillside chanting beauty into the world.

He stood, turned, and looked up the mountain. "Chant beauty into my heart, old man." He sat on the rock for a moment. The pain eased some. "Thank you, Father," he said softly. He became conscious of Tent Town below him. He noticed four women going into Tom's tent. He got up and trotted toward it. As he entered he saw the Relief Society ladies from church. Tom was lying on his cot propped up by extra pillows.

"Come in, Dan. Seems as how I went and got myself sick. Got some pretty bad pains in my gut, and been throwing up," Tom wheezed. "Trouble breathing. All my muscles hurt."

"I'll bet you got appendicitis," one of the ladies said. Another opined maybe Tom was poisoned, by eating some bad meat or something.

"Mind if I do my own diagnosing?" Doc Dowd said as he entered the tent.

"Glad to see you, Doc," Tom said. "Wondered if those killers at the guard shack would give you the message you was needed."

Doc got busy taking Tom's temperature, and other necessary things to diagnose him. As he did so, he quizzed Tom about his symptoms. Finally, he pressed on Tom's stomach, Tom moaned. "Hard as a rock," Doc said. "Let me see your arms." Doc looked at them closely, then he pulled one of Tom's legs out from under the covers and began examining it. "Aha," he said. "Anything bite you yesterday?" Tom said he felt something, a pin prick on his leg while burying Turk. He'd reached down, slapped it, and pretty much forgot about it. "Look here," Doc said.

Dan looked at Tom's leg and saw an ugly spot that was bluish red in the middle surrounded by a whitish area. "That's where she got you,"

Doc said. "You've got a black widow spider bite."

"Oh, my," one of the ladies said. Another said she heard that you can crush cedar berries and make a paste that will help. A third volunteered to go get some jointfir to make Brigham Tea. The last lady said jointfir can also be crushed to make a poultice out of it to drain away the poison. She added that if it didn't do Tom any good, it wouldn't do him any harm.

Doc seemed to be paying no attention at all to the ladies' suggested remedies. But the moment the last one stopped speaking, he turned to Dan. "Dan, I need you to go to some neighbors and find someone who has a square of butter. Have them cut it in four pieces, lengthwise," Dowd commanded. "Put the pieces on a plate and get it back here right away."

Dan wasted no time. What Doctor Dowd wanted, Doctor Dowd got. Proudly, he returned with the butter sectioned off on the plate, just as the doctor had prescribed.

Doc said Dan did well. Dan was confused for a moment by the smile on Doc's face as he took the plate. The doctor extended the pieces of butter to the ladies. "Here you are, ladies," he said. "Shove it up your collective butts. If it don't do you any good, it won't do you any harm."

Dan stuffed his fist in his mouth to keep from laughing out loud, as the ladies scurried from the tent in a huff. He might have made it had not Tom broken out into a loud guffaw, in spite of his pain. Dan joined him till both of them were howling with laughter. Doc smiled. "That little show was for the two of you. Dan, you look like crap. I'll bet you didn't sleep last night. And Tom, if you think you're in pain now, wait until tonight."

"Doc, I take my hat off to you," Tom said. "Two old duffers such as us have a lot of experience with people and things dying, but I been worrying about the lad, here. In less than a couple of minutes you showed him there could still be laughs in his life. Thanks."

These words brought yesterday's events crashing back into Dan's consciousness. Dan realized as badly as he felt, Tom was right. "Thanks, Doc," he said.

The three of them were still chuckling when a voice from outside called, "Doctor Dowd, are you in there?" Doc invited them in. Two strangers dressed in suits entered the tent. Each held his hat in his hands. One seemed to be just into middle age, and the other was older. Doc asked what he could do for them. They said they were on their way into Sunnyside to see Doc. But when they asked at the guard shack they told them they could find him at troublemaker Carr's tent.

Both Tom and Doc had quizzical looks on their faces. "Let us introduce ourselves," the older man said. Pointing to the younger he said, "This is Major Johnson, my representative in the area, and I am Governor Maybe."

Dan couldn't believe it. Governor Maybe? Himself? Dan got hurriedly to his feet, and Tom sat up in his bed, grimacing. In his whole life Dan'd never met anyone so important.

"How can I be of service, Governor?" Doc asked. The Major said they needed information on yesterday's shootings.

Tom turned to the governor, "Governor, my name is Tom Carr, and the lad there is Dan Cook. Please, won't you gentlemen take a seat?" The men accepted Tom's offer. "Doc, sit here," Tom said as he patted the bed alongside him. As Doc sat, Tom looked at Dan and patted the other side of the bed. Dan sat and now the three townsmen were facing their guests. Tom continued, "I know how busy you must be, Governor. We'll certainly help in every way we can."

Both men nodded, and the governor spoke. "Sorry to intrude on your illness, Tom, but it's important. The major and I already have the company's side of the story. But some things don't add up, so we've come to ask you, Dr. Dowd. From a medical point of view how was Mr. Tennis shot? What wounds did Mr. Tennis suffer, and what were their entry points?"

Doc thought for a minute. He leaned forward toward the governor. "There were two bullet wounds. One in the groin, and one in the back. The most logical explanation is that the first bullet hit him in the groin, spun him around, and the second bullet got him in the back. It is also possible, however, that he was shot in the back, then spun around. It is my judgment that the shot in the back was the lethal one causing massive injury to the lungs and heart, and a rapid death."

Major Johnson removed a notebook from his pocket and started taking notes. The governor nodded, pensively. "Thank you, Doctor.

Please describe Mr. Lorenzo Young's wound, and give me your medical opinion as to how he received it." Tom and Dan shot quizzical looks at each other. They'd heard nothing of Young being wounded.

"Well, I didn't have much of a chance. When I got back from examining Dan here, and Tennis' body, Ovie Rasmussen brought Young in. He had a reasonably minor flesh wound to the outside part of his thigh. He was wearing a long leather overcoat, and there were powder burns on the outside of the coat. This indicates to me that whoever fired the shot had to be no more than eighteen inches from him, maximum."

Johnson was scribbling rapidly. Governor Maybe thought for a moment, then asked if the wound could have been self inflicted. Doc paused a moment to consider it. "In my judgement it's more than possible, but from the evidence I saw, I can't prove it one way or another."

"Good," the governor said. "Did Mr. Young give you an explanation as to how he was shot?" He said Young reported he was walking up the road toward Sunnyside when John Tennis came out of a lane in the orchard, and pointed a pistol at him. He said John ordered him back to Sunnyside. But before Young could respond, John fired once and hit him in the leg. Young said he pulled his pistol, fired twice, hitting John both times. Then he hurried back to find me to treat his wound."

The governor looked into Doc's eyes. "Explain how come you didn't mention powder burns on Mr. Tennis, and yet you found them on Young's overcoat." Doc answered readily. There weren't any. "Okay," the governor went on. "Then what happened?"

Doc sat back on the cot. He told how when he was cleaning his equipment, Rasmussen said he was taking Young into protective custody. His plan was to sneak him out of town, so the strikers wouldn't try getting to him. Rasmussen figured best way to protect him would be to put him in jail.

Apparently the governor was satisfied. He turned to Major Johnson. Johnson leaned over, and whispered something into the governor's ear. The governor nodded, and turned back to Doc. "Did you remove Mr. Young's overcoat to fix his leg?" the governor asked. Doc nodded affirmatively, and added he also split his pant leg up above the wound. "Do you still have the overcoat?" The governor asked as the major scribbled.

Doc said Rasmussen took it with him when they left.

Once more the major whispered into the governor's ear. And once more the governor nodded in agreement. The governor pursed his lips. "We weren't particularly looking for a coat, because I didn't know of the powder burns until you told me. But in Price we asked to see all of Mr. Young's effects. His pants were there with one leg split, but there was no overcoat."

The governor stopped, crossed his arms over his stomach and interlaced his fingers "Another peculiar thing, from his supposed long walk up the road, why wouldn't blood have drained down onto his shoes and socks? Can you explain that?" Doc said he couldn't explain it.

Apparently the governor had finished. "Thank you. Anything else you want to tell us?"

Doc thought for another moment. "No, not medically. But when I got to the scene of the shooting there were several witnesses that told me what they saw." Apparently, the governor was more interested in Doc's medical opinions than second hand witness reports. He did not remove his hands from his stomach. He looked only mildly curious and asked what the witnesses said. "They all told pretty much the same story. Young was walking up the road. John came out of the orchard and onto the road. He saw Young and stopped. Young pulled his gun and fired at John twice. Then Young ran up the road toward Sunnyside."

Once again, as Doc spoke, Major Johnson was making rapid notes. Johnson looked up from the notebook. "Good. If you remember anything else you feel is at all significant, get in touch with me at your earliest convenience." Doc heaved a sigh of relief at being let off the hook.

Johnson flipped through the notes he'd just taken. "One more thing, will you give me the names of those witnesses, and the name of anyone else who might have information as to what happened?" Doc gave them the names of four women. Doc said since their husbands didn't work in the mines and were not strikers, they would probably be the best witnesses. Then Doc gave the names of several Greeks from the coffee houses who said they saw it. Doc said they wouldn't be as good as witnesses because John was a long-time friend of theirs. Even so, Doc said, they pretty much all told the same story.

Tom cleared his throat. "Governor, Dan here was the first one to get to John."

The governor nodded his head. "Oh, yes, Dan Cook. When I first heard your name I didn't recognize it. You must be the boy whose horse was killed when you tried to run Young down."

Dan was shocked. "Yes, Sir, I'm the one. But I wasn't trying to run Young down. He was already gone by the time I got there." The governor cocked his head, then he asked what Dan was doing running his horse into Sunnyside. Now Dan was embarrassed. "I don't know." The governor continued to press him for an explanation. Dan did the best he could to explain. "What I was feeling was hate. John was a close friend, I considered him a second father. I just set out after Young. I never figured on running him down." The governor seemed to understand. "I can accept that, under the circumstances. To the best of your recollection, tell me what happened."

Dan told the governor in as much detail as he could what he could remember from the time Andy came and said Young was looking for trouble. Then the governor asked how Dan could be certain there were only two shots, and not three as Young reported. It was possible shots from two guns fired simultaneously might sound a single shot.

Dan looked puzzled. "Yeah," he said and paused. "I guess that's possible. But according to Young's own story, John shot him first, then he shot twice."

Dan then told the Governor of the talks he had with John about Ludlow, and John's insistence that carrying a gun not only caused trouble for the union, but could cause a man to get killed. This definitely interested the major. "Nobody ever saw John with a weapon? Is that right?"

Tom cleared his throat again. "I've known John ever since I came to Sunnyside. The only time I ever saw him with a weapon of any sort was when we went hunting." Then he added, "John was always telling fellow Greeks to take their guns home and leave them there. When he saw someone with a gun, he would get upset. Governor, I'll swear in court that John was not armed." When the major said they believed him, Tom mentioned a railroad engineer, by the name of George Harmer, who also saw the whole thing and would be a good witness.

Doc nodded. "I forgot to mention George. But I also talked with George later. I told him John shot Young in the leg. George just laughed.

He said Young sure wasn't running the way a man shot in the leg would. He said if Young was shot, somebody else shot him."

Both men stood up. "We've kept you long enough," the governor said. There were handshakes all around. After the governor thanked them again and left, Doc gave Tom some morphine for his pain, and promised to return as soon as possible with some anti-venom.

"What was that all about?" Tom asked after Doc had left. Dan asked Tom what he was talking about. "Him, the Guv himself. Kind of questions he asked showed he figured Young was lying."

Dan thought it all over. "He seemed a nice man. And seemed to be on our side."

Tom snorted. "Don't let first impressions fool you, kid. We'll see whether or not he's on our side. I'll bet when the chips are down, he ain't with us although he'll mealy mouth it around to seem like it." Dan couldn't believe Tom could doubt this well-dressed man, who spoke in such soft, pleasing tones. Then he thought of what John said about the analtos.

CHAPTER 24

WHITE MAN IS MISERABLE

Benton pulled the Packard around behind the courthouse and parked by a no parking sign. There was always an abundance of parking places along the sidewalk in front, but not today. It seemed every Greek from four states had gathered for Tennis' burial. Thank heavens Saxton's body had been shipped back to Wyoming.

"Damn," he said as he got out of the Packard. "What a mess."

"Come in, Bob," Commissioner Santschi called from the inner meeting room.

Benton entered and saw the three men seated at a conference table. They stood and exchanged hand shakes. Benton greeted Santschi and William Emerson who, in addition to being elected a County Commissioner and Cameron's snitch, was also one of Benton's employees at Utah Fuel. Benton knew him well. The third commissioner was A. E. Gibson who was an employee of Knight Fuel. Except for meetings and socials, Benton knew little about him.

The meeting went pretty much as Benton expected. First was the concern that one of his men had shot a striker. Santschi expressed the thought that because of it the governor seemed to be turning a cold shoulder to anything they tried to tell him. Emerson said the night of the shooting the governor came down on the train and stayed the night in Helper. When they tried to have a meeting with him, he refused at first, then said they could come to Helper if they wished.

"We wanted to give him some pretty strong evidence of the trouble we've been having," Emerson said. "But he just asked if there was anything new we had not already given to Major Johnson. We mentioned the shooting, and he just told us to write it up, and give it to Johnson."

Gibson said the next day was worse. "We tried all day, but we couldn't even find out where he was." When he returned to Price, they only got a twenty minute audience standing on a sidewalk.

Benton had listened carefully without saying much except an occasional comment to let them know he was listening. But now it was time for him to take the offensive. "My opinion is that you boys have the right spin on what is happening. He probably had his mind made up even before he came to the county. I know for sure he made it up before he ever got to Sunnyside."

Santschi mentioned that they couldn't talk much longer because there would be a parade of strikers after Tennis' funeral, and they still had to make arrangements to control it so there would be no violence. "Jimmy Morgan is using the funeral to stir up strikers," Santschi commented.

Finally, however, Emerson brought up the subject Benton knew he was itching to report to Cameron. "Congratulations, Bob, we understand your daughter is getting married to that Cook boy. Isn't he the one who got his horse shot out from under him?"

Benton had been working on a plan to answer this all the way from Sunnyside. "You boys let word of what I'm telling you now slip out, and I'll let Art Webb have a talk with you," he said, put his hands behind his head and leaned back in his chair. "When you're a Dad, what can you do? She's expecting." He'd figured he might as well tell them now because once the baby was born, everybody would figure it out anyway. "But that's only half the problem. Cameron called me and said that Maybe is a big horse lover. He said I'd better be buying Cook a new horse so as not to get the governor mad at us." Putting on what he hoped was a look of humility, Benton paused, and lowered his head. "I'm kind of glad to tell you about this. It's a heavy load to have to carry by myself." The sounds of a lively band going by outside interrupted for a moment.

Benton didn't want to push it by waiting for any show of sympathy which may or may not be forthcoming. He lifted his head, the pained look off his face. "Well, boys, I still work for Cameron. I'd best be getting back."

On his way back to Sunnyside, a car honked at him. Looking, Benton recognized his daughter's Star, then saw his daughter and Dan wave to him as they passed going the other direction. I hate them both, he thought.

Dan began to worry. For some reason, on the trip down, Elizabeth would talk only in short, polite sentences. Now at the cemetery, she stood silently, hardly uttering a word. He tried to get her to relax during the parade, and at least enjoy the music. But he had no more luck as they watched the huge parade with over 3,000 marchers in it, than he'd had all the way from Sunnyside. No matter how often he asked her what was wrong, she would reply it was nothing and she didn't want to talk about it right now. After the parade he suggested they go back to the Greek church where food would be served to the mourners. She turned him down.

"I just need to get home."

"Why, Elizabeth? The day is still young and maybe something'll happen to make us feel better."

"I don't want to talk about it right now. Please, Dan, let's just go."

They got in the car. "You've changed your mind about marrying me, haven't you?" he blurted out when the car was barely out of Price. Instead of answering him, tears began rolling down her cheeks, and she kept on driving. She did not stop until they came to some big cottonwood trees a couple of miles from Wellington. She pulled the car over under the shade of the trees. She looked at him with melancholy eyes. Dan's heart sank. Tears began streaming down his face as well. He barely noticed them, it had happened so often lately.

"Is it that obvious?" she asked.

Dan wiped at the tears. "I couldn't think of anything else that would make you tear yourself up as you have been." He started to speak, but she put her hand to his lips and stopped the words.

"I swear to heaven," she said, "if you say one word before I finish I will never be able to get through this." She paused, then added, "and you'll never know why. First thing, I am the very worst sort of liar. Second thing, the child I am carrying is not yours."

A stab of pain hit Dan's chest. He tried to speak, but again Elizabeth's hand gently stopped him. Tenderly, she wiped a tear from his cheek. "Be still, I'm not through yet. The night before I left college I was stupid enough to let one of the friends I would never see again make love to me." Again, she paused, but this time to try to wipe her own tears away. It was no use, but she did her best to keep talking. "I swear that was the first and only time." She continued to explain how she didn't know she was pregnant that first time with him. When she found out, she made plans to leave, but their love made her willing to lie and let him believe the child was his.

"When I saw how much it hurt you to lose Turk, I knew I couldn't take the chance that someday you would find out the child you loved wasn't yours."

Little of what she was saying made much of an impression on Dan. His mind just kept screaming, "Not mine!" Dan's sobbing stopped. He went cold inside. He felt empty, empty and cold. Mitch, John, Turk, and Elizabeth? It was just too much.

"Now," she said, and took a deep breath. "Now I've said it all except one more thing. Dan Cook, I will still marry you if you will learn to love the child in my belly as you would your own."

Now Dan was stammering. "I . . . I don't know . . ." But Elizabeth cut his answer off. "Don't try to tell me right now. You don't know what you really feel. Take a few days to think it over, and be absolutely sure. I couldn't stand it if you said you'd marry me out of duty, or out of pity."

Once more Dan tried to speak, and once more she stopped him. She said he had to decide things on his own. She said if they talked to each other, later maybe one of them might feel they got talked into something they really didn't want. She put the car in gear and sped off.

All the way back to Tent Town she drove as if she was alone in the car. She hunched over the wheel. She took some turns much too fast. She wouldn't look at Dan, and did not speak till Dan got out of the car. Before he closed the door, she looked at him. "Let me know what you decide, one way or the other," she said in a flat tone with no more emotion than would be used to ask him what he wanted for dinner. Then she let out the clutch before he could answer.

Dan stood numbly watching the car speed away until the dust settled. He had lost so much on that road toward Sunnyside. First John, then Turk, and now, probably Elizabeth. He wished he had never seen that horrid stretch of road where so much he loved had been snatched from him.

He looked around. Even Tent Town seemed dead except for a few children playing here and there. Every man and most of the women had gone to the funeral, and were still there. He could not bring himself to go sit in his tent in solitude. It would be hot and stuffy and close him in. It resembled a grave too much to suit him just now.

He headed for the corral. He would ride up the mountainside and maybe go see Billy. Why do I think of Billy when trouble comes? Dan stopped short. He had forgotten about Turk. He had no horse. Then Dan decided that even though Tom wasn't around to ask for the loan of his horse, Tom wouldn't mind. He decided to leave Tom a note. That done, he saddled Tom's sorrel and headed up the trail.

He tried to focus himself on his problem. How can I get Elizabeth to marry me even though I can't promise to learn to love her child? I will take care of it, and maybe come to love it sometime in the future. But how can I promise I will love it? What will I say when someone asks if the child is mine if it doesn't look anything like me? Should I just lie, say I'll learn to love it?

He looked down and saw the horse heaving and sweating under him. He reached down and patted the horse's neck. Even though the horse didn't know Dan, it was doing its best for him. "Sorry, boy. I don't even know your name," he said to the horse. "I'll ask Tom later."

He topped the rise, and Billy was waiting for him. He got off the horse and Billy started walking with him to let the horse cool down. "I see you're riding a new horse," Billy remarked.

The words came pouring out of Dan's mouth involuntarily. "Two of my friends have been shot and killed, Turk was shot and killed, and now Elizabeth will not marry me."

"I wondered," Billy said turning to look at the horse behind them.

"How long since you ate?" Billy asked. Dan said he'd only had a quick bite for breakfast. "I thought so," Billy said. "First thing, we'd better feed you."

The food was simple. Some bread, some of the jelly left over from one of Dan's previous visits, and a little sheep's milk was all Billy offered him. But it was satisfying to Dan. The food also had a calming effect on him. He didn't feel quite so empty now.

"Your friends and your horse," Billy said, and looked sad. "Was it because of the strike?" Dan just nodded. Now Billy looked worried. "I was afraid so."

Billy knows things, Dan thought. Maybe he can help me. "Is the killing over, Billy?" Billy just shrugged his shoulders. Dan thought about the stupidity of running Turk by the guard shack. He began to have a new feeling of guilt. If I'd only stopped when Webb shouted, Turk'd be alive.

Billy got up, removed the coffee pot, returned, poured some in their cups and sat down. "When I was younger each spring we used to go to fish. I would sit and watch a fish surface. Sometimes it only surfaced a little bit, and I could not tell what kind of a fish it was so as to know how best to catch it. Sometimes I tried to catch it anyway. But my movement always scared the fish, and it went away. Then Mother Earth showed me if I did not move while the fish was at the top, it would surface again later. Then I could see what kind it is and how best to catch it."

Dan sat thinking for a while. By now Dan knew that however far fetched it seemed, every story Billy told had an answer to a problem Dan was having at the time. He only needed to figure out how. This one was obvious to him. "I don't know how many stories you have told me about letting things work themselves out. And I just got another one. You're not only mystical, you're persistent. Maybe someday I will be able to let things work themselves out."

"Who knows," Billy said and began to laugh as he always seemed to be doing.

Dan just wasn't in a laughing mood. "Billy, this is important, be serious." Billy asked why one should be serious when one knows things are working themselves out the way Mother Earth and Father Sky wanted them worked out.

Dan had about enough. He looked at Billy. "Oh, yeah? How about this. Elizabeth won't marry me unless I can promise to learn to love the child she got pregnant with when some guy in college knocked her up."

Billy turned suddenly serious, himself. "Is this a problem?"

Dan couldn't believe the question. "Of course it's a problem. How can I promise to learn to love something I may not be able to learn to love?"

"No, I mean is it a problem for you to love the baby now?"

"Of course it is. No man wants . . ." Dan started to say, but Billy's sudden movement startled him. Billy jumped up, began whooping and hollering, and started to dance around the fire. Everything Billy was chanting was in Paiute so Dan had no idea what was going on. He waited for Billy to stop and explain it to him. But Billy did not stop. Dan watched in fascination, and from time to time he went to gather wood to keep the fire going. Each time he came back he hoped Billy had stopped, but he hadn't.

He kept dancing and chanting till the sun went down. He kept at it till the moon came up. And he was still going when Dan was finally overcome by weariness and lay down to sleep alongside the fire. His last thought before drifting off was to wonder who would keep the fire going now that he was going to sleep. A hand placed gently on his shoulder woke him up. He opened his eyes and saw Billy standing over him. The glow of first light was off to the East. Dan realized the night had almost passed.

Billy looked directly into Dan's eyes. "Thank you, my son," Billy said in a tired voice.

"Thanks for what, Billy?"

"Thanks for giving me the answer to my question."

"I did?"

Billy spoke a little sadly. "Yes. But I used to think if I could find the answer I could teach it to the white man so he could be as happy as the Indian. Then maybe he would leave us alone."

Wide awake now, Dan gave Billy his full attention as Billy continued speaking. "Then Mother Earth sent you to me. I discovered you are intelligent and still young enough to learn. More important, however, I discovered you have a good heart. So we talked of many things. We talked of how hard it seems to be for your people to love one another and take others as your fathers, or sons. I thought if anybody could learn how to do this, it would be you."

Dan thought of his calling John, Father, and Turk, Little Brother. He felt he had learned this, and started to protest. Billy just held his hand up to stop him. "But not being able to love even a neighbor, let alone his enemy, is so strong in the white man. I know, now, it is hopeless. The white man sees himself as separate from the community; it is not his family. The Paiute sense of himself is only as family member within his community. While you think others are separate from you, we know we are not only related to others, but to the trees, and rocks, and birds, and waters, and animals, and especially Mother Earth and Father Sky from whom all things flow. The white man is so miserable, and so unrelated, he cannot even call the child in his own maiden's belly, Son. Or love it now, no matter how it got there."

"I can't . . ." Dan started to say. But he stopped. "I don't . . ." he started to say again, then he fell silent. Something happened inside him, and he also had his answer. He would not be able to promise he would learn to love the baby, he already did. With great joy, he accepted Billy's suggestion they chant beauty into the world. How can this old man dance after all he's already done? Dan asked himself. It amazed him. But dance he did and watching him was a joy.

As he returned to camp, he blessed the day Mother Earth brought him to Billy. He unsaddled the horse, and hurried over to Tom's tent. He knocked on the tent pole, and was invited in. Tom was boiling his luncheon dishes, and he still limped a little as he walked. But Dan could see the effects of the spider bite had all but disappeared. Tom pointed to a chair. "Take the load off your feet. What's up?"

Dan sat. There was no way Dan could tell Tom what had transpired on the mountain the night before. He played it safe. "Thanks for the loan of your horse."

Tom came over, sat in the other chair, and wiggled it around until he was facing Dan. "Don't mention it. Any time you want him, he's yours." Dan thanked him again, and then he remembered his promise to the horse to find out what his name was. Tom snickered. "I call him Pancho, after Pancho Villa. He came up here from Mexico. Belonged to some big ranchero down there." Dan said he thought Pancho was a fine horse. Then he brought up what was really on his mind and asked if anyone saw Elizabeth leave Sunnyside today.

Tom didn't know, and suggested he go ask Andy. Tom mentioned that with John's passing, Andy was now the head of the security crew. With that, Dan said good-bye to Tom and set out to look for Andy. Finding him was easy. He was sitting on a chair in front of his tent and looking up the road. As Dan approached he moved some.

Andy's posture caught Dan's eye. "What you looking for, Andy?" Andy replied he was just looking. Dan didn't have much time for chit chat. He had to find Elizabeth. "Anybody see Elizabeth leave town today?" Andy nodded, and said about four hours ago she left and looked as though she was headed for Price. Dan thought for a minute. "I figured today was her day to go get the galleys. She should be coming back soon." Andy just grunted, never taking his eyes from the road. Then he added that Dan could ride out and meet her because for some reason, the goons had abandoned the road block.

With that problem settled, Dan's curiosity got the best of him. "What are you looking for?"

Andy now had a somewhat puzzled look. "The train came by with a cattle car on it a little while ago. There was a flurry of activity on the other side where they unloaded something from it, but I couldn't see what it was because the guard shack was in the way. I'm watching to try to figure it out, or see if something else happens." Dan asked if maybe they were bringing in scabs. Andy shook his head and pursed his lips. "Don't seem likely. Otherwise, the pickets at Mounds would have let me know by now."

"When you figure it out, let me know if you need me for anything," Dan said and took his leave. Maybe Tom would let him borrow Pancho again, and he could ride out to meet Elizabeth. Then he had a disquieting thought. He wanted Elizabeth to see him standing alongside the road so she would be sure to stop. If he had a horse, maybe she would pass him by. He returned to the road and started off at a brisk walk, then broke into a slow jog.

Barely more than a mile out of town, he saw dust coming up the flats. His heart quickened when he recognized the Star. She glided smoothly to a stop. Dan opened the door and got in. "Thanks for stopping. I've got to talk with you," he said. She started the car forward, and in a pleasant voice, said it would have to wait. Dan didn't want to have to wait, but he didn't want to make Elizabeth angry either. "Something pretty important?" he asked. Elizabeth smiled. She said it was so important that she had grabbed her galleys, talked with Ann a short time, and come straight back in the hopes of finding him. "Okay, what's going on?" he asked.

"You'll see," she said as she picked up speed. Dan figured they'd talk when they got to Tent Town, but to his surprise, she didn't stop there either. When she stopped at the guard shack, he started to get out but she stopped him. "We're going into town now," she said to Deputy Cook. He waved and she drove off.

"What in the heck is this all about?" Dan asked in bewilderment.

But Elizabeth just looked smug. "Is Deputy Cook a relative of some sort? He's a decent sort."

Dan relaxed some. She seemed so happy about something, he was grateful for whatever it was. "No, Cook's a common name around here. I can think of at least four families in the county."

She pulled up to the stables and stopped. She pointed toward the corral. "Look over there. What do you see?" Elizabeth asked. He took a quick look and said he just saw Bonnie. "Okay, Cyclone," she called as she got out of the car. "He's here." Cyclone stepped from the other side of the stable, leading a beautiful, big buckskin. He had a jet black mane and tail.

Elizabeth was almost dancing up and down with excitement. Dan was in awe. "He's beautiful."

Elizabeth looked into Dan's eyes. "His name is Showboat, and he's yours!"

As he was about to speak, Art Webb came limping out of the blacksmith shop carrying a saddle, and walked toward them. Webb stuck out his hand as he approached. Dan refused to take it.

"Sorry about shooting your horse, Dan," Webb said. "Mister Benton wanted me to apologize to you personally. To make amends, he had the horse and saddle sent up on the train. Said since I'd caused the trouble, I should give them to you. No hard feelings?" he asked.

"The hell there ain't," Dan spat and then jabbed a straight right fist into Webb's face. The force of the blow split Webb's lip and knocked him to the ground. The fury in Dan was so great he would have kicked Webb if Elizabeth were not there to see it. Webb rolled over on his left side. His right hand made a quick move to his holster. Hate on his face he drew his pistol.

"Art!" Elizabeth screamed.

At Dan's punch, Cyclone dropped the reins and came running. "Remember what Big Boss be sayin'!" Cyclone shouted.

Webb put the pistol back in it's holster and got to his feet. He turned to leave. "Still no hard feelings?" Dan taunted him. Webb just glared and continued walking.

"Cyclone, please saddle Bonnie, too. I'll ride with Dan for a ways." Then she turned to Dan and smiled. "Nice punch," she said softly.

Elizabeth explained to Dan about Showboat. She said her father had chewed Webb out royally for shooting Turk. "He told me he was getting you the finest horse he could find on such short notice, and giving him to you as a wedding present. He also mentioned something about showing Webb he couldn't go around shooting horses without somebody having to pay for it."

Now's as good a time to tell her as any, Dan reasoned. "I can't promise to learn to love the baby, because I love it already."

CHAPTER 25

THANK YOU SPIRITS

Benton was kind enough to let Dan back into town to talk with his family about getting married. Steve, of course, made it plain that he wished he could find a, "good lookin' babe" like Elizabeth when he got married. Dan's mother was thrilled and his dad was disappointed. Mary was thrilled because at the dance Elizabeth seemed genuinely nice and down to earth. Carl was disappointed because Dan was marrying outside the church. Both parents agreed that, because of her station in life, he could have done a lot worse picking a wife. They seemed to be looking forward to the wedding, but both worried about how Mr. Benton would act toward them. "At least I shouldn't have to worry so much about getting fired," Carl observed.

The day of the wedding there was no noticeable status difference between the two families. Mrs. Benton could not have been more cordial and Mr. Benton not only gave his daughter away, to indicate his support, but he also seemed reasonably friendly as well. Judge Fred Woods pronounced the couple man and wife, and the couple enjoyed their first wedded kiss. Thereafter, Benton mentioned he had to leave right away, sorry. Something about urgent business.

The party left the judge's chambers and stood outside in the antechamber. It pained Dan to see how longingly his father looked out the window at the Packard as Mr. Benton drove off. Mrs. Benton noticed his look. "You know," she said, "that Packard is Bob's pride and joy. Sometimes I wonder if he doesn't care more of it than he does of his family." She put her arm around Mary Cook's shoulder and looked straight at Carl. "And now we've got more family than ever."

With Mr. Benton gone, before the party left for the wedding breakfast at the Queen City, everyone was calling everyone else by their first names and seemed almost a family that had been together for years. On the way out Elizabeth reached her arm around Dan, and gave him a side-ways hug. "I'm so happy," she said. A huge smile made its way to her face. Her voice became almost seductive. "Let's get out of here before I do something shameless."

Parents on both sides of the family had offered to host a wedding dinner for the newlyweds, but Elizabeth refused, saying she was anxious to get going on their honeymoon.

During the breakfast, wedding gifts were presented to the couple. Carl and Mary gave them a fine set of carving knives. Katherine was a little embarrassed when she presented a beautiful silver tea service. She looked at Elizabeth, "I respect your decision to move into Dan's tent," she said. "I'll just hold this for you until this strike is over."

Elizabeth reached over and kissed her mother. Then, on impulse, she leaned across the table and kissed Mary as well. She smiled happily, "Thanks for the knives. They're a beautiful gift."

When the couple started home in the Star, Dan slid across the seat and sat close to Elizabeth.

They'd agreed they would exchange their own gifts privately. Dan reached in the back seat. He brought out a small, neatly wrapped box. First, Elizabeth held it, she noted it was heavy for its size. She tore away the wrapping eagerly. Nestled inside she found a small leather bag. Inside the bag were a number of small, beautifully polished stones. "Oh, Dan, I love them," she said.

"Those will have to do as your jewels until I can get you the real thing."

Elizabeth looked eagerly at him. "Where on earth did you get them?" she asked.

"Being out of work and all, I don't have much money," Dan said. "At least not enough to buy you any sort of decent gift. I was wandering along the creek, wondering what I could do. I saw a stone glistening in the water, and that gave me an idea. I walked along the creek bed picking up different ones I thought you'd enjoy. Billy gave me the bag, an old man in town polished them."

Elizabeth turned to look Dan directly in the eyes. "Real jewels? Decent Gift?" she asked. "Darling, don't you know that anything you could ever buy in a store would never equal this? These are one of a kind! I'll cherish them always." Dan could feel a blush creeping up on him. He didn't know what to say, but hoped she really meant it because he, too, had liked the stones.

She reached into her purse, and brought out a somewhat larger package. He opened it eagerly, and discovered a Meerschaum, a small box of matches, and a pouch of tobacco. "Well, I'll be..." Elizabeth looked crestfallen, "I thought you'd enjoy it".

"To use your words, I love it!"

Not convinced, Elizabeth asked, "Then why the, I'll be...?"

Dan hastened to explain. "A short while ago, Billy, my Indian friend up on the mountain asked me if I smoked. I said, no. He said, too bad, we needed to smoke together. Then he said never mind, Mother Earth is taking care of that." He looked at Elizabeth,

"But it seems Mother Elizabeth beat her to it."

Elizabeth felt a little embarrassed. She had other reasons for getting Dan the pipe. "One reason I got the pipe was I thought you might want to quit chewing tobacco."

Dan shook his head slowly. He mumbled, as if under his breath, that they'd been married barely an hour, and already she's trying to change him. "I am not!" Elizabeth shot back sharply.

"Are we having our first fight?" he asked with a grin. "Not only do I want to smoke the pipe, but the next time I'm on the mountain, Billy and I will smoke together. It will please him as much as it does me." Elizabeth sighed. She said she thought she would enjoy meeting this Billy of his, and he promised her when they returned from the honeymoon, she would.

Back at Sunnyside, Dan felt genuine love and gratitude for all the people in Tent Town. Little as these people had, they helped prepare for the honeymoon as they would for their own sons or daughters getting married, and Tom graciously lent Pancho for a pack horse.

It seemed that everyone in camp chipped in with what they'd need for their honeymoon—their own tent. And some men pitched in to help saddle the horses and pack Pancho.

Dan's heart swelled with pride as they left Tent Town. A beautiful bride, Showboat, Bonnie, Pancho showing his strength as a pack horse, and a wonderful early afternoon to start their trip. But best of all, it seemed everyone in camp came out to cheer, and wave good-bye as the little caravan headed out. Elizabeth laughed, smiled, and waved back. Apparently, she felt love from these people and gratitude for them. Dan headed east, passed the coke ovens, then turned south when they cleared company property.

The honeymoon itself was not a disappointment, either. Castle country was everything Dan said it was and more. Truth be told, they did far more love making and resting up afterwards, than they did sight seeing. Dan observed, "We should've seen twice as much." Elizabeth suggested she'd not trade what they did see for a trip to Niagra Falls.

When they got back to Sunnyside, yet another surprise was waiting for them. The people of the camp, with the union's help, had set up a special tent for the newlyweds. It was larger than even Tom's. There was an old carpet on the plank floor, faded, but able to keep some of the dust from seeping between the cracks in the planks. They also had a real bed! And an old vanity for Elizabeth! But she looked ruefully at the cook stove that burned kerosene. "Guess I'll have to learn to cook," she said. Dan chuckled, "I know more than enough to start."

Ann had brought the paper which had been published while they were gone, and the galleys needing correcting for next week's paper. Elizabeth wished she could have been here to visit with her. She spread the papers and galleys out on the bed and began to digest them.

While she worked, Dan sat watching her and looking around the tent. The reality of the circumstances to which he had brought her, struck him forcefully. "Honey, I'm sorry I can't provide a better place for you to live right now. I know how much you must miss your stuff."

"For heaven's sake, Dan, please stop that. Don't want to hear any more of that sorry stuff. Don't you have anything better to do than sit here while I get caught up on what's been happening?"

He smiled in mock agreement. "Yes, Massa. Yo' slave, with yo' kind permission, will go out and do a little catching up of his own." Dan started out, raised the tent flap and threw it outside over the side of the tent. "Maybe that'll cool it down a bit," he said as he left.

She picked up one article, and read it. It said Jack Dempsey was starting his own coal company here in Carbon County, hiring County Commissioner A. E. Gibson to head it up for him. On June third, the paper reported that one day after a picket camp was established at Kenilworth, some strikers ambushed a man trip. The trip was full of miners leaving the mine after their day's work. The strikers fired fifty to a hundred shots at the man trip all along the path of its journey. Elizabeth thought it strange. That many shots and nobody hit?

Justice A. J. Webber of the State Supreme Court praised the way the Governor was handling the strike so far. But The Advocate reported that they could agree with Webber only if he thought "doing nothing" was actually handling violent situations in the county. The Advocate then went on to call, once more, for the governor to have the courage to send in the Guard, especially in light of a man trip full of men fired on. It derided his statement that he was sending another representative to look into it. They wondered if this "flunky" would do a better job of reporting the real violence going on here than the rest of the governor's flunkies had.

As she finished this article, Elizabeth could no longer ignore the pressure on her bladder. She had needed to go since before Dan left, but just could not bring herself to it. Now, she had no choice. She left the tent and headed for the nearest outhouse. She had to wait a bit because it was occupied. Finally, a Mexican lady came out, smiled, and said, "Buenos dias, Señora Cook."

"Good morning to you, too," Elizabeth said as she hurried inside. As she sat in the crude closet, the tears began streaming down her cheeks. Here she was. A part of her knew she'd chosen this because of Dan and the baby. But another part could not help mourning all she'd given up by that choice. She sat there thinking, wiping her eyes with sheets of paper torn from a Montgomery Ward catalog, throwing it down the hole, and trying to get herself under control. But her thoughts would not let go of her. This outhouse is worse than my friends said. I've even lost my name.

Several minutes after she finished what she came to do, she got up and left. She hoped Dan wasn't back in the tent. Even though she was no longer crying, she knew her eyes were red. Back at the tent, thankfully, Dan was not there. She sat down in the chair facing the bed. The next article really caught her eye. Deputy Sheriff Lorenzo Young had been charged with first degree murder. A cousin of Tennis brought the charge. Elizabeth shook her head as she read the next part. The paper described

Young as a deputy shot in the leg trying to keep order. It described Tennis's death as "an outcome of Young's quick reaction in the pursuit of his duty." It continued on to say the charge was welcomed by the sheriff's office as it will serve to put on record the real facts in this case. County Attorney Henry Ruggeri would be prosecuting the case. He vowed that he would prosecute thoroughly so there will be no doubt as to the truth when the jury was given the case for consideration. "Yeah, I'll bet," Elizabeth said to no one in particular.

She turned to the galleys of the paper coming out this week. The first was an editorial calling for new immigration laws. It stated there were three thousand Greeks in the county and only a hundred or less had their wives here. The paper accepted it as a certainty that the men with their wives still in the old country were sending all their money home to Greece. The minute they had built up what would be a fortune back there, they would abandon this country.

Dan came rushing back in. Apparently, he was bursting with news to give her. "Did you hear they got Young in jail?" Elizabeth nodded and said she'd just finished reading about it. "Did they say anything about all the witnesses who told Rugerri that Young shot John in cold blood? Or did they tell the truth, that when Young ran up the road he had nothing wrong with his leg?"

"Not a word. Glad to hear what you said. It helps remind me of how biased they are." She paused for a moment. "I guess I forgot about the mess we're in while we were in the San Rafael."

Dan asked her what she wanted to do now, and she replied whatever he wanted.

"I kind of thought maybe you would enjoy going to see Billy, if you're not too tired from our trip." When she said she wasn't they saddled the horses once again and were on their way.

Elizabeth was all eyes on the way up, and remarked how different everything down there seemed from this high up. It changed how things looked about as much as . . . She struggled for a way to describe it. Then it came to her, as much as the paper distorts the truth. That reminded Elizabeth of one article in the paper. "Dan, did you hear anything about a man trip getting shot up at Kenilworth?" Elizabeth asked. He said he had, leaning to one side a little as Showboat side-stepped to miss a rock in the trail.

"The day after a picket line was set up, the men on a trip coming out of the mine heard a few shots. After the trip stopped, they looked and saw some places where a couple of the cars had been hit by bullets. Frank Bonatti said the company tried to blame it on the picketers, so the governor sent one of his men down to check it out. The governor's investigator said the man trip couldn't be seen from anywhere in the picket camp. The men in the trip testified to him they only heard shots. They said nobody actually saw anybody shooting at the trip. Also, all of them denied hearing any bullets hitting the cars. That's all I know."

Just then, Dan and Elizabeth topped the rise, and Dan looked around, bewildered. The camp was not where it used to be. Then he relaxed as he saw that Billy had moved it even further along the mountain side. He raised his arm and pointed so Elizabeth could see the new camp. As they approached, all was quiet and no one could be seen. But soon a figure moved along the hillside where sheep were grazing. It took just a moment for Dan to realize that the figure wasn't Billy. "Something's wrong," Dan said, "That's not Billy." The man approached them. "Where's Billy?" Dan blurted out without even asking the man's name.

"Are you Señor Dan?" the man asked.

Dan was getting even more upset. "Yes. Where's Billy?" he asked again. But this time his voice carried a tone of command. Dan got off his horse, and the man before him hung his head, and said he did not know. But he added that Billy had left some of his stuff and said to give it to him. All of this was reported in a heavy Mexican accent, the man unable to speak English well.

Dan looked around, disbelieving. "What you mean, stuff?" Dan demanded. The man took a step back, and seemed to look afraid. Elizabeth got off Bonnie.

"My name is Elizabeth," she said in a pleasant tone of voice. "What's your's?"

He said his name was Juan Guzman Arteaga, and he was at her service. Elizabeth smiled. "Pleased to meet you, Juan. You already know my husband Dan. Dan, shake hands with Mr. Arteaga. "Dan curbed his anxiety long enough to shake Juan's hand.

"Long time wait, Señor. Maybe you not come, I think." Dan did his best to relax, and let things work themselves out. But what this man was saying wasn't helping any. "Three weeks I wait."

Dan thought fast. That was almost the entire time since he had last seen Billy. What with the plans for the wedding, and the honeymoon, and all, he hadn't been able to visit Billy till they got back. "And he didn't tell you where he was going?"

"No, Senor," Juan said. Then, continuing as best he could, he explained in a little more detail. "He send message my boss. I must come quick here. Take care of sheep. He say he must go. I come, he give me stuff. A palo. Sorry, not know Engles. Wood, long wood."

"You mean stick?" Dan asked.

"Si, stick. And a sack, for, for, just a minute, I no can say in Engles." Juan turned, went into his tent and came back out carrying the items. Dan saw Billy's stick, but it had been changed. Now instead of a number of feathers adorning it, there was only one. It was a big feather, mostly white, with a black tip. Also tied to it was a rattlesnake rattle. Also, there was Billy's medicine bag.

Grief gripped Dan's heart. He knew that unless Billy was on the trail of the spirits, he would never give up these things. He felt Turk had been shot all over again, or he just saw Harry Carpenter dead. A sob escaped from his throat.

"Please, honey. What's wrong?" Elizabeth asked.

"Billy's dead."

Juan shook his head back and forth in denial. "No, no, Señor. He is not dead. He say tell you take better care of stick than last." Dan was a little angry at himself when he remembered he hadn't even thought of the stick after Billy gave it to him. He didn't even know where it was.

Elizabeth was getting impatient to get to the bottom of this. "If he isn't dead, and he didn't say where he was going, how come you keep acting as if it's some sort of mystery?"

"He no say nothing. We stand front of tent, he go get stuff, give me, say keep for Dan. He call me hijo, say tent and other stuff for me keep. He say Senor Dan come but I must wait. I go in tent, put stuff on bed, come back quick, he gone. He nothing take."

Impossible, Elizabeth thought, gone? Just gone? How could that be? You can see for a hundred yards in all directions.

"I not know," Juan said, but his answer seemed evasive.

Elizabeth was not about to let this drop, but before she could say anything, Dan almost exploded. "You mean he just disappeared?"

"Señora, Señor, we civilized people. We know nobody just disappear," he said, although his tone carried no conviction. "But Señor, when I looked, all I could see was coyote walking down trail."

CHAPTER 26

MONEY IN YOUR POCKET

The phone on the office wall began ringing the moment Benton stepped into the office. He lifted the ear piece, and almost his entire conversation consisted of phrases similar to, "Yes, Sir," and "No, Sir," and "I'll do that." Benton hung up the phone, and began swearing silently to himself. When Frank Cameron told him to get to Salt Lake fast, be ready to stay a couple of days, and bring the other three Supers with him, Benton knew it was not going to be a fun day.

Benton walked into the outer office, told Ganz to ring up Tom Parmley, Mark Haywood, and Hank Thompson. Ganz was to tell them to cancel everything and get ready for a trip to Salt Lake. Ganz was also to tell them Benton was on his way and would get there as quickly as he could.

Benton rushed home and began throwing stuff in a suitcase. In less than thirty minutes, he was pushing the Packard out of town, and within an hour he picked up the others and was on his way.

At headquarters, Hotchkiss ushered them into Cameron's office.

"You made good time, Bob," Cameron said. Benton smiled and nodded. Cameron waved off the coffee proffered by Hotchkiss. He pointed to the chairs. "Take a load off your feet. Big problem right now," he began, "Governor Maybe is definitely giving all the operators the cold shoulder." He paused as the men finished seating themselves. "We've tried to meet with him several times. Each time we're told his schedule is full right now. We figure he's avoiding us."

Tom Parmley leaned across the table. "Hotchkiss says the Governor is out of town. How are you going to get him to meet with you?"

Cameron leaned forward as well, getting closer to Parmley than the usual etiquette would permit. "Never mind the governor. He's my problem. I called all of you in to discuss your problem—the production of coal—or in this case, the lack thereof." Here it comes, Benton thought.

Cameron looked at Benton. "Bob, this strike is eating into corporate profits badly. Unless we do something quick to get production at all four mines back on track, we just can't afford a General Super." Bob hoped he hadn't turned white as Cameron sat back in his chair and just glared at the other men. Then he looked toward Benton again. "Of course, if we are forced to make that move, you're welcome to stay on as Super of Sunnyside, if you choose to."

Benton felt queasy, but he didn't display any outward sign. He hadn't been fired, but Cameron was putting responsibility for poor production squarely on his shoulders. Further, it sounded as though his resignation wouldn't cause them a great deal of unhappiness, either. When he spoke, there was acceptance in his voice. "Thanks for clearing that up for me. How long have I got?"

Cameron leaned back, folded his hands across his stomach, and didn't answer right away. Benton felt slightly relieved. A quick answer would mean the situation was already decided.

Cameron let out a deep breath. "The way things stand now, three weeks, maybe, a month tops."

"Man, I hope this strike is over before then," Parmley interjected.

"Not likely," Cameron shot right back. "In the West and Central Districts, things are going the union's way. But strike or no strike, Utah Fuel will produce coal. Do I make myself clear?"

The Supers all nodded, gravely. Cameron unclasped his hands, leaned forward again. "Good. Now let's see what we can do to get more coal."

Thompson fidgeted in his chair, and cleared his throat. "Boss, we are already doing everything we know how. We are working our men over-time, some even double shifts. We're even cutting back on some of the safety measures, we just don't have the man power to do it. We discussed making overtime and some double shifts mandatory. We're afraid if we do that, however, even more of the men would join the strike as they did at two other mines that tried it."

Cameron just stared at him with fish-cold eyes. "Who cares about all of that? What I'm paying you for is to produce coal." He didn't add, or else, but Benton got that message.

Cameron looked down, and thought for a moment. "When I was running things in Carbon County we didn't handle trouble-makers with kid gloves as you all seem to be doing. Make no mistakes, I'm not advocating you do anything that will be interpreted as breaking the law. But in my day we made it so miserable for those jerks in their coffee houses and Tent Towns that many of them left the union to come back to work. How many men have you had break their strike?"

Nobody looked at Cameron. They were all looking down at the table. Cameron snorted. "I thought so. Reason you're here is to see if I can put some spine into you gutless wimps."

Benton wanted to smash him in the face. In his entire life he had never been talked to like this. How dare he? Benton had about enough. Job, or no job, he had to put an end to this. "Listen, Frank. Times change. Jimmy Morgan and JD what's-his-name from over in Wyoming have our men so brow-beaten that they are afraid to even think of going back to work. And as for kid gloves, you know what happened to Saxton."

Rather than the "Get out of here" Benton had been expecting, Cameron smiled. "See," Cameron said, and continued smiling. "It's working. At least Benton is starting to develop guts."

Parmley asked if maybe he didn't mean get down to brass knuckles. Cameron nodded his head. "That's the spirit, Tom."

The atmosphere as they continued was almost friendly. Cameron told them he had been doing his part. While the Mormon Church took no official stand, all the bishops advised everyone that there were good jobs waiting in Carbon County. Nearly fifty Mormon men had applied for work.

"And that's not all," Cameron said. "We've hired a couple of labor agents, they promise that within two weeks we'll have another fifty men," he said. Turning to Benton he added, "We even got you that armature winder Strang said he needed. A Czech named Fred something or other. Hotchkiss contacted his old friends at the Denver and Rio Grande. They can get me four private cars here by the time we need them. That way, we'll load a separate car for each mine. It can be switched off and taken to you without the men ever having to get off till they're in your camps."

Cameron was looking mean again. "I don't want any pickets even close to those cars, peaceable or otherwise. We've worked too hard to get 'em to have 'em scared off. Clear?"

Again the heads nodded. Benton thought for a moment and turned to the other three Supers. He figured now was as good a time as any to exercise his authority as General Super over the other three men. "Parmley and Thompson, I want you to send security crews to Thistle. Have them board the train there and ride with the men. Their job will be to control any pickets. But more important, they are to see that nobody gets out of those cars until they arrive in your camps. Haywood you have your security people board the train at Helper, mine will board at Price."

The three men nodded once more. Then Cameron reached into his coat pocket again and brought out some folded sheets of paper and handed them to Benton. "This concerns you." Benton took the proffered papers and saw immediately that they were legal papers. He began reading rapidly and finished in a little over a minute.

"What's it say?" Parmley asked.

"We had a boy named Carpenter killed awhile back. The Industrial Commission paid the parents the usual monthly death benefits. Utah Fuel lawyers contested it on the grounds that there was no proof that Carpenter contributed any money to his parents, so they were not his dependents and not entitled to any benefits. Secondly, and most interesting to the appellate board, was that Carpenter did not have a release from the principal to go to work in the mine, and lied about his age on his application. Therefore, he wasn't a legal employee."

"Thanks, Bob. I want you to advise the Carpenters of the board's decision right away." Benton said he could since Mr. Carpenter was a faithful employee not on strike.

Cameron took some water, and changed the subject. He began complaining once more about the non-availability of the governor. He said there was no guarantee the governor would be any more willing to meet with the operators when he got back than he had been before he left.

Benton sat thinking rapidly as Cameron said he must find some way to meet the governor, even if he had to do it without the other operators. He smiled. I know they're trying to set up separate meetings themselves.

Benton looked at Cameron, "Frank, do you know what time the governor's train reaches Wendover?" He was smiling inside, but he kept a serious look on his face.

Cameron looked puzzled, "Why?" he asked.

"If the train arrives there at any reasonable hour in the morning, we could drive out and board it when it stops to take on water." Cameron didn't even hesitate. He shot a look at Hotchkiss and nodded his head toward the door. Hotchkiss got up, and was back in a couple of minutes with word that the train would arrive in Wendover at 8:00 a.m.

"Good," Cameron said and began to smile. "Good idea, Bob. We'll leave here at about five in the morning. Think the Packard can make the hundred and twenty miles in three hours?"

Benton now let the smile show on his face. "Once we get past the lake, there are a lot of straight stretches. There's one stretch along the salt flats that's thirty-seven miles without a single turn, and flat as a pancake. We'll make it with enough time to spare for breakfast and coffee."

"One other thing," Cameron interjected. "Is it all right with you if Charley drives your Packard back to Salt Lake from Wendover?" Benton said that would be fine, and Cameron added that was good. He wanted Benton at the meeting on board the train.

The other three Supers asked whether they should take the evening train back to Carbon county, but Cameron said that idea was baloney. He wanted each and every one of them penned up with the governor for the two hour train trip back to Salt Lake. That way the governor could hear first hand what trials and tribulations were forced on the operators by trouble-making union flunkies.

When they boarded the train in Wendover, Governor Maybe allowed them an immediate audience, seemed interested in what they had to say, and promised to look into the matter more fully. As they rode the taxi from the train station back to the office, Cameron was all smiles. It was a feather in his cap to talk with the governor when none of the other operators had any luck.

At the office, Cameron put his arm around Benton's shoulders, and even told him not to worry too much about the company having to drop the General Super's job, "Till we see how things develop." They made general conversation for a few more minutes, until Hotchkiss arrived with the Packard. As the Supers prepared to leave, Cameron said it had been a good meeting.

The trip back to Carbon County in the Packard was uneventful. Parmley didn't want to get off in Winter Quarters. He said something about having business in Price. Benton thought Parmley looked worried, and the moment the other two men were let off, Benton found out why.

As Benton drove, Parmley looked at him. "You know that bastard would fire us just for pleasure, don't you?" Parmley asked. Benton slowed to take the turn through Blue Cut, then said there wasn't a doubt in his mind. "You know those other two bootlickers aren't going to help you one bit," Parmley insisted. "In fact, do you realize the jump switch Cameron has put you in?"

Benton chuckled. "Come on, Tom. You don't really think I wouldn't catch on to the fact that by laying the blame on me, Cameron's got those other two waiting for a shot at my job, do you?"

Parmley sat back and relaxed. "Just checking to see how you'd answer. If you pretended not to know, I'd have figured you were including me in those you've got to watch out for now." Parmley rolled the window down, and spat out into the air rushing by. "You know I'll help you all I can, Bob," he stated simply, but convincingly.

"Sure, and thanks. But in the end, I know, it's up to me."

When Benton got back to Sunnyside, it was still early enough to get some work done. He called in Rasmussen and the security crew. He wanted to make plans for the successful run of special cars as soon as possible. First thing at the meeting, Rasmussen started acting the big shot, and began giving the other deputies orders about what he did, and did not want happening.

Benton held up his hand. "Just a minute, Ovie. With most of our deputies on the train, that leaves us pretty naked here in town. I want you to make sure we're safe here." Benton turned to Webb. "Art, this train trip will be your baby. When we learn its timetable, we'll meet for final plans. "Webb didn't conceal his pleasure very well. "Sure thing, Boss. I won't let you down."

Benton said the only other item of importance on the agenda was the big union rally that was happening in Price tomorrow. He wanted Rasmussen to talk with his men and decide which ones could be spared to go to the meeting. "If anything important happens, I want to know about it immediately," he said. He didn't add, so Cameron can't blind side me with it again.

With that, Benton dismissed the security crew and waited for his next appointment to arrive. He was not looking forward to it. As Mr. and Mrs. Carpenter came into the room, Benton rose, greeted them, and shook hands with Mr. Carpenter. He motioned them to a chair and sat down behind his desk. He picked up the legal papers and looked at the Carpenters. "Sorry, folks, I've got some very bad news for you. The review board for the Industrial Commission has denied you any claim on your son's death." Mrs. Carpenter started weeping softly. Mr. Carpenter looked as if he'd been struck between the eyes with a baseball bat. He closed his eyes, and shook his head back and forth a couple of times. He opened his eyes, but did not look straight at Benton. Instead, he looked at his shoes.

"I don't understand, Sir. Our boy was killed in your mine while he was on the job. How can the Industrial Commission do this to us?" Benton told him that he felt just as badly about this as they did. What he did not tell them was that the Industrial Commission ruling was in response to a brief filed by Utah Fuel attorneys requesting such an action.

Benton looked sad. "My hands are tied," he said. "Once the Industrial Commission makes a ruling, that's it. As to why, there are a couple of reasons, but I'll only go into the most important one. Your boy was not a legal employee of this company."

Carpenter looked badly confused. "Not an employee? I don't understand. He worked in the mine and the company paid his wages." Benton explained to him about the release from the principal. Without that the company could not legally hire him, and only did so because he lied and said he was eighteen. "I told him," Carpenter said as Mrs. Carpenter continued crying. "I told him not to lie, but he said if he didn't, you wouldn't hire him."

"But, but . . ." Mrs. Carpenter started to stutter, "But you did hire him, and he turned eighteen before he was killed. Doesn't that make him a legal employee?" Benton became evasive and said he wasn't an attorney, but the Commission had all the facts before they made their ruling.

"What's worse," Benton said, looking at the papers, "his lying on his employment application is now going to force you folks to pay back what you've already been given. But don't worry, my friends, Utah Fuel has a big heart, and we'll work out a schedule to help you pay it back without too much trouble on your part."

Then Benton looked straight at Carpenter and smiled. "I'll tell you what I'm going to do. I'll even let you work all the overtime you want. Why, in no time you'll have the award paid back, and have extra money in your pocket to boot!"

As Benton went home that evening, he was troubled by the predicament the Carpenters were in, but he'd seen worse. He knew that if the attorneys didn't scrutinize every claim with a magnifying glass, the company would be so overwhelmed with phony claims, they'd soon be out of business. Even so, he slept fitfully.

"What a beautiful morning," Elizabeth observed as they headed out for Price the next day.

"Pull over and stop," Dan said.

She looked at him quizzically, but did as he asked. "What's up?" she asked.

"Bout time you taught me to drive." Without another word, Dan got out of the car and headed for the other side. Elizabeth slid over as he got in. Dan sat behind the wheel, grasped it with both hands, and looked at Elizabeth. "Okay, Professor, what do I do?"

She explained the basics, had him practice a few important items such as shifting while they sat there. She looked as serious as she could, but her voice held an undertone of jest. "But if you wreck us, you'd better make sure you kill me. If you just cripple me, I'll make the rest of your life hell." She reached up, forced her hands against the dashboard, and braced herself firmly against the seat. "Okay," she said, pretended fear in her voice, "Let 'er rip."

Before it was over, however, Elizabeth no longer felt it was a laughing matter. Dan ground the gears time and again, let the clutch out so fast he stalled the engine at others, and made such lurching and jerky starts, she got a headache. When finally he could get the car in motion without too much trouble, he had a hard time steering, and began weaving back and forth over the road. Finally, she reached over and held the wheel with one hand. "Keep your hands on the wheel and feel it as I steer," she said. At last he understood what she meant by over-correcting.

Dan slowed as he drove the Star over Nickerson's Hill.

"Hey, Dan," Tom called from the sidewalk as the car started to pass by him. "Why'd she let you drive? Give her something special, did ya?" Elizabeth smiled and waved to Tom. Dan tried to shift down, but ground the gears. He jammed his feet on the clutch and brake, and the car came to a shuddering stop.

Tom slapped his knee in a gleeful gesture. Elizabeth waved to him again, this time beckoning him to the car. Tom came over and Elizabeth slid over to let Tom get in. "Thanks for the lift," he said. "Where we going?"

"Don't know," Elizabeth answered. "Where we going, honey?"

"Where we going? Who says that's my responsibility? My job is to get us there."

Tom thought for a moment, and said it would be a good idea to go up to the park where the parade would soon be starting. Dan chuckled, and tried to pay close attention to letting the clutch out slowly and smoothly. "Yes, Massa. Park okay with you, Missy?" With her agreement, they were off, as if Dan had been driving for years. Dan was so busy shifting, working the clutch, and all the rest, he barely had time to make sure he was taking the right route to the park.

Men from all the different coal camps were already gathering. They parked and got out of the car. Tom took his leave and said there was union business he needed to attend to. Elizabeth and Dan mixed with other people there, and Dan introduced her to friends and acquaintances. Again, he was feeling proud. Showing Elizabeth off was better than driving the Star.

Soon the parade was underway. It was at least three times bigger than the parade held in John Tennis' honor. There were four different bands, and each camp marched in a group. Signs identifying each group and carrying union slogans abounded everywhere. Dan's favorite was, "WIN or LOSE, UNION FOREVER." He discussed it with Elizabeth, and she agreed.

Finally, the parade brought them back to the park. Everyone sat on the grass and benches to get ready for the speeches they were all looking forward to. Sam King stood up first. "We all know how hard this strike has been on us," he said amid rounds of applause. "And I know how sick and tired you must be of your leadership harping on not committing acts of violence." The crowd murmured their agreement. King turned, and reached down to JD Ramsey who was sitting beside him. Ramsey handed him Salt Lake's Evening Telegraph newspaper. King opened it up, and held it high above his head for all to see.

The front page headline read, "MASSACRE IN BLOODY WILLIAMSON COUNTY." King pulled the paper down and read excerpts from the long article. The dateline was Herrin, Illinois. Superintendent C. K. McDowell and between twenty-seven and forty-five persons were slain when striking union miners stormed the mine.

"This," King fairly shouted, "This is what happens when things get out of hand. We warned you about the damage that would result. Listen to these reports."

The Carbon County strikers were horrified to hear that according to witnesses, McDowell, with only one leg, was beaten to death with stones before being riddled with bullets. Wounded men were kicked around in the scorching sun on dusty roads.

Sam held up the newspaper again. "We told you how they'd distort the truth. Listen to this, and see how much of it you believe." He pulled the paper down and began reading one "eye-witness" account about miners' wives taking little children to the morgue, pointing out the dead bodies. "Look, look what your pap did," the paper reported they had said.

Most of the crowd sat in subdued, stunned silence. Various comments muttered here and there indicated most of them didn't believe the papers. Others said they couldn't imagine how bad things got there to cause the strikers to do such a thing.

King folded the paper and handed it back to Ramsey. Then he faced the crowd again. "You know it's got to be a bunch of crap, start to finish, and I know it. But what do the people in New York know? What do the people in Chicago know? What do the people in San Francisco know? I'll tell you what they know. They know what they read in the papers. They know miners are a bunch of illiterate, brutal beasts. That's what violence brings." With that, he sat down.

Almost to a man, the assembled strikers pledged to prevent this from ever happening in Carbon County. On the spot they called for the creation of law and order committees to police each camp. JD Ramsey acceded to their demands and groups were set up to discuss the possibilities. Before it was all over, union officials had appointed Dan, Andy Vullis, and Frank Bonatti to head up the Sunnyside law and order committee.

All this was time consuming and left little time for others to speak. Sam King's display had put a damper on the whole afternoon. The next morning the Salt Lake papers would report that instead of violence and rowdyism, in Carbon County, the whole parade and meeting which followed had been as quiet and as orderly as a church gathering. As they left, Dan assured Elizabeth he'd had enough excitement for one day. So she got behind the wheel of the Star.

CHAPTER 27

WHO'S NEXT

The night of the rally, a loud commotion woke them shortly after midnight. Dressing hurriedly, they left their tent to discover frightened and angry men running into Tent Town. Dan rushed to Andy's tent. Tom and Frank were already there. Quick conversations indicated that about two dozen masked men raided the coffee houses. Each coffee house down the road was being hit. Apparently, it was still in progress. Quickly, Dan said it would be better if Elizabeth stayed, and the group started up the road. Other men from the camp joined as they rushed up the road.

They were slowed as more victims of the raid came fleeing toward camp. More hurried questions to which there were panicked answers: flour sacks over their heads, masked men wielded guns and clubs; said they would kill if the Greeks didn't get out of the town; they beat up some.

Again the rush toward the coffee houses, but this time more wary. A short distance further, and the men from camp were stopped again by other victims. They said some of the coffee house owners and some of the strikers were being held hostage. Dan and the rest took off at a dead run. The sight at the first one sickened them. A number of battered and bleeding men were lying on the floor, or sitting on chairs. One was Andy. He was sitting and trying to wipe the blood off of himself. "Are you all right, Andy?" Dan asked in an almost pleading voice. Andy said he wasn't hurt bad, and asked Dan to see to the other men who were hurt worse.

Dan looked but saw every hurt man was being tended by others from Tent Town. He turned back around to Andy, and began checking him out to see how badly he was hurt. Andy winced as Dan touched his left side. "Kicked me in the ribs-hurts like hell." Dan discovered the cut on his head was relatively small. However, the cut was bleeding profusely. He took a napkin off a table and placed the napkin on top of Andy's head. He began to apply pressure. Andy grimaced.

Doc Dowd came bursting through the door. Dan ran over to him quickly, pointed to Andy. Doc took a quick look, then brushed Dan aside. Obviously, other men were hurt worse. Doc began tending them first. Dan walked back over to Andy. He sat down across from Andy. "Doc will be here in a minute. He's taking care of some others first."

"Good," Andy said. He let out a big sigh. "I think the pain in my ribs is easing up some." Dan stood up, and looked at the top of Andy's head. Dan sat back down, and asked what made the cut. "Don't know," Andy replied. "So many people in here. So much was going on. I couldn't follow it. Then somebody hit me from behind, or from the side with a club of some sort."

Dan asked if he recognized any of them. "No, they had small flour sacks on. But though I can't identify them, I recognized some of the voices. I think they were all from town. No hired goons from outside." Andy asked Dan for a drink. Dan found a glass and poured Andy some wine.

Doc Dowd was passing by and stopped. "Good idea. Give everybody else a drink, too," he said.

After returning from giving the wine, Dan looked at Andy. "Why did they do this?"

"They pretended they just didn't like Greeks, but it had something to do with the strike. They kept shouting they were citizens doing what has needed to be done. They cursed us and told us all to go back where we came from. Seems they'd rehearsed it. All repeated the same things."

Doc's coming to tend Andy stopped more conversation. He cut some hair away from Andy's scalp. "Needs a couple of stitches," he said and began fishing around in his bag. Doc said he didn't have time for anesthesia, and began closing the wound. Thank heavens it was over fast. Andy hadn't reacted badly at all, but as Doc began to put a bandage on, Andy was breathing heavily and sweating profusely. Then Doc made Andy stand up. He had Andy raise and lower his arm a couple of times. He asked Andy some questions, and probed here and there along his chest. He confirmed Andy's own diagnosis, bruised but not broken. He looked at Dan, "Help me get that guy up," he said pointing to a man on the floor. "Got to set his broken arm."

Other people began cleaning up the place and talking with the half dozen or so hurt men. Soon somebody brought a pitcher of wine to the table. Both Andy and Dan availed themselves of the opportunity. Dan talked with Andy some more, but there was not much more to be learned. Once Dan was sure he could no longer be of any help, he returned to Tent Town. Elizabeth was waiting for him down the road, she was in a near panic. "Oh, Dan," she said, "I was so worried." She rushed into his arms, and the hug she gave him made him glad there was nothing wrong with his ribs.

Dan told her all he could remember of what had happened. He told her how worried he was. Not just about what happened to the Greeks, but that if it happened to them, it could happen to anybody. "Who's next?" he asked Elizabeth, but she had no answer. "Will they come busting into our tent and break our heads too?" She had no answer for this either. They went to bed for the second time that night, but this time sleep didn't come easily.

Dan and Elizabeth were just finishing the breakfast dishes when someone knocked on the tent pole. It was Andy Vullis, and they invited him in. When they inquired about his injuries, Andy said his ribs were a lot better this morning. The bandage on his head still had dried blood on it, however. They offered him something to eat, which he declined. Elizabeth asked him what brought him to their tent so early in the morning. He said. "I want to run down to Mounds this morning and keep an eye on my Greeks. They're pretty upset over what happened last night."

Dan nodded. "Yeah, I imagine so. We're pretty upset ourselves." He turned to Elizabeth, "Aren't we?" he asked. She agreed. Dan thought for a moment, and then turned to Elizabeth. "Would you mind driving us down? I want to stay there with Andy for a while."

"Sure, Honey," she agreed quickly. "How long will you be staying?" Dan asked if she'd mind coming back down and picking him up for lunch, and she agreed. They piled into the Star. On the way down Andy said last night's episode showed the company must really be getting desperate.

"Exactly!" Dan agreed. "And even worse for them, we didn't fight back as they expected." Andy said he was real proud of his countrymen.

Elizabeth cranked the wheel, barely missing a dead rabbit lying in the road. "Have you thought about the possibility that since they didn't get the desired response last night, they'll try something else?" Andy suddenly became even more upset and said he hoped they would have time to figure out the company's next move, and prepare for it. Dan agreed, and said they'd better really be on guard. The next one will be so big it'll probably bring in the Guard for sure.

Elizabeth was looking extremely unhappy. "You guys got to know I love my dad and my mom." The two men looked at her. Dan tried to figure out what this had to do with the conversation. "But," Elizabeth continued, as she pulled the Star up to the depot at Mounds, "I know my father better than either of you. Also, I know his friends, and I've over-heard a lot of their conversations. Anxious to get the Guard in? They're on it like a bird dog on a quail."

Before Elizabeth dropped Andy and Dan off, they all agreed she should tell Frank and Tom what they'd been talking about as soon as she got back to camp. The boys said good-bye and went up to the pickets. By staying a couple hundred yards above the terminal and well away from the tracks, they were off both railroad and company property and could picket legally.

Dan left Andy and walked down to the depot to see about the morning train when it stopped.

Besides the engineer and a fireman from the D&RG crew waiting at the depot to take the train into Sunnyside from the main line, there was also a Utah Fuel railway engineer and fireman sitting in the lobby as well. Since the train wasn't due in yet, he stopped to talk with the D&RG crew. Their union was planning its own strike soon, and Dan felt a kinship with them. Finally, the station master came out of his office. For some reason he seemed jumpy, and not his usual talkative self. Dan felt something was wrong. He left the depot and headed back to the pickets.

Andy greeted him, and asked what was up. Dan cocked his head to one side. "Something's wrong. There's a company engineer and fireman there, and the station master seemed almost jumpy to me." Just then they heard the first whistle of the approaching train. As Dan turned to leave,

Andy said thanks, and began to warn the men to keep their eyes peeled for trouble.

"See ya," Dan said. "If anything's going on, I should be able to get back to warn you in plenty of time before the Sunnyside cars get switched off the main line." The train pulled in, and stopped. The D&RG men got in their small engine and hooked onto their cars just switched off the main line. Everything went smoothly until the Sunnyside train pulled back up to the depot and stopped. Dan was surprised to see the two D&RG men get out of the engine, and head for the depot. Suddenly, another figure started climbing out of the cab of the engine, it was Art Webb.

"It's a scab train," the D&RG engineer said to Dan. "We won't take it in."

The two company train men were already coming out of the depot, as though they expected to operate the engine all along. "Hey, you two!" Webb shouted to them, "Get in this cab, and get this train moving, and I mean now!"

The men were barely there when Dan was on his way to tell Andy. Andy listened intently, then made a quick decision. He began shouting to his men in Greek. "I told them to stay back until the train started moving. Then I want us to get as close to the right of way as possible," he said. Everybody scurried to pick up picket signs. "Here," Andy said, handing Dan a sign.

In but a moment, there was a puff of steam, and the wheels of the engine spun, throwing sand from the sanders under the primaries. With a chug, chug, chug, the engine started forward.

The train picked up speed and approached the first of the pickets, Andy shouted and waved once more and the men backed away from the train a little. By now, the train was about half way up the picket line. Andy was a little closer to the train than Dan, and was a little higher up the bank from the railroad bed. Andy raised his sign and wiggled it back and forth. Dan started to raise his sign, but froze.

With horror, Dan saw Art Webb, rifle in hand, leaning out the back of the cab of the engine. He aimed at Dan, and fired. Dan didn't even have time to flinch; the shot hit Andy's upraised arm and knocked him to the ground. Now, as when Turk was shot, time went crazy on Dan. He dived for the dirt, still falling, he saw Andy hit the ground and bounce off it once.

When at last Dan felt the relative safety of the ground, he rolled over, heard slow blasts of sound, and saw powder smoke erupting from inside the train. A few men on the picket began pulling pistols, and returning fire. As Dan continued to look up, the engine and cars seemed to move slowly past. Webb was still leaning out the side of the cab slowly firing shot after shot.

Then, strangely, Art slowly raised his hand and his rifle went gracefully arching into the air. Art continued the motion of his hands until they were behind his head. They seemed to pull him backwards onto the floor of the cab of the engine. Dan got the impression that blood was splattering. The train passed. Although it seemed to Dan to take forever, the truth was that the train was actually accelerating rapidly. As quickly as the gun battle started, it ended.

Dan got to his knees and looked over to Andy, who lay moaning and bleeding on the gravel of the railroad bed, hit bad in the shoulder. Dan got to his feet. Andy's Greeks were there. Rudely, they brushed Dan aside, picked Andy up in their arms, and started off with him. Dan just stood there, aware of everything around him. None of it seemed real, yet it all seemed to be happening at the same moment: men running off with Andy, other Greeks high-tailing it toward the mountains, some going in other directions, and the D&RG engineer and fireman running toward him. He stood as a statue, taking it all in, and not really knowing what any of it meant.

"Git," the engineer was screaming at him. "Git out of here."

"Station master's already called Sheriff Kelter, and Benton's goons," the fireman was shouting.

The engineer took Dan by the shoulders and shook him. "You better be long gone before they get here." Without a word, Dan started running up the tracks.

"Hey!" the D&RG engineer shouted. Dan stopped and looked back. "Get off these tracks, and stay clear of the road, too," he called.

"Oh, yeah," Dan said and headed off at a dead run. When he reached Big Spring Ranch road, he realized he'd come over seven miles at a dead run. His heart swelled with gratitude. Elizabeth was driving so fast along the bumpy road, she was being thrown back and forth inside the car. She had a hard time holding onto the wheel. Dan turned and ran toward her. She braked the car to a stop, jumped out and came running toward him.

Her face was streaked with tears, dust, and mud where the two had joined. "Thank heaven, thank heaven," she was repeating over and over as they threw themselves into each other's arms. Dan held on tight, gasping for breath. Elizabeth looked up at him. "I almost missed you. I almost missed you." Dan was still panting so heavily, he couldn't speak. But he nodded his head in agreement. "Are you hurt?" She asked. Dan tried to speak, then just shook his head back and forth. He pointed toward the car, and Elizabeth understood. They began walking the few yards back to the car. Dan opened the door, got inside, and collapsed on the seat. "All hell's broke loose," Elizabeth said, her tears gone. She reached out and took Dan's hand. "Word is that Andy's hurt bad." Her words brought the horror of the moment back to Dan. He hadn't thought of it since he started running. He opened his mouth to tell her about it, but only wheezing came out. Elizabeth reached up and touched the side of his face with the palm of her hand. "Shh, just rest. I don't know for sure about Andy. That's just what the company fireman said."

Dan was able to gasp a single word, "Webb?"

"He's dead. Couple more are wounded. Why, Dan? Why'd the Greeks shoot up the train?"

"Didn't," Dan gasped, breathed heavily a couple more times, then added, "Webb shot first." Again he breathed heavily. "Aiming at me."

Elizabeth couldn't believe it. "The company engineer said it's too bad Webb had to shoot from a moving train, or the trouble-making Greek would be dead instead of shot in the shoulder."

"Aiming at me," Dan insisted. "Andy's arm up," he said, still gasping "Shoulder, arm over my head." He kept struggling for breath. The pace of his breathing slowly began to decrease. Elizabeth started the car, and began to turn around. Dan grabbed the wheel. "Where you going?"

"Back to town."

Dan was shaking his head back and forth violently, "Can't, they'll get me."

"No, Dan. The train stopped at the guard shack. I ran over when we saw them taking Webb's body out of the engine." Again Dan started to protest and tell her Sheriff Kelter was coming. Elizabeth put her hand to his mouth. "You rest. Don't talk till I'm finished," she said. Dan nodded. "When I ran over, nobody stopped me. Guess it's 'cause I'm his daughter. Anyway, in no time Doc was there and so was Rasmussen. Rasmussen got everybody from the train together near where I was helping Doc, and started questioning them about who was on the picket line. Almost everybody named Andy. Some said just the Greeks, and some said a specific name or two, but nobody mentioned you."

Dan looked puzzled. "Webb knew . . ." he started to say, then stopped. "The company engineer and fireman knew." Elizabeth looked perplexed, and asked why. "They were in the depot when I was there." Hopefully, Elizabeth said maybe they hadn't seen him. Dan didn't answer for a moment. He was getting his breath under control, and needed just a little more time. "Saw me," he said, after another pause. "Didn't mention me?" Elizabeth shook her head in wonderment.

"Only answer I can think of is they're protecting me because of you," he said.

"That's silly, why . . ." Elizabeth began. "Let's drive back. Bet nobody's looking for you."

On the way back Elizabeth explained that right after Rasmussen read the list from the depot, a couple of cars arrived, and several deputies and other men got in. They all had rifles as well as pistols. Before Rasmussen got in, he told the ones waiting that soon a string of horses would arrive. They were to search the foothills and arrest any Greek they found.

Elizabeth pulled up in front of their tent. Dan was still sweating heavily, and his clothes were wet and stained, but his breathing was almost normal. They went inside, and Dan started to change. There was a knock on the tent pole. Elizabeth's head jerked toward the front of the tent. Dan put his finger in front of his mouth. He lowered his finger and mouthed the word, "Who?"

Elizabeth looked afraid. "Who is it?" she asked.

"Tom. Dan here?" he asked. Dan finished dressing as Tom came in. "Have a seat, Tom, I'll be with you in a minute." Just then there was another knock on the tent pole. All three heads in the tent jerked toward the tent pole.

Elizabeth acted calm. "Yes, who is it?" she asked. It was Frank and they asked him in.

When Frank was seated as well, Dan and Elizabeth sat on the bed. They told Frank and Tom everything they saw and heard. Both Tom and Frank had many questions. Tom said he thought the whole thing was a set-up. The Greeks being raided the night before was a part of it, as was Dan not being named. Both Elizabeth and Dan had trouble following it until Frank explained.

"Tom's got to be right. They knew when they brought in the scabs, the Greeks would be on the picket line; knew if they shot first, the Greeks would shoot back. Now they're going to claim the Greeks shot up the train as an act of vengeance for last night."

Dan was nodding his head in agreement. "And having the Big Boss's daughter and husband involved just wouldn't fit that picture." Dan heaved a sigh of relief at not going to jail.

Tom looked concerned, however. "When the Guard gets here, you're going to have to tell them you were at the shooting, and that you saw Art Webb shoot first."

Frank nodded. "And when Andy's arrested, Sam King will call Dan as a defense witness."

After Frank left, Tom agreed with what Frank had said. Tom said he believed that for once the union had the right people in the right place at the right time. He was no sooner out of the tent, when Dan turned to Elizabeth. "Let's start on lunch. We won't have much time later."

"What shall we fix?" she asked. Dan suggested beans. Elizabeth shook her head in exasperation. "I know we're having beans. I meant how'll we fix them?" They warmed up some of the leftover beans in a pot, and put a few small scraps of ham in for flavor. Dan went to the box at the side of the tent and got out some cheese and the butter for the bread.

They were just finishing their lunch when a tent pole knock announced they had visitors. "Come," Dan said, chewing rapidly to finish. He was still in the process of swallowing when Morgan, Ramsey, and King came into the tent. These the couple had expected, but to their surprise Major Johnson was also with the union men.

The Major informed them that the Guard was indeed being sent in by Governor Maybe. Dan's heart sank. There goes the strike, he said to himself. Now they'll be able to bring in all the scab strike-breakers they want, and have the military protect them.

The discussion which followed was along similar lines as the earlier conversation with Frank and Tom. The officials agreed that Tom's assessment of it as a set-up looked more and more plausible. The major said, unless definite proof of this was discovered, it'd remain an allegation.

Before they left, Jimmy asked Dan and Elizabeth if they would be willing to go to Price and get the special edition papers from Salt Lake. The union men and the major were anxious to see them. The couple agreed. The train had already arrived when they got there, and the papers were going fast. The dispatcher for the newspapers said it was a good thing Salt Lake sent down four times more papers than they usually did. Dan could only get ten copies of each

Dan read the articles to Elizabeth as she drove. "The Telegram says, the National Guard units from Salt Lake City and Ogden have been ordered to move to Carbon County." He held up the paper so she could see the headline. She glanced quickly at it. "BULLETS RIDDLE TRAIN CARRYING STRIKE BREAKERS"

Dan continued, "First Fatality in Coal Strike War Results When Armed Forces Attack Special Train. They're already calling it a war." He scanned the rest of the article. "They claim there were thirty-five strike-breakers on the train. It says one man was brought to the doctor with his arm practically shot off." Dan paused at the horror. "That must be Andy." Dan stopped reading. Elizabeth noticed and asked him what was wrong. Dan blinked away a tear. "I was just thinking about Andy," he said and resumed reading. "It says Major Elmer Johnson came to investigate." He paused. "So Elmer's his first name. Don't remember ever hearing him called anything but Major Johnson." Dan didn't speak for a few minutes while he read a long section where it described what occurred during the attack. "They've got it all wrong," he said. "The train didn't speed up the track to escape a hail of bullets. Only two or three Greeks were carrying pistols."

"Take it easy, honey. Did you really think the paper would be reporting facts?"

Dan continued. "Well here's another one. It says the strikers knew the train was coming and were lying in ambush for it to arrive. Baloney. We were expecting a normal train, till I said different."

Again he began reading directly from the paper, "When word of this latest outrage reached Governor Charles R. Maybe in Salt Lake City he was apparently convinced that no credence could be placed on the repeatedly broken promises of the strike promoters that their men would cease to commit acts of violence and the state militia was ordered to the county."

The reports in the *Deseret News* and the *Salt Lake Tribune* were pretty much repeats of what Dan had read. "Listen," he said as he read an article with something new about the governor's orders, to send in the Guard. "He'll exercise his prerogative impartially, with an absolute determination that the troops shall afford all the rights and privileges guaranteed by the constitution."

Elizabeth snorted. "Sure, and my favorite places in the world are outhouses."

Dan chuckled. He continued summarizing. "Then, he issues General Order Number One: Patrols are specifically ordered to prevent street meetings and assembling in large crowds. At the freight depots the patrol will stop all incoming vehicles and pedestrians to search for weapons."

"Oh!" Dan exclaimed excitedly as he resumed reading, "Listen to this. 'Governor Maybe also issues orders forbidding the mass importation of strike-breakers under company escort but individuals will be permitted to seek and accept employment.'"

CHAPTER 28

THE LONG ARM OF MARTIAL LAW

The next morning Dan was hardly able to move, so stiff and sore were his leg muscles from yesterday's run. Elizabeth stretched her arms up above her head. "I'll start breakfast."

They talked as they ate, but their conversation was interrupted by the sound of several people coming to the front of their tent. "Troops, halt!" a voice commanded. "This is Captain Young of the Utah National Guard," the voice said. "In one half hour all persons in this tent will assemble at the baseball field. Any person not attending will be arrested. Troops, forward, march!"

Elizabeth snickered. "Officious sounding little bastards."

Dan frowned. "Elizabeth, it's not funny. Let's clean up and get going." Elizabeth lifted the flap.

"Think I should invite them in for coffee?" Dan did not appreciate the humor, and reminded her they were the National Guard. Elizabeth reminded him that no matter what they were called, they were still just men. She said they put their pants on one leg at a time, as do the rest of us.

Dan thought for a moment. She was right, as usual. She'd just changed his nameless fear, "National Guard," into a more manageable concept: they were just a group of human beings.

The Major Johnson at the meeting, however, seemed a different man than the Major Johnson Dan and Elizabeth had met. In his capacity as a military man, he was all business, and no nonsense. "Be advised," the Major began, "these troops will maintain law and order. Under martial law, they'll arrest any person or persons engaged in any and all acts which are unlawful."

Somebody behind Dan shouted, "Hey! We thought they were here for a parade."

The Major just stood and looked toward the area of the comment.

266

Apparently he decided to ignore it. He continued, "Be advised that an eight o'clock curfew has been established and all streets both here and in Sunnyside will be patrolled regularly; and anyone found there will be arrested."

He said it as though this was going to be a big problem to the strikers who usually had their kids in bed by that time. But now, the humorous comments behind Dan were subdued, and could barely be heard. "Whoopdeedoo" someone said. "Think a couple of us should go out at night just to give them something to do?" someone else asked.

"Be advised, you have one hour to turn in any weapons in your possession. After that time, anyone who is found in possession of fircarms of any kind or description will be arrested."

Dan heard rumblings behind him, but could not make out any particular comment. Then he saw the Major point to one of the Coccimiglio boys, who began translating the Major's orders into Italian. After that Peter Darlkaris did the same in Greek. During the translations, the women in the crowd were talking, the children were playing around, and the soldiers were doing their very best to keep order and to quiet everyone down. Major Johnson was standing there stiffly, occasionally waving his hand to get his soldiers to where order needed restoring.

Dan was watching all this in amusement. The meeting seemed to be falling apart. Elizabeth was laughing. "Look how hard Major Johnson and the soldiers are trying to make everybody take this seriously." Dan observed it seemed everybody was having more fun than they did at the park the day of the parade. Finally, the Major said some of his troops would stay here for the hour to receive, tag, and issue receipts for all arms turned in. That seemed to conclude the meeting.

But instead of leaving, most people wanted to hang around to talk and visit with the soldiers. Dan and Elizabeth decided they would wait as well, and see how many arms were turned in. Before it was over a strange assortment of modern and ancient weapons were collected. They ranged from large bore hunting rifles to small caliber pistols, including a German Luger said to have been taken from a German officer on the battlefields of France.

Dan and Elizabeth decided to go back to their tent. But on the way, they were intercepted by Frank Bonatti. "Dan, now that Andy's gone, I guess you're head of security."

Inwardly, Dan squirmed. Doing whatever he was asked to do was one thing, being in charge and telling others what to do was quite another. Outwardly, however, he acted confident. "Check," he said. "What's up?" Frank said Johnson wanted three men to go with them to search the coffee houses and pool halls. Dan asked why, and Elizabeth observed she felt that was their job.

Frank shrugged his shoulders. "Guess he figures if we go, people being searched will cooperate more. Anyway, he said he wanted some-body to speak English, Italian, and Greek. I got Kismatakis for the Greek part, and I'll do the Italian." Elizabeth said she'd go back to the tent.

I sure wish I had a cigarette, she said to herself as she walked.

When Dan got back, Elizabeth wanted to know how it went. First thing he told her was that Captain Young, the man in charge of searches, said the Guard was very serious about making sure the company didn't bring in strike-breakers recruited elsewhere by the company.

Then Dan reached into his pants pocket and brought out a packet of cigarettes. She wanted to know how he knew. Dan was grinning. "Don't think I got a nose? Think I didn't know what you and Ann did every time you got together? Every coffee house was filled with smoke, and it reminded me. Thought you might be wanting one since you haven't been with Ann for awhile."

Elizabeth'd just lit up when they heard Tom ask if Dan was in the tent.

"Come," Dan called and Tom took a chair when he entered.

"Found out about Andy," Tom said. Suddenly, Tom had their undi-vided attention. "Too soon to tell if the arm's a goner. Maybe they can save it, if gangrene don't set in. Not much they can do about gangrene besides amputate. Doc says even if Andy don't lose it, there's so much nerve damage, it will probably never be much use to him anyway. But Doc is trying to save it."

Nobody spoke. At such times, the best thing friends could do was just be with each other.

Dan forced his mind back to Tom. "Where's Andy now? They got him?"

"Interesting thing, that. First they did, now they don't." Elizabeth decided if her husband already knew she smoked, everybody might just as well know. She came to the table, sat down, and lit up a cigarette. Tom barely glanced her way. "Andy was hurt so bad his friends figured he'd die if they didn't get him to Doc. They brought him in and then they hightailed it right back out again. Doc hadn't even started his examination yet when Rasmussen and Wally Cook came busting in."

"They arrested Andy but Andy was so weak from loss of blood, every time they tried to move him, he passed out. Doc said to stop it, and nobody was going anywhere until morning."

Tom paused, "Can I have one of your cigarettes, Elizabeth?" he asked. Elizabeth reached out the pack and Tom took it. Dan looked surprised, and mentioned he didn't know Tom smoked. Tom looked down, as he lit the cigarette. He coughed at the first puff. "Don't usually," he said. "But I'm runnin a little short on the where-with-all for a plug of chew. Going without's made me a mite edgy lately, what with everything that's been going on."

Elizabeth looked at Tom, got up, and went over to a box that served them as a cupboard. She took out three plugs of tobacco, held them up a little, and looked at Dan. He nodded. As she headed back toward the table, Dan put his hand on Tom's arm. "Old Buddy, ever since I started smoking a pipe, Elizabeth has been pestering me to get my chewing tobacco out of the tent. She says it stinks up the place. Been meaning to see if you'd take it off my hands."

Elizabeth could see Tom was delighted, and a little embarrassed all at the same time. She felt a little badly about having lit the cigarette, and arousing Tom's craving. Tom reached up, took the tobacco, and offered Elizabeth his barely smoked cigarette.

"As I was saying," Tom said, then he put the chew in his mouth and looked content, "Doc said nobody could move Andy till morning. Anyway, from here on, the story gets real strange. Wally promised Doc he would see that Andy was taken good care of, and wouldn't be hurt. He said he'd take him to the guard shack, and stay with him personally until Kelter arrived. But on the way, it seems Andy passed out by John Buzos' coffee house. Wally took Andy in there, told Buzos to watch Andy. Then Wally high-tailed it down to the guard shack to call Sheriff Kelter."

Elizabeth looked startled. "You mean Wally left Andy in the care of a fellow Greek?"

Tom was looking pleased as punch. Dan couldn't tell whether it was because of the story, or the tobacco. "For some reason, I always liked Wally. He talked to us like human beings," Dan said.

"Yeah," Tom agreed. "Upshot is, Andy's gone, Buzos is under arrest for aiding and abetting, and Wally is fired. Plus . . ." Tom started, but never got to finish.

"Dan, is Tom in there?" Frank Bonatti called from outside the tent. He sounded highly agitated. Dan invited Frank in. As he came in, Dan pointed to an empty chair. Frank spoke almost frantically, "No time! Come quick! The soldiers took over the guard shack! They're setting up a machine gun!" The four of them made a rush for the front of the tent. They ran out, down the road toward the main part of Tent Town, then headed up the road toward Sunnyside, they saw a large group of people standing, looking toward the guard shack.

Looks of fear were rampant on every face, man, woman, and child alike. Dan, Tom, Frank, and Elizabeth made their way toward the front. They stood where they could plainly see a machine gun in the road. Soldiers were digging dirt and filling bags, making a barricade around the gun.

A couple of soldiers left the front of the guard shack and headed toward the assembled people. Some of the people from camp scattered, and headed back toward Tent Town. But to Dan, the soldiers seemed almost to be sauntering, and didn't look upset at all. As they approached, one of the soldiers inquired in a pleasant voice, "Who's in charge here?" Tom told them they weren't soldiers and nobody was in charge of anybody else. The soldiers laughed. "Okay," the one speaking said. "Then, where are your union leaders?"

Frank was getting suspicious. "Who wants to know?" he asked.

The soldiers stopped smiling. The second one spoke up. "I sure as heck don't care, one way or the other. But Captain said to come down here and bring back the union leaders so he could explain things to them." After a brief discussion, Frank, Tom, Dan, Peter Darlkaris, old man Lupo, and a few of the other men started forward with the two soldiers as escort. When they arrived near the machine gun, Captain Young stepped out of the Guard shack. Atten hut! Somebody called, and all the nearby soldiers came to attention and saluted. The captain returned their salute, "At ease," he said. Then, he turned his attention to the men from the town.

He spoke in a friendly enough way, but the words left no doubt as to his seriousness. "This morning you all thought it was rather funny when Major Johnson said we were sent here to maintain law and order. Look at that machine gun, and see how funny you think it is now."

Dan stepped forward. "Captain Young, today you said the Guard'd make sure there were no scab trains, or crews of strike breakers recruited by the company. I thought you were on our side."

"Yeah," Tom interjected. "And now you point a machine gun at us. That ain't friendly."

Captain Young smiled. "Look again," he said, nodding his head toward the machine gun. "It isn't pointed at anyone. It's pointed toward the mountain up there. And before we took over the guard shack, our officers told Mr. Benton that this machine gun could point either at Tent Town or back toward mine workings, Sunnyside, and the searchlight. We will keep the opposing sides apart," he said. "We will train the gun on whomever threatens that. We'll do our level best to be even-handed in all this, that was the governor's orders."

Dan felt a sudden sense of relief. And relief spread to the faces of the other strikers as well. The Captain nodded, and, once again, the soldiers began the task of filling and placing bags of dirt. "When you men go back to report on this," the Captain said, "I hope you make it very clear that as long as your people remain peaceful, there is nothing to fear here." Then he looked at Dan. "And as to our being on somebody's side, forget it. We are on nobody's side. Yes, we will stop strike trains or men recruited by the company. But rest assured, we will be just as active if any striker tries to interfere with any man who, on his own, comes to this town looking for work."

Tom's nostrils widened. "You mean we can't picket?" he demanded.

The Captain remained as calm as before. "I surely didn't say that. Picketing is your right under the Constitution. What I said was, interfering with. That means no touching, no blocking, no obstructing in any way any man looking for work. Looking for work is his Constitutional right. Dismissed!" the Captain said, and returned to the guard shack.

"All in all," Dan said as they were walking back, "the long arm of martial law could be worse."

The next morning seemed the biggest holiday of the year. The Guard had it's patrols established, and everyone in Tent Town was allowed to go into Sunnyside. They could go as far as the post office, as long as they stayed on the main road. Elizabeth and Dan strolled arm in arm through the lower part of town. Dan stopped a dozen or so times to introduce Elizabeth to people.

Dan's whole family was waiting for him, and they'd brought so much food that Steve had to go back home and get a basket and gunny-sack to help carry some of it. Nor was this an isolated scene. Elizabeth looked around and saw literally dozens of such little groups with people from the town sharing what they had. Sometimes it was only two or three people in a group, but at other times it was a huge family from grand-mothers right on down to grandchildren. Elizabeth's observations were interrupted when Mary spoke to her. "Elizabeth, we have been worried sick that you and Dan might be having a pretty hard time of it."

Elizabeth was not only feeling gratitude toward's Dan's family, but love for Mary as well. "Mom, if I tried to lie to you, you'd know. Can't say it has been fun, but we've been getting by."

Carl put his hand on her shoulder, and Elizabeth began to have feelings of warmth for Carl.

"Mom, Dad," Dan interjected. "As Elizabeth said, it hasn't been easy. But people in Tent Town are sharing what little they have, and they've made sure we took some of their food because of the baby." Dan saw the shocked look on his parents' faces.

Mary reached out and folded Elizabeth into her arms. Elizabeth shot an "if looks could kill" glance toward Dan over Mary's shoulder. She had planned to break the news in a far different way than this. Then Elizabeth smiled at the love in Mary's embrace, and just enjoyed it. Now, instead of the greatest catastrophe in her life, the baby inside her was bringing joy to others.

The three of them started out, loaded down. To their surprise, two

Fred Civish

Guardsmen even volunteered to help carry some of it. As they walked, Tom came rushing up to them. "Now they got something else to blame on us," he said. "While the post office was closed for lunch, somebody broke in and robbed it! Now Benton will insist it's the Guard's fault for letting us into town."

273

CHAPTER 29

WELCOME BROTHERS

Ganz walked into Benton's office, and gave him the news about the post office. He told Ganz to find Ovie and tell him to request the major come to his office. When Ganz left, Benton began smiling. This robbery was an opening he had been hoping for. Benton had been furious about how Sunnyside people had helped the strikers. Probably already gave them enough food to prolong the strike a month. Benton had been on the phone to his three Supers. They reported the same kinds of food exchanges going on at all the camps. So far, it seemed every advantage had gone to the union, but the robbery gave him an edge. On his legal pad, he listed the problems the Guard caused in carrying out the governor's orders. They set up patrols to make it possible for strikers to get into town. The company could not recruit outside the mine area. The Guard made him discharge all his extra deputies.

Benton let out a big sigh, stopped writing, and placed his hands on the table. So much for what the Guard did. Now it was time to play the card the robbery gave him, to convince the major that the robbery proved the governor had indeed been misinformed, that strikers were lawless men.

Benton stood up as he heard people entering the outer office. He headed in that direction and saw Major Johnson and Captain Young. They were frowning. Benton figured he'd better do something quick. "Major, Captain, thank you so much for coming. It was very gracious of you." Benton looked at Durrant. "Ganz, will you see that refreshments are sent in for the gentlemen?" Then Benton looked at the major. "Please come this way." He turned and headed for his office. The military men followed him without comment. Once seated the major said they hoped this wouldn't take too long because they were working on finding who robbed the post office. Benton jumped on it. "You don't have enough men to be everywhere at once, and such things are bound to happen. That is why I asked to speak with you. I wanted to offer my services and the services of my constabulary in this matter in any way which might serve you."

The major smiled. "That's very kind of you Mr. Benton. "What type of assistance?"

Benton thought fast. "The man will try to spend what he stole. The few law enforcement people you so graciously allowed us to keep know everyone in town. They can report anyone who seems to be spending extra money." Benton noted both the major and the captain were nodding.

Benton continued, "Letting everyone move back and forth from Sunnyside to Tent Town would strain the Guard's capacity to prevent similar situations in the future. That robbery was just the first proof you have that lawless strikers must be controlled." The major agreed, and said he would talk with the governor about keeping strikers out of Sunnyside.

As a parting favor to them, he even advised them that if they were on their toes, the major's patrols would even find moonshine stills the strikers had set up all over the place.

Immediately on arriving back at his headquarters tent, the major told his officers to instruct the soldiers to search for illegal alcohol. And as it turned out, it was a good night for such a search. Some people of the camp, having eaten all they wanted for the first time in weeks, were ready to celebrate. Tom, Frank, and a couple of others came by Dan's tent shortly after dusk. They informed him that, rather than wait for the sometimes uncertain delivery of moonshine, they were headed for a still above Pessetto's old place. Elizabeth was as eager as Dan for the adventure. Upon arriving, they built a small bonfire to warm their outsides while they warmed their insides.

The first anyone around the campfire was aware of potential trouble was when they heard the cocking of three rifles. "Nobody move!" Every head turned toward the sound.

"Party's over," the soldier said. "Disperse immediately," he commanded. "Our orders are to destroy the equipment, and arrest anyone who interferes."

"Hey," Dan said. "I know you two guys. You're the guys helped us carry our stuff." Two of the three soldiers hung their heads. "Doesn't matter," the other soldier said. "We are going to destroy all alcohol we confiscate. Then we'll break up the equipment."

"Okay," a man with a little too much to drink spoke up. "I'll help you, wa . . . tchsssh me destroy some," he said as he raised a cup full of moonshine and drank it in one long gulp. After which he fell backwards off the log he was sitting on. Even the soldiers laughed.

Dan extended his tin cup of booze toward a soldier. "Hey, want to start destroying a little yourself?" The soldier, named Larry, took it and without hesitating joined the destruction process. Soon a full-fledged party was in progress. Everyone agreed this was a fine way to destroy illegal alcohol. After most of it was gone, the soldiers began the second part of their duty and began breaking up the equipment of the still. Then Dan began to look around. Nowhere could he see the "remains" of the boiler, the hardest to replace of all the equipment.

As the fires began to die down, and most people were gone, Dan started toward camp, clasping Elizabeth's hand. She stumbled along behind him. The last thing Dan heard was a Guardsman thanking the people of camp for their help. Someone else from Tent Town pretty well summed it up for Dan. "You're welcome, Brother. Call us when you have more of this kind of work to do."

A week later, Benton was agitated as he walked toward the command tent. The soldier accompanying him had been cordial enough in his request that the major wanted to see Benton. Nevertheless, it was an affront. The major could just as easily have come to the mine office. He knew Benton was usually there. "Morning," the major said to no one in particular and placed several papers he was holding on the long map-reading desk serving as a conference table.

"These papers contain some names I want to run by you," the major said. Benton did not like the tone of his voice. He sounded arrogant and patronizing. "We didn't find it necessary to wait for your help on that post office robbery. The post office sent down an inspector. The workers in the post office, Nicholas Patterson and Mary Reese, both cooperated with him." Benton said he was familiar with them. Mary Reese was the clerk who kept the post office open while Post Master Patterson worked in the mine. The major continued. "The postal inspector determined that $562 was taken from a money sack. The thief left $127 in the sack untouched, and made no effort to take other valuables in the office at that time."

Benton felt the need to show he had a good grasp of deductive reasoning. "Then we're dealing with someone not too bright, or someone who got spooked before he could do more damage."

The major just grunted his acknowledgment, and continued on with the information he seemed so willing to show off. "Miss Reese remembered a particular man who had been standing around talking to no one in particular. Some of the union officials were very cooperative. They questioned their people and reported seeing the same man hanging around. We arrested a man named Benjamin England," the major said triumphantly.

Benton smiled. But Benton's smile faded as the major continued. "He is not a striker, nor is his father. He's only sixteen years old. Obviously, this changes our plans to speak with the governor about keeping people out of Sunnyside." Benton felt as if he'd been slapped in the face.

Major began, but had trouble with some of the pronunciations, "Do Anton Kambourakis, John Dantes, Delabanis, Pete Kukis, Domunini, Ellian Konterakis, George Kontaros, Harry and George Kocolakis or John Kriaris mean anything to you?"

Benton had enough. "Major, the last time we met you reminded me how busy you are. Need I remind you that I am no less busy? Now, unless I know why I am listening to all these names, and you are ready to tell me why they're important, I will return to my own duties."

The major looked smug. "I was just trying to establish if you had any previous trouble with any of these men?" Benton shot the major a questioning look. "With the cooperation of Sheriff Kelter, all these men have been arrested for the murder of Art Webb."

Benton showed his pleasure, "Splendid, Major. How many more are there?" Benton asked. What was more important to him was the major's use of the word "murder." This meant the governor was buying the company's side of the story the strikers shot first.

Rather than count them, the major just read off the rest of the names.

"Nick Maris, George Petros, a man whose last name is Siatrous, Peter Prazzi, Andreas and Mike Zulakis, and, finally, Andreas Vullis. However, we expect more arrests." Benton was angry he hadn't been informed of any of this by the sheriff, or others he expected to keep him informed. He felt he was being shut out of what was going on. That could be deadly to him.

Leaving shortly, Benton headed out in a near rage. His first order of business would be to make some phone calls. One way or another he must find out what was going on! It only took him a couple of calls to discover his fears about being shut out were unfounded. Everyone was being kept in the dark until the Guard chose to announce something. Sheriff Kelter was threatened with charges of interference if he revealed to others what the Guard had him doing.

Benton stopped by the file clerk's desk, said he wanted some coffee, went into his office and sat down. The coffee had not arrived when he heard Rasmussen come busting into the office and telling Durrant he had to see the boss right away. Benton called for Rasmussen to come on in, and looked up at him as he entered. "What is it Ovie?" Rasmussen hurriedly told him that three of the six men coming in on the train today were turned back as illegally hired strike-breakers.

Benton jumped up. "Come with me," he commanded Rasmussen. Then he headed straight for the command tent he had so recently left. No time now to request the major come to his office. Plus, Benton reasoned, after this morning's little demonstration by the major, working cordially with the goon was impossible. He might as well learn right now that I'll be in his face.

Finding the major was in the mess tent, Benton headed that way. They entered and saw Major Johnson and Captain Young sitting at a long mess table, drinking coffee. Benton strode rapidly to the table, and sat down across the table from the major before the major was even aware of his presence. "Would you please explain the actions of your men in keeping potential employees away from Sunnyside?" Benton demanded without any preliminary greeting.

The major looked startled. "We, Sir, are following the governor's orders to deny strike-breakers access to coal mines. I suggest you take up problems you have with that with Governor Maybe."

Benton no longer made any attempt to hide his real feelings. "Listen, Major, you may be hot shit in the governor's office, but here you are a nuisance we have been putting up with," he said. "Our job is to provide the people of the state of Utah with coal to keep them from freezing this winter. The Guard was only sent here in the first place to help get that job done."

"Well I never!" the major said, and looked at the Captain. "Captain, have this man removed."

As the Captain started to get up, Benton looked at Rasmussen. "Ovie, write in your book that Major Johnson refused to listen when it was explained to him the governor's prime concern is that the people of his state don't freeze this winter."

The major motioned the captain to sit. Benton pursued his attack. "No need to throw us out. I, for one, don't intend to stay here one moment longer than necessary, once our business is finished. You surely must know we will protest formally to the governor about your removing workers. My only purpose for being here is to get your response to include in that report." The major asked what response, and there was none of the previous arrogance. Benton thought fast. He had the major on the defensive, and he wanted to keep it that way. "How, exactly, did you determine that the three men of the six men you blocked were strike-breakers?"

"We let three men pass," the Major said, defensively. "Thought you'd be pleased with that."

But Benton was not one who could easily be distracted. "As you said earlier, I'll get to that in a moment. But for now, I'm sure you wouldn't want the governor informed that you refused to disclose on what basis you are classifying some as strike-breakers while you let three men go."

"Well," The Major said, and reached up with his fingers to loosen his collar. "I can't be everywhere at once, and have to rely on my officers. If you'll wait a few minutes, I'll find out."

Benton tried not to show how pleased he was. "Sorry, I have urgent business waiting. When you find out, have the lieutenant run the infor-mation over to my office. This report to the governor has to be forwarded as soon as possible."

The major was now sounding business-like, "I'll do that," he said, unemotionally.

"Good," Benton said as got up. "Oh, by the way, I will be pleased with the number of new employees you let pass when we have enough to produce the coal necessary to keep the people of Utah from freezing this winter." Then he added, "I'm sure you remember the coal famine a couple of years ago, and the misery that caused." Benton even said good-bye cordially.

He even had to laugh at Rasmussen's question on the way back. "Boss," Rasmussen said hesitantly. "Why did you say our coal goes to keep people warm? We make coke out of it all."

"Ah," Benton replied, "but much of the coal in the county does. The major has no idea how much of ours might, if he bothered to think about it at all. The governor should never have sent such a greenhorn into a serious card game. The major may know military procedures, but he doesn't know crap about coal mining. I will send the report to the governor."

Later, sitting in his office, Benton smiled as he read the communique the Major sent over with the lieutenant. It said simply that the three strike-breakers had been turned back because they heard about jobs in Salt Lake, and the three of them were traveling together, and thus seemed to be a crew recruited by the company illegally. The other three were traveling as individuals, and judged to be individuals seeking work, which was allowed.

Benton was doubly pleased while he was writing to the governor. Not only would this part make a fool of the major, but Benton requested the governor spell out in detail the criteria for identifying men as strike-breakers. He added that without such criteria, carrying out his orders to let men seeking employment through would be impossible. Then, on impulse, he added the bit about the coal famine, and said he was certain the governor did not want to be a part of bringing such calamity on the people of Utah again.

When he finished the report, he was so proud of it he decided to forward it to Frank Cameron. Benton knew that if the governor ever saw it, Cameron would take credit for it. But this just might keep the General Super job secure a little bit longer. Cameron would love to keep the governor and his staff busy trying to figure out exactly what did justify stopping enough workers to create another coal famine. Besides, much of the coal from the other Utah Fuel mines did go to the people of the state. Benton thought a bit. Perhaps the situation isn't hopeless; perhaps this will show Governor Maybe that prolonging the strike only hurts all of us, even the miners.

CHAPTER 30

IDENTIFY YOURSELVES

Elizabeth drove to Price, did some shopping with a little money her mother had given her, and arrived at the newspaper in the late afternoon. Now she sat at a desk looking at the galley she was going to take home. One was the usual castigation of the governor for interfering with the hiring of men to produce coal, and for not keeping the lawless element under control. Another article bemoaned the fact, once again, that good honest people were being badgered and bullied by both the union and the pickets, and thus were afraid to go to work. Hal Cooper interrupted her reading. "Keep an eye on the place, will you Elizabeth? I've got to meet some people for coffee."

Elizabeth agreed, and kept busy correcting the galleys. She finished before Cooper returned, and wished she could leave. She sat there restlessly awaiting his return. She began to look around, and saw the several clipboards hanging on the wall. This is where Cooper kept his teletype UPI news dispatches. She walked over to them, hoping she would find something interesting.

Nothing much seemed worth bothering to read until she got to an item buried near the back of one clipboard. She couldn't believe her eyes. "The entire responsibility for the murders of both nonunion workers and union miners resulting from the riots and massacre in bloody Williamson county are laid upon the slain Superintendent McDowell and upon the officials of the Southern Illinois Coal company." She knew this piece of news would never see the light of day.

"Can I help you find something?" a voice asked. Elizabeth jumped. Cooper had returned.

Elizabeth turned. "Oh my gosh," she said. "You scared the living daylights out of me." She took a deep breath, hoping he hadn't noticed she was sneaking a look at the dispatches.

"Looking for anything in particular?" he asked again, still standing just inside the door.

"Yes," Elizabeth said. "I finished the galleys. I was looking for something else to work on."

Cooper didn't look convinced. "I think we had a discussion once before what I print is my job."

Elizabeth put on her most coy look. "Gee, Mr. Cooper, did I do something wrong? I just figured if I read some of those, whatchamacal-lits, I would be able to proofread the galleys faster."

Cooper came the rest of the way into the office. "If I didn't have reasons you will never know about, you'd be looking for a new job. For now, let's say it was my fault for leaving you alone."

Elizabeth could hardly wait to get out of there so she could breathe again. For some reason Cooper seemed way more upset than seemed called for. She couldn't understand it. Once outside, she began to calm down. She wished she hadn't promised Ann she would meet her at the Queen City for lunch. Elizabeth wanted to get back to Tent Town with her news about McDowell while it was still news. By tomorrow it would probably be in at least one Salt Lake newspaper.

She drove to the restaurant and sat waiting for Ann to arrive. She lit up a cigarette. It was barely finished when Ann came down the sidewalk. Elizabeth rolled down her window. As Ann approached, Elizabeth spoke in an urgent tone. "Get in, I've got something to tell you."

Ann got in. Elizabeth proffered her pack of cigarettes and Ann took one. She lit up, took a drag, and Elizabeth continued. "I almost got fired! Cooper left the office, and I started looking at the wire dispatches. He caught me, and got furious." Elizabeth told Ann about the McDowell story, and said she had to get back to give the information to the union.

Ann looked at Elizabeth. "I've got the day off, I'll go to Sunnyside with you. As they drove Ann took a bottle out of her purse. A stiff drink later, she proffered it to Elizabeth. Elizabeth took a sip. She really didn't know why, but she felt sort of, well, naughty. A couple of drinks later, Elizabeth suggested they get Dan, come back, and paint the town red. Ann said it was a fine idea.

As they crossed over the bridge at Twelve Mile Wash, they stopped at a Guard road block. A couple of soldiers stepped into the road, and one held up his hand signaling the car to stop. "Identify yourselves, please," one of the soldiers commanded.

Elizabeth could see no harm in a little banter.

On impulse, rather than answer, Elizabeth let out the clutch and stepped on the gas. The Star shot forward leaving the two soldiers just standing. Ann began to giggle, and Elizabeth was laughing loudly. Bursts of light, and the sound of shots being fired froze Elizabeth's laughter. She hit the gas and the Star lurched again. Once safely away, the two girls laughed all the way to Tent Town. When Elizabeth told Dan about their adventure at the road block, Dan didn't think it was funny. Not being half swacked, as they were, he thought it had been a foolish thing to do. When she told him about McDowell, Dan left to give the news to Tom. He was back in no time at all, but threw cold water on their plans to go to Price for a party. "We'd never get back in time for curfew," he said. Elizabeth protested that she had to get Ann back.

"Why?" Ann asked. "If I stayed I could brag that during the strike I slept in a tent."

After sharing a couple of drinks with the girls, Dan gave up trying to join the party. The girls were having so much fun with each other, he could hardly get a word in edgewise. He decided the girls would have to sleep in the bed. He took a couple of spare blankets and made his bed on the rug. He crawled between the blankets and turned his back on them so they could undress.

"If I wasn't afraid they'd try something else stupid, I'd sleep outside," he mumbled to himself. But sleep didn't come easily for Dan. The girls in the bed continued to disturb him with their whispering, laughing, and giggling for what seemed hours. "Women," he said.

That night the girls had enjoyed themselves so much that every time they met during the next two weeks, this private little party dominated their conversations. Elizabeth's twice weekly trips to Price to work on galleys gave them plenty of opportunities to reminisce.

It didn't surprise her that the galleys were attempts to step up the pressure on the governor. This week's editorial called for the removal of outsider union agitators and strict control of the strikers. The *Deseret News*, too, carried this same theme, but it's language was more harsh.

Elizabeth had no doubt that what the anti-union newspapers printed really made a difference with people outside the coal camps, although by now the strikers didn't seem to be influenced much by them. The mood of the people in Tent Town was definitely optimistic. The strikers were looking on the Guard as protectors and felt the strike was now, "in the bag."

Her thoughts returned once again to finish reading the galleys so she could be with Ann. The main editorial read, "MABEY'S PLAN PROVES BIG FIZZLE IN STRIKE CONTROL." Elizabeth found the subhead confusing: "Governor Must Now Make Another Guess." Strangely, the editorial didn't specify just what new guess the governor must now make. It did assert, however, that the governor's plan to have arms turned over by non-citizens developed into a "huge joke." Claiming that it was, "a well known fact in the county that these people, almost to a man, are provided with weapons," it then went on to make light of the situation where the request to relinquish weapons, "did scare up three or four antiquated pieces of armament." Interesting, she thought. Cooper didn't have the guts to come right out and say the union was giving guns.

She continued to read. "For weeks people have been terrorized and intimidated; men who have been willing to work have reluctantly run the gauntlet of groups of armed and muttering foreigners; while worst of all some have actually lost their lives."

How much they had twisted the truth! By putting a semi-colon between the sections "run the gauntlet" and "lost their lives," they connected separate events in a way which made it seem men trying to get to work had been killed. Which, Elizabeth knew, was absolutely false.

She forced her mind back to the article. "The governor's promise that all who wanted to work in the mines would be protected was only the governor's pretty phrase."

Finding nothing more of importance, she set it aside and perused another article. She read, "Coal is going to be mined in sufficient quantity to prevent any fuel famine next winter. This is the assertion of a high government official tonight following the disclosure of steps being taken by President Harding to bring the operators and striking miners into conference on a settlement of mine wage dispute. Peaceful means will be tried first to end the coal mine strike, it was stated. If those should fail, more drastic action will be taken."

Elizabeth noted that no mention was made of what that drastic action might be, but judged it did not bode well for strikers. She noted that Cooper was now even mentioning the president to show the strikers how high up opposition to the strike reached. As she read a small item, Elizabeth began to chuckle. Under a subhead of, "Shots Bring Results," she found, "Two women in an automobile attempted to drive past the Guards on the road into Sunnyside. They disregarded the order to halt, the Guard fired warning shots over their head." I wonder how long Ann and I would be working if these people knew we were the mysterious "two women."

A wrap up of the post office story was also entertaining. "According to Postal Inspector, E. L. Jackson, of Provo, Benny England is said to have made the steal when he ran to the assistance of Miss Mary Reese, postmistress, when she was frightened by a mouse. However, Mr. England has given no clue as to the whereabouts of the missing funds." Elizabeth almost burst out laughing. Where do they get this garbage? Enough, she thought. I can find more truth in the funny papers. She advised Cooper she was leaving. She took the time for a leisurely lunch with Ann before she went on her way with the information she was sure would be valuable to the union. Back in Sunnyside, Tom briefly scanned the galleys.

"It's a new ball game since the Guard came," Tom said. "They've pretty well figured out how to put pressure on the governor."

After Tom left, Dan just sat looking at Elizabeth. "What?" she asked.

Dan smiled, "You, that's what. I'm the one out on strike. I help with security, I man picket lines, I attend union meetings and all the rest." In spite of his serious tones, Elizabeth could tell he was pleased about something. "You bring home a few sheets of paper, you get Tom jumping as if he had ants in his pants. Married me some kind of woman, I did."

A few days later, at daybreak on the morning of the Fourth of July, the sound of a cannon blast woke Dan. He sat up, stretched, yawned, and then looked down at Elizabeth. She was lying there wide-eyed. He smiled at her. "Get up, Honey. We're burning daylight."

Elizabeth was not smiling. Now she could hear what now sounded like gun fire. She demanded to know what it was. "Did you forget? It's the Fourth of July."

Elizabeth's eyes relaxed, but only a little, as she continued to hear the gunfire sounds. She tried again. "The little noise is firecrackers, but what was that big noise?"

Instead of answering right away, Dan first leaned over and gave her a peck on the forehead. "Dynamite. It's an old tradition around here. Sunnyside starts off the Fourth with a bang."

Elizabeth got out of her side of the bed and started dressing as well. "Well," she said, "you could have warned me. When it went off it almost made me pee my pants. Speaking of which," she said, "I've got to go, and I mean now!" By the time she got back, Dan was folding a blanket. "What are you doing?. I thought we were going to make breakfast."

Dan smiled. "Another tradition is for everybody in town to have a chuck wagon breakfast." Dan looked pleased. There was not much he could offer Elizabeth in the way of worldly goods. But miners knew how to celebrate, and today she would see another reason why life with him wasn't going to be all that bad. "Let's go," he said.

After they'd spread the blanket on the lawn for breakfast, many more surprises were in store for Elizabeth. All of the veterans had their hats on, and so many of them had on uniforms it seemed the Guard was putting on the breakfast. Elizabeth was pleased. Somehow, it touched her that people in as bad shape financially as they were could celebrate the birth of the nation so enthusiastically. But that was only part of it. Most celebrants were also the so called foreigners.

After breakfast, the early hours were devoted to the children. There were the usual races, complete with ribbons for winners. But Elizabeth thought she would die laughing at the greased pole climb, and the catch-a-greased-pig event. The winner of the pole climb got a five dollar gold piece, and the winner of the greased pig event got to keep the shoat.

Finally, it was time for Dan and Elizabeth to be more than spectators. Their first event was the three legged race. After that came the spoon and egg relay, and then the horseshoe pitching contest. If Dan wasn't so good at pitching horseshoes, they would certainly have finished last. "If you had even a half decent partner, you'd win easily," she said to him.

Dan's mood turned reflective. "I had a wonderful time playing horseshoes with you. I'd rather lose with you than win with somebody else."

Shortly thereafter, Elizabeth had a new experience. Playing with Dan and playing with this strange variety of people gave her a sense of belonging. She was more at home here in a tent and on the dirt field than she had ever been in the fanciest house with the most carefully groomed grounds. These people were more than friends, they seemed her family.

Lunch was another treat. Each group had set up its own serving tables and all who wished could sample from each of them.

Afternoon brought relaxation and speeches. The first speaker was a Justice of the Utah Supreme Court, A. J. Weber. It's not that Elizabeth wasn't interested, just tired. She fell asleep.

Dan nudged her awake while the union people spoke. It hardly seemed worth attention-except for the bad news one speaker mentioned. He said it seemed the Guard had started letting strike-breakers into the various camps. When people in the crowd began to moan and complain, the speaker said he figured it wasn't really a big problem. District leaders would speak with Major Johnson, and advise him Guards in some camps were not keeping the governor's guidelines.

For a change, Dan was interested in what Attorney Sam King had to say. He reminded everyone of the upcoming trial for Andy and some of the others arrested in the train shooting. He asked that anyone who had further information, to come forward as soon as possible.

The highlight of the union speakers was William Houston, International Representative of UMWA. He told the assembled miners that the union had come up with a set of conditions on which they thought the strike in Carbon County could be settled.

First, the company was to discharge any armed Guards still employed in the various camps. Secondly, the company must promise not to discriminate against either union miners or non-union miners. Thirdly, miners would return to work under the reduced wage. However, a new wage would be set by negotiations in the Central Mining District, and would be retroactive to April first once those negotiations were concluded. Loud applause followed the announcement.

Dan stood up, reached down to help Elizabeth up, and snatched the blanket from the ground. Elizabeth asked where they were going. "Back to the tent for supper before the dance and fireworks," he said. Elizabeth groaned, reached down with both hands, and placed them on her stomach. She said he must be kidding if he thought she could eat anything after that feast at lunch. Dan chuckled. "Don't forget, you're eating for two."

Back at the tent, Dan made himself a sandwich, and Elizabeth relented enough to have a cup of coffee. Then they took a nap. Soon both were asleep, but sweating in the late afternoon heat.

It was dark when Dan awoke. For a moment he wasn't sure what day it was, but the sound of music reminded him. The dance had already begun. He reached over and kissed Elizabeth softly on the forehead. As quickly as possible, they washed their faces in cold water to refresh themselves and headed for the dance.

Finally, just before curfew, fireworks were set off. As they ended, everyone headed for their tents. On the way Elizabeth began wondering where all the money came from for the fireworks extravaganza. Dan said that people saved all year for this, and the union chipped in with a little money as well. At the tent, Elizabeth lit a cigarette, and Dan began his last pipe of the day. Elizabeth reached out and put her hand on his. "I just never realized that having a wonderful time really has nothing to do with how much money a person has . . ."

CHAPTER 31

NO CHANGE IN POLICY

Five o'clock in the morning was an awful hour to begin a trip anywhere, Benton thought as he headed the Packard for Salt Lake. The proposed settlement of the strike was impossible. He wanted to be there in person to find out how Cameron wanted to handle it. By leaving this early he would get there shortly after everybody got to the office.

Benton was practically alone on the road. At places he pushed the Packard so fast he was afraid he might wreck it. By the time he entered Utah Valley, he was white-knuckled from gripping the steering wheel so hard. He was at the office in the Judge Building by ten. Charley Hotchkiss looked up, and didn't seem at all surprised to see him. Hotchkiss smiled.

Benton returned his smile. "Kept the Packard purring," he said. "Is Frank in?" The smile faded from Hotchkiss' face, as he told Benton not only was Frank in, he'd phoned Benton at eight, and was sitting there waiting for him. Benton heaved a sigh. He nodded his head toward Cameron's office. "Lead me to him." Hotchkiss got up. Hotchkiss knocked on Cameron's door.

"Come in," Cameron said, and Benton didn't care for the sound of it. The two of them entered, and Benton saw Cameron sitting at his desk with newspapers scattered all over it. "Have you read these ridiculous newspapers?" Cameron demanded. "How could you let them blind-side us?" Benton didn't have the foggiest idea what Cameron was talking about, but knew he'd better find out, and quick. He explained he had been on the road before the papers arrived. Cameron shoved a paper at him, "Here, look at this." But he gave Benton no chance to read it. "The union has released a proposal to put everybody back to work and the crazy papers are jumping up and down with joy that the strike is all but settled." Benton explained he had found out about the settlement offer only yesterday, when Houston announced it. "Why didn't you call me the minute you knew?" Cameron asked, frowning an ugly frown.

"I don't have your home phone number, Frank, and the operator said it is unlisted." Cameron said he should have called Commissioner Emerson to get his number. Benton knew his job was on the line again, but there is only so much a man can take. Without being asked, he sat down across from Cameron. Out of the corner of his eye, he saw Hotchkiss sitting in a chair in the corner of the office. He looked at Cameron and was about to speak.

Cameron looked strangely guilty. "Sorry," he said. "I get so peeved I forget my manners."

Benton was starting to learn something. Cameron seemed more than willing to push someone hard until they showed signs of pushing back. Then he would haul in his reins a bit. This was not the first time Cameron had done just this when Benton had about had it. Benton spoke with more confidence, "Frank, I know how important all this is. That's why I drove the Packard at a speed I worried might kill somebody to get here. If I'd known the union was going to release it to the newspapers before they ever told us, I'd have walked here last night if I had to."

Cameron seemed pleased. "I know you would have, Bob. It's a good thing you came so fast. Our answer to the union about this so-called offer is simple: get off our backs."

Benton had been worried that the company might be weakening at high levels. What Cameron just said pleased him. He leaned forward toward Cameron. "Glad to hear you say that, Frank. Lately the strikers have been acting as if they had everything in the bag." Cameron looked smug and said the strikers were a mite premature, and that he knew a few things they didn't.

Continuing to look smug, he continued. "Tell you about it in a bit. First, how would you like thirty more men in each mine?" Benton almost didn't believe it. "Did your people tell you the union was preparing a complain to Major Johnson about some strike-breakers getting in?"

Benton was hoping he wasn't wrong about where all this was leading.

Again the smug look on Cameron. "They were practice runs to see how the Guard would react." Benton remarked that thirty more men would help production a lot. "That's only for starters," Cameron said. "There'll be another fifty as soon as we can get them."

Benton knew news such as this meant there'd been an accommodation far above Major Johnson's level. In the end, Johnson was nothing more than a flunky for the governor. "How'd you get to the governor?" Benton asked with real admiration.

Cameron took another puff and knocked some ashes off into the ash tray. He looked at Hotchkiss. "Charley, do you think we could get some coffee?" Hotchkiss stood and said the coffee would be right in

The moment Hotchkiss was out the door, Cameron laid his cigar in the tray and leaned toward Benton. "I didn't want Charley to hear all of this because some of it isn't any of his business, but you need to know. We had the governor as soon as we started screaming coal famine."

Cameron paused and lowered his voice a little more. "Why you need to know about this is that your daughter is a union informant. She has been tipping them off in advance what *The News Advocate* was going to print. Cooper caught her going through some wire service releases."

Benton grew ashen. First chance he had-daughter or not-he'd kill her. Cameron would fire him for sure. "I'll handle it, Frank," was the best he could manage, turmoil churning his guts.

Cameron sat up straight. "You'll do nothing of the sort. I thought you understood. She's a God-send to us." Benton was totally confused. "Don't you see," Cameron said. "The union thinks it's got us by the nuts. But thanks to your daughter we let them see exactly what we want them to see, and not a thing more. We wanted them to see tirades against the governor. That way, they will have to believe so many people have complained, the governor has no choice, and the union won't be able to raise the issue of the governor selling out to big business."

Hotchkiss came back into the room and sat down before Cameron could continue. Benton had about a dozen questions, but so far Cameron had only seemed pleased about the whole situation.

"Where were we before you left, Charley?" Cameron asked, then answered his own question. "Oh, yes. Bob, you'd asked how we got to the governor. There has never been any real question about which side he'd end up on. He's got to get re-elected. To do that he needs two things: support of people with money, and the illusion he's on the side of the common man."

Hotchkiss leaned forward and looked at Benton. "Of course," he said, "It didn't hurt any that Utah Fuel and the other coal companies made a healthy contribution to his campaign through our association." Benton nodded, but he was losing respect for the wishy-washy ways of politics in Utah. During the last strike in Colorado the governor had flat out said unionism was bad for all honest, hard-working people, and that was that.

"Bob, when you get back to Carbon County, you will find Major Johnson has an entirely different attitude, although what he will be saying will sound pretty much the same." Charley nodded, and Benton was curious. "When the union complains to Johnson, he will say that Adjutant General Williams made it clear to him there has been no change in the policy observed by the Guard. The Guard never has undertaken to prevent men from entering the coal camps of Carbon county for the purpose of working. If the strikers felt otherwise, they were mistaken."

"Say," Benton said. "That's beautiful. Not only will that let Johnson off the hook, workers can be brought in while proclaiming there has been no change in policy."

Smug no longer described Cameron. If he had been standing, he would have been swaggering. "And the governor is clear to stand stead-fastly on the side of working people everywhere. But, believe it or not, that's not the best part." Benton looked at Cameron expectantly. "Next Thursday's *News Advocate* will carry an article quoting the President of the United States. It will say that the president in his proclamation sets forth a principle which is about as fundamental to our social order as any we could name. He says that the men who take the places of the striking men have the same indisputable right to work that others have to decline work."

"And, because of my daughter being where she is, the union will learn that the big guns are now taking off their kid gloves," he said, and watched closely for Cameron's reaction. The only thing he could observe was, if possible, an improvement in Cameron's already good mood.

"Exactly, and they'll have to start scrambling to try to cut the damage they've caused by telling their people they had the ear of politicians this time." Cameron finished the last of the coffee.

Cameron was not smiling when he put his cup down. "It's all great, except for the Salt Lake papers are calling on us to accept the union's proposal."

Benton was almost stunned. He'd almost forgotten the tirade Cameron had about the papers when he first came in. He could see the problem. If the papers didn't change their tune, neither could the governor, gracefully. Cameron just sat there staring at him, as though it was Benton's fault.

"Think about it, Frank. Our options here are limited," Benton began to give himself time to think. He realized he didn't know the first thing about how to get papers to reverse a stance. Then he had an idea. "The only thing I can think of is if the governor," he paused for more time. "Yes, uh, if we could get the governor to make a statement on the subject, to, uh, say the offer was ridiculous because it meant virtual recognition of the union, then, uh . . ." he tried to continue but Cameron jumped on it.

"Exactly," Cameron almost shouted. "The governor could say that virtual recognition of the union would mean other working men would have to kowtow to the demands of a few." Cameron jumped up. "You guys stay here," he said. "I've got to go make a couple of phone calls." When Cameron came into his office, he was all smiles. "You can go home, now," he said to Benton. "The governor agrees to it. The papers will fall in line because they're no more anxious to have unions take over their papers than we are to have unions taking over our mines."

Bob knew he would be late getting home, but he didn't care. He had to get back. This time in Salt Lake he'd not only felt a small fish swimming with sharks, he'd felt a fish out of water. Finally, because of his early start and the pressure he was under, he felt very tired. He didn't want to doze at the wheel, so he pulled over for a short nap. He arrived home near midnight, but Katherine was waiting up for him. "I've been so worried," she said. "How did things go?"

The question brought everything rushing back in on him. "Well," he said and paused. "You might say I learned a lot."

The next morning he began opening up sections of the mine that he'd had to close down for lack of workers. Every day for the next two weeks what started as a trickle of strike-breakers became a flood. People were coming in from all the surrounding states to take the miners' jobs.

That, plus the trial of their friends for the train shooting had people in Tent Town downhearted. The joy of the Fourth of July was long gone. The day of the trial, Dan, Elizabeth, and Tom left for Price early. On their way, no one spoke. Dan drove the Star carefully so Tom would think he was a good driver. Elizabeth sat between the two men with her legs on either side of the gear shift.

Finally, Elizabeth broke the silence. "From the looks of you two, they're hanged already." Coming to the junction at Twelve Mile Wash, Dan slowed, then turned right and began picking up speed again. "What's to say?" he asked. "Except for Andy and a couple of other guys, the men they arrested don't even work here. They've got the wrong men. Yet they're still going ahead with a trial? Don't make any sense to me." Tom grunted, and said he guessed they would just have to put their faith in Sam King, and the justice system. Tom said that a lot of people didn't like old Sam, but nobody could say he wasn't a good attorney.

Once Dan was inside the courthouse, Sam King went over with Dan what questions he would ask, and told Dan he wouldn't be called till late in the day. When they did get in the court room, Dan, Tom, and Elizabeth found seats up front, on the opposite side from the jury. Apparently, because of pre-trial maneuvering, and the fact that Andy was still too weak to stand trial, only five of the accused were being tried at this time.

Then Henry Ruggeri got up and advised the court that The Honorable Isaac Blair Evans, former United States District Attorney, would be assisting him in the trial. He went on to say that Otto Morris of the United States Fuel Company would also be assisting as the representative of the coal mine operators association. Ruggeri said neither man was acting as counsel of record. He asked them to be here for him to confer with on important questions which might arise.

Sam King objected to this saying that changed the trial from one being prosecuted as a state case into a contest between the operators and the strikers. This objection was overruled. Then there were a number of motions. Sam King's first motion was that the trial of these men should be moved to a court martial because at the time of their arrests by the National Guard the area was under Martial Law. When that was denied, King moved for a change of venue in that feelings against strikers ran so high they could not receive a fair trial in Carbon County. He presented seven hundred affidavits in support of this request from people of all classes, obtained from every section of the county. This motion was also denied. Then King insisted that under Utah statutes the men demanded their right to separate trials. Elizabeth noticed a quick conference underway by the three men at the prosecution table, but the Judge spoke before they had finished. He said that right was clear, but the request was untimely since the men had previously agreed to come before this court as a group, and were, in fact, now before the court.

Ruggeri's opening statement painted a picture of the accused as being a group of fiendish foreigners lying in ambush to do vicious murder upon honest men trying to get to a job so they could earn a living for their families.

Also, Ruggeri said the motive for the killing was also an act of revenge. The night before the attack on the train, a couple of friends and countrymen of the accused had been roughed up some by people tired of their trouble-making foreign ways. He ended by saying the jury must listen to the evidence from the point of view that such men were among those whose answer to a civil disturbance was to kill as many people as possible on a train.

"Thank heaven," he said, for the good deputies on the train who prevented these foreigners to whom murder is second nature, from fully carrying out their nefarious plot. "Thank heaven," for one such good and honorable man, doing his duty to protect all good people. But as his reward he was to be so foully shot down in cold blood.

Boiled down, Sam King's statement was that he would prove that except in one instance, these men were neither from Sunnyside nor on the picket line. And the one man from Sunnyside was not at the scene of the shooting. He asserted that anyone testifying otherwise would be shown to be a perjurer. He would also prove the deputies fired first, those returning fire did so in self defense.

The coroner was called for the prosecution's first witness and described the wounds suffered by Art Webb, and the time of his death. King had no questions for the witness. Next a civil engineer by the name of James Block was called, and testified he was working near the train when the shooting occurred. He showed maps of the area, and pinpointed where the attack took place. When Ruggeri had finished, Sam King asked Block if there were any boulders, brushes, trees, or anything else the men at the train could hide behind. Block said there were not. He asked Block how far he was working from the incident when it took place. Block said about two hundred yards. He asked what Block's position was: was he at the side of the picketers, or behind them? Block said his crew was mostly behind them. Then King asked Block if, being on the scene, he could swear who fired the first shot. When Block said he could not, Sam dismissed him.

Ruggeri then called another civil engineer by the name of Neve who was working with Block. He identified the five defendants in the court room as being among those who fired on the train. He seemed sure of his identification. When the prosecution asked him how he could be so sure, he answered that his work as a civil engineer was to pay close attention to detail.

When it was his turn, King arose. His first question was to confirm from Neve that he'd testified close attention to detail was important. Then, after a pause, King continued. "Mr. Neve, can you tell us who fired the first shot?" Neve said he couldn't. "Was there anyplace the men could hide in ambush such as rocks, trees, or brush?" Again Neve said no. Sam walked back to his table and shuffled through some papers on his table. He returned to the witness stand. "Mr. Neve, how many of these men that you identified did you know prior to this incident?"

Neve looked a little surprised by the question. "Why, none of them. I'm not a coal miner, and I hardly hang out in their social circles." His answer brought chuckles throughout the audience.

King pursed his lips. "If you didn't know them, by name, how did you first identify them to authorities?" Neve said the sheriff had a bunch of suspects lined up and he pointed out these five. King put his hands behind his back. "As a person trained in paying close attention to detail, how long did this entire incident last?" Neve pursed his lips, then said maybe thirty seconds. "Thank you," King said and turned as if to go back to the table. Finally, he turned around again to face the witness. "Oh, by the way, will you describe your own actions when the shooting started?"

"You better believe I dove for the ground," Neve said quickly, then paused. "But I, uh, raised my head and paid close attention to what was happening."

King's voice got hard. "Let me get this straight. From behind these men, lying in a prone position, two hundred yards away, with about two dozen men, shooting or running, or diving to the ground, during an interval of thirty seconds more or less, you can positively identify these five defendants you had never seen before?"

Neve became defensive. "No matter how you make it sound, I was there, I saw it, and I saw those five men." King nodded his head as though agreeing with Neve, and suggested Neve was so positive because he pays such close attention to detail. "Absolutely right," Neve shot back.

"Then tell us how any of the men you saw were dressed. Not in detail, just any one thing you noticed, maybe an identifying mark, or some other thing by which you could make an identification." Neve just glared. Contemptuously King said, "No more questions."

Next Ruggeri called Sheriff Kelter. Kelter testified how and where the suspects were apprehended and placed in custody by the National Guard. Kukis was arrested based on information developed by his deputies. Zulakis was seen near the scene of the crime. Pagialakis, Kamourakis and Kriaris were seen near the scene within fifteen minutes of the shooting.

King didn't even pretend to be nice to Kelter. He put him on the defensive right from the start. He asked Kelter if, in all the searching he testified about, he or any of his men had made a search of both the site of the shooting, and inside the train for empty shell cases. When Kelter said he had not, King made it clear that Kelter had no idea whatsoever who did the most shooting.

When King tried to establish that Kelter had supplied Art Webb with rifles the morning of the shooting, Ruggeri objected on the grounds that this was not even remotely related to anything the sheriff had testified about, and the judge sustained that objection as well.

King switched to another subject. He asked where Kukis was arrested. The Sheriff said in Winter Quarters. King had Kelter admit that was over sixty miles from the scene. King asked which deputies gave information leading to Kukis's arrest, and Kelter said it was deputies J. R. Boren, and W. F. Abbot, both of whom were on the train at the time of the shooting. Then King asked similar questions about who gave the

Guard information on the others arrested, and each time Kelter's answer was Boren and Abbot.

Next, King wanted to know how many men all told had been arrested based on these expert witnesses so close to the scene of the shooting. Kelter said twenty-two. When King asked why only sixteen were held for a preliminary hearing and bound over for trial, Kelter said the six men released had sufficient alibi's and there wasn't enough other evidence against them to hold them.

"So," King said to Kelter, "based on the identical information given by these two deputies, six were released because they could prove they were somewhere else?" Kelter said that was true.

The Judge called an hour and a half recess for lunch. Everyone left the courtroom. On the way out of the building, Dan saw King. Elizabeth and Tom accompanied him as Dan went over to him to ask how much longer it would be before he testified. King said a couple of things were developing, so it might be a little later than he thought. Tom asked how it was going, and King just shrugged, "The judge is making many strange rulings. Good grounds for appeal. If we lose."

CHAPTER 32

JUSTICE IS SERVED

Next Ruggeri called Deputy Abbot, who testified that, on orders from Art Webb, he was armed with a rifle. He sat on the steps on the right hand side of the front platform of the coach carrying the men seeking work. Abbot said Boren was on the left side and Henry Fiack was standing in the vestibule at the rear of the train. He testified he heard shooting, stood, and began firing himself. He said he then saw the picketers shooting as the train rushed by, and identified the five in the court as being among those he saw shooting.

King approached him. "Tell me, Mr. Abbot. Can you give us a description of anything any of these men were wearing the day of the shooting, or any marks, or any other means by which you identified them?" Abbot said he just recognized their faces. King thought for a moment, "Can you tell me who you saw fire first?" Abbot admitted he could not. "Do you know if the first shot could have come from where Mr. Webb was, up in front at the engine?" Abbot was sweating, and said maybe it could have. "You testified that you had a rifle. What kind was it?" Abbot said it was a 1903 Springfield 3006. King looked at the jury when he asked the next questions. "Had you, personally, ever seen a 1903 Springfield 3006 among the weapons at Utah Fuel?" Abbot said he had not. Now King turned and looked toward Kelter. "So how did you acquire that rifle?"

"Boren said . . ." Abbot started but was interrupted by Ruggeri.

"Objection, hearsay."

The judge still had not looked up, "Sustained."

"You said you had a rifle and were sitting at the front of the coach. You said when you heard shots, you rose and began firing. At what were you firing?"

Abbot scowled, "At the Greeks, of course."

King nodded. "Of course. Were you shooting over their heads to scare them, were you shooting to wound them, or were you shooting to kill?"

Abbot squirmed in his chair, and seemed uneasy at the question. "I was shooting to kill."

"Would you tell the court why you were carrying a rifle, and sitting outside the train car?"

Abbot shifted in his chair. When he spoke, he spoke with a little more confidence. "We were expecting trouble, and we were prepared for it."

King pursed his lips. "You said you were expecting trouble, and were prepared for it. To your knowledge had this train ever been shot at before?"

"No," Abbot answered curtly.

"Ever been stopped or molested in any way?"

"No," Abbot said, and seemed confused by the questions.

King turned to Abbot, "To your own knowledge, who told you the strikers were going to shoot at the train, or threaten it, or in any other way do any illegal action this time?"

Abbot was sweating again. "Why, uh, nobody said that. We, uh, this was the first time we brought in a car full of scab, uh, men, and we, uh, were just taking precautions."

King faced the jury yet again. "I will remind you, Mr. Abbot, you are under oath, and if it is necessary to refresh your memory, I can have His Honor instruct you on the penalties for perjury." Wiping off sweat with his handkerchief Abbot said that wouldn't be necessary. King's voice grew cold. "Just now you said you were only taking precautions. Earlier you said you were expecting trouble and you were prepared for it. Were you lying then, or are you lying now? Which, exactly, was it?"

Abbot just looked down at his handkerchief, as he spoke. "Expecting trouble." King never looked toward Abbot again and said simply, "No more questions."

Ruggeri called Boren who testified much as Abbot had, except that he stated he'd definitely seen Pagialakas with his pistol in hand, shooting at the train, then ducking under a fence.

King asked Boren to demonstrate with his hand how he held his rifle when he was aiming it to shoot. Boren held one hand by his cheek with his other hand at arm's length. King asked Boren if it was his testimony that with a field of vision for only a few seconds as the train raced by, with his hand and rifle in front of his face, he could identify a man ducking under a fence two hundred yards away. Boren said he'd seen him all right.

Then King started on yet another tack. "Mr. Boren, let's look at those orders you testified you were under. Could you elaborate on that a little bit?"

Boren stated the orders came from Art Webb. They were to do everything possible to make sure the train got to Sunnyside safely. King looked into Boren's eyes. "Let's get more specific, Mr. Boren. Exactly, what were the words used in giving orders to you regarding the pickets?"

"Mr. Webb said we were not going to let this train be picketed, peaceably or otherwise."

King turned to the jury. "Mr. Boren, how, from a speeding train, did you propose to keep men on the ground from picketing that train?" Boren mumbled something. King may have heard it, but he didn't let on. He stayed facing the jury. "Would you please speak up, Mr. Boren?"

Boren's face turned mean. He spoke loudly. "I said by shooting at them." King dismissed him.

Shortly thereafter, the prosecution rested, and King began calling witnesses. First was the engineer running the train. King got the court's approval to treat him as a hostile witness, because he said he was busy running the train and didn't see nothin. Once he started speaking, however, he said when Webb saw the picketers, he said, "Here they are," and started firing.

"Did you hear any shots fired before Webb fired after he said, 'Here they are.'?"

"Objection. The witness has already testified he could not."

"Sustained," said the judge.

When King dismissed the engineer, he called twelve witnesses who all swore they knew Pete Kukis and during the time of the shooting, he was in his tent in Tent Town. These witnesses were never contradicted nor shaken by Ruggeri. Then King brought witnesses to prove Mike Zulakis had come from Greece only a few months before, and didn't speak a word of English, so Boren couldn't possibly have had a conversation with him. Further, he lived in one of the coal camps near Helper, and had never left that area.

In rapid order seventeen other witnesses testified that Tony Kamourakis and John Kriaris lived in Kenilworth, and had not left there since the first day of June. Then he presented over twenty sworn affidavits to the court backing up what the witnesses had said.

At that point the Judge adjourned the court until nine the next morning. Dan looked at Elizabeth for the first time in a while, she was dripping with sweat. "What's wrong honey?" he asked, but she just patted her tummy. "It ain't just that," he said. "It's a furnace in this courtroom. Are you sure you want to come back tomorrow?" She said she wouldn't miss it for the world.

On the trip home, nobody said much. They each had their private thoughts. Dan was going over his testimony again and again in his mind. After seeing Ruggeri at work, he was not at all anxious to be cross-examined by him.

Even during supper that night, breakfast in the morning, and the trip back to Price, there was little except polite conversation. At least it was cool in the courtroom as they took their seats.

King's first witness was the station master who testified that all messages about the scab train had been in code, so the union men couldn't possibly have known there were scabs on the train. King asked, if the picketers couldn't have known, why would they set up an ambush?

The objection from Ruggeri was on the grounds of calling for a conclusion, the judge sustained it, ordered the court clerk to strike the question and the jury to disregard it.

Another witness asserted that he was in Helper the night the Guard arrived, and the Guard rounded up a whole bunch of men as suspects in the shooting. Later the Guard released all but a few. Most of those detained could not speak English, so they couldn't give an alibi.

Other witnesses testified that Zulakis was a total stranger to every other defendant charged in the shooting, and could have had no part in planning or carrying out any part of the shooting. Elizabeth gave up trying to keep track of it all, and just sat, and looked down as the judge was doing. What was mostly on her mind was just how hard the chairs in the courtroom had become, and how uncomfortable they were making her bottom.

Finally, Dan was called. But to her disappointment, his testimony was fairly brief. King asked him to describe what he did before, during and after the shooting. After Dan finished with this background, King zeroed in on seeing Webb shoot first.

After Dan testified about that, King asked about Webb having shot Dan's horse before Webb was killed on the train. Ruggeri objected that this had nothing to do with this trial, and King explained that for the jury to get the full picture of Dan's testimony, they needed to understand that Dan had motives for lying about seeing Mr. Webb shoot first. King said he wanted it brought out in open court what everyone knew privately, and establish that Dan's testimony would be truthful in spite of that.

"This should be interesting," the judge said. "Overruled."

After Dan answered about Turk, King brought up another incident. "Isn't it true you also had a fist fight with Mr. Webb after he shot your horse?" Dan said that was true. "Yet you are telling this jury that the only reason you're saying Webb shot first was because it is the truth?"

"Yes, Sir," Dan answered.

"I'm not convinced yet," King said. "Let me play the devil's advocate for a moment. You're a union member on strike, right?"

Dan fidgeted in his chair. "Yes, I am."

King pursed his lips, "The company threw you out of your place of domicile, caused you to live in a tent, shined a spotlight on your tent, and all the rest. And then they killed your horse?"

Dan seemed uncomfortable. He reached up and loosened his collar. "Yes, Sir. That is correct."

King put his hand on the side of the witness box, and looked into Dan's eyes. "What would keep a person with all that happening to him from hating the company and Art Webb, and lying about who shot first?"

Dan sat up straight in his chair. He looked directly back at King. "Because a man I admired as a second father, and who was murdered, said that what he hated most was lies, and for us to lie about the company makes us worse than they are."

"No more questions," King said abruptly, and sat down.

Ruggeri didn't even try to shake Dan's testimony about who shot first. As near as Elizabeth could tell, Ruggeri was trying to discredit his whole testimony by harping on why he didn't turn himself in to the sheriff as having been on the scene.

Dan simply recounted all the company men who had seen him at the depot. He said the deputies who testified they were on the train must also have seen him. He said while he ran from the scene of the shooting, he never tried to hide. He went straight back to Tent Town and assumed they didn't want to talk to him or they would have come to question him. He said he would have been glad to tell the sheriff and anybody else who shot first. But nobody asked him.

That was the end of the trial for Elizabeth, the chair was just too uncomfortable, the heat too intense. When Dan got up to leave the witness box, she got up quietly, nodded her head toward the exit, and went out. They left the courthouse and sat in the car on a seat which was less uncomfortable. Still, it was hot as blazes even there, so they went and sat in the shade on the courthouse lawn. An hour or so later, people began streaming from the courthouse. Tom came out and told Dan and Elizabeth how brilliant King's summation had been.

Tom said as King finished his summation, he told the jury that they needed to decide if there was a reasonable doubt in their minds. He said if there was a reasonable doubt, they had not been paying attention because logic, facts, and testimony proved there was no reasonable doubt whatsoever that the company had set up this entire thing, a company man had shot first, and that the company was responsible for any death. Further, there was no reasonable doubt whatsoever that the witnesses who identified these men were lying through their teeth. He pointed to the almost mountain of written affidavits that he had presented and said all of them fairly shouted these men were innocent and must be found not guilty.

Seated on the lawn, they eagerly awaited some sign that the jury had reached a verdict. In less than half an hour people began streaming back into the courthouse. Tom, Dan, and Elizabeth could only find standing room at the back, so they didn't even have to rise when the bailiff called, "All rise." The men of the jury were already present, and rose to their feet with everyone else. When they were seated again, the foreman of the jury stood and called the names of the defendants off one by one. "We the jury find Peter Kukis, guilty of Second Degree Murder." Those in the courtroom seemed stunned. A deadly quiet settled in as the foreman continued. "Mike Zulakis, guilty of Second Degree Murder." The quiet gave way to angry murmurs. The foreman continued, "Mike Pagialakis, guilty of Voluntary Manslaughter." The murmurs grew to open expressions of anger and hostility. The judge banged his gavel, then banged it again. He threatened to clear the courtroom immediately unless quiet prevailed. The foreman looked afraid. Hurriedly, he combined the last two verdicts, "Tony Kambourakis and John Kriaris, both guilty of Involuntary Manslaughter."

Murmurs of discontent turned into a roar. "Liars!" and "Fakes," and screams of, "You call this justice," blared out. The judge's banging of the gavel did no good. One man apparently stepped on the foot of another, and a fight broke out between them. People were so angry and frustrated they began lashing out at each other. In seconds bedlam prevailed. Brawls began in all sections of the court. It was all the bailiff and deputies could do to keep the incensed mob away from the jury, who were rapidly being hustled out the back door of the jury box. Dan and Tom did their best to get Elizabeth out, but not before someone punched Dan in the eye. They headed for the door, but were momentarily blocked as more deputies came rushing in amid curses in half a dozen languages. The courtroom was finally cleared.

During the next few days it became obvious that nothing that had happened during the strike discouraged the people of Tent Town as this verdict did. At the killings they had felt hate, or anger, or grief, but now there was just hopelessness and despondency. People hardly seemed to care when the Guard closed the road into Sunnyside and they could no longer get extra food.

The last part of July and the first part of August was also miserable because of the heat. The occasional monsoon-type cloudbursts during the period cooled things off for a short time. But as soon as they passed, unlike the usual dry air, the humidity was intolerable. Elizabeth got so she couldn't stand sweltering in the tent during the heat of the day. She didn't know if it was extra hot, or if she just suffered more because she was pregnant. She figured if it wasn't for the cool, pleasant evenings, she would just die.

Sometimes, during the heat of the day, they would go somewhere in the Star, but the trip to a place that was cooler, such as Nine Mile Canyon, was long, gas was short, and the heat in the car was almost as bad as in the tent. Because of her pregnancy they could no longer even ride Bonnie and Showboat. This was Elizabeth's favorite way to try to beat the heat, but even this was not always pleasant.

Dan suggested they go down to the creek and sit under the shade of a tree. As usual, at such times, they would splash some fresh cool water over themselves. Elizabeth agreed, but today, finding a spot under a tree wasn't easy. All the good places were taken up by others.

They removed their shoes, and waded in the creek while Dan tried to figure out what to do. Finally they came to a place where the bank was steep and high, casting a shadow over one side of the creek. Dan pointed out some rounded boulders they could sit on. They waded over to them and sat dangling their feet in the cool water. "This is real luxury," Elizabeth exclaimed. "We've got shade, rocks to sit on, and a babbling brook at our feet. What more could we ask for?"

But even this didn't last. After a while, the movement of the sun put them out of the shade and Elizabeth was beginning to have difficulty sitting on the hard rock. "Time to be getting back," he said. "Wet down your dress," he said as he got off the rock and began soaking himself.

Back at the tent, Elizabeth asked him if he wanted lunch, but Dan refused, saying it was just too hot to eat. He didn't mention that what they might eat could present a problem. Supplies were running low. Instead, they both went to the bed. Lying there in their still damp clothes, they definitely were more comfortable. When they started getting too warm again, Dan went to the creek for a bucket of water.

About the time they were ready to get up and cook supper, Elizabeth looked at Dan. "You know something?" she mused, and Dan just looked at her. "This is the best afternoon I've had in a week, and I owe it all to you. Don't think I haven't noticed how you work to take care of me."

Dan blushed. "I love you, too," he said. "Now let's get supper. I'm starving." There wasn't much, beans, four ears of corn from the garden, and a couple loaves of bread.

They were just sitting down to eat when a knock on the tent pole interrupted them. "Come on in," Dan said, then chuckled. "It ain't locked," he added. Tom came in, sat, and looked at the beans.

"Have you eaten yet, Tom?" Elizabeth asked. Tom indicated he usually ate later than this. "Want to eat with us?" Elizabeth volunteered. Tom said it looked like a feast.

Dan wondered why Tom was visiting them. "What brings you visiting tonight, Tom?" he asked.

"Wanted to talk about the president," Tom said. Tom looked gloomy. "The strike's all but busted. Production is up high enough so that the company can keep going," he said.

Dan dipped a piece of broken bread into his beans, then looked at Tom. "With all the scabs coming in, Tom, that's hardly news. A lot of the guys been askin' me when the district is going to get off it's duff and admit we ain't got a chance. I don't have a good answer for them."

Tom took a few more spoonfuls of beans. "I been tellin' everybody it ain't quite time to give up yet. The president has finally forced the operators and national union officials to meet in Washington. Jimmy Morgan sent me word that while no agreements have been reached yet, things seem to be moving along."

"I sure hope so. Seems that conference is our last chance," Dan offered.

CHAPTER 33

A MANAGEMENT DECISION

When he was finally through talking and eating, Tom offered his thanks and left. Dan opened his arms and beckoned Elizabeth into them. He gave her a good, long, loving hug. As he finished, he kissed her on the neck.

"My," she said as she came out of his embrace. "What was that all about?"

Dan looked at her with love in his eyes. "While we were talking, I got to thinking about how bad some of the others have it. But no matter how this strike comes out, we've won, you and me."

Now it was Elizabeth's turn to be puzzled. "How can you say that?" she asked.

Dan reached both hands up and put them on her shoulders. He looked deep into her eyes. "If it wasn't for this strike, I never would have got you. No matter what we've gone through, and ten times worse to boot, you're more than worth it."

Elizabeth didn't know what to say. Tears came into her eyes. "I feel the same," she finally stammered. "You're right, we've won." She came into his arms for the second time.

A week later in Price she began to read her galleys. Not much new was there, but an editorial interested her. The headline read, "Utah's Striking Miners Are Victims Of Delusion Imposed By Outsiders." Elizabeth realized that once more the operators were pushing hard to drive a wedge between the workers and the union leaders.

She continued to read. "What an utterly foolish thing this so-called coal strike here in Carbon county has been! What dupes these poor blind followers of a few outside agitators have proven themselves! What a waste of time and personal energies these strikers have imposed on themselves and on their families," the first paragraph read. It went on to insist there had been no discontent among Utah miners till outside agitators and "strike-makers" so badly deceived them.

The only thing new was the catchword, "strike-makers," which was splashed liberally throughout the article. Better let the union know about this, she reasoned. Especially that part which called on the governor to take action in Carbon county to send the labor leaders from Wyoming packing because, "the removal of the agitating strike-makers from other states would go far toward a solution of the whole matter."

The whole tone of the item confused Elizabeth. She couldn't figure out why this was being printed at this particular time. The only thing which had changed since the governor started letting strike-breakers in was the convening of the negotiations at President Harding's insistence.

When she'd done enough proofreading, she said good-bye to Mr. Cooper. She met Ann at the cafe by the train station. They each ordered the marinated pot roast. While they were waiting to be served, Elizabeth began sharing her concerns about the article with Ann. But all the time she was telling Ann about it, she remembered Tom asked her if she would drop by the train depot on her way home and get early copies of the evening papers so they could follow the progress of negotiations back East. Lunch finished, she advised Ann of her errand and took her leave.

Quickly she went to the station, got the papers, and headed once more for home and Dan. She couldn't believe the headlines. Back in tent town, she got out of the car, grabbed the newspapers and rushed into the tent. She threw the newspapers on the table. Dan was lying on the bed. He looked up at her. He thought she looked as if she'd just won a million dollars. Dan got up and headed for the table.

"My Lord!" he shouted. "Why didn't you tell me?" he asked as he looked at the headline. "BOTH SIDES RATIFY AGREEMENT TO SIGN MINE CONTRACT." "We're going back to work!" Dan said, joy in his voice. He jumped up, paused a moment to read the first few details of the settlement, then his grin widened. "We've won! We've won!"

Benton sat on the train going over yesterday's newspaper accounts so he would be up to speed when he met Cameron.

According to the *Salt Lake Telegram*, the governor was "pleased as punch" and told the newspaper he was, "tickled to death." He went on to say there was never any real trouble in Utah during the strike, and state authorities agreed the strike had been managed well. Phony no-good liars, Benton mumbled to himself. Benton was a little surprised at the number of states where both sides had ratified the agreement and were going back to work immediately. Ohio, West Virginia, Pennsylvania, Indiana, Illinois, and Michigan had caved in to the union. Those included the largest coal producers in the country.

Benton sat for a while going over the ramifications of it all in his mind. He literally felt sick that now a Super would no longer be in complete charge of how his mine was run. At least the union hadn't won a wage increase. They were all going back to work at the old wage scale, before the wage cut twenty weeks ago. A commission was to be set up to consider the possibility of an increase. Worst of all, however, it was now the company's job to collect money for the union dues from its workers. They're forcing us to cut our own throats, he thought. We collect the money, hand it over to them, then they use it to fight us with. What the hell is this country coming to, he wondered. It's un-American to have to kowtow to unions that way.

The conductor interrupted his thoughts, announcing they had arrived in Salt Lake. Hotchkiss was again waiting for him. Hotchkiss said all the major operators in the state were gathering in Cameron's office to discuss the situation, and the meeting had already started.

When they got to the Judge Building, there was not even a place for Hotchkiss and Benton to sit in the large conference room. However, the secretary brought in a couple more chairs, and Benton sat uneasily in front of the doorway-no other space was available. The man speaking had been a participant at the contract negotiations held in the negotiations back East. He looked terrible. His coat looked rumpled, his pants needed a press, and he looked tired. He must have been awake on the train all night to get back here for this meeting.

"It was the I.W.W. Them, and their one big union idea, has the operators scared shitless."

Cameron spoke up. "Hell, Ken, the IWW isn't anywhere near as powerful as the miners' union, or the railroads', or almost any of the others including the steel workers' and the teamsters' for that matter. Why should we be so afraid of them?"

"First," Ken replied. "They're not as powerful as the others because they're newer. They didn't start till after the revolution in Russia, but they're growing fast. Second, we should be afraid of them because if they ever get that one big union idea of theirs going, we're up a creek without a paddle. They won't just shut down the coal mines, or the railroads. They'll be able to shut down the whole country all at once any time they want to."

Murmurs of dismay ran through the assembled men. Ken reached into his coat pocket and withdrew a sheet of paper. "Listen to this," he said, and held the paper up so the others could see it. "Chester Rowell, president of the California State Railway Commission says that if the purpose of business is to destroy capitalism, stalling the individual craft unions and letting I.W.W. get a good foothold amongst American workers is the way." Ken stopped to breathe, then continued. "Rowell says if we don't do something to stop the I.W.W., expect the break-up of many of today's successful business empires. If the purpose of business is to survive, they had better sign contracts with the likes of the U.M.W.A., Rail Road Operating Engineers, and the other individual craft unions. Once these individual unions are recognized, they and their workers will become our allies to fight the I.W.W. and the whole one big union idea."

"Makes a heck of a lot of sense to me," a company official observed. "We'd probably better ratify the agreement."

"I disagree," another said. "Now that those eastern pencil-necks have turned yellow and sold us out, they've already got most of the miners in the country against the Wobblies. What would be our advantage in knuckling under here?"

Benton was surprised at the arguments which followed. Somehow, he had always assumed that the operators were one hundred percent behind squashing the union, as was any company he had ever worked for. But obviously they were a divided group. At one point, Benton was almost sure these men would give in as the people in the Central District had. The argument against ratification which seemed to gain the most favor, however, was that production in all the local mines was up enough to get by. Once it became evident the local union had lost the strike, and wouldn't be getting any more help from the national union, enough current strikers would return to work to bring production up to its pre-strike levels.

Slowly but surely, the arguments against ratification gained strength. Finally it was decided they would issue a statement to the press from their association that business conditions here in Utah made it impossible for Utah operators to ratify agreements signed elsewhere since conditions there were vastly different than conditions in Utah.

Benton could not have been more pleased. There was only one part of the whole discussion against ratification he did not personally agree with. That was putting the strikers back to work in the mines. He felt this was a terrible mistake. When the big meeting broke up, Benton and Hotchkiss went into Frank's office and sat down. At his first opportunity, Benton raised his objection, but Cameron seemed surprised. "Why on earth would you want to keep the inexperienced and inefficient men we brought in, when there's a Tent Town full of experienced miners waiting to go back to work?"

Benton observed that all men are inefficient when they first come into the mine, but the newly hired men were learning. He brought up that if they put the union men back to work, there would be extremely hard feelings between them and the miners who had stayed loyal to the company. He mentioned that the union had been so well organized this time that only by refusing to take the union miners back could they break the union at Utah Fuel mines. Plus, he had another suggestion. "It's not that we won't hire anybody out on strike anywhere. Utah Fuel will just not hire someone who struck against that particular mine."

"I see," Cameron said and seemed to agree. "Somebody at Castle Gate could get a job at Winter Quarters, and you'd hire somebody from Clear Creek." Benton said that was the gist of it, and in this way they could still hire as many experienced miners as they needed. "Okay, you go on back and tell the other Supers that it is the management's decision that we will not put men who struck their mines back to work. But this is your baby, Bob. You had better make it work, or it will be a management decision to overrule you if problems occur."

On the train trip back Benton wished he hadn't been so against the union. He had only brought up not putting the men back to work and breaking the local union because he had been sure Cameron would love the idea. Naturally, when Cameron objected, Benton was left with no choice but to defend his idea. Still, the thought of hiring back the likes of Tom Carr made his blood boil. Maybe getting rid of that crafty devil would make it worth the risk.

Tired he sat listening to the clicking of the wheels on the track, and feeling the slight swaying as the train went around curves. He relaxed into the steady rhythm until the conductor called the train into Price.

He got off the train, and headed for the Packard, sitting there and shining in the sun, as if greeting him. Benton knew it was probably irrational, but inside the Packard was the only place he felt at home and really in charge. It was so luxurious, and so typified what he sought in life. And, best of all, it responded instantly to his every action to control it. Perhaps even better, it could never ever even think of organizing a strike against him as that devil Tom Carr, or put him under its thumb as the contemptible Frank Cameron.

Benton started the engine and headed for Sunnyside.

Two days later, after Benton's announcement of the company's management decision, Elizabeth's heart hurt with the sorrow and pain of the other people of Tent Town. They were making preparations to move to other towns to find work. A few left almost overnight, and in a few other tents only women and children remained. The fathers had gone seeking work.

Saddest of all was when Tom came by. He and Dan discussed the possibilities of finding work. Dan was extremely anxious to find out from Tom which Utah Fuel mine was good to work for and might need employees. Tom said, hands down, Winter Quarters. Superintendent Parmley was death on unions but he was a fair and honorable man.

Elizabeth said she'd drive them all up there the next day to see if they could get on. But Tom declined. He said if he couldn't work in Sunnyside, working anywhere else in Utah would bring back too many memories of friends he'd lost and the bad things which happened here. He guessed he would head for Colorado or Wyoming. He figured it would be better to find work there, and start over where the hatred of unions wasn't so intense.

Elizabeth said fair treatment of people and the union in Utah looked totally impossible to her, remembering that even a fifteen-year-old girl could be brought in and coerced into sex in this state.

Tom had a higher viewpoint, "Look what happened back east," he said. "If the operators in Utah don't give in, eventually they'll lose all their good workers to union mines in other states. Sooner or later they'll have to recognize the union."

Dan disagreed and said as far as he was concerned, even if the unions did get a minor foothold in Utah, the Church's position against them would cause overall wages here to end up the equivalent of wages in the deep south where most working people were ex-slaves."

As Tom prepared to leave, he promised to drop by in the morning to say good-bye before he left. "Maybe by then I'll have figured out where I will make my new life," he said, then added, "Much as I hate leaving you good people here."

As Tom left, Dan and Elizabeth sat, looking at each other. There was no joy on their faces, and without saying anything Elizabeth got up and started packing things into some powder boxes. "I'm only putting away things I'm sure we won't need till we find out for sure where we're going." Dan said that was a good idea, and he began doing the same with items of his. He said they would probably end up at Winterquarters, however. If Tom said that was best, Dan knew it must be true. He put his flute and medicine bag in a powder box and took it outside where he had his stick lying alongside the tent wall. He went inside, raised the plank over his rifle, and took it outside as well.

Once they'd done about as much as they could, Elizabeth suggested they take a break for supper. But even eating made them feel no less somber. They hardly spoke to each other. What was there to say? Even if they had wanted to say something to cheer each other up, the misery of others in Tent Town would have made it a hollow gesture.

After supper, Dan helped Elizabeth with the dishes. "Well, at least," he said, "I won't keep having to make runs to the creek for water."

"Yeah," Elizabeth agreed. "And truth be known, it won't break my heart to be able to use an indoor toilet again." That brought a quick thought to her mind. "Dan, when we go to Winter Quarters tomorrow, I refuse to let you take a job there unless we can live in a newer house with inside plumbing." Dan agreed completely and said if they couldn't get one, they'd leave the state and go with Tom.

After dinner each of them smoked, and there was no joy in this, either. Mostly, they still just sat, looking at each other, occasionally smiling at each other, but even the smiles made them feel sad. Occasionally, one of them would get up for something and pass by the other, giving them a loving pat of consolation.

Shortly after the sun went down, Dan asked Elizabeth if she would mind if he went out alone for a while. "I've just got to think, Honey. I need some time by myself to try to sort it all out." Elizabeth nodded, and said maybe she'd go over to Tom's tent and take him the remaining food they had left over from supper. Maybe she'd help him pack. As Dan passed by the side of the tent, he noticed the box containing the flute, stopped, and got it out. He took the flute out of it's leather sheath and replaced the sheath in the box.

He climbed up the hillside and sat on a rock. It was a warm evening, and he began trying to play the flute. As it got darker, Dan remembered Billy saying this was the magic time when it was past day, and not yet night. It was then Dan noticed that while his flute playing was not even close to being as beautiful as Billy's, at least he was making Indian sounds. Shortly thereafter, the sounds he made were pleasing to him. Soon, he was playing music. Unlike any music he had ever heard before, but music nevertheless.

Tired, he stopped playing and laid the flute on the rock alongside of him. He lit a pipe and watched the darkness take over the world, only to give way a little itself as a big full moon came up over the mountain. Before the pipe was done, he smiled to himself and began fanning smoke toward himself as Billy had done. Finished, he knocked the ashes out on his heel as he had seen Billy do so many times. Then he began to ponder the strike and all that had happened since then. He wanted desperately to be able to make some sense out of it. To find even one thing, if he could, that would make it all worthwhile.

The thought of finding Elizabeth helped, but that was a selfish thing. It did nothing for the others who had lost so much. This brought to his mind Turk, and John, and Mitch. Dan knew that even with all he had personally suffered and lost, they had given up far more. And for what?

That was the question which came back to his mind again and again. For what? He thought of the union and Jimmy Morgan, and Andy with his bad arm. His mind was alive with memories, vivid pictures of the past. And the sorrow. And for what? There was no answer to that.

Finally, he realized it was getting late, somewhere past midnight. He figured he'd better be getting back to Elizabeth. But before he left, he picked up the flute and began playing again. As he played, pictures of Billy dancing and chanting and talking returned to him. It was almost as if Billy was there with him.

Dan lay the flute down and lit his final pipe for the night. But the pictures of Billy did not go away. Dan began puffing, and fanning the smoke toward himself again. It baffled him, but he noticed he was getting calm, and more clear-headed. Once, as he puffed and reached up for more smoke, he noticed the glowing tobacco inside the pipe bowl. Power of fire, he thought.

He had no idea where the plan came from. It wasn't something he had reasoned out, it was all there at once, and he knew what he was going to do. He walked slowly back to the tent, and he smiled as he walked. He replaced the flute quietly into its sheath, being careful not to wake Elizabeth. Then he headed for town. He didn't even take pains not to be seen, but walked boldly up the road. It was the middle of the night, and while the National Guard wouldn't leave till the weekend, they had stopped their patrols. As near as Dan could tell, the whole town was asleep, except for him.

As he approached the carriage house, his smile broadened. Quietly, he opened one of the doors and went inside. The bright moon even made it easy for him to find a can of gasoline. When both the inside and outside of the Packard was drenched, Dan sprinkled a little around the rest of the place as well. Then he made a little trail outside and up the driveway a bit. His first inclination was to light the trail with a match, but he reconsidered. Instead, he heaped his pipe up until tobacco was bulging out over the top, and used the match to light that. Then he took a couple of big puffs, got the tobacco glowing hotly, and touched it to the trail of gasoline.

When the trail burned inside, there was a loud, "whump!" and some of the windows of the carriage house blew out. Dan could see inside the doors, and the Packard was beginning to burn brightly. He turned toward the house, and as he approached it, he saw lights coming on. He walked up to the back door and knocked. Half dressed, Benton came to the door, in his right hand he carried his forty-four pistol.

"I just burned up your Packard," he said to Benton.

Benton pointed the forty-four at Dan's chest. "You're dead, you're dead," he spat.

"Go ahead," Dan challenged. "If you want everybody knowing your son-in-law burned you out, go ahead and shoot."

Benton stood and looked at Dan. He cocked the pistol. Dan did not flinch. Everything in Benton cried out to pull the trigger, but he hesitated. "You better listen to me," Dan said in a calm, reasoning tone. "This fire is just the first. More are coming unless you put all the strikers back to work."

Benton lowered the pistol. "You . . . no-good," Benton threatened, "I'll have you locked up. I'll . . . I'll tell every body the baby isn't yours."

Dan knew having him arrested was a bluff born out of desperation. Dan smiled at the feebleness of telling people the child was not his. "Of course the kid's mine. It's caught in my trap, ain't it?" However, Dan had come on far more urgent business than to discuss the parentage of his child. "If you have me locked up, others will see. I've shown them the way. They'll understand the power of fire themselves. Don't forget, a mine can burn better than a Packard. Then what will you be Super over?"

Benton had not moved. He was still standing there in the doorway, half-dressed, pistol hanging at his side, looking at Dan with hate in his eyes. His agony over the Packard was matched by his fury at being dominated this way. But he understood the force in what Dan said. Benton's mind raced to figure some way out, but the town siren interrupted his thoughts.

"Make up your mind quick! Or I'll tell the first person to get here I burned your Packard to get their jobs back. What's it going to be? Strikers rehired and a tragic accident, or the burn-out everybody'll say you got coming after Pessetto's?"

Benton looked down the road and saw some men hurrying toward his place with a hose cart. He looked back at Dan. Dan was not bluffing. Anybody who would burn up a Packard was capable of anything. "A tragic accident," he said in a tone that would have killed if it could. "All except Tom Carr, I won't hire him back."

"You ain't said nothin' yet," Dan said. "Okay," Benton hissed as the men with the cart arrived, "Tom, too."

Happily, Dan helped the men hook up the fire hose, and then stood by as they put down the flames. When the fire was enough under control to make sure nothing else would catch on fire, he walked over to Benton standing there shivering in the heat.

"You'd better tell them about going back to work right now," Dan said softly, "or I start talking this minute." Again Benton looked at Dan with total hatred. He knew if the little fiend opened his mouth, he was through. Cameron would fire him for sure.

"Men . . ." Benton started to say, but his voice cracked. He covered his mouth and coughed. "Men," he started again. "Your help in this tragic accident has touched me deeply. Management decision, or no management decision, I cannot deprive such fine people of the right to work in Sunnyside. Everyone who wants a job can come back."

Cheers and joyous shouts broke out among men, women, and children alike. One woman even ran up and hugged Benton. Dan could not help but notice there was not a striker in the group. "Bye, Dad," Dan said loudly, and Benton cringed at the word. "I'm sorry about all this, but I better be getting back to Elizabeth."

He had barely started down the road when he met people from Tent Town swarming toward him. A minute later, Elizabeth and Tom came up to him. "People are saying the Packard's gone?" Tom asked.

Trying not to laugh, Dan said it was a tragic accident.

Elizabeth looked at him. "You did it, didn't you?"

"I did," Dan admitted softly, "But for heaven's sake, don't tell anybody." Tom asked why not tell, and added it was a glorious deed. "I did it so he'd put you all back to work. If word gets out I started the fire, I'll lose leverage with him. He made the announcement everybody was going back to work a little while ago."

Tom and Elizabeth were both puzzled as they walked back to Tent Town, but Dan would say no more about the subject. When they got there, the first rays of a new day were beginning to light up the eastern sky. Tom returned to his tent. At theirs, Dan stopped Elizabeth long enough to point out the coming light. Then, without a word, he walked over to the side of the tent and picked up his stick.

"Where are you going with that?" Elizabeth asked.
"To chant beauty into the world," Dan replied.

EPILOGUE

The next morning Benton called Cameron and advised him that he decided to take his advice. It was really much better to put experienced men to work. The men who worked this mine knew this mine, and it would take others too much time to learn how to mine it productively and safely.

The following Thursday *The News Advocate* published an editorial under the headline, CAHILL WHINES TO PUT MEN TO WORK. "Matt Cahill, one of the Wyoming ginks who has been helping keep some of the Carbon County miners from working, has now addressed a letter to the operators begging for a chance to get some of the men back on jobs as the funds for feeding idlers have been exhausted and winter is not far away. The miners want to find out through Cahill on what terms they can go to work. *The News Advocate* has not inquired from any source what answer, if any, may be given by the operators, but it is hard to see why any answer is needed. Those who really want to work can easily find out on what terms they can get jobs. All they have to do is to apply at the mine offices and find out the wages and working conditions and take the job, if there is one for them."

On September the first, Utah coal mine operators angered everyone in the state by raising the price of coal by one dollar a ton. Since they all made this raise at the same time, charges of monopoly were filed. On that same day, Dan and Elizabeth got a new little sister named Mary Elizabeth Cook. She would be called Liz. Mary lay in bed looking at her newest addition to the world. "This one will never be hurt or killed in a mine," she said to Carl.

Within a month, the scabs brought in during the strike were petitioning the union to do something for them. When the company hired them on, they were promised that if the pay scale was raised back to its pre-strike cut, they would be paid that wage retroactively from the date they hired on. Now Utah Fuel was reneging on that promise. Plus a lot of the scabs were being laid off as the more skilled union men returned to take their old jobs back. They felt this unfair, and wanted the union to do something about it.

Lorenzo Young died before ever coming to trial for the murder of John Tennis.

On the twenty-ninth of November, the Cooks were blessed with a seven-pound, blonde, blue-eyed boy. Doc Dowd said he could stop delivering kids now, he'd finally delivered the perfect baby. Showboat and Bonnie were happy as well. Bonnie was expecting in the Spring. Dan announced it would be a male, and its name would be Turk.

In 1924, Democrat political unknown, George Henry Dern defeated Gov. Charles Maybe by a vote of 81,308 to 72,127. His campaign slogan was, "We want a Dern good governor, and we don't mean Maybe!"

APPENDIX

UTAH COAL MINE CASUALTY LIST
IN THE 19TH & 20TH CENTURIES

Pleasant Valley Coal Company was owned by the Denver & Rio Grande railroad. It later became Utah Fuel Company. They had mines in Scofield, Winterquarters, Castle Gate, Sunnyside, and Clear Creek. The Winterquarters mine blew up on May 1, 1900, with the loss of over 200 lives and was the worst coal mine disaster in the United States for nearly half a century. The Castle Gate mine blew up March 8, 1924. I personally saw the actual explosion of the Sunnyside mine on May 9, 1945.

The following is a work in progress in that, prior to this, no comprehensive list of fatalities existed anywhere in the state. Further, as reported by the State Mine Inspector, many of the small, or "family" type of mines had fatalities which were never investigated, or included in the fatalities which can be found. Also, the date shown is usually the date of the accident which resulted in a fatality, not necessarily the date of death, although in a few cases the dates are approximate.

Old records with difficult to read spelling of names, the possibility that first and last names have been reversed, incomplete information about when the accident took place, or where, and the fact that different newspapers sometimes report different names for catastrophes, all add to the certainty that this list is not 100 percent accurate. Yet faith can be placed in it because it is the most complete and accurate record available. Finally, I included the explosion in the Moab potash mine on Aug 27, 1963, because while it was not a coal mine, the mines in Carbon County were closing up at that time, and many of the men killed in Moab were coal miners from Carbon county who had gone to Moab for work and met a miner's death.

Many of the old records researched were Industrial Commission Rulings where a particular dependent or family was awarded or denied a payment on the death of a relative. Such records frequently give only the date of the award, not the date of the death, or the name of the company, and not the name of the mine. Where the company name was given, and they had a number of mines, I listed it thus: Unk U.S. Fuel mine.

If anyone has information about inaccuracy here, or names of miners not included, contact Fred Civish at **www.bullofthewoodsbooks.com** and advise him of any additions.

While the actual total likely exceeds 1,500, here are the current 1,383 names on this memorial list, including one woman:

19TH CENTURY

NAME:	DATE:	MINE:
Anderson, Charles	11/24/1896	Castle Gate Mine
Bishop, Joseph J.	08/09/1897	Winter Quarters #1 Mine
Davis, William C.	05/28/1898	Castle Gate Mine
Duerdon, William	11/18/1896	Castle Gate Mine
Jensen, Peter	07/18/1896	Castle Gate Mine
Kranwurkel, Theodore	07/08/1898	Castle Gate #1 Mine
Martin, George H.	01/14/1897	Winter Quarters #1 Mine
Tyler, Lorenzo	08/04/1898	Castle Gate Mine

20TH CENTURY

NAME:	DATE:	MINE:
A		
Accord. S.V.	03/08/24	Castle Gate Mine (Explosion)
Acroterianakis, E	03/17/19	Winter Quarters Mine
Adams, Gus	05/07/23	Rains Mine
Adams, Orson	04/14/26	Mutual Mine
Adamson, Andrew	05/01/00	Winter Quarters (Explosion)
Adamson, Phillip	10/09/76	Deer Creek Mine
Adda, John	03/07/16	Black Hawk Mine
Adrian, Elton	1952	Unk

Aeillo, James	11/21/12	Hiawatha #1 Mine
Aho, Oscar	09/06/16	Kenilworth Mine
Aho, Victor	05/01/00	Winter Quarters (Explosion)
Aicaguerre, John	11/06/25	Rains Mine
Aimo, Batista	12/20/01	Castle Gate #1
Alamazan, Simon G.	01/31/23	Kenilworth Mine
Albarado, Nito	02/27/51	Sunnyside #1 Mine
Albino, Ivona	09/09/03	Castle Gate Mine
Alexander, Prince	03/08/24	Castle Gate Mine (Explosion)
Alfred, Voel	08/13/42	Dugout Mine, Nine Mile (Explosion)
Alger, Mayo	07/19/54	Horse Canyon Mine
Allison, James	02/18/29	Standardville Mine
Allred, C.W.	10/23/20	Black Hawk Mine
Allread, Harry	05/04/29	Castle Gate #2 Mine
Allread, William	08/10/36	Castle Gate #2 Mine
Alonzo, Gustavo	07/21/97	Railco Coal Loading facility
Ambrosia, Joe	03/08/24	Castle Gate Mine (Explosion)
Ambrosia, Nick	03/08/24	Castle Gate (Explosion)
Ampliotis, George	07/09/11	Grass Creek Mine (Surface)
Anderson, Burdell	01/05/20	Sego Mine
Anderson, Claire C.	01/10/47	King #1 Mine
Anderson, Dell	03/07/41	Am. Fuel Hunting Canyon Mine
Anderson, D.R.	03/08/24	Castle Gate Mine (Explosion)
Anderson, George	04/14/14	Winter Quarters #1 Mine
Anderson, Irvin	05/07/23	Rains Mine
Anderson, J.R.	03/08/24	Castle Gate Mine (Explosion)
Anderson, Joseph	05/01/00	Winter Quarters (Explosion)
Anderson, Joseph	11/05/29	Utah Fuel Mine
Anderson, June	04/19/27	Sweet Mine
Anderson, Keith	01/17/58	Spring Canyon Mine
Anderson, Outney	06/14/23	Standardville Mine
Anderson, Richard L.	03/10/82	Southern Utah Fuel Mine
Anderson, William	11/05/28	Spring Canyon Mine
Andrakis, Steve	03/08/24	Castle Gate (Explosion)
Andrezzi, Ernest	12/04/57	Sunnyside Mine

Anesi, Otto	04/18/06	Pariette Mine
Angelo, Louis	12/11/35	Standardville #1 Mine
Angotti, Antonio	10/16/29	Kenilworth Mine
Angotti, E.	03/15/13	Unk
Angus, Barney	11/10/19	Rains (Explosion)
Angus, Ray	01/18/61	Carbon #2 Mine
Anselmo, Nicolo	05/01/00	Winter Quarters (Explosion)
Antoniou, Nikaloas	02/22/18	Castle Gate Mine
(AKA Nick Anton)		
Aplanalp, William L.	10/14/30	Peerless Mine
Apostolakis, John	08/14/20	Hiawatha Mine
Archuleta, Cristobal	05/24/45	Horse Canyon Mine (Surface)
Ardohain, Mike	12/16/63	Carbon Fuel Mine (Explosion)
Argyle, Mark	11/23/26	Mutual Mine
Aramaki, Matakumi	04/04/36	Hiawatha Mine
Arikane, Chojiro	11/11/24	Mohrland King #2 Mine
(AKA Arkana)		
Arnold, Lawrence	03/01/15	Storrs #1 Mine
Arnold, Orson A.	02/19/20	Wasatch Mine
Arvanitakis, Kionisios	08/29/21	Kenilworth Mine
(AKA Dan Tikas)		
Asay, Charles	04/26/45	Hiawatha Mine
Asdrobolini, Antonio	02/10/19	Mohrland Mine
Askern, Carroll John	01/29/59	Sunnyside #1 Mine
Aquila, Nick	03/08/24	Castle Gate Mine (Explosion)
Averett, W.A.	09/09/25	Wattis #2 MINE15
Avery, Kenneth.	03/08/24	Castle Gate Mine (Explosion)
Azbe, John	04/23/14	Sunnyside #1 Mine

B

Babcock, Ben. J.	05/14/02	Winter Quarters #5
Babionitackis, Mike	09/11/19	Standardville Mine
Backlund, Lee	11/04/19	Kenilworth Mine
Badiertakis, George	12/03/27	Castle Gate Mine
Baich, Mike	03/17/32	Sweet Mine
Bailey, James	05/09/45	Sunnyside (Explosion)

Bailey, Westley	07/18/57	Castle Gate Mine
Baird, Dave	01/29/60	Sunnyside #2 Mine
Baldini, Sam	06/25/27	Spring Canyon Mine
Bamanakis, Mike	03/08/24	Castle Gate Mine (Explosion)
Barber, Wesley J.	08/27/63	Moab Mine (Explosion)
Barbieux, Emil	10/13/34	Unk Mine
Barney, Angus	02/06/30	Standardville (Explosion)
Barra, Santiago	02/06/30	Standardville (Explosion)
Bastion, Michael Leo	08/31/71	Southern Utah Fuel Mine
Batiste, Milano	02/21/10	Kenilworth #1 Mine
Baumann, David	10/23/28	Spring Canyon Mine
Bearnson, Gunner	05/01/00	Winter Quarters (Explosion)
Beck, Levi	03/08/24	Castle Gate (Explosion)
Behunin, Cecil	09/09/40	U.S. Fuel King Mine
Bell, Philip E.	12/19/84	Wilberg Mine Huntington (Fire)
Bellalis, Conslatenon	12/15/34	Columbia Mine
Bench, Sheldon	01/04/41	Royal Mine
Bende, Antone	11/14/06	Castle Gate Mine
Benedetta, James	04/25/05	Sunnyside #1 Mine
Benedict, John	12/28/43	Hiawatha Mine
Bennett, Bert	12/19/84	Wilberg Mine Huntington (Fire)
Bennett, David	03/14/45	Kenilworth (Explosion)
Benson, Reed	01/24/49	Kenilworth
Bentley, Brigham	01/15/31	Columbia Mine
Berkley, George J.	10/27/22	Standardville Mine
Berg, Cyril	03/08/24	Castle Gate Mine (Explosion)
Berg, Emil	03/08/24	Castle Gate Mine (Explosion)
Bergera, Pete	09/16/44	Latuda Mine
Bernard, John	06/15/26	Castle Gate #1 Mine
Bernard, Henry	05/01/00	Winter Quarters (Explosion)
Berry, Charles T.	10/24/46	Royal Mine
Berry, W.A.	03/08/24	Castle Gate Mine (Explosion)
Bertoglio, Dominic	03/08/24	Castle Gate Mine (Explosion)
Bertoglio, Mike	03/08/24	Castle Gate Mine (Explosion)
Bertuzzi, James M.	12/19/84	Wilberg Mine Huntington (Fire)
Betterson, Harry	05/01/00	Winter Quarters (Explosion)

Bianco, August	03/25/41	Royal Mine
Biandich, Matt	05/21/32	Spring Canyon Mine
Bigelow, Emery	02/04/26	Spring Canyon #1 Mine
Billalis, Constantenon	11/05/34	Sweets Mine
Bills, John Edgar	06/22/46	Spring Canyon Mine
Binch, Robert S.	01/04/41	Royal Mine
Bintala, Andrew	05/01/00	Winter Quarters (Explosion)
Bintals, Matt	05/01/00	Winter Quarters (Explosion)
Birch, John	03/10/41	Am. Fuel Hunting Canyon Mine
Birch, Leo	11/05/28	Mutual Mine
Birch, Thomas	11/06/02	Grass Creek Mine
Bird, Rulon J.	12/12/37	Wattis #2 Mine
Bishop, Arthur	09/06/04	Winter Quarters #1
Bjarnson, Henry P.	10/19/18	Schofield Mine
Bjarson, M.C.	10/14/16	Sunnyside #2 Mine
Black, Raymond	06/02/41	Unk
Black, Walter	03/06/31	Cleer Creek Mine
Blackham, Archie Mack	04/25/57	Huntington Mine
Blackham, Charles	11/26/19	Clear Creek #4 Mine
Bluck, Frank	10/12/20	Clear Creek #3 Mine
Bobo, Robert W.	08/27/63	Moab Mine (Explosion)
Bocook, David William	12/19/84	Wilberg Mine Huntington (Fire)
Boita, Thomas	10/02/28	Chesterfield Sego Mine
Bolonakis, Steve	12/18/12	Castle Gate Mine
Bonaquista, Tony	04/29/16	Sunnyside #1 Mine
Bonchlakis, Angelo (AKA Angelo Buhles)	11/06/24	Columbia Steel at Sunnyside
Bonterakis, James	02/07/20	Castle Gate #1 Mine
Boris, (Boral) Pete	09/18/50	Royal Mine
Borich, Andrew	11/24/09	Sunnyside Mine
Botanakis, Tony	03/08/24	Castle Gate (Explosion)
Bouhlakis, Angelo (AKA Angelo Buhles)	1923	Columbia Steel at Sunnyside
Boyetto, Jim	11/29/14	Standardville #1 Mine

Bozas, Christ	10/13/19	Wattis Mine
Bozun, Charles (Chris)	01/25/46	Kenilworth Mine
Brace, William	11/23/03	Sunnyside Mine
Bradley, Jefferson	01/08/19	Storrs Mine
Bradock, M.	05/09/45	Sunnyside (Explosion)
Bradshaw, Claude D.	09/30/41	Unk Utah Fuel Mine
Bradshaw, David Claude	03/31/41	Castle Gate Mine
Brady, C.H.	02/06/30	Standardville Mine (Explosion)
Brady, Ilo	07/18/57	Castle Gate Mine
Brannon, Joseph	08/03/27	Castle Gate Mine
Brecho, Joseph	10/12/11	Winter Quarters #1
Brek, Levi	03/08/24	Castle Gate Mine (Explosion)
Brennan, Guy	05/01/00	Winter Quarters (Explosion)
Briest, Steve	10/04/37	Spring Canyon #1 Mine
Briggs, Leroy	02/06/30	Standardville Mine (Explosion)
Brinkerhoff, George L.	09/29/27	Spring Canyon Mine
Broderick, A.C.	09/07/26	Sunnyside #1 Mine
Brooks, Walter	10/13/20	Am. Fuel at Sego Mine
Brogden, Thomas	05/01/00	Winter Quarters (Explosion)
Brotherson, Nels	04/03/47	Wattis Mine (Surface)
Brown, Carl	04/02/62	Unk
Bruketa, Martin	11/08/16	Standardville Mine
Bruno, Daniel	12/09/60	Columbine #1 Mine
Bruno, Mike	02/06/30	Standardville (Explosion)
Buffmire, Gus	04/10/33	Mutual Mine
Buffo, Stephano	01/29/41	Royal Mine
Burdis, Frank	01/22/51	Sunnyside (surface)
Burns, John M.	05/01/00	Winter Quarters (Explosion)
Burns, Ralph	05/01/00	Winter Quarters (Explosion)
Burnside, Mitchell	08/28/46	Kenilworth Mine
Burr, William H.	09/01/37	Consumers Mine
Burton, John	04/29/32	Spring Glen (Surface)
Burton, William	01/20/19	Spring Canyon Mine
Burton, William	10/14/24	Storrs Mine

Busas, John	03/08/24	Castle Gate Mine (Explosion)
Busato, Jack	01/31/50	Royal Mine
Busker, Lloyd G.	01/65	Geneva Horse Canyon Mine
Byrge, Thomas R.	08/07/81	Valley Camp Belina Mine

C

Caillet, Vincente	07/30/12	Sunnyside #1 Mine
Caldwell, John E.	11/22/29	Kenilworth Mine
Caliguri, Dom.	07/31/16	Storrs #1 Mine
Callvas, Gust	03/08/24	Castle Gate Mine (Explosion)
Caloway, Leland	06/13/44	Horse Canyon Mine
Cambalone, John	11/18/10	Mohrland Mine
Camprides, Mike	03/08/24	Castle Gate Mine (Explosion)
Canelos, Tom	10/14/20	Castle Gate Mine
Cangerlango, Ricci G.	12/19/84	Wilberg Mine Huntington (Fire)
Capelletti, James	03/08/24	Castle Gate Mine (Explosion)
Caperletti, M.	03/08/24	Castle Gate Mine (Explosion)
Cappas, Antone	06/08/16	Sunnyside #2 Mine
Carlson, John	01/02/14	Kenilworth Mine
Carnivole, Nick	11/16/16	Sunnyside #1 Mine
Carpio, Jose	09/18/26	Unk Utah Fuel Mine
Carr, Sam	09/11/45	Columbia
Carter, Curtis A.	12/19/84	Wilberg Mine Huntington (Fire)
Carver, Donald Lewis	01/25/63	Unk (Emery County)
Carvounis, Mike	10/30/19	Clear Creek #1 Mine
Casaday. William	09/27/23	Unk Utah Fuel Mine (Surface)
Casaril, James	01/07/25	Grass Creek Mine
Casselli, Joe	03/08/24	Castle Gate Mine (Explosion)
Cassidy, Martin	05/01/00	Winter Quarters (Explosion)
Chapman, James	06/30/45	Sunnyside Mine
Chappell, Merl	10/11/68	Chappel Coal Co. Mine
Charles, James	03/08/24	Castle Gate Mine (Explosion)
Charter, Thomas William	02/28/25	Hiawatha King #1 Mine
Chavis, A.J.	11/17/37	Clear Creek Eagle Mine

Choingas, Tax	04/09/09	Castle Gate
Chokas, Gus	10/13/11	Kenilworth
Christensen, Andrew	10/24/01	Winter Quarters #1
Christensen, Andrew	09/09/30	Hunting Canyon Mine
Christensen, Edward	10/17/30	Standardville Mine
Chirstensen, Myrlen H.	08/27/63	Moab Mine (Explosion)
Christensen, Nels A.	07/08/57	Huntington Mine
Christensen, Peter Angelo	10/01/24	Clear Creek Mine
Christensen, Ralph C.	10/17/27	Unk U.S. Fuel Mine
Christensen, Robert S.	12/19/84	Wilberg Mine Huntington (Fire)
Christensen, Troval	04/14/70	U.S. Fuel Mine
Christian, Ralph	10/18/27	Castle Gate #2 Mine
Cibairo, Bert	03/08/24	Castle Gate Mine (Explosion)
Cihurra, (Cihuras) Charles	10/17/46	Royal Mine
Cingolani, Victor A.	12/19/84	Wilberg Mine Huntington (Fire)
Clark, George	05/01/00	Winter Quarters (Explosion)
Clark, S.W.	05/01/00	Winter Quarters (Explosion)
Clark, William	05/01/00	Winter Quarters (Explosion)
Clark, William, Jr.	05/01/00	Winter Quarters (Explosion)
Clavora, Antonio	09/21/29	National Mine
Clintis, James	10/21/20	Mohrland Mine
CoClet, Peter	05/01/00	Winter Quarters (Explosion)
Coffey, Sam	05/24/15	Unk
Coleman, Jack A.	09/08/47	Columbia Mine
Collias, George	09/06/24	Hiawatha #2 Mine
Colis, Nick	03/17/19	Kenilworth Mine
Collins, Abner	12/12/43	Horse Canyon Mine
Colzani, Joseph	11/09/43	Latuda Mine
Como, Frank	07/11/17	Spring Canyon Storrs Mine
Conover, Gordon P.	12/19/84	Wilberg Mine Huntington (Fire)
Conrado, Joseph Eugine	04/23/51	Sunnyside
Cooper, Edward L.	01/04/94	Plateau Co. Star Point Mine
Cordon, Jack	08/14/42	Hiawatha Mine

Cowley, Ted	02/25/30	Consumers Mine
Coulthard, George W.	05/01/00	Winter Quarters (Explosion)
Cox, Archibald Lyman	07/28/42	Standardville
Cox, Earl	12/26/56	Trial Mountain Mine
Cox, Ed B.	03/08/24	Castle Gate Mine (Explosion)
Crandall, N.B.	09/16/32	Unk
Crawford, Dave	11/10/48	Columbia Mine
Cresto, Frank	01/13/00	Castle Gate Mine
Crocco, Stanley	12/15/48	Independent Coke Mine
Crosby, William	01/02/04	Sunnyside #2 Mine
Crow, Robert	03/08/24	Castle Gate (Explosion)
Cruchi, Frank	11/03/14	Cameron Coal Mine
Cullam, Ernest	02/17/44	Unk (Carbon County)
Cunningham, James	10/03/01	Sunnyside #1 Mine
Cunningham, John	10/10/13	Spring Canyon Mine
Cunningham, John	01/16/14	Kenilworth Mine
Cunningham, Michael	10/03/23	Storrs Mine
Curry, Randall P.	12/19/84	Wilberg Mine Huntington (Fire)
Curtis, Lester	03/08/30	Peerless Mine (Explosion)
Curtis, Owen K.	12/19/84	Wilberg Mine Huntington (Fire)
Curtis, William	03/08/30	Peerless Mine (Explosion)

D

Dakovich, Louis	06/28/19	Hiawatha #2 Mine
Dale, James	04/23/08	Grass Creek Mine
Dallas, Jim	03/08/24	Castle Gate Mine (Explosion)
Damanakis, Mike	03/08/24	Castle Gate Mine (Explosion)
Daniels, William	01/17/58	Spring Canyon #4 Mine
Dantis, Mike	01/30/30	Rolapp Mine
Dark, Richard	10/21/19	Kenilworth #1 Mine
Dashos, Steve	06/12/12	Winter Quarters Mine
Davidson, Lawrence I.	08/27/63	Moab Mine (Explosion)
Davis, Christian	08/27/12	Castlegate #2 Mine
Davis, Cyril	11/13/13	Black Hawk Mine

Davis, D. D.	05/01/00	Winter Quarters (Explosion)
Davis, Daniel	05/01/00	Winter Quarters (Explosion)
Davis, David John	05/01/00	Winter Quarters (Explosion)
Davis, Ephraim	04/06/28	Peerless Mine
Davis, George O.	05/01/00	Winter Quarters (Explosion)
Davis, John	03/08/24	Castle Gate Mine (Explosion)
Davis, John N.	05/01/00	Winter Quarters (Explosion)
Davis, John O.	05/01/00	Winter Quarters (Explosion)
Davis, John T.	05/01/00	Winter Quarters (Explosion)
Davis, John Q.	05/01/00	Winter Quarters (Explosion)
Davis, John Wade	04/26/78	Braztah #3 Mine
Davis, Richard T.	05/01/00	Winter Quarters (Explosion)
Davis, Roger B.	05/01/00	Winter Quarters (Explosion)
Davis, William	05/01/00	Winter Quarters (Explosion)
Davis, William P.	05/01/00	Winter Quarters (Explosion)
DeAngeles, Eugene	02/14/48	Columbia Mine
Debesson, Emile	07/01/21	Sunnyside Mine
DeCarpio, Jose	09/18/26	Unk Utah Fuel Mine
Decker, Bernel Frances	05/31/20	Liberty Mine
Defreiz, Charles	03/28/46	King #2 Mine
Degner, Elmer	03/24/50	Horse Canyon Mine
Dekleva, Mike	08/22/20	Hiawatha Mine
Delaby, Hippolyte Ernest	03/08/24	Castle Gate Mine (Explosion)
Della Corte, C.	05/09/45	Sunnyside (Explosion)
Delklef, J.	05/01/00	Winter Quarters (Explosion)
DeMarco, Dominic	07/10/14	Mohrland Mine
DeMartini, Tom	12/19/40	Rolapp Mine
Demille, Rick D.	06/25/81	Valley Camp Belina Mine
Devicak, Nick	07/19/30	Consumers Mine
Diambrosio, Paul	07/08/53	Spring Canyon
Dimick, Jerry Lee	03/07/86	Kaiser #1 Sunnyside Mine
Diston, John	12/17/15	Grass Creek Mine
Dixon, Richard.	05/01/00	Winter Quarters (Explosion)
Dixon, Thomas	06/29/26	Kenilworth Mine
Dixon, William	01/09/29	Kenilworth Mine
Docemos, Mike	03/08/24	Castle Gate Mine (Explosion)

Dodd, Harry	03/08/24	Castle Gate Mine (Explosion)
Dodd, Robert	03/08/24	Castle Gate Mine (Explosion)
Dolni, John	11/21/22	Utah Mine
Donaldson, David C.	10/01/27	Clear Creek #3 Mine
Donohue, Wade Monroe	03/08/47	Castle Gate # 2 Mine
Dougal, W.B.	05/01/00	Winter Quarters (Explosion)
Douglas, George	03/01/10	Sunnyside #2
Douglas, W.K.	05/01/00	Winter Quarters (Explosion)
Dragon, Dan	12/04/57	Sunnyside #1 Mine
Drakakis, Mike	03/09/29	Peerless Mine
(AKA Mike Drakis)		
Drakos, Mike	03/09/27	Peerless Mine
Drosos, Gust	12/07/36	Castle Gate #3 Mine
Duke, Austin	02/06/30	Standardville (Explosion)
Duke, Grover	02/06/30	Standardville (Explosion)
Duke, J.D.	02/06/30	Standardville (Explosion)
Duke, Nick Del	09/13/20	Latuda Mine
Dumis, Pete	03/08/24	Castle Gate Mine (Explosion)
Duros, Tony	04/02/35	Clear Creek Mine
Durrant, Tony	09/14/50	Sunnyside Kaiser Mine
Dye, Lloyd Burton	01/21/70	Co-op Mining Co. Mine

E

Elwood, William J.	04/14/28	Standardville #1 Mine
Estrado, Antonio	10/18/29	Castle Gate #2 Mine
Edson, William Elliott	10/06/08	Castle Gate
Edward, Andrew	03/30/28	Unk U.S.Fuel Mine
Edwards, Charles	05/01/00	Winter Quarters (Explosion)
Edwards, Edward A.	10/03/17	Hiawatha Mine
Edwards, R.W.	04/09/26	Hiawatha King #1 Mine
Edwards, Thomas	03/21/31	Standardville Mine
Edwards, William W.	12/15/47	King #1 Mine
El???, George	03/08/24	Castle Gate Mine (Explosion)
Elder, William D.	03/06/23	Spring Canyon Stoors Mine
Eliomanousakis, Nick	10/06/20	Castle Gate Mine
Elkins, Henry H.	06/01/50	Spring Glen Mine

Elliott, A.B.	09/28/14	Storrs Mine
Ellis, Roger G.	12/19/84	Wilberg Mine Huntington (Fire)
Ellis, Thomas	08/12/42	Sunnyside
England, George	10/16/16	Winter Quarters Mine
England, Leonard	02/09/22	Winter Quarters Mine
Erichson, Eric	05/01/00	Winter Quarters (Explosion)
Erickson, Herman	05/01/00	Winter Quarters (Explosion)
Erkkila, William E.	10/05/35	Clear Creek #3 Mine
Eesuki, Abe	10/14/09	Clear Creek Mine
Equinta, Joseph	01/18/16	Hiawatha Mine
Etzl, Romeo	10/16/15	Sunnyside #2 Mine
Evans, David R.	03/08/24	Castle Gate Mine (Explosion)
Evans, David T.	05/01/00	Winter Quarters (Explosion)
Evans, Evan E.	05/01/00	Winter Quarters (Explosion)
Evans, Franklin R.	03/08/24	Castle Gate Mine (Explosion)
Every, Ralph	05/27/47	King #2 Mine

F

Faddis, R.H.	03/02/18	Standardville Mine
Faddis, Thomas R.	11/17/23	Unk U.S. Fuel Mine
Farren, John	04/03/25	Panther Mine
Farrimond, James	07/15/16	Cameron Mine
Farrish, Robert T.	05/01/00	Winter Quarters (Explosion)
Farrish, Thomas	05/01/00	Winter Quarters (Explosion)
Farron, John	04/03/25	U.S. Fuel Panther Mine
Fassaris, John	03/08/30	Hiawatha Mine
Faubain, James	06/07/47	Sunnyside Kaiser Mine
Faure, Andrew	08/19/20	Hiawatha Blackhawk Mine
Fechiko, John	01/24/36	Spring Canyon #1 Mine
Fere, Aime	05/21/27	Spring Canyon Mine
Ferguson, Byron Kent	07/28/55	Sunnyside Mine
Fernand, B.	08/04/13	Sunnyside #1 Mine
Ferrens James	05/01/00	Winter Quarters Explosion)
Ferrens, Robert	05/01/00	Winter Quarters (Explosion)
Ferrish, Robert	05/01/00	Winter Quarters (Explosion)

Figueroa, Lawrence	05/09/45	Sunnyside (Explosion)
Finari, G.	05/01/00	Winter Quarters (Explosion)
Fiora, Emil	02/02/32	Mohrland Mine
Fjelsted, Frank	03/08/24	Castle Gate Mine (Explosion)
Fjelsted, George	03/08/24	Castle Gate Mine (Explosion)
Flemetakis, Joseph	08/19/08	Cleer Creek Mine
Fletcher, David	06/15/81	Soldier Creek Ninemile Mine
Forest, Peter	01/25/22	Sunnyside #1 Mine
Forman, W.H.	04/18/06	Pariette Mine
Forester, Thomas	06/08/19	Castle Gate #1 Mine (Surface)
Forrester, William	08/08/14	Bear Canyon Mine
Forsyth, Clell	05/09/45	Sunnyside (Explosion)
Fossat, Victor	12/16/63	Carbon Fuel #2 Mine (Explosion)
Fowler, Lester	07/19/54	Horse Canyon Mine
Fowles, Udell	02/06/30	Standardville (Explosion)
Fox, Jessee	08/27/63	Moab Mine (Explosion)
Fragadaks, George	05/13/12	Sunnyside #3 Mine
Frandsen, Burke	03/07/47	Huntington Co-op Mine
Frangudakis, Mannus	12/02/19	Sunnyside #2 Mine
Franklin, A.J.	05/01/00	Winter Quarters (Explosion)
Franklin, John R.	08/30/49	Sweets Mine
Frederico, Guy	02/06/30	Standardville (Explosion)
Frederiea, O.	02/06/30	Standardville (Explosion)
Fredrickson, Eli	01/20/21	Kenilworth Mine
Fredrickson, Ross	12/26/79	Southern Utah Fuel Mine
Freeze, Ruben R.	07/09/40	Unk Utah Fuel Mine
Frulakis, Steve	06/18/27	Sunnyside #1 Mine
Fuero, John	05/08/11	Scofield Mine
Fugihara, K.	02/16/16	Black Hawk Mine
Fulmer, George	03/08/24	Castle Gate Mine (Explosion)
Fulmer, Grant	07/23/22	Rains (Surface)
Fulmer, Loren	03/08/24	Castle Gate Mine (Explosion)
Fulton, B. F.	10/23/03	Sunnyside Mine

G

Gaddis, Charles	10/17/49	Spring Canyon Mine
Galanis, Tony	06/15/20	Sunnyside Mine
Gallian, John	08/14/41	Royal
Gallaway, Leland	01/14/41	Horse Canyon
Garcia, Anselmo	04/12/27	Castle Gate #3 Mine
Garcia, Cecilio	01/17/58	Spring Canyon #4 Mine
Gardner, George	07/28/19	Clear Creek Mine
Garegnani, Toni	03/08/24	Castle Gate Mine (Explosion)
Garfola, Peter	01/12/07	Sunnyside Mine (Wellington)
Garlick, Earl	06/11/29	Hiawatha King #1 Mine
Garroch, Peter	03/08/24	Castle Gate Mine (Explosion)
Garroch, William Sr.	03/08/24	Castle Gate Mine (Explosion)
Garvais, John	02/12/08	Black Dragon Mine
Gatherum, Jason W.	05/01/00	Winter Quarters (Explosion)
Gatherum, Thomas	05/01/00	Winter Quarters (Explosion)
Gatherum, William W.	05/01/00	Winter Quarters (Explosion)
Gavaldon, Pedro	05/09/45	Sunnyside (Explosion)
Gentry, Robert Darrell	11/25/57	Latuda Mine
Gentry, William H.	08/24/79	Plateau Co. Star Point #1 Mine
Georgropoulos, George	1915	Unk
German, Frank	08/20/20	Peerless Mine
Germanich, Frank	05/02/16	Sunnyside #2 Mine
Giaconne, John	03/25/13	Utah Mine
Gialitakis, Louis	03/08/24	Castle Gate Mine (Explosion)
Gibbs, Richard R.	01/24/02	Sunnyside #2 Mine
Gibbons, C.G.	06/10/25	Kenilworth Mine
Gienidas, Andrew	03/08/24	Castle Gate Mine (Explosion)
Gilbert, Andrew	03/08/24	Castle Gate Mine (Explosion)
Gilmour, James	05/09/45	Sunnyside (Explosion)
Gines, Randy	08/12/88	U.S. Fuel King Mine
Gioni, Steve	03/08/24	Castle Gate Mine (Explosion)
Gittins, Basil	03/08/24	Castle Gate Mine (Explosion)
Gittins, Brimley	03/08/24	Castle Gate Mine (Explosion)
Godeness,	07/06/57	Castle Gate Mine
Gomez, Tony	10/02/29	Columbia Mine

Gonzales, Seferino James	02/15/57	Royal #2 Mine
Good, James	05/01/00	Winter Quarters (Explosion)
Good, William	05/01/00	Winter Quarters (Explosion)
Goodrich, Howard	11/03/60	Spring Glen Mine
Gordin, Gus	05/01/00	Winter Quarters (Explosion)
Gordin, Leon	05/01/00	Winter Quarters (Explosion)
Grodon, Jack	09/12/41	Hiawatha
Gorsick, Tony	01/12/31	Kenilworth Mine
Grahm, William	03/16/20	Castle Gate Mine
Grange, Edward Vance	01/25/46	Kenilworth Mine
Grange, Kerry R.	08/24/79	Plateau Co. Star Point #1 Mine
Graves, Joseph N.	05/01/00	Winter Quarters (Explosion)
Gregerson, Heber	02/22/10	Hiawatha #1 Mine
Gregerson, Vernon	08/20/41	Hiawatha Mine
Grehek, John	12/06/29	Spring Canyon Mine
Grozdanich, Rudy	08/30/41	Spring Canyon Mine
Gruber, Andrew Edward	03/30/28	Hiawatha Mine
Grukovich, Steve	01/17/07	Sunnyside Mine
Grundvig, Daniel	02/16/22	Wattis Mine
Gubler, Walter	01/08/23	Spring Canyon Storrs Mine
Guillen, Jesus	03/10/43	Sunnyside
Guzman, Michael S.	08/24/79	Plateau Co. Star Point #1 Mine

H

Hajianis, John	01/30/20	Black Hawk Mine
Hakkinen, Victor	06/23/20	Hiawatha Mine
Hall, Littleton, T.	10/20/14	Nelson #2 Mine
Hall, Lynn	12/01/83	Geneva Horse Canyon Mine
Hall, Tom Pearson	04/29/10	Winter Quarters Mine
Hamby, Isaac Nelson	09/29/36	Castle Gate #2 Mine
Hamlin, James	12/19/84	Wilberg Mine Huntington (Fire)
Hancock, Donald Verne	12/23/42	Mutual Mine
Hanson, Milton H.	05/26/41	Unk
Hanson, Wilford C.	11/16/29	Mohrland King #2 Mine
Haraguchi, George	06/23/53	Spring Canyon
Haravyis, Dimitrios (AKA Jim Kallas)	11/08/23	Panther Mine

Hardee, Edward M.	05/01/00	Winter Quarters (Explosion)
Hardee, Thomas J.	05/01/00	Winter Quarters (Explosion)
Hardy, Alma	03/08/24	Castle Gate Mine (Explosion)
Harriman, John	02/06/30	Standardville (Explosion)
Harrison, George	03/08/24	Castle Gate Mine (Explosion)
Harrison, Norman	03/08/24	Castle Gate Mine (Explosion)
Harrison, Thomas	03/08/24	Castle Gate Mine (Explosion)
Harsah, Harold W.	07/18/41	Columbia Mine
Hartman, Charles R.	01/16/46	King #1 Mine
Harvey, William B.	11/08/66	O'Connor Clear Creek Mine
Hatai, Kazuto	11/28/18	Spring Canyon Mine
Hauta, Andrew	05/01/00	Winter Quarters (Explosion)
Hawks, Clem	03/14/45	Kenilworth (Explosion)
Haycock, William H.	01/15/70	Castle Gate #5 Mine
Haycock, Robt. W.	11/02/66	O'Connor Clear Creek Mine
Hays, William H.	06/04/86	Little Dove Mine
Head, Earnest	03/08/24	Castle Gate Mine (Explosion)
Head, George Washington	05/05/47	Geneva Horse Canyon Mine
Heikkila, Alex	05/01/00	Winter Quarters (Explosion)
Heikkila, John	05/01/00	Winter Quarters (Explosion)
Helsten, Gus	01/12/30	National #1 Mine
Henderson, A. J.	03/08/24	Castle Gate Mine (Explosion)
Henderson, Walter	02/07/30	Standardville #3 Mine
Henrico, Gio	06/17/03	Castle Gate Mine
Herrera, Don L.	12/09/70	Kaiser #1 Sunnyside Mine
Herring, H. Ray	10/12/36	Kenilworth Mine
Hersh, LeRoy M.	12/19/84	Wilberg Mine Huntington (Fire)
Hicks, Joseph	10/09/22	Sunnyside Mine
Hill, Ira	05/09/45	Sunnyside (Explosion)
Hillyard, Melvin Ambrose	01/28/45	Geneva Horse Canyon Mine
Hilton, John, Sr.	03/08/24	Castle Gate Mine (Explosion)
Hinkins, Earl	07/28/54	Sunnyside
Hiraska, S.	10/30/23	Rolap Mine
Hirotsu, K. (AKA Kirotsn)	05/24/27	Castle Gate #2 Mine

Hirst, William	12/31/13	Utah Mine
Hitchcock, Willard	03/08/04	Sunnyside #2 Mine
Holbrook, Sherman	03/08/71	Kenilworth Mine
Hollinger, James N.	08/27/63	Moab Mine (Explosion)
Hollos, Charles Mills	09/15/47	Sunnyside Kaiser Mine
Honkala, Charles	05/01/00	Winter Quarters (Explosion)
Honkala, John	05/01/00	Winter Quarters (Explosion)
Hopkins, Elmer	04/18/06	Pariette Mine
Hotchkiss, Warren	05/09/45	Sunnyside (Explosion)
Howard, Brian	12/19/84	Wilberg Mine Huntington (Fire)
Hubbartt, Dale	04/29/55	Horse Canyon
Hudson, Walt	09/21/24	Rains Mine (Explosion)
Huff, John	03/08/24	Castle Gate Mine (Explosion)
Huff, William	03/08/24	Castle Gate Mine (Explosion)
Hughes, Edward	10/03/01	Sunnyside #1
Hull, Walter	02/15/41	Sunnyside
Humberto, Leon	07/08/78	Co-Op Mine (surface)
Humphrey, Dee H.	02/22/61	Unk
Hundus, Matt	05/01/00	Winter Quarters (Explosion)
Hurskainen, John	01/02/32	Castle Gate Mine
Hunter, Adam	05/01/00	Winter Quarters (Explosion)
Hunter, David	05/01/00	Winter Quarters (Explosion)
Hunter, James A.	05/01/00	Winter Quarters (Explosion)
Hunter, Jason C.	05/01/00	Winter Quarters (Explosion)
Hunter, John	05/01/00	Winter Quarters (Explosion)
Hunter, John S.	05/01/00	Winter Quarters (Explosion)
Hunter, Robert	05/01/00	Winter Quarters (Explosion)
Huntsman, Leland	June 64	Kaiser #1 Sunnyside Mine
Hutchinson, Thomas W	09/06/04	Winter Quarters #1
Hutula, Elias	05/01/00	Winter Quarters (Explosion)
Hutula, Nicholas	05/01/00	Winter Quarters (Explosion)
Huzil, William	08/27/63	Moab Mine (Explosion)

I

Ihler, Ben	12/26/56	Trial Mountain Mine

Illingsworth, David	05/01/00	Winter Quarters (Explosion)
Imanaka, M.	1906	Castle Gate Mine
Immoneu, Herman	07/09/34	Standardville Mine
Ingram, Joe	03/08/24	Castle Gate Mine (Explosion)
Ingram, T. L.	03/08/24	Castle Gate Mine (Explosion)
Inouyem F.	03/08/24	Castle Gate Mine (Explosion)
Isa, K.	12/17/27	Mutual #3 Rains Mine
Ishibashi, Yosuke	10/26/26	Peerless Mine
Ishizue, W.	02/06/30	Standardville (Explosion)
Isom, Chester S.	09/23/47	Sego #1 Mine

J

Jaccobucci, John	07/01/14	Sunnyside Mine
Jackson, Charles	02/15/41	Kenilworth Mine
Jackson, Ivan Russel	03/14/45	Kenilworth (Explosion)
Jacobs, Barry	12/19/84	Wilberg Mine Huntington (Fire)
Jacobsen, Jacob	02/12/29	Castle Gate #2 Mine
Jacobson, Matt	05/01/00	Winter Quarters (Explosion)
Jacobson, William	05/01/00	Winter Quarters (Explosion)
Jacoby, Sam	03/08/24	Castle Gate Mine (Explosion)
James, Charles	03/08/24	Castle Gate Mine (Explosion)
James, Frank	02/06/30	Standardville Mine (Explosion)
James, George Jos.	05/01/00	Winter Quarters (Explosion)
James, John	05/01/00	Winter Quarters (Explosion)
Jansen, Lyman	01/03/41	Unk Utah Fuel Mine
Jardine, James	05/09/45	Sunnyside (Explosion)
Jenkins, Andrew David	06/13/48	Hiawatha Mine
Jenkins, James	05/01/00	Winter Quarters (Explosion)
Jenkins, Samuel Walton	08/24/97	Bear Canyon #2 Co-op Mine
Jennings, Gary Kay	12/19/84	Wilberg Mine Huntington (Fire)
Jensen, Alton	12/27/27	King #2 Mohrland Mine
Jensen, Ivan	03/14/45	Kenilworth (Explosion)
Jensen, J. L.	02/06/30	Standardville (Explosion)

Jensen, James	03/08/30	Peerles Mine (Explosion)
Jensen, John G.	12/29/27	Unk U.S. Fuel Mine
Jensen, Rosel Zen	04/25/57	Huntington Mine
Jensen, Samuel	02/07/31	Columbia Mine
Jensen, Vernal	02/03/36	Clear Creek Eagle Mine
Jensen, Wallace	11/01/78	Deseret Mine (surface)
Johansen, Lee	12/19/84	Wilberg Mine Huntington (Fire)
Johansen, Ruel	01/17/53	Hiawatha
Johnson, Barney	02/06/30	Standardville Mine (Explosion)
Johnson, Brian	03/08/24	Castle Gate Mine (Explosion)
Johnson, Charles	10/13/19	Unk
Johnson, Christ	05/01/00	Winter Quarters (Explosion)
Johnson, Clayton F.	08/10/54	Royal Mine
Johnson, Clell	08/27/63	Moab Mine (Explosion)
Johnson, Homer B.	04/06/36	Columbia Mine
Johnson, John	05/01/00	Winter Quarters (Explosion)
Johnson, Merril	02/12/29	Castle Gate Mine
Johnson, Robert W.	10/15/24	Wattis Mine
Johnson, Roy W.	09/17/33	Unk Utah Fuel Mine
Johnston, Kenneth	03/27/24	Standardville Mine
Jolly, Boyd	04/20/94	Ut. Fuel Sevier Mine
Jones, Edward	05/01/00	Winter Quarters (Explosion)
Jones, Edward L.	03/08/24	Castle Gate Mine (Explosion)
Jones, Ira R.	07/25/22	Mohrland Mine
Jones, John T.	05/01/00	Winter Quarters (Explosion)
Jones, K.S.	11/24/22	Standardville Mine
Jones, Levi	05/01/00	Winter Quarters (Explosion)
Jones, William D.	06/26/04	Soldier Summit Mine
Jones, William G.	05/01/00	Winter Quarters (Explosion)
Jones, Willis Sr.	04/21/54	Nine Mile Mine
Jolley, Boyd	04/20/94	Southern Utah Fuel
Jorgensen, Gunnar	02/28/25	Spring Canyon Storrs #3 Mine G14
Judd, Wayne	05/17/44	Coalville Mine

Juvan, Andy	12/16/63	Carbon Fuel #2 Mine (Explosion)

K

Kankonen, George	09/05/26	Wattis Mine
Kakos, William	02/12/08	Black Dragon Mine
Kallas, Nick	04/03/50	Sunnyside
Kanakis, Karas	03/08/24	Castle Gate Mine (Explosion)
Kanelakis, Mihael	04/07/26	Sunnyside #1 Mine
Kangas, Alex	05/01/00	Winter Quarters (Explosion)
Kangas, Mike	05/01/00	Winter Quarters (Explosion)
Kappas, George	03/08/24	Castle Gate Mine (Explosion)
Karogis, Jim	03/08/24	Castle Gate Mine (Explosion)
Kasimatis, Mike	08/10/45	Royal Mine
Kassler, Jesse C.	08/27/63	Moab Mine (Explosion)
Katagiri, Tom	1921	Hiawatha Mine
Katsanevis, Mike	03/08/24	Castle Gate Mine (Explosion)
Kavros, Louis	08/18/30	Peerless Mine
Kelakis, Tony	01/09/20	Clear Creek Mine
Kelly, Melvin C.	06/06/57	Sunnyside #1 Mine
Kenekalis, Michael	05/07/26	Sunnyside Mine
Kenner, Richard	02/03/82	Trail Mountain Mine
Kerkos, Louis	07/11/19	Castle Gate Mine
Ketola, Alex	05/01/00	Winter Quarters (Explosion)
Ketros, Angelo	02/09/20	Clear Creek #1 Mine
Keraner, Jacob	05/01/00	Winter Quarters (Explosion)
Kichikawa, Tom	12/03/27	Mohrland #2 Mine
Kilian, Franklin Lloyd	11/28/59	Geneva Horse Canyon Mine
Kimball, Martin	03/08/24	Castle Gate Mine (Explosion)
King, Douglas D.	05/29/24	Spring Canyon Mine
Kirby, Joseph	03/08/24	Castle Gate Mine (Explosion)
Kirby, Walter	03/08/24	Castle Gate Mine (Explosion)
Kirotsn, K	06/24/27	Castle Gate #2 Mine
Kitton, John	05/01/00	Winter Quarters (Explosion)
Kivicht, Herman	05/01/00	Winter Quarters (Explosion)
Klemola, Antti	05/01/00	Winter Quarters (Explosion)

Klemola, Leander	05/01/00	Winter Quarters (Explosion)
Klemola, Westeri	05/01/00	Winter Quarters (Explosion)
Knezovich, George	02/02/32	Sweet Mine
Knezovich, Sam	11/21/36	Sweet Mine
Koda, J.	03/08/24	Castle Gate Mine (Explosion)
Kogianakis, Vaselick	03/28/25	Castle Gate Mine
Kohakis, Jim	03/08/24	Castle Gate Mine (Explosion)
Kokogianakis, Andrew	04/02/25	Castle Gate #3 Mine
Kolenas, Charles	03/08/24	Castle Gate Mine (Explosion)
Kolmpistardas,	09/06/24	Unk U.S. Fuel Mine
(AKA Mpistardas, Collias, Koais, and Colleas)		
Kologianakis, Andrew	03/28/25	Castle Gate Mine
Kolson, Frank	05/01/00	Winter Quarters (Explosion)
Kompoc, Andrew	03/08/24	Castle Gate Mine (Explosion)
Kontoimas, John	03/08/24	Castle Gate Mine (Explosion)
Korbela, John	05/01/00	Winter Quarters (Explosion)
Korpi, John	05/01/00	Winter Quarters (Explosion)
Koski, Charles	05/01/00	Winter Quarters (Explosion)
Koski, John	05/01/00	Winter Quarters (Explosion)
Koski, Matt	05/01/00	Winter Quarters (Explosion)
Koski, Oscar	04/13/32	Clear Creek Mine
Koslakis, Mike	04/20/12	Sunnyside #2 Mine
Kosmos, Mike	11/22/23	Castle Gate Mine
Kostello, George	12/24/07	Sunnyside (Surface)
Kotsenaris, Eraklis	10/28/10	Castle Gate #2 Mine
Koukourakis, Nikalaos	03/17/19	Kenilworth Mine
(AKA Nick Colis)		
Koukurakis, Angelo	03/08/24	Castle Gate Mine (Explosion)
Kourgastis, John	03/08/24	Castle Gate Mine (Explosion)
Koutras, Pete	05/27/11	Clear Creek #2 Mine
Krajnc, Frank	01/09/59	Latuda #1 Mine
Kravanja, John	08/12/26	Hiawatha Mine
Krook, John	05/01/00	Winter Quarters (Explosion)
Kruzich, Tom	08/30/18	Standardville Mine
Kuaritch, Frank	09/20/10	Sunnyside #4 Mine
Kulezakis, George	03/08/24	Castle Gate Mine (Explosion)

Kubota, Tom R.	02/11/92	Ut.Fuel Skyline #1 Schofield
Kulie, Nicholas	01/02/35	Standardville Mine
Kumbola, Israel	05/08/02	Winter Quarters #1
Kuskar, John	07/19/09	Winter Quarters
Kytrakis, Alexandres	02/09/20	Clear Creek
(AKA Angelo Ketros)		

L

Labbe, John	06/30/33	Unk Utah Fuel Mine
Lacasse, Joseph	05/01/00	Winter Quarters (Explosion)
Lakinedakis, Steve	05/01/12	Sunnyside #3 Mine
Lager, William	03/25/01	Sunnyside (Surface)
Lahey, John	05/01/00	Winter Quarters (Explosion)
Lakso, Christian	05/01/00	Winter Quarters (Explosion)
Lamph, William James	09/22/30	Rains Mine
Langeros, Harry	10/11/25	Hiawatha #1 Mine
Langford, C.	11/25/48	Hiawatha Mine
Langstaff, George	05/01/00	Winter Quarters (Explosion)
Langstaff, Robert	05/01/00	Winter Quarters (Explosion)
Larimor, Bernie	02/16/20	Latuda Mine
Larsen, Archie A.	12/16/63	Carbon Fuel #2 Mine (Explosion)
Larsen, Charles Russell	05/12/75	Deer Creek Mine
Larsen, Harry	07/29/14	Storrs #3 Mine
Larson, John L.	11/18/36	MacLean #2 Mutual Mine
Larson, Merril Alfonso	01/24/61	Deseret #1 Mine
Larson, N Orville	09/10/25	Spring Canyon #1 Mine
Law, Clyde	05/01/00	Winter Quarters (Explosion)
Lawhorn, Mont C.	12/12/24	Standardville Mine
Leamaster, Delbert	10/12/46	King #1 Mine
Leamaster, Eli O.	06/25/63	Cane Creek Mine
Leavitt, John	01/13/27	Rains Mine
LeBlanc, Emile J.	08/27/63	Moab Mine (Explosion)
Leonard, Irving	05/09/45	Sunnyside (Explosion)
Leonard, Ronald	01/28/83	Plateau Co. Star Point Mine
Lermusiax, Arthur	03/14/45	Kenilworth (Explosion)

Leyshon, Louis	05/01/00	Winter Quarters (Explosion)
Liangoura, Harry	10/10/25	Hiawatha Mine
Likich, Jim	12/05/35	Rolapp #2 Mine
Liljenquist, Le Monte	09/05/13	Kenilworth Mine
Lilikas, John	07/10/13	Clear Creek #1 Mine
Lind, Emil	01/04/12	Kenilworth Mine
Liin, Henio	12/16/63	Carbon Fuel #2 Mine (Explosion)
Lindback, Oscar	05/01/00	Winter Quarters (Explosion)
Lindsey, Odel	03/28/75	Kaiser #1 Mine Sunnyside
Livingston, Arnold	08/05/26	Hiawatha Mine
Llewelyn, Bertie	07/16/48	Kenilworth Mine
Lloyd, Ben	05/01/00	Winter Quarters (Explosion)
Lloyd, J. N.	05/01/00	Winter Quarters (Explosion)
Lobasky, Victor	08/12/41	Raines Mine
Lobbe, Charles	05/01/00	Winter Quarters (Explosion)
Locke, James	05/05/02	Castle Gate
Logias, Gust	03/08/24	Castle Gate Mine (Explosion)
Loman, John R.	02/07/30	Standardville explosion rescuer
Londrakis, Poledeukis George	1923	Hiawatha Mines
Long, Duane A.	12/12/34	Castle Gate #2 Mine
Long, S.E.	1919	Winter Quarters Mine
Lopez, Antonio	02/27/51	Sunnyside
Lopez, Jesus F. (Father of 11)	07/18/69	Horse Canyon
Lopez, Joe D.	06/05/68	No. Amer. Coal Castle Gate #5
Lopez, Tony	02/27/51	Sunnyside #1 Mine
Lorimer, Bernie	02/16/20	Latuda Mine
Lorince, Nicholas M.	03/25/53	Sunnyside
Louma, A. A.	05/01/00	Winter Quarters (Explosion)
Louma, Abe	05/01/00	Winter Quarters (Explosion)
Louma, Alex	05/01/00	Winter Quarters (Explosion)
Louma, Gust	05/01/00	Winter Quarters (Explosion)
Louma, Henry	05/01/00	Winter Quarters (Explosion)

Louma, Henry J.	05/01/00	Winter Quarters (Explosion)
Louma, Leander	05/01/00	Winter Quarters (Explosion)
Louma, William A.	05/01/00	Winter Quarters (Explosion)
Lucas, Gust	03/08/24	Castle Gate Mine (Explosion)
L???, Charles	03/08/24	Castle Gate Mine (Explosion)
Luke, Roger	05/12/75	Deer Creek Mine
Lulich, Joe	09/22/28	Standardville Mine
Lund, Vernon	09/30/57	Sunnyside Mine
Lynch, F.W.	03/10/16	Clear Creek Mine

M

Mabbut, Fred	08/03/52	Price River Coal #1
MacBeth, Alaxander M.	03/20/25	Standardville Mine
MacDonald, Ramsay	05/05/76	Geneva Horse Canyon Mine
Macki, Andrew	05/01/00	Winter Quarters (Explosion)
Macki, Issac	05/01/00	Winter Quarters (Explosion)
Magnusen, Monroe	04/13/28	Spring Canyon Mine
Magnusen, Paul	04/21/66	Carbon Fuel #1 Mine
Maine, Arnie	01/12/20	Unk U.S.Fuel Mine
Maio, Giuseppi	05/01/00	Winter Quarters (Explosion)
Malax, Tony	03/08/24	Castle Gate Mine (Explosion)
Maler, Ed	12/14/29	Spring Canyon Mine
Manchester, LeRoy	01/19/28	Kenilworth Mine
Manchester, Paul H.	11/23/73	Swisher Mine
Mandos, Mike	08/29/12	Sunnyside #3 Mine
Manos, Tom	03/08/24	Castle Gate Mine (Explosion)
Manzanares, Efran	05/09/45	Sunnyside (Explosion)
Marasco, Joe	02/23/14	Nelsen Mine
Maranges, John	02/05/30	Kenilworth #1 Mine
Marcen, Martin	02/04/32	Latuda Mine
Marcen, Rudolph	12/08/30	Latuda Mine
Marchello, Charles	04/26/78	Bratzah #3 Mine
Marchetti, John	03/08/24	Castle Gate Mine (Explosion)
Marcovich, John	12/30/19	Sunnyside #1
Mardrovitr, Nick	11/09/11	Castle Gate #1 Mine
Marianakis, George	02/10/10	Clear Creek #1

Markakis, George	03/08/24	Castle Gate Mine (Explosion)
Markakis, Mike	03/08/24	Castle Gate Mine (Explosion)
Markovich, John	02/02/28	Spring Canyon Mine
Marlotte, John	10/03/00	Castle Gate Mine
Marshall, Alex	12/20/24	Standardville Mine
Marshall, James P.	08/27/24	Wattis Mine
Marshall, John A.	03/18/25	Panther Mine
Martucci, Charles	10/07/24	Rolapp Mine
Mascaro, Nick	07/11/52	Spring Canyon
Masearo, Ben	03/08/24	Castle Gate Mine (Explosion)
Martell, Thomas, C.	03/10/13	Black Hawk Mine
Martin, J. C.	05/01/00	Winter Quarters (Explosion)
Martin, James Wylie	12/23/57	Sunnyside #2 Mine
Martinez, Christobol	08/11/18	Storrs #1 Mine
Martinez, Joe	08/38/35	National Mine
Martinez, Juan	05/09/45	Sunnyside (Explosion)
Martini, James	12/01/39	Wattis Lion Mine
Martucci, Charles	10/07/24	Rolapp Mine
(AKA Charles Moncuso)		
Marzo, Morris	June 64	Kaiser #1 Sunnyside Mine
Mathindakis, Spellis	12/23/10	Kenilworth Mine
Mathiodes, Gust	03/08/24	Castle Gate Mine (Explosion)
Matsamas, Tony	03/31/44	Columbia
Mattievich, Matt	01/19/40	Sweet Mine
Mattingly, Robert Monroe	07/02/29	Hiawatha King #1 Mine
Mavinsel, Matt	12/09/10	Sunnyside #1 Mine
Mayo, Alger	07/19/54	Horse Canyon
McArthur, Claude	02/03/49	Hiawatha
McClanihan, Clyde	12/19/18	Wattis Mine
McCluskey, John	03/08/24	Castle Gate Mine (Explosion)
McDermaid, James	05/09/29	Unk
McDermaid, William	07/22/20	Hiawatha #1 Mine
McDonald, Otto	03/08/24	Castle Gate Mine (Explosion)
McGuire, William	02/06/30	Standardville Mine (Explosion)
McIntyre, Bernard	10/13/43	Sunnyside

McKee, Thoma	06/25/04	Castle Gate Mine
Medina, Raymond	12/04/57	Sunnyside #1 Mine
Melgaard, John	09/21/24	Rains Mine (Explosion)
Melling, Allen S.	Oct. 64	Webster #2 Mine
Memanich, Frank	01/15/30	National Mine
Menotti, Mark	08/15/19	Sunnyside #1 Mine
Merenkovich, Spero	01/13/55	Spring Canyon #4 Mine
Metrakis, Peter	12/03/29	Mohrland Mine
Mihos, T. A.	03/08/24	Castle Gate Mine (Explosion)
Milkovich, Joe	06/16/27	Standardville Mine
Millarich, Martin	03/03/31	Spring Canyon Mine
Miller, Grant S.	03/01/15	Black Hawk Mine
Miller, H. A.	05/01/00	Winter Quarters (Explosion)
Miller, Isaac A.	05/01/00	Winter Quarters (Explosion)
Miller, John	05/01/00	Winter Quarters (Explosion)
Miller, Leib H.	08/27/59	Columbine Mine
Miller, Morgan	05/01/00	Winter Quarters (Explosion)
Miller, Thomas B.	12/13/46	Independent Coal & Coke
Miller, V. R.	05/01/00	Winter Quarters (Explosion)
Miller, William	05/01/00	Winter Quarters (Explosion)
Mills, Alfred	06/07/34	Rolapp Mine
Mills, Gerald	11/15/46	Wattis #2 Mine
Mills, Hollis Charles	09/15/47	Sunnyside Kaiser Mine
Milton, Kenneth	08/27/63	Moab Mine (Explosion)
Minton, Fred	09/30/37	MacLean Mine
Miredos, James	08/19/14	Hiawatha #1 Mine
Mitchell, George	03/08/24	Castle Gate Mine (Explosion)
Mivec, Frank	12/17/08	Winter Quarters
Moffit, Wells W.	04/28/30	Kenilworth Mine
Moffitt, Donald	12/20/42	Kenilworth (Surface)
Moherino, Domico	09/24/08	Sunnyside (Surface)
Monroe, Roy	11/19/18	Hiawatha mine (Surface)
Monson, Arthur	11/06/27	Kenilworth Mine
Montoya, Benino	12/16/63	Carbon Fuel #2 Mine (Explosion)
Montova, Joe	05/09/45	Sunnyside (Explosion)

Moore, James	08/11/19	Hiawatha Panther Mine
Morishigi, Schoichi (Soichi)	07/30/24	Castle Gate Mine
Moore, Hamilton H.	02/20/28	Gordon Creek Mine
Moros, Nick	07/19/30	Consumers Mine
Morrison, Dan	03/08/24	Castle Gate Mine (Explosion)
Morrison, William, Sr.	03/08/24	Castle Gate Mine (Explosion)
Moskeno, Harry	04/23/21	Winter Quarters Mine
Motte, Kanny Joe	01/15/79	Deer Creek Mine
Moudndakis, Louis	06/01/46	Royal Mine
Mower, Francis	08/13/25	Spring Canyon
Mower, Joseph A.	09/24/68	Plateau Star Point #1 Mine
Mower, Lavor Paul	08/25/49	Horse Canyon
Moxin, William	03/09/09	Winter Quarters Mine
Muanla, Ieri	05/31/02	Clear Creek Mine
Muir, Daniel	05/01/00	Winter Quarters (Explosion)
Muir, George	05/01/00	Winter Quarters (Explosion)
Muir, John	05/01/00	Winter Quarters (Explosion)
Mullen, Theodore	01/24/48	Horse Canyon Mine
Murch, Clarence H.	08/05/14	Castle Gate #1 Mine
Muring, Peter	01/17/53	Hiawatha
Murphy, James	03/08/24	Castle Gate Mine (Explosion)
Murray, N. I.	10/23/33	Hiawatha Mine
Musig, Charles	02/07/00	Morrison Mine

N

Nagayama, H.	01/07/10	Kenilworth Mine
Nakamura, T.	03/08/24	Castle Gate Mine (Explosion)
Narumiya, Kumatara	03/06/37	Kenilworth Mine
Naskel, John	11/19/02	Winter Quarters #1 Mine
Naturle, Matt	09/04/41	Raines King Mine
Navarich, John	09/23/33	Hiawatha Mine
Neadonich, John	08/04/39	Sweet Mine
Neil, Oscar	03/08/24	Castle Gate Mine (Explosion)
Neilson, Carl Eric	10/10/61	Unk (Near Orangeville)

Neilson, Gerald L.	12/16/63	Carbon Fuel #2 Mine (Explosion)
Neilson, Russell	01/17/58	Spring Canyon #4 Mine
Neimi, Maknus	05/01/00	Winter Quarters (Explosion)
Neimi, Oscar	05/01/00	Winter Quarters (Explosion)
Nelson, William A.	05/01/00	Winter Quarters (Explosion)
Newland, Francis	08/26/21	Sego Mine
Newren, Merril Clifford	02/27/25	Scofield Mine (Surface)
Nichols, Benjamin Booth	09/12/28	Standardville Mine
Nichols, Gary	02/27/73	Kaiser #1 Sunnyside Mine
Nicolaris, Steve	03/08/24	Castle Gate Mine (Explosion)
Nielsen, Bean	01/17/58	Spring Canyon Mine
Nielsen, Carl Eric	10/10/61	Deseret Mine
Nielsen, Gerald L.	12/16/63	Carbon Fuel #2 Mine (Explosion)
Nielsen, Gilmer	03/14/45	Kenilworth (Explosion)
Nielson, Jack	10/31/52	Huntington
Nielson, Wilford Leroy	07/16/52	Peerless
Nieminen, Victor (AKA Niemi)	10/30/22	Standardville Mine
Nightingale, Tim	08/24/79	Plateau Starpoint #1 Mine
Niitsuma, Denshir	05/09/45	Sunnyside (Explosion)
Nikaido, C.	04/30/27	Rains Mine
Nokovich, Nick (AKA Novich)	04/04/25	Grass Creek Mine
Nose, Kiyoshi	12/11/22	Spring Canyon Mine
Norton, Glen	07/12/74	Geneva Horse Canyon Mine
Noys, Ben J.	08/30/77	Deer Creek Mine
Noys, Walter H.	04/15/58	Wattis #1 Mine
Nojumi, Ichigoro	08/16/19	Kenilworth #2 Mine
Nevitt, Joel T.	12/19/84	Wilberg Mine Huntington (Fire)
Nucci, T	07/30/33	Clear Creek Mine
Nucich, Frank	10/14/30	Castle Gate #2 Mine
Nukovitch, Emil	11/16/29	Mohrland Mine

O

Oblak, Jerry	07/27/11	Winter Quarters #1 Mine
O'Branovicz, Andro Matt	02/18/42	Rolapp Mine
Ochi, S.	02/26/20	Hiawatha #1 Mine
Oddinino, Peto	01/18/45	Hiawatha Mine
Oja, Vic	12/02/29	Peerless Mine
Ojan, Leander	05/01/00	Winter Quarters (Explosion)
Ojan, Victor	05/01/00	Winter Quarters (Explosion)
Okuji, K	02/07/20	Mohrland Mine
Oloskovitch, Pete	11/23/29	Sweet Mine
Olsen, Edwin	09/11/34	Standardville Mine
O'Neil, Richard	07/21/65	Kaiser #1 Sunnyside Mine
O'Neill, Cornelius J.	08/18/58	Columbia Mine
Onodera, K.	03/27/14	Sunnyside #2 Mine
Ontiveros, Antonio C.	10/10/25	Winter Quarters Mine
Oliver, Jed	08/05/86	Deer Creek Mine
Olsen, Antonne	08/12/23	Columbia Mine
Olsen, John	12/27/15	Cleer Creek Mine
Olson, William N.	10/30/33	Spring Canyon
Osumi, S.	05/23/29	Unk U.S. Fuel Mine
Otterstrom, Joe	04/18/56	Kaiser Sunnyside Mine G81
Otterstrom, Gene	12/26/52	Kenilworth Mine
Otteson, Leo	02/04/30	Kenilworth Mine
Ottoson, Roy	09/27/24	Wattis Mine (Surface)
Owen, Thomas	12/13/82	Kaiser #1 Sunnyside (Surface)
Ozeki, K.	05/23/24	Storrs Mine

P

Pack, Richard	05/01/00	Winter Quarters (Explosion)
Padfield, David	05/01/00	Winter Quarters (Explosion)
Padfield, S. J.	05/01/00	Winter Quarters (Explosion)
Padfield, Thomas	05/01/00	Winter Quarters (Explosion)
Padilla, Joe	05/09/45	Sunnyside (Explosion)
Paizakis, Nick	03/08/24	Castle Gate Mine (Explosion)
Pajala, John	06/17/04	Clear Creek Mine
Paliatseas, Peter	10/18/29	Hiawatha Mine

Pallos, John	03/08/24	Castle Gate Mine (Explosion)
Pallos, Steve	03/08/24	Castle Gate Mine (Explosion)
Paloni, Jim	07/16/20	Sunnyside Mine
Panas, Pete	10/17/16	Cameron Mine
Pantakos, Angelo	11/11/09	Castle Gate Mine
Papagerorio, Sotiro	12/17/21	Sunnyside Mine
(AKA Tom Pappas)		
Pape, B. W.	10/11/36	Clear Creek Eagle Mine
Papgourides, Nick	11/30/11	Kenilworth Mine
Pappadogianne, Miltiades	02/12/21	Sunnyside Mine
(AKA Milt Pappas)		
Pappas, Angelos	03/14/16	Storrs #1 Mine
Pappas, George	06/10/10	Clear Creek #2 Mine
Pappas, John	05/31/16	Sunnyside #2 Mine
Pappas, Nick	07/26/28	Unk U.S.Fuel Mine
Pappas, Steve	03/08/24	Castle Gate Mine (Explosion)
Pappas, Tony	02/15/82	Tower Resources Pinnacle Mine
Parish, Joseph	04/18/01	Winter Quarters
Park, Y. S	03/08/24	Castle Gate Mine (Explosion)
Parkin, Ronald P.	02/11/92	Skyline #1 Mine
Parmley, William	05/01/00	Winter Quarters (Explosion)
Pascoe, Sam	11/20/05	Sunnyside Mine
Pasquale, Aurable	10/22/06	Sunnyside #2 Mine
Patrick, Louis	03/08/24	Castle Gate Mine (Explosion)
Patterson, William Hunter	05/01/00	Winter Quarters (Explosion)
Pattinson, Mathias	05/01/00	Winter Quarters (Explosion)
Paulso, Samuel	07/28/34	Standard Ville Mine
Paulson, H. V.	10/26/33	Kenilworth Mine
Peacock, Homer	08/25/20	Hiawatha Panther Mine
Pechinino, August	09/14/43	Peacock Mine
(Also, Pegninio)		
Pecorelli, Martin	09/11/33	Unk Utah Fuel Mine
(AKA Michele)		
Pelly, Thomas, Jr.	1925	Unk Utah Fuel Mine
Perdue, Fred	08/04/39	Sweet Mine

Perkins, Ed	03/08/24	Castle Gate Mine (Explosion)
Perkins, Neil	03/08/24	Castle Gate Mine (Explosion)
Perkins, R. D.	07/26/17	Sunnyside Mine
Perpene, Tony	03/08/24	Castle Gate Mine (Explosion)
Peterson, Loren	06/23/51	Castle Gate #2 Mine
Peterson, Rodney J.	08/20/88	Valley Camp Belina #2
Petricco, Joe	03/07/22	Castle Gate Mine
(AKA Pucco)		
Petterson, Nicholas	02/01/32	Castle Gate Mine
Pesola, John	05/01/00	Winter Quarters (Explosion)
Pessetto, Wayne	07/02/82	Cementation King #4 Mine
Petty, Glen	01/04/41	Royal
Piccolo, Frank	03/08/24	Castle Gate Mine (Explosion)
Piccolo, Joe	04/25/57	Huntington Mine
Pierce, Howard	08/24/79	Plateau Star Point #1 Mine
Pilton, David	08/30/09	Winter Quarters Mine
Pinerelli, Sam	04/21/66	Carbon Fuel #1 Mine
Pino, Frank	11/01/24	Castle Gate #2 Mine
Pinterelli, Joe	03/01/35	Sweet Mine
Piro, Philip	01/04/10	Kenilworth Mine
Pitman, Daniel	05/01/00	Winter Quarters (Explosion)
Pitman, John	05/01/00	Winter Quarters (Explosion)
Pitman, John D.	05/01/00	Winter Quarters (Explosion)
Pitman, Meshick	05/01/00	Winter Quarters (Explosion)
Phelps, Thomas	05/17/10	Sunnyside #1 Mine
Plakarakis, S.	02/23/16	Castle Gate #1 Mine
Plese, Matt	02/23/16	Sunnyside #1 Mine
Polhronakis, Spiros	11/06/12	Mohrland Mine
Pollock, W. W.	03/08/24	Castle Gate Mine (Explosion)
Polly, Thomas, Sr.	03/08/24	Castle Gate Mine (Explosion)
Polly, Thomas, Jr.	03/08/24	Castle Gate Mine (Explosion)
Polostro, John	07/17/07	Castle Gate Mine
Polvie, James	01/28/11	Kenilworth Mine
Popejoy, James D.	12/19/95	Scofield White Oak (surface)
Potocnik, Jerry	08/18/33	Maclean Mine
Poulos, Alex T.	12/19/84	Wilberg Mine Huntington (Fire)

Powell, Clarence	05/14/48	Lion Coal Co. Mine
Pratt, T.	09/08/00	Winter Quarters Mine
Priano, James	03/08/24	Castle Gate Mine (Explosion)
Price, Benjamin	1901	Sunnyside Mine
Price, John R.	05/01/00	Winter Quarters (Explosion)
Price, Norman (13 Years Old)	07/07/09	Winter Quarters Mine
Pritchett, E. F.	02/06/30	Standardville Mine (Explosion)
Pritchett, T. L.	02/06/30	Standardville (Explosion)
Pritza, Eli	03/21/27	Rolapp
Protachnik, Frank	07/13/12	Winter Quarters #1 Mine
Proukos, Christ	08/09/23	Sunnyside #1 Mine
Psario, John	03/08/24	Castle Gate Mine (Explosion)
Pugh, William	05/01/00	Winter Quarters (Explosion)

Q
Quilter, Charles	03/08/24	Castle Gate Mine (Explosion)

R
Ramage, Thomas	05/01/00	Winter Quarters (Explosion)
Randall, Harvey Albert	12/23/96	Bear Canyon #2 Mine (Co-op)
Raroden, B. L.	04/08/06	Pariette Mine
Rappley, G. A.	08/13/10	Clear Creek #2 Mine
Rasmussen, Lawrence	07/18/60	Kenilworth Mine
Rasmussen, Wilmot Earl	01/15/47	Wattis (surface)
Reese, Thomas L.	03/08/24	Castle Gate Mine (Explosion)
Reese, William	07/15/22	Latuda Mine
Reese, William C.	05/01/00	Winter Quarters (Explosion)
Reichert, E. F.	02/06/30	Standardville Mine (Explosion)
Reilley, Thomas H.	05/01/00	Winter Quarters (Explosion)
Renberg, Joseph	05/04/12	Clear Creek #2 Mine
Renner, Edward	11/12/43	Sunnyside
Renni, Angelo	09/17/09	Sunnyside Mine
Retchert, C. F.	02/06/30	Standardville (Explosion)

Reve,Theodore	03/08/24	Castle Gate Mine (Explosion)
Ricci, Albert	03/09/53	Moore
Rice, Alfred, Sr.	03/08/24	Castle Gate Mine (Explosion)
Rice, Alfred, Jr.	03/08/24	Castle Gate Mine (Explosion)
Rich, Clark	02/28/44	U.S. Fuel Mine
Rich, Orvin	06/14/20	Rains Mine
Richards, J. M.	03/17/13	Sunnyside #2 Mine
Richards, Thomas	01/20/30	Spring Canyon Mine
Richards, Walter	03/08/24	Castle Gate Mine (Explosion)
Riches, William	02/06/64	King Mine
Riches, William G.	Unk	U.S. Fuel Mine
Richetts, James Moyer	04/09/58	Sunnyside #1 Mine
Riddle, Kelly	12/19/84	Wilberg Mine Huntington (Fire)
Rigby, Charles M.	10/22/20	Unk Utah Fuel Mine
Rigby, Charles Martin	10/22/20	Clear Creek #3 Mine
Riley, Thomas	05/01/00	Winter Quarters (Explosion)
Riser, Edward	11/25/21	Spring Canyon Mine
Rizutto, Tony	03/08/24	Castle Gate Mine (Explosion)
Rizzi, Emil	1915	Mohrland Mine
Robertson, Bret	11/14/96	Deadman Canyon Mine
Robertson, Ted O.	12/26/56	Trial Mountain #2 Mine
Robinson, James	12/22/06	Grass Creek Mine
Robinson, Leonard	12/17/37	Timothy Mine
Robinson, Lynn	12/19/84	Wilberg Mine Huntington (Fire)
Rogers, Lucius T., Jr.	07/02/46	Sunnyside #2 Mine
Rollins, O. H.	03/08/24	Castle Gate Mine (Explosion)
Rollo, Antonio	05/01/00	Winter Quarters (Explosion)
Romero, Joe	03/03/30	Sweet #1 Mine
Rossi, Joe	11/06/25	Spring Canyon Mine
Rowley, Fred	08/27/63	Moab Mine (Explosion)
Rowley, William Kevin	05/26/64	Hiawatha King Mine
Roy, Joseph Rene	08/27/63	Moab Mine (Explosion)
Ruffena, Frank	10/07/03	Sunnyside Mine
Rupakais, Gust	01/28/07	Sunnyside #4 Mine

Rushton, Lamar C.	08/27/63	Moab Mine (Explosion)
Rutherford, William	06/14/26	Spring Canyon #1 Mine

S

Safford, Orville Phillip	11/06/45	Castle Gate Mine
Sakiloris, Nick	10/28/10	Clear Creek #2 Mine
Salido, Jamie	01/29/85	Co-Op Mining Co. Mine
Salliano, Joe	08/14/42	Royal Mine
Salma, Matt	08/19/01	Winter Quarters #4
Salme, Ralph	09/16/24	Black Hawk Mine
Salo, My (Henry)	12/05/41	Scofield Mine
Samples, Blue	03/24/95	White Oak Clear Creek Mine
Samuels, William	05/01/00	Winter Quarters (Explosion)
Sanchez, Joe	08/23/29	Spring Canyon Mine
Sanders, Harry	03/08/24	Castle Gate Mine (Explosion)
Sanders, O. E.	03/08/24	Castle Gate Mine (Explosion)
Sanders, O. R.	03/08/24	Castle Gate Mine (Explosion)
Sandoval, Nick	05/09/45	Sunnyside (Explosion)
Sanipolo, Frank	03/21/11	Scofield Mine
Santi, Louis	12/04/37	Wattis Lion Mine
Santon, Gust	12/08/25	Latuda Mine
Saracisom, Joe	09/28/42	Kenilworth Mine
Sargent, George Lorenzo	04/23/08	Grass Creek Mine
Sarsfield, Henry	02/02/22	Rains Mine
Sasaki, Y. (S.)	02/22/22	Castle Gate Mine
Sasso, Peter	02/26/29	Chesterfield Sego Mine
Satatakis, John	08/05/24	Standardville #1 Mine
Satato, K.	06/26/43	Sweets
Sato, Sataro	04/17/36	Columbia Mine
Satyetch, John	10/29/15	Storrs #1 Mine
Scalise, James	06/28/13	Sunnyside #2 Mine
Scharf, Rex E.	07/23/86	Small Fry Mine
Schear, Keith	08/27/63	Moab Mine (Explosion)
Schneider, John	11/01/09	Sunnyside Mine
Scordes, Chris	05/14/12	Kenilworth Mine
Scott, Robert	02/15/94	Star Point #2

Scrubis, John (AKA Scruby)	11/25/30	Standardville Mine
Seely, Mill	03/08/24	Castle Gate Mine (Explosion)
Seibert, Antoni	01/28/10	Utah Colleries Co. Mine
Selan, Frank	12/24/28	Peerless Mine
Senechal, John, Jr.	12/16/63	Carbon Fuel #2 Mine (Explosion)
Seperas, John	02/14/27	Spring Canyon Mine
Serapis, John	02/14/27	Castle Gate Mine
Sickinger, Harper H.	02/18/29	Weber Coalviille Mine
Simons, John	04/06/19	Utah Mine
Shaw, James E.	02/23/43	Wattis
Shiner, Oran E.	12/05/60	Geneva Horse Canyon Mine
Shirtliff, George	03/08/24	Castle Gate Mine (Explosion)
Sicillia, Sam	10/23/37	Mohrland Mine
Sichinger, Harper W.	02/18/29	Coalville Weber Mine
Siddoway, Ross	05/17/43	Coalville Mine
Silien, Jacob	05/01/00	Winter Quarters (Explosion)
Sillitoe, Samuel Leroy	04/14/39	Castle Gate Mine
Silo, William	05/01/00	Winter Quarters (Explosion)
Silvestri, Luigi	05/28/20	Hiawatha #1 Mine
Simmons, Forrest	11/23/60	Sunnyside #3 Mine
Simmons, Simone	04/06/44	Hiawatha Mine
Simone, Angelo	02/02/43	Columbia Mine
Simonich, John	02/12/14	Sunnyside #3 Mine
Simpson, Clarence	03/08/24	Castle Gate Mine (Explosion)
Simpson, Horace	03/08/24	Castle Gate Mine (Explosion)
Singer, Frank	02/18/43	Castle Gate Mine
Sitterud, Douglas O.	01/29/73	Huntington Coal Mine
Skain, Alger Larsen	09/09/18	Clear Creek Mine
Skerl, Adam	03/03/23	Standardville Mine
Skerl, Matt	01/28/43	Latuda Mine
Skersies, Danial	05/01/00	Winter Quarters (Explosion)
Skipworth, W. T.	04/27/29	Sunnyside (Surface)
Skofk, Andrew	02/02/28	Spring Canyon Mine
Slobenski, John	03/08/24	Castle Gate Mine (Explosion)

Sluga, George	03/08/24	Castle Gate Mine (Explosion)
Smith, Abraham Owen	02/20/57	Sunnyside Mine
Smith, Arthur	03/14/45	Kenilworth (Explosion)
Smith, Carlisle	02/06/30	Standardville Mine (Explosion)
Smith, Clarence	02/07/30	Standardville explosion rescuer
Smith, James	08/11/05	Winter Quarters Mine
Smith, James M.	1988	Banning Load Out (Wellington)
Smith, Joe	10/24/55	Royal
Smith, Abraham Owen	02/20/57	Sunnyside Mine
Smith, Steve	03/08/24	Castle Gate Mine (Explosion)
Smith, Thomas	09/23/04	Castle Gate Mine
Smith, Tony	03/08/24	Castle Gate Mine (Explosion)
Smith, Woodrow T.	10/28/39	Kenilworth #2 Mine
Snow, Ray	12/19/84	Wilberg Mine Huntington (Fire)
Sompa, Jack	05/23/11	Utah Mine
Soter, George	07/26/18	Clear Creek Mine
Sorka, Joe	11/09/09	Sunnyside Mine
Southerland, Peter	05/01/00	Winter Quarters (Explosion)
Soye, Joseph M.	09/09/05	Sunnyside Mine
Spenda, Tony	03/08/24	Castle Gate Mine (Explosion)
Speros, Steve	03/08/24	Castle Gate Mine (Explosion)
Spigarelli, Cecil	01/14/41	Hiawatha Mine
Spigarella, John	11/09/09	Scofield Mine
Springer, R. E.	02/06/30	Standardville (Explosion)
Srajakis, Steve	03/08/24	Castle Gate Mine (Explosion)
Staffon, Mike	03/08/24	Castle Gate Mine (Explosion)
Staikos, Enagelas	08/05/11	Castle Gate #2 Mine
Staker, Earl J.	11/16/28	Kenilworth Mine
Stakos, James	05/15/13	Castle Gate #1 Mine
Staley, Esmond E.	06/05/23	Spring Canyon
Staley, Irvin	01/19/25	Grass Creek Mine
Stamation, Sam	03/18/12	Thompson Mine

Stamblakis, Mike	08/14/20	Hiawatha #1 Mine
Stamitalis, George (AKA Stamos)	11/24/22	Sunnyside #2 Mine
Stamper, Virgil	05/09/45	Sunnyside (Explosion)
Stankovic, Dane	01/04/22	Unk Utah Fuel Mine
Stapley, L. C	03/08/24	Castle Gate Mine (Explosion)
Stathakis, John (AKA Satakis)	08/05/24	Standardville Mine
Stavarakis, E. L.	03/08/24	Castle Gate Mine (Explosion)
Stavrianakin, Eli	03/08/24	Castle Gate Mine (Explosion)
Stavros, Mike	10/19/33	Kenilworth Mine
Stavyos, Theros	03/08/24	Castle Gate Mine (Explosion)
Stevens, Ben	03/08/24	Castle Gate Mine (Explosion)
Stevens, Charles	10/08/29	Standardville Mine
Stevens, H. B.	10/14/18	Cleer Creek Mine
Stevens, Serrill	10/31/22	Mohrland Mine
Stevenson, James C.	02/07/77	Soldier Creek #1 Nine Mile Mine
Stewart, Duane	06/28/35	Castle Gate #2 Mine
Stewart, Richard	05/01/00	Winter Quarters (Explosion)
Stewart, William Preston	10/27/45	Kenilworth Mine
Stocks, Thomas L.	11/26/30	Columbia Mine
Stokes, James	04/06/44	Hiawatha Mine
Stone, K.	01/23/14	Castle Gate #2 Mine
Strang, Frank, Sr.	05/01/00	Winter Quarters (Explosion)
Strang, Frank, F. Jr.	05/01/00	Winter Quarters (Explosion)
Street, Ed	05/01/00	Winter Quarters (Explosion)
Strong, Asa	09/28/14	Storrs Mine
Struhs, Irvin J.	09/30/30	Peerless Mine
Stubblefield, Orvil	05/09/45	Sunnyside (Explosion)
Subab, Andrew	01/02/13	Sunnyside #1 Mine
Sublett, Mike	10/06/41	Standardville Mine
Succuardo, Sam (AKA Succro)	06/24/42	Spring Canyon
Sugimura, Kanhishi	1922	Standardville Mine
Sviscsu, Peter	08/27/63	Moab

Swazer, John | 06/11/26 | Spring Canyon #1 Mine

T

Name	Date	Mine
Tachibana, Ishi	03/25/24	Columbia Mine
Tagliabee, Joe	03/08/24	Castle Gate Mine (Explosion)
Takagi, Shosuki	06/29/22	Rains Mine
Takahashi, Nideo Harold	12/23/56	Wattis
Takaya, Kenzio	08/11/21	Sunnyside Mine
Takeuchi, Tom	03/08/24	Castle Gate Mine (Explosion)
Tallereco, Joe	03/08/24	Castle Gate Mine (Explosion)
Tanaka, S.	05/20/27	Castle Gate Mine
Tangaro, Frank	03/05/41	Hiawatha Mine
Tangaro, Giuseppi	11/06/27	Kenilworth Mine
Tango, Joe	09/26/27	Castle Gate #2 Mine
Taslich, John	02/05/23	Wattis Mine
Taujisako, Isuki	04/24/23	Rains Mine
Taylor, Chester	06/20/23	Wattis Mine
Taylor, Jesse	01/20/42	Kenilworth
Teasdale, William H.	02/25/29	Castle Gate #1 Mine
Tennefer, Paul	06/29/43	Hiawatha Mine
Thimakis, K	08/11/14	Clear Creek #2 Mine
Thomas, B.F.	03/08/24	Castle Gate Mine (Explosion)
Thomas, Daniel	03/18/24	Kenilworth Mine
Thomas, Evan D.	05/01/00	Winter Quarters (Explosion)
Thomas, F. D.	05/01/00	Winter Quarters (Explosion)
Thomas, Fred	12/07/14	Storrs #1 Mine
Thomas, John	05/01/00	Winter Quarters (Explosion)
Thomas, Johnathon	03/08/24	Castle Gate Mine (Explosion)
Thomas, Joseph P.	05/01/00	Winter Quarters (Explosion)
Thomas, Joseph S.	05/01/00	Winter Quarters (Explosion)
Thomas, Matt	11/02/09	Sunnyside Mine
Thomas, Richard P.	05/01/00	Winter Quarters (Explosion)
Thompson, George (AKA Grant Thomas)	07/16/26	Rains
Thompson, John, Jr.	04/06/03	Morrison Mine
Thorpe, John	03/08/24	Castle Gate Mine (Explosion)

Tidwell, Elden S.	08/19/63	Geneva Horse Canyon Mine
Tinall, John B.	08/27/63	Moore
Tite, John	04/09/13	Utah Mine
Tollestrop, Alvin	11/12/26	Unk U.S. Fuel Mine
Tomac, Matt	11/23/09	Sunnyside Mine
Tomlinson, William	05/01/00	Winter Quarters (Explosion)
Torno, August	12/01/38	Kenilworth #2 Mine
Turen, Gust	12/12/20	Standardville Mine
Turner, Ben	04/09/85	Kaiser #1 Sunnyside Mine
Turner, Clement	03/08/30	Peerless Mine (Explosion)
Turner, Daniel	03/08/30	Peerless Mine (Explosion)
Turner, Elijah	02/06/05	Grass Creek Mine
Turra, Joe	01/20/30	Spring Canyon
Trauntvein, Nelson J.	08/19/46	Castle Gate #2 Mine
Trikouris, George	09/02/42	Hiawatha Mine
Troupis, George	03/08/24	Castle Gate Mine (Explosion)
Trow, Thomas	03/08/24	Castle Gate Mine (Explosion)
Trujillo, Aniano Jose	03/28/43	Sunnyside
Trujillo, Manuel	05/09/45	Sunnyside (Explosion)
Trujillo, Willie	01/13/54	Horse Canyon
Tziblakis, Mike	09/27/20	Clear Creek #3 Mine
Tsoouroupakis, Mike	07/17/19	Winter Quarters Mine
Tsujisako, Isuke	04/24/23	Unk Carbon Fuel Mine
Tyrer, Matt	03/08/24	Castle Gate Mine (Explosion)
Tzegounakis, Angelo	04/02/24	Unk Utah Fuel Mine

U

Ulerthorn, William	05/01/00	Winter Quarters (Explosion)
Underakis, Steve	03/08/24	Castle Gate Mine (Explosion)
Ungericht, Orson	03/08/24	Castle Gate Mine (Explosion)
Unknown Miner, The	Many dates	Many mines
Uppa, Eric	05/01/00	Winter Quarters (Explosion)
Urtrdo, Frank	02/15/57	Royal #2 Mine

V

Valdez, Benjamin	12/16/63	Carbon Fuel #2 Mine (Explosion)

Valdez, Joe C.	12/27/46	Sunnyside #2 Mine
Valasquez, Ben	03/17/23	Sunnyside #1 Mine
VanDerHelp, Lewis	03/17/70	Deseret Mine
Van Wagoner, Del	09/07/26	Sunnyside Mine
Varitti, Samual	08/21/03	Sunnyside Mine
Varner, C. A.	06/18/42	Columbia Mine
Vendos, Tom	02/26/16	Sunnyside #2 Mine
Verde, Tony	06/23/51	Castle Gate #2 Mine
Verges, Kanaz	03/08/24	Castle Gate Mine (Explosion)
Vericolli, Rocco	12/14/14	Standardville Mine
Vesoynick, Joseph	05/16/07	Winter Quarters Mine
Via, Joe	03/02/43	Independent Coal & Coke Mine
Vigil, Sam	04/14/70	Kenilworth Mine
Vigil, Tom	05/09/45	Sunnyside (Explosion)
Voen Duer, M.	05/01/00	Winter Quarters (Explosion)
Vrondakis, Mike	03/16/12	Hiawatha Mine
Vrontakis, Ross	07/22/15	Castle Gate Mine
Vucinich, Nick	08/26/25	Latuda Mine

W

Wahlin, Albert C.	03/12/04	Winter Quarters #1 Mine
Waldoch, John	12/19/84	Wilberg Mine Huntington (Fire)
Walkama, Herman	05/01/00	Winter Quarters (Explosion)
Walker, Parley P.	05/05/25	Rains Mine
Wallace, James Sr.	05/01/00	Winter Quarters (Explosion)
Walls, Lester Jr.	12/19/84	Wilberg Mine Huntington (Fire)
Walton, Bud	05/09/45	Sunnyside (Explosion)
Ward, Heber W.	09/01/25	Clear Creek #3 Mine
Ward, James	04/23/51	Sunnyside
Ward, John Edward	07/21/41	Standardville
Ward, Ray	10/15/77	Swisher #3 Mine
Warila, Alfred	05/01/00	Winter Quarters (Explosion)
Warren, Floyd	08/25/49	Geneva Horse Canyon Mine

Warren, William Alonzo	12/11/43	Sunnyside
Watanabe, Y	03/08/24	Castle Gate Mine (Explosion)
Wateri, J.	11/27/15	Sunnyside #2 Mine
Watson, A. E.	05/01/00	Winter Quarters (Explosion)
Watson, William	02/06/30	Standardville (Explosion)
Waymon, Move	07/06/65	Kaiser #1 Sunnyside Mine
Webber, John	05/01/00	Winter Quarters (Explosion)
Webber, Thomas	05/01/00	Winter Quarters (Explosion)
Webber, William	05/01/00	Winter Quarters (Explosion)
Werrett, Alan B.	09/23/53	Castle Gate Mine
Werrion, Maurice	05/12/42	Kenilworth Mine
Wheeler, Nanette M. (First female)	12/19/84	Wilberg Mine Huntington (Fire)
Whitby, Leo L.	11/06/25	Standardville Mine
White, Richard	07/30/00	Castle Gate Mine
Whittaker, James H.	01/03/25	Rains Mine (Surface)
Wilberg, LaMar	11/14/64	Wilberg Mine
Wilcox, David	05/01/00	Winter Quarters (Explosion)
Wilde, James	11/26/19	Cleer Creek #4 Mine
Wilde, William H.	07/31/12	Grass Creek Mine
Wilga, Andrew	12/08/10	Scofield Mine
Wilkinson, Arlo A.	12/13/83	So. Utah Fuel #1 Mine
Williams, Daniel	05/01/00	Winter Quarters (Explosion)
Williams, Evan	07/28/00	Winter Quarters
Williams, Isaac (First in 1900s)	01/13/00	Winter Quarters #1
Williams, Llewellyn	05/01/00	Winter Quarters (Explosion)
Williams, R. A.	03/08/24	Castle Gate Mine (Explosion)
Williams, Robert	05/01/00	Winter Quarters (Explosion)
Williams, Thomas W.	06/21/12	Winter Quarters #1 Mine
Willis, Alfred Lee	05/12/75	Deer Creek Mine
Willis, Ed	03/08/24	Castle Gate Mine (Explosion)
Wilsey, John	12/19/84	Wilberg Mine Huntington (Fire)
Wilson, Earl Dean	08/22/77	Deseret Coal Mine
Wilson, George	05/01/00	Winter Quarters (Explosion)

Wilson, Henry	05/01/00	Winter Quarters (Explosion)
Wilson, Jame	05/01/00	Winter Quarters (Explosion)
Wilson, John L.	01/12/25	Standardville Mine
Wilson, Sandy	05/01/00	Winter Quarters (Explosion)
Wilson, Willie	05/01/00	Winter Quarters (Explosion)
Wilstead, Robert D.	05/01/00	Winter Quarters (Explosion)
Wilstead, William	05/01/00	Winter Quarters (Explosion)
Wimber, Melvin	01/24/30	Spring Canyon #1 Mine
Wimber, Tobe	02/06/30	Standardville (Explosion)
Winders, Bernard	01/18/45	Hiawatha Mine
Winkler, Ray	08/13/26	Standardville Mine
Woods, A.	03/08/24	Castle Gate Mine (Explosion)
Wooten, Clayton	01/28/44	Columbia Mine
Wright, Robert Ray	06/14/84	Deer Creek Mine
Wright, Scott	03/10/53	Moore
Wycherley, James	05/09/45	Sunnyside (Explosion)
Wycherley, Ted	07/19/30	Consumers Mine
Wyndham, Thomas	08/24/01	Winter Quarters #1
Wynineger, Thomas E.	02/12/34	Unk Utah Fuel Mine
(AKA Thomas Glenn)		
Wyou, K.	03/08/24	Castle Gate Mine (Explosion)
Wzrd, John Edward	07/20/42	Standardville Mine

X

Xedonas, George	10/14/09	Winter Quarters Mine

Y

Yadao, Valentin	09/02/30	Peerless Mine
Yadrosich, John	02/12/29	Standardville Mine
Yamada, K.	01/15/19	Carbon Fuel Mine
Yietz, Frank	08/22/29	Castle Gate #1 Mine
Yoshido, Kenzio	04/12/44	Sweets Mine
Yoshimoto, Y.	11/04/18	Hiawatha #1 Mine
Young, Fred	01/14/19	Sunnyside #2
Young, James, Jr.	03/08/24	Castle Gate Mine (Explosion)
Young, Joseph Alfred	01/14/19	Sunnyside Mine

Yum, S. C.	03/08/24	Castle Gate Mine (Explosion)
Yuzna, John	10/01/31	Standardville Mine

Z

Zabriskie, Charles	05/19/43	Kenilworth Mine
Zagarakis, E	03/08/24	Castle Gate Mine (Explosion)
Zaikawa, S.	01/24/28	Sunnyside Mine
Zakaris, Paul	03/08/24	Castle Gate Mine (Explosion)
Zanis, Mike	03/08/24	Castle Gate Mine (Explosion)
Zdunich, John	03/03/23	Standardville Mine
Zellars, Frank	02/06/13	Black Hawk Mine
Zeprian, Andrew	03/01/11	Sunnyside #1 Mine
Zervas, Angelo	11/11/30	Kenilworth Mine
Zidar, Martin	07/06/09	Winter Quarters Mine
Zizich, Mike	01/24/22	Rains Mine
Zmerzilkar, Albert	11/20/31	Castle Gate Mine
Zogmaster,	02/14/48	Columbia Mine
Zorka, Joe	11/02/09	Sunnyside Mine
Zwahlen, John Frederick	02/09/66	Deseret Coal Mine
Civish, Steven P.	07/26/75	Killed on mission for LDS Church in Argentina

About the Author

Fred Civish is a professional journalist living in West Jordan, Utah. He is also a fourth-generation coal miner, having worked in the mines as a teenager, including a summer spent swinging a sixteen-pound spike hammer in 100 degree heat.

Being a fourth-generation miner meant he was raised in a coal camp and heard mining stories all his life. Thus began a lifelong belief in the greatness and nobility of the so-called "common working man."

Fred has always had a desire to write, and he has written more than a thousand articles for dozens of trade journals. He received a bachelor's degree in Journalism and later a master's degree in Educational Psychology, which led to a position as an associate psychologist at the Utah State Training School for the mentally handicapped.

His broad range of activities and interests include such diverse things as parachute jumping and diving for abalone in the Pacific.